Markets and Diversity

Markets and Diversity

- Sherwin Rosen

Harvard University Press
Cambridge, Massachusetts
London, England
2004

Library of Congress Cataloging-in-Publication Data

Rosen, Sherwin, 1938–2001.
    Markets and diversity / Sherwin Rosen.
        p.   cm.
    Includes bibliographical references and index.
    ISBN 0-674-01075-2 (alk. paper)
    1. Labor market. 2. Diversity in the workplace. I. Title.
    HD5706.R67 2004
    331.1—dc22   2003067633

Contents

Publisher's Note

Sherwin Rosen was elected president of the American Economic Association for the 2001 term but unfortunately died a few months after taking office. At the time of his death on March 17, 2001, he had selected the papers and written a final draft of the Introduction to this collection. He felt that these papers represented his best work on heterogeneous labor markets, which was the topic he was chiefly interested in and to which he made lasting contributions.

The Publisher would like to thank Edward Lazear for vetting the Introduction and for preparing the figures. He subsequently presented this piece at the annual meeting of the American Economic Association in January 2002 as Rosen's presidential address. The Publisher would also like to thank Luis Garicano for reading the proofs and preparing the index.

Markets and Diversity

Introduction:
Markets and Diversity

Diversity is the staff of economic life. Interpersonal differences in tastes and talents, whether naturally endowed or environmentally produced, give us the unique "propensity to truck, barter, and trade" that improves our standards of living. Every elementary economics student knows how different endowments in an exchange economy create potential gains from trade, and how competitive markets efficiently intermediate and exhaust those gains. In production activities, work is organized in highly specialized ways to use our human resources to the fullest.

All this is so elementary that economists largely take it for granted, yet much of the complexity of modern economic life is built upon these foundations. The variety of choices that confront us is astonishing. No consumer buys more than a tiny fraction of goods that are available to be purchased. The average person is unable to identify by name more than a handful of goods because most are irrelevant to anyone's personal economic behavior. And in work activities, each of us masters hardly any of the immense varieties of skill required in a modern economy. Out of the totality of what is known by society at large, a single person knows practically nothing, no matter how well educated or how brilliant! Work and production knowledge are even more specialized than consumption choices and activities.

How do decentralized markets accommodate the diversity of choices, tastes, and productivities that are so important in economic affairs? The choice of quantities (the intensive margin) by a typical

Sherwin Rosen passed away on March 17, 2001. The final draft of this Presidential Address was prepared by Edward Lazear of Stanford University, with comments from Gary S. Becker and Robert E. Lucas, Jr. of the University of Chicago. The address was delivered by Edward Lazear at the one hundred fourteenth meeting of the American Economic Association, January 5, 2002, Atlanta, GA. It subsequently appeared in the *American Economic Review* 92, no. 1 (March 2002): 1–15.

buyer or seller has dominated neoclassical economics. Most of price theory focuses on the determination of price and quantities of already-defined goods, but does little to examine the extensive margin by which the nature of the goods is chosen. Price theory does not provide a rich enough structure to analyze these issues, which require a framework that takes heterogeneity and diversity as a fundamental, primitive construct. Location or spatial theory is specifically designed for that task. It is a theory of choice based on interpersonal differences in willingness to pay for differentiated objects perhaps best known from Adam Smith's theory of equalizing differences.[1] Differentiated products are valued according to their various qualities and product characteristics. Comparing reservation prices with market prices determines specific choices of buyers and sellers out of the vast varieties that are available. Many successful examples have clarified how spatial models can be applied to the economics of variety and diversity.

Much of my research reflects my attempt over the years to work out some of the economic issues associated with diversity and the implications of heterogeneity for markets and prices.[2] There are three main themes: the determination of value in the presence of diversity, the sorting or allocation of diverse buyers to diverse sellers, and the effects of heterogeneity and sorting on inequality.

I. Value, Assignment, and Inequality

How do markets accommodate inherent differences in goods, jobs, and productive talents of people? How are these things valued? Just as the value of land depends on its location, it is often possible to think of goods, jobs, and people in terms of their addresses in a map of productive attributes or characteristics. Some addresses are more desirable than others, and market prices equate the supply and demand for the latent characteristics of goods at each location on the map. Thinking spatially proves especially useful when there are many more varieties of goods than attributes that each contains. Because there are fewer attributes than goods, the dimensionality of the problem is greatly reduced and analysis can proceed on conventional cost-benefit terms.

---

1. Adam Smith (1776).
2. The paper in which most of the theory is formalized is Rosen (1974).

Examples of applications include hedonic indexes of quality change needed to correct price indexes for changing product characteristics; among such products as automobiles and computers; regression analysis of housing prices on house characteristics, used for real estate assessments in urban economics; the capital asset pricing model, where asset characteristics are the means and covariances of their rate of return distributions; studying how labor markets evaluate jobs of varying quality, useful for estimating the social value of safety and environmental goods that are not directly traded; and how and why labor markets sustain enormous differences in rewards and rents among people of different talents. All are manifestations of almost exactly the same basic spatial problem: valuing diversity.

Market values are an important part of the story. The allocation of diversity in the economy is another. How are buyers and sellers matched or assigned to each other in market equilibrium? These marriage-type questions bear importantly on the economic consequences of diversity because stratification of agents is inherent in spatial equilibrium. Certain kinds of buyers come to be associated with certain kinds of sellers, even when there are no externalities and social influences in preferences. Rich people tend to ride in a better class of automobiles than poor people. They are more likely to live on the lakeshore and in other high-rent districts, to eat in fancy restaurants, wear designer clothes, send their children to better schools, and work in more pleasant environments. But there are many other manifestations of the same basic sorting or assignment issues in the presence of diversity. Widows and orphans tend to hold their wealth in relatively safe assets. People from similar ethnic groups tend to live together in city enclaves, more talented students are apt to be found in colleges and graduate schools that have more talented teachers, higher-quality lawyers work on the largest legal claims, and people exposed to higher unemployment risks tend to live in the same neighborhoods.

The address analogy in spatial equilibrium often extends to these kinds of matches or assignments: goods with special attributes appeal to buyers with specific kinds of tastes. In product markets, sellers design their goods to cater to specific types of customers. And in labor markets, each of us in our career choices and work activities seeks a niche in the incredibly complex machinery of modern production and the division of labor. The number of people seeking these slots and the nature of the technologies that affect the personal scale of operations affects the distribution of rewards in society.

Markets accommodate diversity by establishing prices that tend to make different things relatively close substitutes at the margin. Adam Smith's insight that market prices tend to equalize their net advantages is fundamental to these problems. If one good has more desirable characteristics than another, the less preferred variety must compensate for its disadvantages by selling at a lower price. Supply is inelastic and exogenous in geographic spatial theory, but in many applications both sides of the market must be considered jointly. Sellers choose their varieties by comparing prices with costs. Higher-quality goods are more costly to produce and must be offered at a higher price. In equilibrium these extra costs can only be supported if their incremental value to some customers is at least as large as their incremental costs. Thus diversity creates *inequality* in prices and values. The reverse statement is also true. Certain kinds of inequality are necessary to sustain diverse outcomes. For example, if higher-quality goods were not more expensive to produce than lower-quality ones and if all consumers had the same relative ranking on the quality of two different goods, then only the higher-quality good would survive in the market. The lower-quality good is driven out by the existence of a superior one that can be produced at equal cost.

What is less obvious is that there are social incentives to *create* inequality, even when agents are initially identical in every conceivable way. This is a third theme of the essay. The basic idea also derives from Smith, who argued that personal investments in skill acquisition, not inherited differences in natural abilities, are the principal causes of wage inequality in society. Since labor-market skills are costly to learn, in market equilibrium their costs must be reimbursed by offering larger expected earnings to potential entrants, otherwise students would not have the proper economic incentives to study them. Since much of the cost of education and learning are in time and opportunities forgone, the force of interest weighs heavily in these decisions and can cause remarkably large differences in observed earnings, as equilibrium phenomena.

But once a skill has been acquired, its economic return is greatest if it is used as intensively as possible. That the costs of acquiring most skills are to some extent independent of how intensively they are utilized makes it efficient for people to specialize their skills and trade with each other. There are huge economies of scale in skills. Once acquired, a skill can be used over and over again without diminishing its stock.

Indeed, the reverse may be true, which provides incentives for students to acquire skills early and to increase their work hours after having become skilled.

Furthermore, individuals have different talents and are better suited to some productive activities than others. The principle of comparative advantage holds true for human-capital production as well as for international trade. It accounts for why work is so specialized and why each person knows such a small amount of what is known in total. It even holds if people are identical ex ante. Similar ideas have received lots of attention lately in the fields of industrial organization and international trade, but are just as important, if not more so, for the organization of work.

The cost basis that supports induced or "voluntary" inequality has other interesting consequences. unequal rewards motivate people to strive for superior performance and influence their decisions to acquire skills. The two interact because new generations of workers replace older generations: the assignment of people to jobs changes over the life cycle. A large share of the growth in personal earnings over managerial and other careers occurs at discrete promotion points to higher-ranking positions. Competition for promotions, to acquire greater skill, show one's stuff, and get more powerful and higher-paying positions, plays an important role both in the internal dynamics of organizations and in the overall economy. Uncertainty of outcomes and the statistical aspects of promotion and job assignments guarantee that competition for superior positions occurs in every form of economic organization. The need to use the record of past performance to assess prospects for other positions automatically gives people incentives to try to influence the measures that will put them in a superior category. The strength of these incentives depends on how much of a difference—in money, prestige, and perquisites—it makes to achieve a better grade and a higher classification.

II. Valuing Diversity

Much of my research consists of applications of the problem of analyzing markets for differentiated products when the measure of differentiation is naturally ordered from best to worst. Market prices reflect both the costs and the values of the underlying attributes of goods. Agents implicitly use cost-benefit analysis to choose locations in the product spectrum, with buyers comparing the market prices of alternative varieties with their relative values in use and with sellers comparing market prices with their relative costs. Equality between demand and supply for each variety sustains the market equilibrium price-quality structure.

Consider a commodity that comes in two different varieties. For example, there are high- and low-quality cars, better and worse houses (or schools or neighborhoods), good jobs and bad ones, fast and slow computers, and so on. Let c represent all other goods consumed and let z_h and z_l measure the high- and low-quality characteristics of the goods in question. The relative prices of the two varieties in terms of other goods are p_h and p_l. In the situation considered, which is typical of many markets, individual buyers and sellers are small compared to the overall market and individually have no market power. Suppose that customers purchase either one unit of the differentiated product or none. This is a leading case. Most people live in exactly one neighborhood, hold one job, and drive one car. Preferences are given by a utility function $u(c, z)$ of the usual kind. The choice set consists of three distinct points in the (p, z) plane, as in Figure I.1. A consumer lives at point A, $(0, 0)$, if neither variety is purchased, at point B, (p_l, z_l), if the low-quality variety is most preferred, and at point C, (p_h, z_h), if high quality is chosen. High-quality goods must sell for higher prices than low-quality goods,

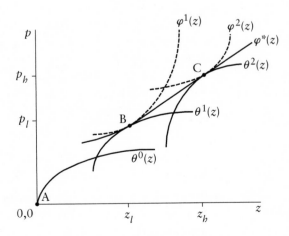

Figure I.1 • Spatial equilibrium

or else low quality is dominated and disappears from the market. Thus, higher z is always associated with larger p if both z_h and z_l are actually traded. Given that some variety is purchased, a consumer chooses z_h if the benefits of its additional quality exceed its additional cost. Once having decided on the choice of variety, the consumer decides whether to purchase it or do without.

The first part of the problem is equivalent to choosing the maximum between $u(y - p_h, z_h)$ and $u(y - p_l, z_l)$, where y is income. The added cost of high quality is $\Delta p = p_h - p_l$. Its added benefit is how much more the buyer is willing to pay for it, $\Delta\theta$, and is defined as a compensating variation:

$$u(y - p_l - \Delta\theta, z_h) = u(y - p_l, z_l). \tag{1}$$

$\Delta\theta$ is the money premium a person would pay for z_h when the lower-quality item z_l is available at price p_l. The optimal choice is z_h if $\Delta\theta > p_h - p_l$ and z_l otherwise. The second part of the problem, whether or not to purchase the good at all, is another cost-benefit comparison. Define θ as the compensating variation that equates the utility of not purchasing anything to that obtained from the best possible variety:

$$u(y, 0) = \max\{u(y - \theta - \Delta\theta, z_h), u(y - \theta, z_l)\}. \tag{2}$$

The consumer does not purchase any z if both $\theta < p_l$ and $\theta + \Delta\theta < p_h$.

This can be neatly described diagrammatically with a spatial *bid function* $\theta(z)$, defined as the amount a person with income y will pay for various varieties at some constant utility index:

$$u(y - \theta(z), z) = \text{constant}. \tag{3}$$

$\theta(z)$ is an indifference curve between money and the measure of quality z. From (3), its derivative $\partial\theta/\partial z = u_z/u_c$, is the marginal rate of substitution between z and c. This is positive and $\theta(z)$ is upward sloping. Diminishing marginal rate of substitution implies that $\theta''(z) < 0$: the marginal willingness to pay for additional quality is decreasing. The curves labeled θ' in Figure I.1 depict indifference curves for three different kinds of buyers. Consumers whose tastes look like θ^0 do not purchase the differentiated product at all because the indifference curve through (0, 0) lies above the available price-quality combinations for z. Analogously, those whose tastes look like θ^1 purchase z_l and those whose tastes are more like θ^2 buy z_h. Choices of differentiated varieties are nicely ordered by the intensity of preferences for quality in this example.

Supply decisions of sellers are similar. The benefit of selling a variety is its market price. Production is profitable if price exceeds production costs of at least some sellers. Parallel with bid functions, these choices are depicted by a spatial *offer function* $\varphi(z)$—the locus of price-quality pairs that result in the same profit. $\varphi(z)$ is the supply price of quality z for that seller. Since higher-quality goods are more costly to produce, $\varphi'(z) > 0$. Offer curves are increasing convex functions of z. Producers either specialize their production in distinct varieties or produce several of them in a product line. Costs and production conditions, indivisibilities, the nature of competition, and competitors' costs factor into these outcomes. Figure I.1 depicts a case of specialization. The offer function labeled φ^1 refers to a seller with comparative advantage at producing the lower-quality variety, and the curve labeled φ refers to a seller whose production conditions are better suited to high quality. Since φ^1 lies everywhere above (z_h, p_h), seller 1 cannot offer the high-quality variety at a profit level higher than that obtained by offering the low-quality variety. Conversely, since φ^2 lies everywhere above (z_l, p_l), seller 2 cannot offer the low-quality variety at a profit level higher than that obtained by offering the high-quality variety. Sellers whose minimum acceptable profit-offer curve cover both prices produce both objects. An example of such a seller is one with offer function $\varphi*$, who is indifferent between selling the two varieties.

Some auto manufacturers produce a full product line and others specialize in niche markets. Research universities cater to students with superior high-school records and achievements, and would not be very cost effective as junior colleges. Climatic and geographic endowments give some California vineyards advantages in producing high-quality wine that is much harder to produce in New York and Michigan, yet some California vintners produce both higher- and lower-quality brands. The prestigious law firms handling large legal claims are careful about which cases they take on and whom they admit as partners. Production activities in which workers directly interact require personnel who complement each other's personal productivity and efficiency characteristics. Because of direct complementarity in most production settings, more interpersonal variation in efficiency within production units can be tolerated by transacting through the market rather than directly in teams. Impersonal transactions are the equivalent of intermediate product markets and reduce the adverse consequences that occur when less efficient workers pull down the productivity of more efficient ones.

Figure I.1 shows how the market sustains diversity as an equilibrium phenomenon. Different kinds of buyers purchase different kinds of goods. Consumers with tastes that correspond to $\theta^1(z)$ buy z_l at price p_l and are supplied by sellers with bid functions that correspond to $\varphi^1(z)$. Consumers with tastes that correspond to $\theta^2(z)$ buy z_l at price p_h and are supplied by sellers with bid functions that correspond to $\varphi^2(z)$. Neither seller has any incentive to try to sell to consumers of the other type, nor does any buyer have any incentive to purchase from the other type of seller. All four types of agents can do no better, given the opportunities available.

A. Interpreting the Implicit Value of Characteristics

Empirical investigations of product and labor differentiation use cross-section data to relate prices p with attributes z. The hedonic regression method regresses product prices on product characteristics. It was initially developed to study real cost reductions in auto and other durable goods manufacturing that were concealed by product design changes and quality improvements. In labor economics, wages of workers are regressed on their personal productivity and job characteristics. In land and housing markets, site and structure prices are regressed on house attributes (size, architectural style, and age) and onsite characteristics (neighborhood, location, and public services). Labor and land market studies are useful for imputing the social value of certain intangible goods, like safety and clean environments. An important use in goods markets is to construct price and quantity indexes that control for changes in the quality of goods over time.

B. Cross-Section Values

Environmental and safety concerns are at the forefront of public policy today. The rhetoric and passions they arouse make it easy to forget that these goods are costly to produce and that rational decisions require comparing their benefits with their costs. Assessing the costs of these kinds of public policies is like finding the costs of any other investment. Assessing benefits requires estimating the willingness of consumers to pay for more safety and better environments. Practice is tricky because there exist no explicit markets where safety and clean air are directly traded, and from which demand values can be directly inferred. Instead, safety and environmental quality often are by-products of other transactions and their valuations must be imputed from the observed packages in which they play a part.

Exposure to risk and pollution are affected by work and residential choices. Some jobs are more hazardous than others and the social and physical environment varies greatly among neighborhoods. Private cost-benefit considerations underlying such choices are the basis for imputing the required values. Housing in crime-free neighborhoods is expensive because people are willing to pay more for greater personal safety and protection of their property and because crime-free neighborhoods are scarce. Wages on hazardous jobs must be higher in order to induce workers to expose themselves to greater risk of life and limb. Observed price differences across jobs and locations are the implicit prices of characteristics, as in Figure I.1, with z interpreted as job safety or neighborhood safety.

Valuations generally vary among agents. People with different tastes and incomes have different bid and offer functions, but more is involved. In most types of economic exchange, the Law of One Price implies that marginal valuations across buyers are identical and that differences in tastes manifest themselves only in differences in quantities consumed. For example, the "last" loaf of bread is worth about the same—its market price—to a person who consumes one loaf per week as to a person who buys one loaf per day.

The Law of One Price always applies to the specific houses, jobs, or goods markets that embody intangible characteristics, but not necessarily to the intangible characteristics themselves. Whether there is a unique market price of a characteristic depends on whether or not the characteristics embodied in existing varieties can be recombined or re-manufactured by buyers into different varieties. The leading example of such "combinability" is asset and portfolio management. Risk and return of any single asset are relevant only insofar as they affect the risk and return on one's total portfolio. A portfolio is a linear combination of various assets, so covariance of risk on one asset compared to others is the key risk component. The implied linear restrictions (or no-arbitrage conditions) imply a unique market price for risk.

But the fact is that combinability of characteristics across varieties is not possible for most other goods. If it is expensive to untie bundles after they have been manufactured, sellers must design their goods for specific tastes and assemble packages of characteristics that appeal to specific market segments. This generally results in differing attribute prices across packages. One cannot buy another unit of comfort for a sports car in an independent "comfort" market. Instead, a larger car must be purchased. A worker on a risky job cannot subcontract little bits of the risk to others in a secondary market. It is all-or-nothing. The only way less risk can be chosen is by finding a safer job. Workers come prepackaged with various combinations of skills and traits, some productive and others counterproductive. Employers cannot detach the less desirable ones from any single worker. Rather, an entirely different person has to be hired. In these cases the market equilibrium price function $p(z)$ usually is nonlinear, and the gradient $p'(z)$ generally depends on z itself. Since there is no single market price for z, different people have different valuations of it at the margin. Type θ^1 and θ^2 buyers in Figure I.1 serve as an example. In principle an average of the two slopes at z_l and z_h is appropriate for assessing the (marginal) benefits of a small independent public project affecting z in some application, with the average weighted by benefit incidence of the project among different types of people.

So many factors determine market prices of goods in practice that the best chance empirically for isolating the implicit value of safety and environment is to examine specific goods or jobs where these aspects dominate other considerations of choice. For instance, my labor-market study with Richard Thaler (1976) on the value of life was one of the first to systematically examine wage premiums on very risky jobs, where risk was measured as excess insurance premiums charged by private companies on worker compensation policies.

The revealed preference argument in Figure I.1 applies directly to that problem. Here z represents job safety and $p(z)$ is estimated by statistically comparing the smaller market wage that workers are paid on safer jobs compared to higher wages paid on riskier ones, other things equal. Examining risky jobs empirically confines the study to jobs with relatively low values of safety, e.g., to those in the neighborhood of z_l in the figure. Since most workers hold relatively safe jobs (located closer to a point like z_h in the figure), people holding risky jobs surely place smaller values on safety than the median person, much like the difference between people of types θ^1 and θ^2 in the figure. Workers choosing safe jobs are willing to pay at least as much for safety as people choosing risky jobs, so the wage premium on risky jobs is likely to be a lower bound on the average person's willingness to pay for safety.

Thaler and I estimated a "value of life" of about $800,000 in dollars of Year 2000 purchasing power. Other labor-market studies using data on a wider range of risks have found much larger values. The broader range of risks in these studies is the most probable reason for the larger estimates: they include more between-variation (e.g., the differences between z_l and z_h), whereas our study was largely confined to within-variation (around z_l). Similar considerations apply to housing and land market studies that impute values for crime, climate, and pollution. Here, too, revealed preference implies that estimated pollution and crime gradients are likely to be lower bounds for the average citizen because they ignore important sorting considerations.

C. Time-Series Imputations

The main practical difficulty in assessing changing standards of living is that goods change their character over time. The prices of tractors and automobiles today differ from 30 years ago, not only because manufacturing productivity and input prices have changed, but also because the products themselves have improved. The nature of the problem is starkest when entirely new goods appear on the market. If their introduction is successful and they supplant older varieties, how should they be linked into a price index?

Conceptually, the only possibility is to think in terms of the costs of providing ultimate services. Technical changes reduce the cost of services. Autos were successful because they were a superior way of producing transport services compared to animals. Electricity produced heat and light more efficiently than steam and lanterns, and radio, television, and movies reduced the cost of entertainment services relative to live performances. In these examples, technical changes should be factored into price indexes for transport services, power, and entertainment services. In practice it is extremely difficult to link entirely new goods to old goods in this way. Adjusting for quality improvements of existing goods is more manageable.

Rising incomes naturally cause product quality to improve over time, because the income elasticity of demand for quality is positive. Even when the prices per unit quality of goods do not change, rising incomes increase the demand for quality is positive. Even when the prices per unit quality of goods do not change, rising incomes increase the demand for quality and raise average transactions prices over time. Offsetting the rise in demand for quality is that some aspects of quality (like ornate detail on early twentieth-century houses) are labor intensive, which causes their prices to rise as incomes rise. As long as the cost factor is not dominant, there is upward bias in measured prices and downward bias in measured real living standards from a change in the composition of goods toward more expensive varieties. Transactions prices rise not because cost has increased, but because the quality of what is being referred to as a particular good has increased. Income effects are represented by movements along a given $p(z)$ locus in Figure I.1. The same envelope of offer functions define $p(z)$, but bid functions shift up and to the right as income rises because the willingness to pay for increments of z increases with income. θ^1 and θ^2 in Figure I.1 could represent two people with the same underlying utility functions but different incomes. With constant returns to scale in production, prices of each variety do not change as income rises, but average quality purchased and average transactions prices both increase. We should not confuse movements along the $p(z)$ locus with changes in the cost of living. Most consumption decisions change as income rises, and these are part and parcel of the same general phenomenon. Standardized comparisons that control for the changing composition of goods eliminate this kind of bias.

To assess changes in the real costs of living, we should account for *shifts* in the price-quality locus or technological changes that extend the real range of choice. Such shifts can cause quality-specific prices either to rise or fall. For example, $p(z)$ and the cost of living go up in the income-increasing experiment above if goods are supplied inelastically. For example, rising real incomes increase the demand for amenities associated with geographic location, raising site values and the costs of housing services in the preferred locations. On the other hand, innovations that extend the quality range of goods tend to reduce the real costs of services and reduce living costs for those who buy them.

Productivity-improving quality changes generally reduce the real prices of goods. Prices and available qualities are always changing. Some sellers are innovating and attempting to increase profits by extending the desirable characteristics in their goods and reducing prices below those of competitors. The prototypical example appears in Figure I.2. The first-period equilibrium is the same as before, where goods are labeled z_{l1} and z_{h1} and equilibria are found at points A and B. In the second period the attributes of goods have changed to z_{l2} and z_{h2} so the price-quality locus has moved down, and the average price per

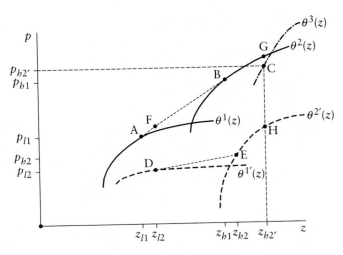

Figure I.2 • Time-series effects

unit quality has declined. (A ray from the origin through A is steeper than one through D and similarly for B and E.) Quality-adjusted price indexes require measuring the *distance* between the two price-quality loci, shown in Figure I.2 as the curve that connects A and B and the one that connects D and E. The distance between F and D is a measure of the quality-adjusted change in price at quality level z_{l2}. When technical change is so large that z could not be produced in period 1 (a 32-bit computer chip did not exist in 1980) shown, for example, by $z_{h2'}$, direct price comparisons of the improved product are impossible. In principle this can be overcome with sufficient structural knowledge of bid functions. In this case, the requirement amounts to knowing the exact shape of $\theta^2(z)$ and of $\theta^{2'}(z)$, which represents different indifference curves for the same consumer. The conceptually appropriate measure of distance is the difference between actual price in period 2 and what type 2 buyers would have been willing to pay for $z_{h2'}$ in period 1 had it been available, shown in Figure I.2 as the distance between G and H. Generally such detailed structural knowledge is unavailable, so distance must be measured by using overlapping varieties whose quality is more or less comparable across adjacent periods. For example, top-of-the-line goods in period 1 might be compared with bottom-of-the-line goods in period 2. Longer period comparisons are made by linking or chaining indexes with common components over the years.

Figure I.2 contains a graphic example of why these adjustments are important. Consider a new good $z_{h2'}$ not previously available, whose current price, $p_{h2'}$ exceeds that of the best prior models. Unadjusted indexes would show rising prices simply because $p_{h2'}$ exceeds p_{h1}. A more accurate distance-based quality-adjusted index would correctly show prices declining because consumers would have been willing to pay more than its period 2 cost in period 1, had it been available. Note that there is a consumer whose bid function, in this case $\theta^3(z)$, reflects higher satisfaction at $(z_{h2'}, p_{h2'})$ than at any other available (z, p) combination.

This example is transparent, but very relevant. Until a few years ago, the National Income and Product Accounts priced computers by the box—by the package in which producers delivered them. In the early years of the computer revolution boxes were getting bigger and more powerful, and their prices were increasing. It was as if soap were suddenly produced in bigger bars and the index used the price per bar, not the price per unit volume or weight. Computer productivity was grossly distorted in the official indexes, though the aggregate consequences of the error were limited because investment in computers was not such a large share of total investment as is true today. But even when box prices were falling, as has been true for many years, unadjusted price indexes distort productivity. Prices are really falling much faster than appears because products are improving so much. The mainframe of yesterday is the laptop of today. Considering that computers currently make up almost half of gross business investment, eliminating these biases is important for getting an accurate assessment of national income. the recent report of the Presidential Commission on Price Indexes shows that more widespread failures to make quality adjustments of goods in price indexes have serious negative biases for assessing real wage and productivity growth, and overstate inflation and the social security and other entitlements that are indexed to them.

III. Sorting and Stratification

In any market equilibrium, interpersonal differences in tastes and technologies affect the locations chosen by buyers and sellers on the attributes map. Some of these differences are inexplicable: sometimes there really is no accounting for different tastes. Others have more proximate causes, but might just as well be summarized stochastically. For instance, the preferences for material goods of a person from humble origins that subsequently makes lots of money often seems to differ from those of her children. Families that are contemplating having children are likely to prefer larger cars to smaller ones and suburban to downtown dwelling units. In the labor market, a person's supply price for physically demanding or dangerous work depends on age, physical condition, and number of dependents, among other things. Different endowments affect productivities in different pursuits. Musicians cannot be tone-deaf; football players tend to be large; while lawyers, and many economists, have a propensity to talk.

What matters for economic allocations in all of these cases are the direct manifestations of tastes. Here, the reservation prices themselves, not the specific causes that make preferences, differ case by case. The distributions of bid and offer functions are sufficient (in the statistical sense) for ascertaining the demand, supply, and equilibrium price of each variety. But when reservation prices are systematically associated with observable traits of buyers and sellers, these markets become stratified in many ways. Stratification and sorting are ubiquitous in spatial equilibrium and have many interesting consequences. Neighborhood, bandwagon, status, and other social externalities are often invoked to account for stratification, but most stratification occurs without them.

Sorting by income is one of the most important forms of stratification in goods, land, and labor markets. As noted above, people who buy high-quality goods, and live in better residences and neighborhoods tend to be richer than other people. Similarly, high-wage people use their higher earning capacity to purchase more job amenities and better working conditions. Stratification of job quality by the skill characteristics of workers can make it difficult to estimate equalizing wage differences for the implicit attributes of jobs. Sometimes the data on job and worker characteristics are so colinear that the ceteris paribus conditions required for identifying taste parameters alone are overwhelmed by income stratification and cannot be observed in the data. Yet it is incorrect to take this as evidence of failure of the equalizing or compensation principle in the labor market.

Stratification and colinearity is itself an implication of the economic theory of preferences when income effects are important. High-wage jobs generally are the good jobs, not the bad ones. They are staffed by skillful workers whose higher incomes make job amenities more valuable and who buy more of them. There is no logical contradiction here. The identifying restrictions for backing out implicit valuations in the data just are not satisfied. After all, sometimes there is not the right kind of variations in the data just are not satisfied. After all, sometimes there is not the right kind of variation in the data to estimate a conventional demand curve, but that does not imply that a demand curve does not exist. These difficulties are less often encountered in imputing implicit prices of characteristics from goods and land market prices. Prices and attributes of goods and land are almost always measured independently of the characteristics of buyers and sellers. Of course many aspects of product attributes may be highly correlated, making it difficult to extract the value of any single one of them. The stratification problem more often arises in labor markets, because observed wages always reflect the total bundle of both job and worker-productivity attributes. The correlation between them can be too large to separate the components. In sum, potential for stratification places limits on the empirical applicability of the hedonic method. Sometimes it cannot be used, but the test is always empirical.

Colinearity affects the precision with which effects can be estimated, but sometimes there is bias in estimating the importance of equalizing differences. It is not that coefficients are noisy; it is rather that they have the wrong sign. This frequently occurs in the labor-market setting when one estimates compensating differences in wage functions. A good example involves the trade-off between pensions and wages. Other things equal, jobs with higher pension benefits should have lower wages because the total amount that employers are willing to pay for a given worker should not vary with the composition of the compensation package and because workers are willing to trade wages for pensions. In Figure I.3, the observed trade-off is shown by the locus AB, which is the estimated market relation of wages to pensions. Note that it is positively sloped, but this is not because workers do not view both wages and pension benefits as goods. Instead, it reflects the fact that more productive workers, who are richer, take some of their income in the form of wages and some in the form of pensions. The $\varphi 1$ offer function reflects the bid by firms to low-productivity workers and the $\varphi 2$ function reflects the bid by firms to high-productivity workers. Even if all workers had the same preferences, as shown by the dotted offer functions (the one to the northeast reflecting higher utility), the market equilibrium would select points A and B. For any given worker, the trade-off would be negative because then the φ or θ curves would be

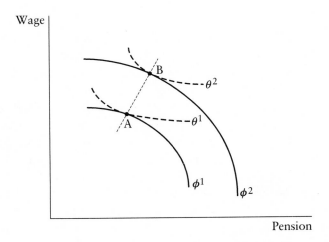

Figure I.3 • Actual versus observed functions

relevant. but the market observes the AB line, because key productivity factors cannot be held constant. The AB line might well be estimated with precision, depending on the amount and nature of the data, but it identifies neither a firm's nor a worker's willingness to trade off pensions for wages.

IV. Diversity and Specialization

Specialization, division of labor, and the organization of work socially create much of the diversity observed in economics. In his compelling discussion, Smith identified scale economies as the principal cause of specialization. Instead of working alone and doing everything by oneself, it is productive for a worker to join teams and assign individual members to a few mutually exclusive tasks. The division of labor is one of the most important bits of economic analysis at the extensive margin. How are productive activities packaged and bundled together into jobs, and who works on them?

For the economy as a whole, the most important reason by far for specialization and division of labor are scale economies in utilizing acquired skills. The returns to investing in a particular skill are proportional to the frequency of its subsequent use. This makes it efficient to use the skills one has already acquired as intensively as possible and not to spread oneself too thinly over a highly diversified portfolio. These same connections between capacity and utilization apply to all capital goods, not only to human-capital varieties. The costs of constructing an office building depend on its size; but once it is built, it is efficient to keep the offices as fully occupied as possible because the marginal cost of an unoccupied office is much smaller than its average cost.

Specialization is optimal if learning new skills involves significant fixed costs that are only loosely linked to the intensity of subsequent utilization. Then it is best to learn a few skills very well and use them all the time. These basic forces produce enormous social gains from trade. We could all build our own houses and educate our own children. Instead, we use markets to buy new houses built by expert house builders and purchase educational services for our children from expert teachers. The houses are better and the children learn more. Specialization and trade are important causes of economic diversity among people in society. Many aspects of economic diversity and its manifestations in economic inequality serve valuable social purposes. The fact is that substantial inequality is necessary for decentralized societies to function. Many components of variance of earnings among persons are sustained by personal activities that would characterize the most free and open societies. They are necessary to sustain both human-capital investment incentives and work incentives.

For example, in almost every society doctors earn more than other people. These wage differentials persist in equilibrium in order to compensate prospective medical students for their arduous and costly training. The number and quality of doctors would fall if earnings were artificially compressed and the rate of return to medical education was reduced. A society with few doctors would score more egalitarian points on a Gini coefficient, but it would not be a better society. This example is trivial, but the point is far more general and often not so obvious. Much inequality in the overall distribution of earnings is attributable to substantial differences in mean earnings among workers of different ages and educational attainments that are associated with occupational choices and human-capital investments over the life cycle. They reflect rational personal choices that change a person's economic status and current incomes over a lifetime.

Rising earnings over working life as well as earnings differences between occupational and educational categories largely reflect returns to human-capital investments. A clear distinction between human-capital (lifetime) wealth and current earnings is needed because learning always involves choosing prospects with smaller earnings now and higher earnings in the future. Observing that a person has low current earnings is no signal of lifetime poverty if future earnings will be high. Similarly, high current earnings are no signal of excess wealth if a person paid the price in low previous earnings. The point is that the distribution of current income is far more unequal than the distribution of human-capital wealth. Inequality indexes based on current data alone give a very misleading impression of true inequality.

The reasoning is most easily understood in terms of an example. Consider a completely equal society in which all workers have exactly the same age-earnings profiles over their careers. Then the distribution of annual earnings is a deterministic function of the age distribution of workers. Societies with more variation in worker age show more inequality, but that is not a very interesting aspect of inequality. In fact, the age distribution makes an enormous difference to measured inequality indexes: earnings data used to assess inequality that are not age standardized are practically worthless for assessing inequality. Remarkably, such adjustments are seldom made. Standardizing current earnings data for education presents more difficult conceptual problems because family backgrounds and personal financial barriers on educational choices distort investment margins and make wage differentials not fully equalizing on costs. Nonetheless, some portion of educational wage differences—and, judging from the remarkable uniformity of estimated rates of return to education in different countries, perhaps a major portion—are equalizing on their costs. They represent productive, socially manufactured diversity and inequality that we cannot live very well without.

V. Personal Productivity and the Distribution of Earnings

Of course, not all differences are willfully created. Many are caused by inherited interpersonal differences in talents and tastes. The hedonic or characteristics approach to labor markets bears similarities to statistical factor-analytic ideas in accounting for earnings differences across individuals. Factor analysis partitions observed variance into a small number of unobserved, latent "causes" or factors. A leading example is intelligence testing, where test scores are thought to reflect the quantitative, analytical, verbal, and mechanical abilities of subjects. Similarly, personal productivity and earning power are ultimately determined by such things as strength, intelligence, dexterity, and attention to detail. Think of a model in which a person's earning power is "scored" as the sum of the amounts of each attribute possessed, times their market prices. If the number of factors is small, important proximate causes of the distribution of earnings are reduced to small dimensions. The economic rationale for compacting the determinants of earnings into a small set of universal factors and prices turns on the existence of unique economywide prices ("loadings") on the factors. Since these price weights are parameters in any factor representation of earnings across persons, dimensionality is reduced only if the same prices apply to all persons.

The implausibility of invariance in any market equilibrium is transparent in the goods market. Is it possible that the marginal value of a unit of comfort in an automobile should be the same as a unit of comfort in an easy chair? Not at all. These commodities represent different, imperfectly substitutable services that cannot be unbundled into such components. We do not see easy chairs in autos and bucket seats in living rooms. No "arbitrage" opportunities are available for trading comfort in one kind of good with comfort in an entirely different class of goods, because those characteristics cannot be untied from the larger bundle of attributes for which the good was designed. Again, the Law of One Price does not apply to characteristics, and their implicit value usually differs among categories of goods. It would be the same only by accident.

Similarly, why should the value of another unit of strength to, say, an accountant be the same as its value to an athlete? It would be the same if there were aggregate markets for such things as strength and intelligence and if a unit of "accounting strength" was a perfect substitute for units of "athletic strength" in all productive activities. The image of accountants on the 50-yard line and linemen running interference against the IRS is not, however, reassuring in this regard. Once again the bundling of personal productivity characteristics and the impossibility of untying bundles and repackaging them into something else is crucial. The marginal products of underlying factors vary across activities—strength is more important to professional athletes than to accountants—and the shadow prices of these factors vary across activities as well. Thus, athletes are stronger than accountants and accountants have more quantitative skills than athletes. This is another important manifestation of sorting and stratification in spatial equilibria.

Activity-specific prices generate comparative advantage. Just as differences in the relative abundance of sunshine to rainfall in Portugal and England give each country its comparative advantage in wine or cloth, so too does strength give people who have it a comparative advantage in some forms of athletics, while arithmetic skills and attention to detail give other people comparative advantage in accounting. Comparative advantage has interesting consequences. For one, people observed in various job and educational categories tend to be selected and stratified by the personal attributes that give them a competitive edge in a specific field. A person's financial self-interest is served by selecting the occupation that maximizes expected earnings. If this is a major consideration in occupational choice (though certainly not the only one), observed earnings of individuals who voluntarily chose an occupation might be a poor estimate of what the earnings of people who avoided that occupation would have been.

Obviously, the earnings of successful athletes or actresses are not representative of the average person's prospects in those fields. But the point is more subtle in other important applications, for instance in interpreting income differences between people with more and less education. As seen above, if all people were identical, the education-earnings premium would be sustained by the supply conditions that pay must compensate for incurring the costs of investment to equalize net advantages across trades. When people differ, things are more complicated. Those who expect the largest returns on their educational investments are more likely to make them. Ability rents persist in equilibrium.

There are two main reasons why rates of return to human-capital investments and human wealth differ among people. First, natural talents complement occupation-specific human-capital investments in different ways. Verbal ability is indispensable for lawyers and quantitative ability for engineers and scientists, for example. People with greater endowments of such traits have better prospects for success in those activities. Another way of saying it is that there are "ability" rents in occupational choices. Wage differences are not fully equalizing on the costs of acquiring skills because natural endowments and premarket investments cause these costs to differ among people. Second, there are substantial financial barriers to educational investments because human capital is not legal collateral for investment loans. The main manifestation of this is traditionally seen in high stratification of educational attainments of children according to parental wealth. Financing difficulties cause inefficiencies and inequities in human-capital investment decisions because some socially desirable investment opportunities are not available to poor people. Here, too, earnings differences are not fully equalizing on educational costs. They manifest the effects of a form of financial "noncompeting groups," as well as the effects of true differences in costs and talents.

The effects of equal educational opportunities on the distribution of earnings depends on the interpersonal differences in talents, abilities, and motivation on the one hand, and on the importance of noncompeting groups and financial barriers on the other. Econometricians have assessed the "ability-bias" in estimated rates of return to higher education. This work is best interpreted in terms of a one-factor representation of skill where individuals are essentially rank ordered from most able to least able, or according to absolute advantage. Then, if financial barriers are not too negatively correlated with ability, people with more education tend to be more able than those with less, and the wage difference between college and high-school graduates is an upwardly biased estimate of what noncollege graduates would have earned had they gone to college. As a practical matter, the estimates of bias typically are rather small. The characteristics model enriches analysis by allowing selection by comparative advantage rather than absolute advantage. Here abilities and talents have different values in different labor-market pursuits.

For example, Robert Willis and I (1979) modeled educational choice by combining traditional human-capital ideas with the theory of comparative advantage, and developed a method to estimate the behavior determinants of actual choices observed in the data. We found that high-school and college graduates do indeed have different comparative advantages across skills that dominate the selection process. Detailed analysis of the earnings patterns of World War II veterans showed the usual result that high-school graduates would not have earned as much as those who actually chose to get their college degrees. But we also discovered that persons who subsequently gained college degrees probably would have earned relatively less as high-school graduates than those who voluntarily discontinued their education after high-school graduation. Positive selection at both levels of school is inconsistent with a simple rank-order interpretation or single-factor model of ability. It is only consistent with two or more dimensions of ability that are negatively correlated across people. Comparative advantage also accounts for why most estimates of ability-bias interpreted as a single factor (absolute advantage) are so small. Those who leave school early do relatively well in their pursuits so that simple cross-sectional estimates are not much different from ability-corrected ones.

VI. Manufactured Inequality

The production of income is not deterministic. Sometimes, random forces play an important role in assigning earnings to individuals. For example, some occupations are risky. The arts come to mind, where only a few individuals can support themselves on the earnings from their trade. Musicians have very skewed earnings distributions, but most young music students who choose to enter the field understand that there is only a small chance that they will end up at the desired end of the distribution.

Somewhat counterintuitively, perhaps, the variance in outcomes that is introduced by this randomness can improve welfare. The idea is rooted in early work by Milton Friedman (1953) and examined again in a different context by Theodore Bergstrom (1986). Indivisibilities play a key role here. Most people live in one and only one house. Area amenities enjoyed depend on the location of the house and on individuals' choices on location that are correlated with income. For example, rich people may choose to live in New York City rather than in Kankakee, Illinois, because there are more ways to spend income in New York than there are in Kankakee. Conversely, the life of a poor person in Manhattan is difficult because the amenities are expensive and tend to be targeted toward high-income people. There is complementarity in the utility function between the quality of housing, in this case proxied by urban amenities, and the level of consumption of other goods. The situation is illustrated in Figure I.4.

A consumer may choose to live in a high-quality house, z_h, or a low-quality house, z_l, with corresponding house prices p_h and p_l. Because of the complementarity in consumption between other goods and housing,

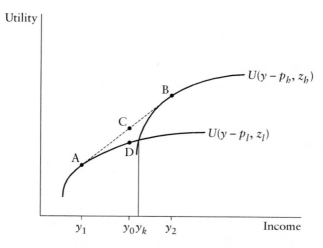

Figure I.4 • Manufactured inequality

those whose incomes are below y_k derive higher utility from living in the low-quality house in a low-amenity location and those whose incomes are above y_k derive higher utility from living in the high-quality house in a high-amenity location. But consumers with incomes between y_1 and y_2 can improve their expected utility by entering into gambles, which would offer them expected utility that lies along the line that connects A and B. For example, an individual with income y_0 who chooses to live in a low-quality house offering utility $U(y_0 - p_l, z_l)$ would prefer a fair gamble that paid income y_1 half the time and income y_2 half the time. Were he to lose the gamble, he would live in the low-quality house and derive utility $U(y_1 - p_l, z_l)$. Were he to win, he would live in the high-quality house and derive utility $U(y_2 - p_h, z_h)$. His expected utility would be at point C, which yields more utility than the certain utility obtained at point D.

Occupational lotteries of this sort manufacture inequality but make the individuals who enter the occupation better off. Because the variance in outcomes give individuals a shot at a much better standard of living, they willingly bear the risk that results in observed ex post inequality. Going to a high-stakes law firm in New York may turn out to be a good option, offering a partnership, high income, and an entertaining city in which to spend income. Those who lose the law-firm lottery accept jobs as corporate counsel in Kankakee, buy a less expensive house, and enjoy fewer amenities. Although it is better to win the lottery than to lose it, the existence of the risky occupation makes all individuals who enter better off in an expected utility sense, primarily because the inequality manufactured by this occupation allows different combinations of income and amenities that are complementary.

VII. Conclusion

Despite the importance of diversity in economic life, only a small part of economic theory is devoted to analyzing differences. Competitive markets value diversity and sort out complex patterns of tastes and technologies that translate into supply of and demand for an enormous variety of products and factors of production. Markets accommodate diversity by establishing values that make differentiated items relatively close substitutes at the margin. The markets match buyers and sellers in marriage-type equilibria where agents sort according to their talents in response to market prices. To bring about the appropriate sorting, markets must create inequality in values. Thus in labor markets, large differences in earnings can result even when individuals are *ex ante* identical.

The theory of diversity applies universally and is manifest in many economic problems. In addition to issues involving earnings inequality, occupational choice, and the differentiation of products, risk analysis of environmental safety concerns and price index problems are analyzable using standard economic approaches to diversity. In such problems, sorting is key, so market valuations understate the average individual's distaste for disagreeable attributes and overstate the average individual's preference for agreeable ones. Sorting plays a role in price index problems, where we seek to ascertain shifts in prices as a result of technology shifts, not movements along a price line that results, say, from increases in real income. Thus, price might appear to rise because richer people buy new varieties of a commodity that has superior attributes that are not captured in standard measurement.

Although tastes may differ, it is the reservation prices themselves and not the causes of the differences that have consequence for economic allocation. Differences in talents are behind much of occupational choice where the theory of comparative advantage is central. Individuals specialize in skills because the fixed costs of skill acquisition is only loosely linked to the levels of utilization. It pays for a worker to learn one thing well and exploit it over and over again. Talents are multidimensional in general, so those who go on to college are better at college jobs than those individuals who do not go on to college. But the converse is also true: Those who opt against college are better at their jobs than those who complete college would be at noncollege jobs. Rather than strict hierarchy, comparative and even some absolute advantage play important roles.

This essay has explored three themes: markets value diversity, markets sort buyers and sellers appropriately to take advantage of heterogeneous talents and tastes, and sorting and choice create income inequality.

Value is determined in diverse markets in the standard way, equating supply with demand. The difference is that there are more margins on which to operate. Not only is quantity a choice variable, but consumers and producers can substitute along varying dimensions of quality. Equilibrium is established when no seller can be made better off by altering the quality of his product and offering it to different buyers and when no buyer can be made better off by substituting a different quality good for the one that he currently consumes.

Just as value is determined by market equilibrium, so too is the allocation of buyers to sellers set by the market. Sellers who have a comparative advantage in producing high-quality products sell to consumers who are willing to pay a sufficient premium for additional quality. Conversely, sellers who have comparative advantage in producing low-quality goods cheaply cater to consumers who prefer to substitute away from high quality so that they can spend the saved dollars on other goods.

Finally, income inequality results from heterogeneity. Some of this is determined by nature as individuals are born with different abilities, but inequality is also manufactured by actions that individuals take. The most obvious actions involve investments in human capital, either through formal schooling or work experience. Such investments create inequality, but are beneficial to individuals and society as a whole because they improve the overall standard of living. A more subtle variant involves gambles that individuals take as they choose to enter risky occupations or make risky investments. Because of indivisibilities, risky payoffs allow individuals to couple the consumption of large amounts of some goods with high-quality versions of others, such as living in expensive cities when income turns out to be high. Losers of occupational lotteries combine their lower consumption with lower-quality indivisible goods, consuming less and living in less expensive cities. Expected utility is higher than it would be, absent this type of inequality.

Markets value diversity. Individuals, using their respective talents and different preferences, respond to these valuations and create important induced differentiation in consumption patterns, earnings, and occupational choices.

References

Bergstrom, Theodore. "Soldiers of Fortune?" in Walter P. Heller, Ross M. Starr, and David A. Starrett, eds., *Essays in honor of Kenneth J. Arrow,* Vol. 2, *Equilibrium analysis.* New York: Cambridge University Press, 1986, pp. 57–80.

Friedman, Milton. "Choice, Chance, and the Personal Distribution of Income." *Journal of Political Economy,* August 1953, 61(4), pp. 277–90.

Rosen, Sherwin. "Hedonic Prices and Implicit Markets: Product Differentiation in Pure Competition." *Journal of Political Economy,* January/February 1974, *82,* pp. 34–55.

Smith, Adam. *An inquiry into the nature and causes of the wealth of nations.* London: Oxford University Press, 1976 [original in 1776].

Thaler, Richard, and Rosen, Sherwin. "The Value of Saving a Life: Evidence from the Labor market," in Nestor E. Terleckyj, ed., *Household production and consumption,* Studies in Income and Wealth 40. New York: Columbia University Press (for NBER), 1976, pp. 412–42.

Willis, Robert, and Rosen, Sherwin. "Education and Self-Selection." *Journal of Political Economy,* October 1979, 87(5), pp. S7–S35. [Reprinted in E. Stromsdorfer and S. Farkas, eds., *Evaluation studies review annual,* Vol. 5. Beverly Hills, CA: Sage Publications, 1980; and in Orley C. Ashenfelter and Kevin F. Hallock, eds., *Labor economics,* Vol. 2. Aldershot, U.K.: Elgar, 1995, pp. 233–62.]

PART I

The Value of Diversity

1

Hedonic Prices and Implicit Markets: Product Differentiation in Pure Competition

I. Introduction and Summary

This paper sketches a model of product differentiation based on the hedonic hypothesis that goods are valued for their utility-bearing attributes or characteristics. Hedonic prices are defined as the implicit prices of attributes and are revealed to economic agents from observed prices of differentiated products and the specific amounts of characteristics associated with them. They constitute the empirical magnitudes explained by the model. Econometrically, implicit prices are estimated by the first-step regression analysis (product price regressed on characteristics) in the construction of hedonic price indexes. With few exceptions, structural interpretations of the hedonic method are not available.[1] Therefore, our primary goal is to exhibit a generating mechanism for the observations in the competitive case and to use that structure to clarify the meaning and interpretation of estimated implicit prices. It will be shown that these data generally contain less information than is commonly supposed. However, the model suggests a method that often can

The substance of this paper arose from conversations with H. Gregg Lewis several years ago. A multitude of other people have contributed advice and criticism. Among them are William Brock, Stanley Engerman, Robert J. Gordon, Zvi Griliches, Robert E. Lucas, Jr., Michael Mussa, and the referee. Remaining errors are my own responsibility. Financial support from the Center for Naval Analysis and the National Institute of Education is gratefully acknowledged.

From *Journal of Political Economy* 82 (1974): 34–55. © 1974 by The University of Chicago.

1. Excellent summaries of the hedonic technique are available in Griliches (1971, chap. 1) and Gordon (1973). Major exceptions to the statement in the text are those studies dealing with depreciation and obsolescence (see Griliches 1971, chaps. 7 and 8) and some recent models based on markup pricing (e.g., Ohta and Griliches 1972).

identify the underlying structural parameters of interest. Also, as a general methodological point, it is demonstrated that conceptualizing the problem of product differentiation in terms of a few underlying characteristics instead of a large number of closely related generic goods leads to an analysis having much in common with the economics of spatial equilibrium and the theory of equalizing differences.

The model itself amounts to a description of competitive equilibrium in a plane of several dimensions on which both buyers and sellers locate. The class of goods under consideration is described by n objectively measured characteristics. Thus, any location on the plane is represented by a vector of coordinates $z = (z_1, z_2, \ldots, z_n)$, with z_i measuring the amount of the ith characteristic contained in each good. Products in the class are completely described by numerical values of z and offer buyers distinct packages of characteristics. Furthermore, existence of product differentiation implies that a wide variety of alternative packages are available. Hence, transactions in products are equivalent to tied sales when thought of as bundles of characteristics, suggesting applicability of the principle of equal advantage for analyzing market equilibrium.

In particular, a price $p(z) = p(z_1, z_2, \ldots, z_n)$ is defined at each point on the plane and guides both consumer and producer locational choices regarding packages of characteristics bought and sold. Competition prevails because single agents add zero weight to the market and treat prices $p(z)$ as parametric to their decisions. In fact the function $p(z)$ is identical with the set of hedonic prices—"equalizing differences"—as defined above, and is determined by some market clearing conditions: Amounts of commodities offered by sellers at every point on the plane must equal amounts demanded by consumers choosing to locate there. Both consumers and producers base their locational and quantity decisions on maximizing behavior, and equilibrium prices are determined so that buyers and sellers are perfectly matched. No individual can improve his position, and all optimum choices are feasible. As usual, market clearing prices, $p(z)$, fundamentally are determined by the distributions of consumer tastes and producer costs. We show how it is possible to recover, or identify, some of the parameters of these underlying distributions by a suitable transformation of the observations.

An early contribution to the problem of quality variation and the theory of consumer behavior has been made by Houthakker (1952) His analysis is designed to take account of the fact that consumers purchase truly negligible fractions of all goods available to them without having to deal with a myriad of corner solutions required by conventional theory. That virtue of Houthakker's treatment is preserved in the present model. More recently Becker (1965), Lancaster (1966), and Muth (1966) have extended Houthakker's methods to more explicit consideration of utility-bearing characteristics. Again, the emphasis is on consumer behavior and properties of market equilibrium have not been worked out, a gap we hope to fill, in part, here. The spirit of these recent contributions is that consumers are also producers. Goods do not possess final consumption attributes but rather are purchased as inputs into self-production functions for ultimate characteristics. Consumers act as their own "middle-men," so to speak. In contrast, the model presented below interposes a *market* between buyers and sellers. Producers themselves tailor their goods to embody final characteristics desired by customers and receive returns for serving economic functions as intermediaries. These returns arise from economies of specialized production achieved by specialization and division of labor through market transactions not available outside organized markets with self-production.

Section II discusses individual choices in the market and the nature of market equilibrium. Some simple examples of analytic solutions for general equilibrium are given in Section III. Section IV presents an empirical method for identifying the underlying structure from the observations, while Section V applies the model to price index number construction in the presence of legislated restrictions. To highlight essential features, the simplest possible specifications are chosen throughout. As a further appeal to intuition, use is made of geometrical constructions wherever possible.

II. Market Equilibrium

Consider markets for a class of commodities that are described by n attributes or characteristics, $z = (z_1, z_2, \ldots, z_n)$. the components of z are objectively measured in the sense that all consumers' perceptions or readings of the amount of characteristics embodied in each good are identical, though of course consumers may differ in their subjective valuations of alternative packages. The terms "product," "model," "brand," and "design" are used interchangeably to designate commodities of given quality or specification. It is assumed that a sufficiently large number of differentiated products are available so that choice among various combinations of z is continuous for all practical purposes. That is, there is a "spectrum of products" among which choices can be made. As will be apparent, this assumption represents an enormous simplification of the problem. It is obviously better approximated in some markets than others, and there is no need to belabor its realism.[2] To avoid complications of capital theory, possibilities for resale of used items in secondhand markets are ignored, either by assuming that secondhand markets do not exist or, alternatively, that goods represent pure consumption.

Each product has a quoted market price and is also associated with a fixed value of the vector z, so that products markets implicitly reveal a function $p(z) = p(z_1, \ldots, z_n)$ relating prices and characteristics. This function is the buyer's (and seller's) equivalent of a hedonic price regression, obtained from shopping around and comparing prices of brands with different characteristics. It gives the minimum price of any package of characteristics. If two brands offer the same bundle, but sell for different prices, consumers only consider the less expensive one, and the identity of sellers is irrelevant to their purchase decisions. Adopt the convention of measuring each z_i so that they all may be treated as "goods" (i.e., so that consumers place positive rather than negative marginal valuations on them) in the neighborhood of their minimum technically feasible amounts. Then firms can alter their products and increase z only by use of additional resources, and $p(z_1, \ldots, z_n)$ must be increasing in all its arguments. Assume $p(z)$ possesses continuous second derivatives. Since a major goal of the analysis is to present a picture of how $p(z)$ is determined, it is inappropriate to place too many restrictions on it at the outset. However, note that there is no reason for it to be linear as is typically the case. The reason is that the differentiated products are sold in separate, though of course highly interrelated, markets. This point is spelled out in some detail below.

A buyer can force $p(z)$ to be linear if certain types of arbitrage activities are allowed. Let z_a, z_b, and z_c be particular values of the vector z. (i) Suppose $z_a = (1/t)z_b$, and $p(z_a) < (1/t)p(z_b)$, where t is a scalar and $t > 1$. Then t units of a model offering z_a yield the same

2. This assumption was first employed by L. M. Court (1941) and allows the use of marginal analysis rather than the programming methods required by Lancaster's (1966) formulation. Following the general rule, it is not without its costs, however (see below).

amount of characteristics as a model offering z_b, but at less cost, ruling out transactions in convex portions of $p(z)$. (ii) Suppose $z_a < z_b < z_c$ and $p(z_b) > \delta p(z_a) + (1 - \delta)p(z_c)$, where $0 < \delta < 1$ and z_b is defined by $z_b = \delta z_a + (1 - \delta)z_c$. Then characteristics in amount of z_b could be achieved by purchasing δ units of a model containing z_a and $(1 - \delta)$ units of a model containing z_c at lower cost than by direct purchase of a brand containing z_b, and products in concave portions of $p(z)$ would be uneconomical. Arbitrage is assumed impossible in what follows (at this point we depart from Lancaster [1966]) on the assumption of indivisibility. This amounts to an assumption that packages cannot be untied. For example, in terms of one characteristic, two 6-foot cars are not equivalent to one 12 feet in length, since they cannot be driven simultaneously (case [i]); while a 12-foot car for half a year and a 6-foot car for the other half is not the same as 9 feet all year round (case [ii]). Similarly, assume sellers cannot repackage existing products in this manner or do not find it economical to do so, as might not be the case with perfect rental markets and zero transactions and reassembly costs.

A. The Consumption Decision

To begin, suppose consumers purchase only one unit of a brand with a particular value of z. Write the utility function as $U(x, z_1, z_2, \ldots, z_n)$ assumed strictly concave, in addition to the other usual properties, where x is all other goods consumed. It would not be difficult to treat z as intermediate goods and relate them to yet more ultimate commodities through self-production functions, but that complication is ignored. Set the price of x equal to unity and measure income, y, in terms of units of x: $y = x + p(z)$. Maximization of utility subject to the nonlinear budget constraint requires choosing x and $(z_1, \ldots, z_n)$ to satisfy the budget and the first-order conditions $\partial p/\partial z_1 = p_i = U_{x_i}/U_x$, $i = 1, \ldots, n$. Optimality is achieved by purchasing a brand offering the desired combination of characteristics. Second-order conditions are fulfilled on the usual assumptions regarding U, so long as $p(z)$ is not sufficiently concave (for a general statement of these conditions under a nonlinear constraint see Intriligator [1971]).

To stress the essential spatial context of the problem, define a value or bid function $\theta(z_1, \ldots, z_n; u, y)$ according to

$$U(y - \theta, z_1, \ldots, z_n) = u. \tag{1}$$

The expenditure a consumer is willing to pay for alternative values of $(z_1, \ldots, z_n)$ at a given utility index and income is represented by $\theta(z; u, y)$. It defines a family of indifference surfaces relating the z_i with "money" (i.e., with x foregone), and has been widely used in urban economics (e.g., see Alonso 1964). Differentiate (1) to obtain

$$\theta_{z_i} = U_{z_i}/U_x > 0, \ \theta_u = -1/U_x < 0, \ \text{and} \ \theta_y = 1, \tag{2}$$

$$\theta_{z_i z_i} = (U_x^2 U_{z_i z_i} - 2U_x U_{z_i} U_{x z_i} + U_{x_i}^2 U_{xx})/U_x^3 < 0, \tag{3}$$

where the inequality in (3) follows from the assumptions about the bordered Hessian matrix of U. Also, strict concavity of U implies that θ is concave in z. Equations (2) and (3) show that the value function is increasing in z_i at a decreasing rate. Alternatively, θ_{z_i} is the marginal rate of substitution between z_i and money, or the implicit marginal valuation the consumer places on z_i at a given utility index and income. It indicates his reservation demand price for an additional unit of z_i, which is decreasing in z_i.

The amount the consumer is willing to pay for z at a fixed utility index and income is $\theta(z; u, y)$, while $p(z)$ is the minimum price he must pay in the market. Therefore, utility is maximized when $\theta(z^*; u^*, y) = p(z^*)$ and $\theta_{z_i}(z^*; u^*, y) = p_i(z^*)$, $i = 1, \ldots, n$, where z^* and u^* are optimum quantities. In other words, optimum location on the z-plane occurs where the two surfaces $p(z)$ and $\theta(z; u^*, y)$ are tangent to each other. One dimension of consumer equilibrium is illustrated in Figure 1.1, where the surfaces have been projected onto the $\theta - z_1$ plane cut at $(z_2^*, \ldots, z_n^*)$. A family of indifference curves, of which only one member (at u^*) is shown, is defined by $\theta(z_1, z_2^*, \ldots, z_n^*; u, y)$. Two different buyers are shown in the figure, one with value function θ^1 and the other with θ^2. The latter purchases a brand offering more z_1.[3]

In general, far less can be said than in the standard analysis about comparative statics, because the budget constraint is nonlinear. Differentiate θ_{z_i} with respect to u, $\theta_{z_i u} = (U_x U_{x z_i} - U_{z_i} U_{xx})/U_x^2$, the numerator of which is recognized as determining the sign of the income elasticity of demand for "good" z_i in standard theory when the other components

---

3. Lewis (1969) employs a similar construction in analyzing the problem of hours of work as a tied sale. Jobs offer a fixed wage-hour package, which varies from job to job. The market establishes a function relating wages and hours on which both workers and employers base their decisions.

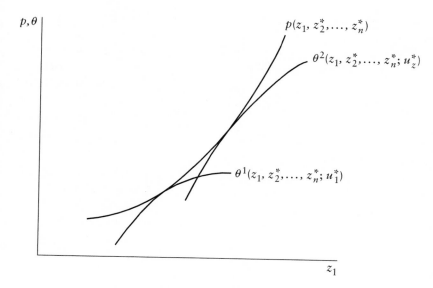

p, θ

$p(z_1, z_2^*, \ldots, z_n^*)$

$\theta^2(z_1, z_2^*, \ldots, z_n^*; u_z^*)$

$\theta^1(z_1, z_2^*, \ldots, z_n^*; u_1^*)$

z_1

Figure 1.1

of z are "held constant." If all these derivatives are positive (z_i is "normal" in this restricted sense for all i), the gradient of θ unambiguously increases as u increases. Additional income always increases maximum attainable utility. Hence if $p(z)$ is convex and sufficiently regular everywhere, we might expect higher income consumers to purchase greater amounts of all characteristics. Only in that case would it be true that larger income leads to an unambiguous increase in the overall "quality" consumed, and differentiated products' markets would tend to be stratified by income. however, in general there is no compelling reason why overall quality should always increase with income. Some components may increase and others decrease (cf. Lipsey and Rosenbluth 1971). Be that as it may, a clear consequence of the model is that there are natural tendencies toward market segmentation, in the sense that consumers with similar value functions purchase products with similar specifications. This is a well-known result of spatial equilibrium models. In fact, the above specification is very similar in spirit to Tiebout's (1956) analysis of the implicit market for neighborhoods, local public goods being the "characteristics" in this case. He obtained the result that neighborhoods tend to be segmented by distinct income and taste groups (also, see Ellickson 1971). That result holds true for other differentiated products too.

Allowing a parameterization of tastes across consumers, the utility function may be written $U(x_1, z_1, \ldots, z_n; \alpha)$, where α is a parameter that differs from person to person. Equilibrium value functions depend on both y and α. A joint distribution function $F(y, \alpha)$ is given in the population at large, and equilibrium of all consumers is characterized by a family of value functions whose envelope is the market hedonic or implicit price function.

The model is easily expended to include several quantities, so long as consumers are restricted to purchasing only one model. Following Houthakker (1952), the utility function becomes $U(x_1, z_1, \ldots, z_n, m)$, where m is the number of units consumed of a model with characteristics z. The constraint is $y = x + mp(z)$, and necessary conditions become

$$\frac{\partial U}{\partial m} = -p(z)U_x + U_m = 0, \tag{4}$$

$$\frac{\partial U}{\partial z_1} = -mp_i(z)U_x + U_{z_1} = 0. \tag{5}$$

The value function is still defined as the amount a consumer is willing to pay for z at a fixed utility index but now with the proviso that m is optimally chosen. That is, $\theta(z_1, \ldots, z_n)$ is defined by eliminating m from

$$u = U(y - m\theta, z_1, \ldots, z_n, m)$$

$$U_m/U_x = \theta.$$

Again, θ_{z_i} is proportional to U_{z_i}/U_x. The logic underlying Figure 1.1 remains intact, and it can just as well serve for this case. However, second-order conditions are now more complex. For example, convexity of $p(z)$ is no longer sufficient for a maximum as it was in the case where m was restricted to be unity. Also, it is necessary to employ stronger assumptions than those used above if the value function θ is to be concave.

Note there is no question of monopsony involved here. Consumers act competitively in spite of the fact that marginal cost of quality, $p_i(z)$, is not necessarily constant—it is increasing in Figure 1.1—because as many units as desired of any brand can be purchased without affecting prices. The function $p(z)$ is the same for all buyers independent of m.

B. The Production Decision

Having set up the formal apparatus above, we give a symmetrical and consequently brief account of producers' locational decisions. What package of characteristics is to be assembled? Let $M(z)$ denote the number of units produced by a firm of designs offering specification z. The discussion is limited to the case of nonjoint production, in which each production establishment within the firm specializes in one design, and there are no cost spillovers from plant to plant. Thus a "firm" is an arbitrary collection of atomistic production establishments, each one acting independently of the others. Analytical difficulties arising from true joint production are noted in passing.

Total costs in an establishment are $C(M, z; \beta)$, derived from minimizing factor costs subject to a joint production function constraint relating M, z, and factors of production. The shift parameter β reflects underlying variables in the cost minimization problem, namely, factor prices and production function parameters. Assume C is convex with $C(0, z) = 0$ and C_M and $C_{z_i} > 0$. There are no production indivisibilities, and marginal costs of producing more units of a model of given design are positive and increasing. Similarly, marginal costs of increasing each component of the design are also positive and nondecreasing. (Ordinarily, there will be some technological constraints that limit the set of feasible locations on the plane.) Each plant maximizes profit $\pi = Mp(z) - C(M, z_1, \dots, z_n)$ by choosing M and z optimally, where unit revenue on design z is given by the implicit price function for characteristics, $p(z)$.[4] Again, firms are competitors and not monopolists even though marginal costs of attributes $p_i(z)$ are not necessarily constant because all establishments observe the same prices and cannot affect them by their individual production decisions: $p(z)$ is independent of M.

---

4. Our inability to treat joint production nontrivially yet simply stems from the spectrum-of-commodities assumption. If a finite number (say v) of packages is available, it would be straightforward formally to specify a standard v-component multiple product cost function for the firm, and proceed on that basis. In the present case, firms engage in joint production only insofar as they own establishments specializing in different packages. However, genuine joint production requires cost dependencies between production units within the firm: the firm must choose a function $M(z)$ describing an entire "product line" offered in the market. The entire function $M(z)$ is an argument in each plant's costs and total costs in turn are the sum (or integral) over all production establishment costs. A complete treatment requires use of functional analysis and is beyond the scope of this paper.

Optimal choice of M and z requires

$$p_i(z) = C_{z_i}(M, z_1, \ldots, z_n)/M, \qquad i = 1, \ldots, n \qquad (6)$$

$$p(z) = C_M(M, z_1, \ldots, z_n). \qquad (7)$$

At the optimum design, marginal revenue from additional attributes equals their marginal cost of production per unit sold. Furthermore, quantities are produced up to the point where unit revenue $p(z)$ equals marginal production cost, evaluated at the optimum bundle of characteristics. As above, convexity of C does not assure second-order conditions due to nonlinearity of $p(z)$, and some stronger conditions, assumed to be satisfied in what follows, are required (see Intriligator 1971).

Symmetrically with the treatment of demand, define an *offer* function $\phi(z_1, \ldots, z_n; \pi, \beta)$ indicating unit prices (per model) the firm is willing to accept on various designs at constant profit when quantities produced of each model are optimally chosen. A family of production "indifference" surfaces is defined by ϕ. Then $\phi(z_1, \ldots, z_n; \pi, \beta)$ is found by eliminating M from

$$\pi = M\phi - C(M, z_1, \ldots, z_n) \qquad (8)$$

and

$$C_M(M, z_1, \ldots, z_n) = \phi, \qquad (9)$$

and solving for ϕ in terms of z, π, and β. Differentiate (8) and (9) to obtain $\phi_{z_i} = C_{z_i}/M > 0$ and $\phi_\pi = 1/M > 0$.

The marginal reservation supply price for attribute i at constant profit, assumed increasing in z_i, is ϕ_{z_i}. Again convexity of C does not always guarantee $\phi_{z_i z_i} > 0$. Since ϕ is the offer price the seller is willing to accept on design z at profit level π, while $p(z)$ is the maximum price obtainable for those models in the market, profit is maximized by an equivalent maximization of the offer price subject to the constraint $p = \phi$. Thus maximum profit and optimum design satisfy $p_i(z^*) = \phi_{z_i}(z_1^*, \ldots, z_n^*; \pi^*, \beta)$, for $i = 1, \ldots, n$, and $p(z^*) = \phi(z_1^*, \ldots, z_n^*; \pi^*, \beta)$. Producer equilibrium is characterized by tangency between a profit-characteristics indifference surface and the market characteristics–implicit price surface.

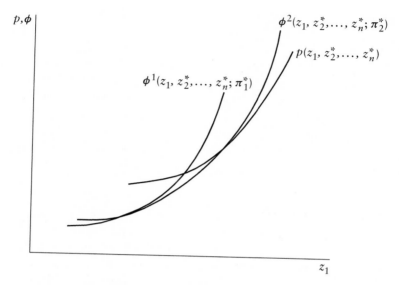

Figure 1.2

One dimension of the solution is depicted in Figure 1.2, where

$$\phi(z_1, z_2^*, \ldots, z_n^*; \pi, \beta)$$

defines a family of curves on the $z_1 - \phi$ plane cut through the indifference surface at the optimum values of the other attributes. Only one member is shown in the figure. The curve labeled ϕ^1 refers to a production unit possessing production and cost conditions making it well suited to produce lesser amounts of z_1, while the one labeled ϕ^2 refers to a firm with a comparative advantage at producing higher values of z_1. That is, the two plants have distinct values of the parameter β. More generally, there is a distribution of β across all potential sellers. Let $G(\beta)$ represent that distribution. Then producer equilibrium is characterized by a family of offer functions that envelop the market hedonic price functions.

What is the empirical content of β? It is anything that shifts cost conditions among firms. Thus differences in factor prices are one possibility. For example, many products are produced in several countries and are traded on national markets (for examples, see Griliches [1971], chap. 5). There is no reason to assume equalization of factor prices in these cases. More generally, anything allowing identification of conventional multiproduct production functions in cross-section data serves to provoke differences in β. Factor price differences across states or regions within a country often serve this purpose and do so here as well. Second, differences in "technology," as reflected by typically unmeasured, firm-specific factors, of production, also act as supply shifters across firms. For example, agricultural production function research often treats education of the farm operator in this manner. Firm-specific R&D expenditure as well as the phenomena of progress-function-learning also serve these purposes.

C. What Do Hedonic Prices Mean?

An answer to the question is an immediate application of the above analysis. Superimpose Figure 1.2 onto Figure 1.1. In equilibrium, a buyer and seller are perfectly matched when their respective value and offer functions "kiss" each other, with the common gradient at that point given by the gradient of the market clearing implicit price function $p(z)$. Therefore, observations $p(z)$ represent a joint envelope of a family of value functions and another family of offer functions. An envelope function by itself reveals nothing about the underlying members that generate it; and they in turn constitute the generating structure of the observations. Some qualifications are necessary, however. (a) Suppose there is no variance in β and all firms are identical. Then the family of offer functions degenerates to a single surface, and $p(z)$ must be everywhere identical with a unique offer function. Price differences between various packages are exactly equalizing among sellers because offer functions are constructed at constant profit. A variety of packages appear on products markets to satisfy differences in preferences among consumers, and the situation persists because no firm finds it advantageous to alter the quality content of its products. (b) Suppose sellers differ, but buyers are identical. Then the family of value functions collapses to a single function and is identical with the hedonic price function. Observed price differences are exactly equalizing across buyers, and $p(z)$ identifies the structure of demand.

III. Existence of Market Equilibrium

Analysis of consumer and producer decisions has proceeded on the assumption of market equilibrium. This section demonstrates some details of equilibrium price and quantity determination. Market quantity demanded for products with characteristics z is $Q^d(z)$, and $Q^s(z)$ is market quantity supplied with those attributes. It is necessary to find a function $p(z)$ such that $Q^d(z) = Q^s(z)$ for all z, when buyers and sellers act in the manner described above. The fundamental difficulty posed by this problem is that $Q^d(z)$ and $Q^s(z)$ depend on the entire function $p(z)$. For example, suppose quantities demanded and supplied at a particular location do not match at prevailing prices. The effect of a change in price at that point is not confined to models with those particular characteristics but induces substitutions and locational changes everywhere on the plane. A very general treatment of the problem is found in Court (1941), and our discussion is devoted to some examples. These examples have been chosen for their simplicity but illuminate the problem and illustrate most of the basic issues. In contrast to the rest of the paper, discussion is specialized to the case where goods are described by exactly one attribute (i.e., $n = 1$). Therefore z_1 represents an unambiguous measure of "quality." When $n = 1$, the location surface degenerates to a line rather than a plane, and products are unequivocally ranked by their z content.

A. Short-Run Equilibrium

Consider a short-run equilibrium in which firms have geared up for the quality (z_1) of goods they can produce and are only capable of varying quantities. The horizon is sufficiently short so that new entry is precluded, and the distribution of firms by quality is given as an initial condition. The market reveals an implicit price function $p(z_1)$, and each firm determines the quantity it supplies to the market according to condition (7). market supply in a small interval dz_1 near quality z_1 is found by weighting firm supply by the quality distribution function. Consumers differ in tastes and income, but all determine optimal quality and quantity as in (4) and (5). Market demand near any quality z_1 is found by using the conditions of consumer equilibrium to transform the distribution of tastes and income into a distribution of qualities demanded and weighting individual quantities demanded by the resulting distribution of qualities. Finally, setting demand equal to supply yields a differential equation in p and z_1 that must be satisfied by market equilibrium, subject to some boundary conditions.

To be specific, assume that $C(N, z) = (a/2)M^2z_1^2$ for all firms. Also, suppose firms are uniformly distributed by the characteristic

$z_1 : g(z_1)dz_1 = kdz_1$ for $z_{1s} \le z_1 \le z_{1l}$, where k is a constant and z_{1l} and z_{1s} are exogenously determined upper and lower limits of the product line. Apply equation (7) to obtain firm supply: $M(z_1) = p/az_1^2$, since qualities cannot be varied by assumption. Therefore,

$$Q^s(z_1)dz_1 = g(z_1)M(z_1)dz_1 = [(k/a)p(z_1)/z_1^2]dz_1. \tag{10}$$

Assume a fixed number of consumers in the population and that only one unit per customer of the optimal model is purchased. Consumers have the same income, and utility is linear in x and z_1, with the marginal rate of substitution, ρ, varying from person to person. Maximize $U(x, z_1) = x + \rho z_1$ subject to $y = x + p(z_1)$. Each consumer purchases a brand for which $dp/dz_1 = p'(z_1) = \rho$. In this case the value functions of Figure 1.1 are straight lines with a different slope, ρ, for each person. The marginal condition characterizes consumer choice so long as $p'' > 0$, which will be shown to be true. Suppose ρ is distributed uniformly, $f(\rho)d\rho = bd\rho$ for $\rho_s \le \rho \le \rho_l$, where b is a constant and ρ_l and ρ_s are, respectively, the largest and smallest marginal rates of substitution in the population. Use the marginal condition $p' = \rho$ to transform $f(\rho)d\rho$ into a distribution of z_1. Then

$$Q^d(z)dz = f(z_1)\left|\frac{dp}{dz_1}\right|dz_1 = bp''(z_1)dz_1. \tag{11}$$

Price must clear the market at every quality. Equating (10) and (11), $p(z_1)$ must satisfy the differential equation

$$(k/ba)p/z_1^2 = d^2p/dz_1^2. \tag{12}$$

Equation (12) is a special case of what is called "Euler's equation" and has a known solution of the form

$$p = c_1 z_1^r + c_2 z_1^s, \tag{13}$$

where c_1 and c_2 are constants determined by the boundary conditions and r and s are defined by $r^2 - r - (a/bk) = 0$: $r = (1 + \sqrt{1 + 4a/bk})/2$ and $s = (1 - \sqrt{1 + 4a/bk})/2$. The parameters r and s are real numbers and $r > 0$ and $s < 0$. Furthermore, $p'(z_1)$ would not be positive throughout its range unless $c_1 > 0$ and $c_2 < 0$, and consumers could not be interior at those points. Equation (13) is graphed in Figure 1.3 on that assumption. Note that p in (13) exhibits an inflection point at

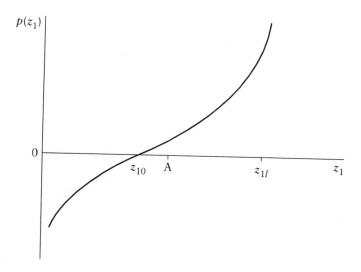

Figure 1.3

$z_{10} = (-c_1/c_2)^{1/(r-s)}$, and it so happens that $p(z_{10}) \equiv 0$. Therefore $p'' > 0$ for $z_1 > z_{10}$.

Boundary conditions. Competition requires there be no masses of consumers at any quality, for there are few sellers located at any point and they would otherwise add nonzero weight to the market. As seen in Section II, consumers with high values of ρ buy higher-quality models, and it must be true that those for whom $\rho = \rho_l$ purchase the highest quality available. Otherwise prices of quality z_{1l} would fall, a great mass of consumers would switch over to them, driving the price back up and causing those buyers to relocate again. Therefore, one boundary condition is $p'(z_{1l}) = \rho_l$, or

$$\rho_l = rc_1 z_{1l}^{r-1} + sc_2 z_{1l}^{s-1}. \tag{14}$$

The other boundary condition is found by examining the lower end of the line. The following three cases cover all relevant possibilities:

1. $z_{1s} = 0$ and $\rho_s > 0$. First choose not to sell at negative prices (see Figure 1.3) and all plants geared to produce qualities less than z_{10} (to be determined) shut down. On the other hand, all consumers value z_1 at least as much as its minimum supply price (i.e., zero) and it must be true that they all buy some value of z_1. individuals for whom $\rho = \rho_s$ consume

the lowest qualities appearing on the market, for if they chose qualities greater than z_{10}, prices of models in the neighborhood of z_{10} would fall to zero, inducing low ρ customers to relocate there and driving their prices back up. Thus a second boundary condition is $p'(z_{10}) = \rho_s$, or

$$\rho_s = rc_1 z_{10}^{r-1} + sc_2 z_{10}^{s-1}. \tag{15}$$

The parameters z_{10}, c_1, and c_2 are determined by equations (14) and (15) plus the definition of z_{10}. It can be shown that $c_1 > 0$ and $c_2 < 0$, as required by the second-order conditions of consumer equilibrium. Therefore, the equilibrium hedonic price function appears as a portion of the curve in Figure 1.3 in the interval (z_{10}, z_{1l}).

2. If $\rho_s = 0 = z_{1s}$, all producers must be in the market, and it follows that $z_{10} = 0$. This only is possible if $p'(0) = \rho_s = 0$ and c_2 must be zero. In this case price is a log-linear function of quality.

3. $z_{1s} > 0$ and $\rho_s = 0$. Now some consumers do not value z_1 very highly, and there is a definite limit to the smallest amount available. Clearly, $p(z_{1s})$ must exceed zero and some consumers must be driven out of the market, finding it optimal not to consume the product at all. If not, consumers with small values of ρ would mass on z_{1s} (there would be a corner solution there), adding finite weight to the market and causing $p(z_{1s})$ to explode. Using the budget constraint, the market rate of exchange between not buying at all and buying z_{1s} is $[y - p(z_{1s})]/z_{1s}$ and must equal the slope of the value function for buyers at that (extensive) margin. That is, the condition $[y - p(z_{1s})]/z_{1s} = p'(z_{1s})$ replaces equation (15)—after substituting for p and p' from (13)—in the determination of c_1 and c_2. The hedonic price function also can be illustrated in Figure 1.3 as the portion of the curve between the points such as those marked $A(= z_{1s})$ and z_{1l}. Again, kc_1 and c_2 have the correct signs and the second-order conditions are fulfilled.

A second type of short-run equilibrium could be considered in which existing firms can alter qualities s well as quantities of their products. When there is a distribution of cost functions, it is necessary to proceed analogously to the treatment of demand in the example above. For example, costs might be described by $(a/2)N^2 z_1^\lambda$ with λ varying across firms. Then $(\lambda/2) = z_1 p'/p$ is used to transform the distribution of λ into a distribution of qualities supplied. The resulting distribution weights firm quantities supplied in the determination of market supply at any quality. A little experimentation will show that the differential equation resulting from setting $Q^d(z_1) = Q^s(z_1)$ is nonlinear in most cases, and closed solutions are not always feasible.

B. Long-Run Equilibrium

Firms may vary qualities at will and also construct establishments of optimum size. No entry restrictions imply the absence of profit ($\pi* = 0$) and long-run offer price for each firm must satisfy $\rho(z; \beta) = C(M, z; \beta)/M$. Plants are constructed to produce models of quality z at minimum cost. Hence scale economies are exhausted under competition and the optimum production unit occurs where $C(M, z, \beta)$ is linear in M, variations of quantity being achieved by changes in the number of establishments. Let $h(z; \beta)$ represent minimum average cost of z for an establishment of optimum size. Then $C(M, z; \beta) = Mh(z; \beta)$ in the long run. Therefore $\phi = h(z; \beta)$ and $p(z) = h(z; \beta)$ is the equilibrium condition for maximum profit and $p(z)$ is completely determined by supply, or by the envelope of the family $h(z; \beta)$ with respect to β. Generalization to n characteristics is obvious in this case.

IV. An Identification Problem

Section III demonstrated that complete solutions for $p(z)$ and the distribution of qualities traded sometimes can be obtained if sufficient a priori structure is imposed on the problem. However, it is not always possible to proceed in that manner. In general, the differential equation defining $p(z)$ is nonlinear and it may not be possible to find closed solutions. Moreover, a great deal of structure must be imposed. For example, the distribution of income follows no simple law throughout its range, making it difficult to specify the problem completely. Finally, partial-differential equations must be solved when there is more than one characteristic. This section sketches an alternative and more efficient procedure, based on the analysis of Section II.

As shown above, derivatives of a consumer's value function, θ_{z_i}, are proportional to marginal rates of substitution. They are reservation-demand prices for additional amounts of z_i at a constant utility index. Therefore $\{\theta_{z_i}(z)\}$ are the inverses of a set of ordinary compensated demand functions for the z_i's. The marginal cost of z_i to the consumer is $p_i(z)$, and optimal z is determined where marginal costs equal marginal values. One dimension of these marginal concepts is illustrated in Figure 1.4. The curves labeled $\theta_{z_i}^j$ are derivatives of θ^j in Figure 1.1 and

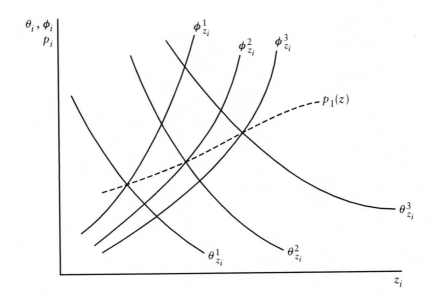

Figure 1.4

reflect compensated demand functions for various buyers. The dashed line labeled $p_1(z)$ is the common marginal cost confronting all buyers. Consumer choice is given by the intersection of demand and marginal cost. It should be emphasized that the functions $\theta_{z_i}(z)$ are compensated demand prices (real income held constant) and can only be derived once equilibrium is determined, as in Section II. For example, a new equilibrium resulting from an exogenous shift in p would not always be given by the intersection of the new marginal costs, $p_1(z)$, and the initial compensated demand price functions. An exception occurs when $\theta_{z_i u} = 0$ and the family of surfaces $\theta(z; u)$, such as depicted in Figure 1.1, are all parallel to each other: $\theta_{z_i u} = 0$ is equivalent to constant marginal utility of money and θ_{z_i} is unique and independent of u only in that case. If $\theta_{z_i u} \neq 0$, the shape and location of the $\theta_{z_i}^j$ functions are determined by the equilibrium conditions of Section II: tangency between $p(z)$ and $\theta^j(z, u*)$.

A similar procedure applies to firms: ϕ_{z_i} is the reservation supply price of incremental z_i and reflects a profit-compensated supply function for characteristic z_i; p_i is the marginal revenue function for z_i facing each firm. One dimension of producer equilibrium is shown in Figure 1.4 as the intersection of a set of compensated supply curves for various firms, ϕ_z^j, with a common marginal revenue function, $p_1(z)$.

Figure 1.4 reiterates the major conclusion of Section II in terms of derivatives of $p(z)$. Equilibrium is described by the intersection of supply and demand functions. However, income effects have been removed, in distinction to the typical case. Observed marginal hedonic prices merely connect equilibrium reservation prices and characteristics and reveal little about underlying supply and demand functions.

However, Figure 1.4 suggests a method that can be used for estimation. In principle, data are available on designs purchased by buyers and also on their incomes and taste variables such as age, education, etc. Denote these empirical counterparts of α by a vector Y_1. Data are also potentially available on the characteristics' content of models produced by sellers and factor price and specific technological differences among them. Denote the empirical counterparts of β by a vector Y_2. Following Figure 1.4, let $F_i(z, Y_1)$ represent the marginal demand price for z_i and $G_i(z, Y_2)$ represent the marginal supply price. Ignoring random terms, the model to be estimated can be written as

$$p_i(z) = F^i(z_1, \ldots, z_n, Y_1) \quad \text{(demand)}, \tag{16}$$

$$p_i(z) = G^i(z_1, \ldots, z_n, Y_2) \quad \text{(supply)}, \tag{17}$$

for $i = 1, \ldots, n$, where p_i and z_i are all jointly dependent variables and y_1 and Y_2 are exogenous demand and supply shift variables. The $2n$ equations determine the $2n$ endogenous variables p_i and z_i. Estimation requires a two-step procedure. First, estimate $p(z)$ by the usual hedonic method, without regard to Y_1 and Y_2. that is, regress observed differentiated products' prices, p, on all of their characteristics, z, using the best-fitting functional form. This econometrically duplicates the information acquired by agents in the market, on the basis of which they make their decisions. Denote the resulting estimate of the function $p(z)$ by $\hat{p}(z)$. Next, compute a set of implicit *marginal* prices, $\partial p(z)/\partial z_i = \hat{p}_i(z)$ for each buyer and seller, evaluated at the amounts of characteristics (numerical values of z) actually bought or sold, as the case may be. Finally, use estimated marginal prices $\hat{p}_i(z)$ as endogenous variables in the second-stage simultaneous estimation of equations (16) and (17). Estimation of marginal prices plays the same role here as do direct observations on prices in the standard theory and converts the second-stage estimation into a garden variety identification problem. There are four cases to consider:

1. There is no variance in β and cost conditions are identical across firms. The variables Y_2 drop out of equation (17) and $\hat{p}(z)$ identifies the offer function. Similarly, the sample observations on $\hat{p}_i(z)$ and the z_i identify compensated supply functions. Suppose several cross sections for different years are available and firms' production functions have been subject to technical change. Then within-year hedonic price regressions identify supply conditions for each year. Changes in marginal prices and qualities induced by changing technology and cost conditions between years approximately sweep out the structure of preferences and compensated demand functions (with due qualification for the nonconstancy of the marginal utility of money).

2. If buyers are identical, but sellers differ, Y_1 drops out of (16) and single cross-sectional observations trace out compensated demand functions.

3. If buyers are identical and so are sellers, offer and value functions are tangent at a single point, and only one quality appears on the market. The observations degenerate to a single point; there is no product differentiation and no problem.

4. In general there is both a distribution of buyers and another distribution of sellers. Both Y_1 and Y_2 have nonzero variance, and the usual identifying rank and order conditions apply. A necessary prior condition for estimation is that $\hat{p}(z)$ be nonlinear at stage one. For if $\hat{p}(z)$ happens to be linear, $\hat{p}_i(z)$ are constants, independent of qualities traded, and display zero variance across sample observations. As shown above, linearity of $p(z)$ is unlikely so long as there is increasing marginal cost of attributes for sellers and it is not possible to untie packages. But it is obvious that the model does not apply if very few distinct products are actually traded.

V. Price Indexes, Economic Welfare, and Legislated Restrictions

This section uses the model to analyze the welfare consequences of quality-standards legislation, a problem not easily handled by conventional methods. The discussion clarifies issues in recent controversies regarding treatment of legislated standards in the construction of price indexes. for example, how should mandatory installation of seat belts

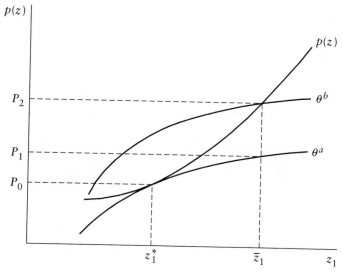

Figure 1.5

and air bags affect the automobile price index? For expository convenience, discussion is confined to the case of one attribute. Generalization to several characteristics is immediate.

A minimum quality standard means that $z \geq \bar{z}$, and brands containing less than $\bar{z}$ are prohibited from the market. Assume constant returns to quantities (as in Section IIIB). Ten the law is irrelevant for all consumers previously purchasing packages containing more than the legislated minimum. The situation for a buyer whose choice is affected by the law is shown in Figure 1.5: z^* was the original choice, whereas $\bar{z}$ is chosen after the law has been passed, since z^* is no longer available. The minimum attainable value function has shifted fro θ^a to θ^b, and the consumer is worse off (see eq. [2]).

Choose the distance $\Delta P = P_2 - P_1$ as a monetary measure of the loss welfare. Since $\partial\theta/\partial y = 1$, ΔP is the bribe necessary for the consumer to purchase $\bar{z}$ when z^* was available. Clearly, this measure is not unique (i.e., if compensation is evaluated at a different amount of z) unless $\theta_{z_iu} = 0$. The welfare loss can be estimated from the implicit price and bid functions. The distance $P_2 - P_0$ is given by

$$\int_{z_1^*}^{\bar{z}_1} p_1(z)dz,$$

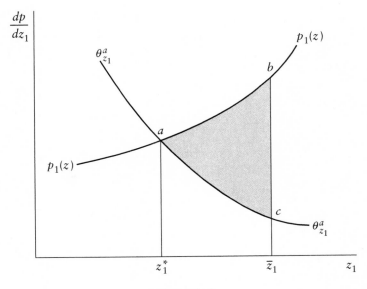

Figure 1.6

or the area under marginal cost from z^* to $\bar{z}$, and is shown in Figure 1.6 as $z_1^*ab\bar{z}_1$. It represents the social opportunity cost of additional resources necessary to produce $\bar{z}$ instead of z^*. The integral

$$\int_{z^*}^{\bar{z}} \theta_1(z)dz,$$

or the area under a compensated demand function (compensated at the original level of real income) between z^* and $\bar{z}$ in Figure 1.6 ($z_1^*ac\bar{z}_1$) measures the amount the consumer would have paid for the increment $(\bar{z}_1 - z_1^*)$ at the unrestricted level of welfare. It measures $P_1 - P_0$ in Figure 1.5 and represents the benefit of the restriction. The difference between costs and benefits is given by $P_2 - P_1$, or the difference between the areas under the marginal cost and compensated demand functions, the shaded area in Figure 1.6. In the general case of several attributes, ΔP must be measured by a line integral. Otherwise, everything else is unchanged.

When the marginal utility of money is constant, ΔP is unique and the price restriction is equivalent to an additive increase in implicit prices in amount ΔP everywhere. In Figure 1.5, $\theta_{zu} = 0$ means that all value functions are parallel, and if the budget constraint was $y = x + p(z) + \Delta P$ instead of $y = x + p(z)$, the consumer would have arrived exactly at θ^b of his own free choice. The real price of the characteristic has risen because choices are restricted, and the price index should rise to reflect that fact. A natural measure of the real price increase imposed by the law is a weighted average of terms such as ΔP (including buyers for whom $\Delta P = 0$), where the weights are expenditure shares among all consumers.[5] This measure overstates the loss insofar as the restriction actually forces some consumers completely out of the generic goods market since they escape the full loss ΔP. Also, standard index number problems arise when the marginal utility of money is not constant.

VI. Conclusions

This paper has drawn out the observational consequences of the construct of implicit markets for characteristics embodied in differentiated products. When goods can be treated as tied packages of characteristics, observed market prices are also comparable on those terms. The economic content of the relationship between observed prices and observed characteristics becomes evident once price differences among goods are recognized as equalizing differences for the alternative packages they embody. Here, as elsewhere, price differences generally are equalizing only on the margin and not on the average. Hence, estimated hedonic price-characteristics functions typically identify neither demand nor supply. In fact, those observations are described by a joint-envelope function and cannot by themselves identify the structure of consumer preferences and producer technologies that generate them.

The formal analysis is complicated by the fact that budget constraints are nonlinear. Consequently, it is not surprising that far weaker

---

5. A complete assessment of the law and its effect on the price index requires balancing the costs calculated above against any externality-induced social benefits of the restriction. In our judgment, seat belts and air bags are in a different category than emission-control devices. In regard to the latter, the apparatus above can be used easily to analyze the effect of the European system of taxing engine displacement. An ad valorem tax increases average and marginal costs of packages with larger liter capacity, and the usual income and substitution effects apply: packages with smaller amounts of this and complementary characteristics (such as size of car) are purchased.

theorems than usual apply. However, a feasible econometric procedure for estimating the underlying generating structure has been derived through the use of derivative transformations. When constraints are nonlinear, marginal prices serve the same role as average prices do in the linear case. Finally, the essential spatial context of the problem means that substitution and income effects must be more carefully distinguished than usual. Indeed, here is a major practical instance where compensated demand and supply functions become the relevant fundamental concepts. These compensated functions are estimated by the econometric method and measures of consumer and producer surplus can be derived directly from them. We anticipate that the basic conceptual framework outlined above will have a variety of applications to many practical problems involving equilibrium in cross-section data.

The analysis has been simplified by assuming divisibility in production. Generalization has to incorporate nonconvexities, and discontinuities must result. When nonconvexities are not small relative to the market, it is obvious that only isolated locations on the characteristics surface will be filled. In other words, such a generalization will naturally incorporate the case of monopolistic competition, and observed "distances" (in terms of characteristics) between differentiated products will be endogenously determined. The methods employed above do not carry through because certain nonmarginal decisions must be analyzed, and far more sophisticated techniques are required.

References

Alonzo, William. *Location and Land Use*. Cambridge, Mass.: Harvard Univ. Press, 1964.

Becker, Gary S. "A Theory of the Allocation of Time." *Econ. J.* 75 (September 1965): 493–517.

Court, Louis M. "Entrepreneurial and Consumer Demand Theories for Commodity Spectra." *Econometrica* 9, no. 1 (April 1941): 135–62; no. 2 (July–October 1941): 241–97.

Ellickson, Bryan. "Jurisdictional Fragmentation and Residential Choice." *A.E.R.* 61 (May 1971): 334–39.

Gordon, Robert J. "The Measurement of Durable Goods Prices." Mimeographed. Nat. Bur. Econ. Res., 1973.

Griliches, Zvi, ed. *Price Indexes and Quality Change*. Cambridge, Mass.: Harvard Univ. Press, 1971.

Houthakker, H. S. "Compensated Changes in Quantities and Qualities Consumed." *Rev. Econ. Studies* 19, no. 3 (1952): 155–64.

Intriligator, Michael D. *Mathematical Optimization and Economic Theory.* Englewood Cliffs, N.J.: Prentice-Hall, 1971.

Lancaster, Kelvin J. "A New Approach to Consumer Theory." *J.P.E.* 74 (April 1966): 132–56.

Lewis, H. Gregg. "Interes del empleador en las horas de Trabajo del empleado" [Employer interests in employee hours of work]. *Cuadernos de Economia,* Catholic Univ. Chile, 1969.

Lipsey, Richard G., and Rosenbluth, Gideon. "A Contribution to the New Demand Theory: A Rehabilitation of the Giffen Good." *Canadian J. Econ.* 4 (May 1971): 131–63.

Muth, Richard F. "Household Production and Consumer Demand Functions." *Econometrica* 34 (July 1966): 699–708.

Ohta, Makoto, and Griliches, Zvi. "Makes and Depreciation in the U.S. Passenger Car Market." Mimeographed. Harvard Univ., 1972.

Tiebout, Charles M. "A Pure Theory of Local Expenditure." *J.P.E.* 64 (October 1956): 416–24.

2

Discrimination in the Market for Public School Teachers

JOSEPH R. ANTOS

SHERWIN ROSEN

1. Introduction

This study examines some aspects of discrimination in the market for public school teachers in the United States, using extensive cross-section data from the Coleman Report of 1965. Our methodological framework is a model of the spatial distribution of teachers based on the theory of equal advantage. Employment contracts in the teachers' market represent a rather complicated variety of tied sale, because both teaching services and conditions of work are not homogeneous.

We examine consequences of the fact that labor market transactions involve mutual, joint exchange of both labor services and consumption attributes at the workplace. Teachers sell the services of their labor, but simultaneously purchase utility bearing characteristics of the schools in which they work. On the other side of the bargain, school administrators purchase desired teacher services and jointly sell characteristics of schools and students to their teachers. Every contract quotes a price for the total package of labor services and on-the-job consumption, and the content of the package varies from school to school. Hence comparisons of wage rates across teacher characteristics and consumption attributes yield a functional relationship from which it is sometimes possible to impute prices for various dimensions of the underlying exchange package. The observed relation between salaries, teacher characteristics, and

Reprinted from *Journal of Econometrics* 3: 123–150. © North-Holland Publishing Company (1975), with permission from Elsevier.

school characteristics is determined by the market in such a way that teachers and schools are correctly allocated to each other and all markets are cleared. In so doing, it serves the same role as, and in fact is analogous to, the familiar concept of the rent gradient in models of spatial equilibrium and urban economics. We estimate the "wage gradient" in the teachers' market and derive its economic implications.

Though our conceptual design relates to a general set of working conditions and teacher characteristics, primary attention is focused on student quality, school neighborhood characteristics, student racial composition of schools, and race–sex classifications of teachers. We ultimately seek to answer the question, "How much additional salary is required to induce a white teacher to teach in a black school?" Also, and as a matter of course, the empirical results allow us to make the usual standardized wage comparisons between race and sex groups, evaluated at a common set of characteristics.

In addition to the possible interest of our study for the theory of equalizing differences and the economics of discrimination, it may also have some practical applications as well. These bear on current discussions of the distribution of public school expenditures among school districts and on some broader issues of public school tax-expenditure policy now under litigation. Many of the key questions in recent debates cannot be answered because information on basis structural relationships is lacking.

Two important issues have remained unresolved and we provide some evidence on one of them. The first and most difficult relates to the nature of educational production functions. For example, it is now widely accepted that students' learning capabilities are proper arguments of the production function. If so, knowledge of substitution possibilities between student abilities and purchased inputs is required to even formulate what is meant by an equitable distribution of expenditures per student. A second set of questions, to which this work is most relevant, is concerned with the distribution of "quality" of purchased inputs across school districts. Certainly, teacher quality is not randomly distributed over the whole student population. But even if all teachers were homogeneous, evidence presented below demonstrates the existence of systematic compensatory differentials in efficiency wages of teachers related to school and student characteristics. Therefore real costs of schooling vary from school to school, and meaningful indexes of expenditure per student only can be computed by pricing out a standard set of purchased inputs within each school. Evidently, what is required here is the wage equivalent of a hedonic price index. Estimation of the wage–school–teacher characteristics function is the raw material for construction of such an index.

2. Nature of the Market

A general organizational principle suitable for the analysis is the notion that amounts of local public goods vary from community to community and, given wealth constraints, individuals make choices among available alternatives by moving to the community most closely matching their preferences. As is well known, local public goods jurisdictions tend to become stratified by family wealth and taste patterns [Tiebout (1956)]. Here the local public good is the "quality" of public education parents desire to purchase for their children. For present purposes it is sufficient to consider the distribution of school quality across school districts as exogenous (though it would not be so considered in a larger context, since the relationships investigated below in part determine output-quality distributions). In such a setting, teachers must also choose among various school districts, applying to schools most closely matching their preferences, in the manner spelled out below.

It amounts to little more than a truism to assert that wage determination in the teacher market always can be described by a general equilibrium system of supply and demand functions. The trouble with a model with so few prior restrictions is that it doesn't offer much assistance for organizing the data. A serious conceptual difficulty arises because different schools and different teachers are very good substitutes for each other, in spite of their heterogeneity. Therefore, supply and demand functions across schools generally are highly interrelated and extremely complicated. However, the nature of substitution provides a clue for simplifying part of the problem and making it more manageable.

If it is possible to decompose transactions into joint trades of characteristics, then both teachers and schools become comparable on those same terms. Supply and demand for teachers determines wages at each school. These prices, along with alternative attributes packages exchanged across schools, reveal a market-determined constraint relating characteristics and money that guides all agents' employment decisions.

The revealed wage constraint in turn determines the system of supply and demand functions that initially generated the observations. In equilibrium, supply and demand functions for teachers at each school and the observed wage-characteristics function across schools and teachers are mutually consistent. Both teachers and school administrators do the best they can on the basis of the market wage-characteristics function and all optimal choices are attainable.

The meaning of market information for both teachers and administrators is knowledge of alternative combinations of characteristics and salaries available in different schools. Teachers seek out schools offering school attributes most closely matching their preferences, comparing subjective valuations of alternative school attributes with opportunity costs, represented by the wage-characteristics function (summarizing prices at other schools), and transportation costs. If a teacher has the requisite package of characteristics desired by the school administrator, itself determined by comparing teaching effectiveness of the person in question in that school with implicit market prices (of other, potential teachers) from the wage-characteristics function, the teacher is hired. If not, the application is rejected and both teacher and school look elsewhere. In equilibrium every teacher finds a school and vice versa. Otherwise the relation between salaries and characteristics must change to incorporate market disequilibrium.

Empirical effort goes into estimating the wage–school–teacher characteristics function, which econometrically duplicates information acquired by administrators and teachers in making rational employment decisions. Of particular interest is the imputed price of race of students. The partial derivative (if it exists) of the wage function with respect to the percentage of black students in a school estimates *marginal* market discrimination. Indeed, the derivative of the estimated function with respect to any school or student attribute estimates the marginal rate of substitution between the attribute and money, applicable to any teacher who found it optimal to work in a school with that amount of the attribute.

These points can be easily illustrated. Let t be an m-component vector of teacher characteristics and s an n-component vector of school characteristics. For example, t would include teacher intelligence, while s would include percentage black students and average student ability. The function $w(t, s)$ gives the wage of teachers with characteristics t in schools with characteristics s, and is revealed to agents by comparison shopping described above. A teacher has a utility function $U(c, s)$, where c is consumption, taken as numeraire, and an "endowed" set of teacher characteristics $\bar{t}$ Utility is maximized by choosing an optimal value of s; that is, by choosing a school with the appropriate package of characteristics, subject to the constrain $c = w(\bar{t}, s) + y$, where y is nonwage income. If the market provides a large enough range of choice, marginal analysis can be used and necessary conditions for a maximum are approximated by

$$\partial w(\bar{t}, s)/\partial s_i \equiv w_{s_i} = -U_{s_i}/U_c, \qquad i = 1, \ldots, n, \qquad (1)$$

all evaluated at the optimal value of s, and at $\bar{t}$. Another teacher with a different utility function or different amounts of nonlabor income or different values of $\bar{t}$ rationally applies to a school with some other combination of characteristics. Be that as it may, if we as outside observers estimate $w(t, s)$ and evaluate the derivatives $w_{s_i}(\bar{t}, s^*)$, eq. (1) shows we also estimate the marginal rate of substitution or marginal demand price applicable to teachers who are at that margin of choice. If $w_{s_i} < 0$, U_{s_i} must be positive and s_i must be a consumption "good." If $w_{s_i} > 0$, U_{s_i} is negative and s_i is a "bad."[1]

To illustrate, suppose the imputed marginal price of percentage black student body is $50, evaluated in schools with 50 percent black students. Then teachers in such schools require receiving about $50 extra annual compensation to move to an otherwise similar school with 51 percent black students. Further, suppose teachers have varying tastes for discrimination [Becker (1957)] in the sense of differing compensated demand price schedules for racial composition. Then teachers working in schools with more than 50 percent black students tend to have lesser tastes for discrimination than those working in 50 percent black schools, and those working in schools with many less than 50 percent black

---

1. It is easy to include transportation costs in the form $\gamma(|s - s_0|)$, where s_0 is the amount of school characteristics readily available in the teacher's present neighborhood. Assume marginal transportation cost γ_{sj} is positive and increasing. The budget is altered to $c = w - \gamma + y$ and $w_{sj} - \gamma_{sj}$ replaces w_{sj} in condition (1). The importance of transportation costs in an unrestricted market is minimal in the long run because teachers can move to their desired location and make s_0 coincide with s^*. However, neighborhood schools and residential segregation by race impose permanent barriers to complete mobility. Since values of s_0 are not randomly distributed between white and black teachers, transportation costs help explain why schools tend to be segregated both by race of students and of teachers.

students tend to have greater tastes for discrimination than the other two groups.

Just as in the familiar theory of equalizing differences with binary alternatives, observed (marginal) market discrimination reflects both the distribution of tastes for discrimination and the number of opportunities.[2] For example, if there are a sufficient number of teachers who do not discriminate against black students relative to the number of black students in the population, no market discrimination need be observed. This would not mean there are no teachers in the population who dislike black students. It would mean that at the margin it is unnecessary to pay wage premiums to attract a few additional teachers into black schools. Those so attracted willingly would work in a black school at no increase in pay, whereas those with strong distastes avoid psychic costs of discrimination by working in schools with many white students.

The foregoing logic suggests a powerful force working toward segregation of *both* students and teachers according to race, in addition to transportation costs. We do not expect teachers to discriminate against members of their own race. Furthermore, there are many black teachers. Therefore, we expect the natural workings of the market to allocate black teachers to black schools and white teachers to white schools, even in the absence of residential barriers. In fact, segregation of this variety works again the presence of market discrimination with respect to school racial composition. However, there is another force working toward segregation that is also consistent with wage discrimination: Parents may prefer members of their own race as teachers of their children. Whether this results in black–white teacher wage differentials (of either sign) depends on the distribution and intensity of parental preferences and the racial distribution of both students and teachers in the population.

Turn now to the demand side of the market. Several plausible specifications are possible and one simple alternative is discussed. It is presented as an illustration of basic principles that must be present in

---

2. The appropriate reference is Friedman and Kuznets (1954). The present model is a generalization for binary choices to a continuum, and the concept of a reservation price relevant to the former must be extended to that of a reservation price *function* defined over the whole range of alternatives. See Rosen (1974) for some details in a more conventional market setting than the one considered here.

more general specifications, and readers are encouraged to supply their own modifications.

For simplicity, assume educational output can be collapsed into a univariate index, z, measured on a per student basis. for example, z might depend on an index of "socialization" and incremental "ability" per student, both in the value-added sense. Define r as the teacher–student ratio and write an educational production function, $z = f(t, s, r)$. School and student characteristics variables s may be partitioned into two parts. Some variables in s are under administrative control, such as air conditioning, laboratory facilities, and the like; whereas others such as racial composition of students, student intelligence, and type of neighborhood in which the school is located are inherent to the school and cannot be changed so readily. They are part of the school's "endowment." further, the list of s variables in $f(.)$ may not correspond precisely with those in $w(.)$. To avoid cumbersome notation the same symbol is used for both, with the understanding that derivatives of appropriate nonoverlapping members in either f or w are defined to be identically zero.

Consistent with the working assumption of an exogenous distribution of school quality across school districts, specify the administrator's task as minimizing per student cost of educational output, subject to the market price schedule for teachers, $w(t, s)$, and the educational production function, $f(t, s, r)$. Ignoring capital, costs per student are

$$\min \{rw(t, s) + V(s) + \lambda[z - f(t, s, r)]\} = C(z), \qquad (2)$$

where λ is an undetermined multiplier (marginal cost) and $V(s)$ is the per student nonwage cost of changing alterable school characteristics.[3] Again, assuming a sufficient range of choice for marginal analysis, necessary conditions for a minimum are:

$$w - \lambda f_r = 0, \qquad (3)$$

$$rw_{t_i} - \lambda f_{t_i} = 0, \qquad i = 1, \ldots, m, \qquad (4)$$

---

3. $C(z; \ldots)$ gives the menu of public goods choices available and serves as a constraint on the determination of the number and type of jurisdictions formed by the political process. Note that within-jurisdiction heterogeneity of both teacher and student characteristics has been ignored. This is an enormous analytical simplification, but it at least is consistent with the observation that cross-jurisdictional differences are at least as large, if not larger, than within-jurisdictional differences.

$$rw_{s_j} + c_{s_j} - \lambda f_{s_j} = 0, \qquad \text{(for a subset of } s\text{)}, \qquad (5)$$

$$z - f(t, s, r) = 0. \qquad (6)$$

If second-order conditions are satisfied, eqs. (3)–(6) determine optimum values of **t**, **s**, and **r**. In particular, they determine a list of teacher requirements, **t***, the administrator insists be embodied in all prospective teachers in his school. Individuals not possessing the desired characteristics are not hired, and the administrator's observations of $w(t, s)$ indicate these requirements can be satisfied. Note that teacher credential requirements are not determined in a vacuum. Rather, they are the result of balancing off the marginal educational value of various teacher characteristics against their marginal cost and availabilities in the market, given the school's own endowment of attributes. Clearly, administrators with different inherent endowments of school and student characteristics choose different values of **t** (as well as **r** and the subset of **s** subject to choice), depending on the precise complementarities among **t** and **s** in both the production function and the market-generated wage-characteristics function. School administrators catering to parents who have chosen different qualities of education for their children (different values of **z**), or who have different beliefs about the nature of the educational production function also optimally arrive at different values of **t***.

The precise relation between demand conditions and observed wages and characteristics can be more easily seen by simple algebraic manipulation of eqs. (3)–(6). Define β as the elasticity of educational output per student with respect to the teacher–student ratio, $\beta \equiv (r/z)(\partial z/\partial r)$. Then (3) and (4) can be expressed as

$$w_{t_i}/w = \frac{1}{z}\frac{\partial z}{\partial t_i} \bigg/ \beta, \qquad i = 1, \ldots, m. \qquad (7)$$

Assuming t_i is measured in such a way as to be productive, (7) shows that relative marginal wage cost of each teacher attribute required by the administrator is proportional to its relative marginal product. For alterable school characteristics, (3) and (5) may be expressed as

$$[w_{sj} + c_{s_j}]/w = \frac{1}{z}\frac{\partial z}{\partial s_j} \bigg/ \beta, \qquad \text{(for alterable } s_j\text{)}. \qquad (8)$$

Hence relative marginal wage costs of nonendowment school characteristics are not strictly proportional to relative marginal products, but are less than that by an amount depending on the nonwage costs of changing them. (8) also shows administrators may alter some school characteristics even if they are not productive in the educational sense (i.e., $f_{sj} = 0$), so long as such expenditures yield returns in the form of reduced teacher cost.

3. The Data

Data used to estimate $w(t, s)$ comes from the Equality of Educational-Opportunity Survey of 1965, a 5 percent sample of public schools in the United States designed in such a way that 50 percent of sampled students were nonwhite. While the defects of this sample for estimating educational production functions are well known, it is useful for the present inquiry because it is the richest source of available data on school characteristics that can be matched to teachers. Moreover, its over-representation of nonwhite students is not unwelcome for studying discrimination.

Each observation in the sample contains three kinds of information. Teachers, principals, and students (in grades 3, 6, 9, and 12) in each sampled school were given detailed questionnaires. Analysis is confined to full-time high school teachers in grades 10 through 12. Particular students were not matched to particular teachers in the original data, and student characteristics could only be defined over schools. Therefore, the relationships estimated are of the form $w_{ij} = w(t_{ij}, s_j)$: the wage of teacher i in school j, w_{ij}, is related to the characteristics of teacher i in school j, s_j. Most of the questions on the student questionnaire were highly subjective and subject to considerable measurement error, and we used principal responses to school characteristics questions wherever possible. The only exception is in measuring student ability, which was computed from the student questionnaire. One very attractive feature of the data is that all students in the sample were given a standard test. We used the mean raw score (unweighted percentage correct answers) on the verbal portion of the test taken by twelfth-grade students to measure student ability in each school.

Contrary to many econometric studies, this one does not suffer from scarcity of data. The EEOS data are so extensive that if anything there is too much data rather than too little! There are 411 variables to work with, many of which are multiple measures of student characteristics. Our selection criteria were as follows. First, the theory requires the content of s to t to be objectively measured. Teachers compare objective market data with subjective values in choosing among schools. Variables indexing tastes serve to locate a teacher at an appropriate point in the (s, t) space, but teachers treat $w(t, s)$ as objective and parametric for their decision. Therefore questions directly asking teacher preferences and opinions should not be included at this stage.[4] Second, some questions were ambiguous and the probable accuracy of response was small. Third, some questions seemed irrelevant to the employment process, while others exhibited little variation across the sample. These too were not used in the analysis.

We decided to fit separate wage functions to each race–sex classification at an early stage of the investigation. To be eligible for our sample, teachers had to report salary, race, and sex. It was still necessary to treat nonresponses to other variables in the records of these individuals. Had we insisted on completely clean data for every observation point (i.e., omitting all observations with at least one nonresponse), each race–sex subsample would have been reduced by at least 20 percent.[5] Such a loss would not be too serious for white teachers, where the samples are relatively large, but would represent an important disregard of information in the case of black teachers, where the samples are much smaller. We have treated all subsamples symmetrically and computed sample sums of squares and cross-products used in the statistical analysis on the basis of *all* available information. This was implemented by assigning mean values (over all respondents in each race–sex class) to missing observations on particular variables of any teacher.

A list of variables selected for analysis is given in Table 2.1. Table 2.2 gives corresponding means and standard deviations, computed over all respondents. If information on a particular variable for a teacher was not reported, that observation was ignored in computing the sample mean and variance for that variable, as above. To economize on

---

4. Levin (undated) analyzed a restricted set of these data and included subjective teacher responses as independent variables in wage regressions. His analysis is not as extensive as ours and is based on a much different view of the market than the one offered here.

5. Of the records where blanks occurred, only a few questions were not answered in each case. The mean response rate for every independent variable selected was well over 95 percent, in spite of the fact that about 20 percent of all records had missing data.

Table 2.1 • Variables used in regressions. (D indicates dummy variable.)

TEACHER CHARACTERISTICS[a]

EDUCATION < BA	Teacher has not earned a bachelor's degree. (D)
EDUCATION BA	Teacher has earned a bachelor's degree. (D)
EDUCATION BA+	Teacher has taken graduate courses beyond the BA, but has not earned a master's degree. (D)
EDUCATION MA	Teacher has earned a master's degree. (D)
EDUCATION > MA	Teacher has taken courses beyond the MA, including those who have earned a Ph.D. (D)
EXP 0–4 YRS	Teacher has 0 to 4 years of teaching experience. (D)
EXP 5–9 YRS	Teacher has 5 to 9 years of teaching experience. (D)
EXP 10–19 YRS	Teacher has 10 to 19 years of teaching experience. (D)
EXP 20+ YRS	Teacher has 20 or more years of teaching experience. (D)
EXP THS SC 0–4	Teacher has 0 to 4 years of teaching experience in this school. (D)
EXP THS SC 5–9	Teacher has 5 to 9 years of teaching experience in this school. (D)
EXP THS SC 10–19	Teacher has 10 to 19 years of teaching experience in this school. (D)
EXP THS SC 20+	Teacher has 20 or more years of teaching experience in this school. (D)
T AGE[c]	Teacher's age, in years.
TCH ASSN MMBR	Teacher is a member of the local teacher association. (D)
TCH ASSN NOT	Teacher is not a member of the local teacher association. (D)
T VERBAL LOW	Teacher answered less than 50 percent of the questions on a test of verbal ability correctly. (D)
T VERBAL MID−	Teacher answered between 50 and 66 percent of the questions on a test of verbal ability correctly. (D)
T VERBAL MID+	Teacher answered between 66 and 83 percent of the questions on a test of verbal ability correctly. (D)
T VERBAL HIGH	Teacher answered more than 83 percent of the questions on a test of verbal ability correctly. (D)
T EXAMS YES	Examinations are administered to teachers applying for jobs in this school. (D)
T EXAMS NO	Examinations are not administered to teachers applying for jobs in this school. (D)
HOW ASSGN SELF	Teacher selected this school to work in. (D)

Table 2.1 • *(continued)*

HOW ASSGN OTHER	Teacher was assigned to this school by an administrator. (D)
CAR COM PERM	(Career Commitment Permanent) Teacher plans to work to retirement. (D)
CAR COM TEMP	(Career Commitment Temporary) Teacher does not plan to work to retirement. (D)
TENURE NO SYS	School does not offer tenure to any teacher. (D)
TENURE LACKS	School does offer tenure to teachers, but this teacher does not have tenure. (D)
TENURE HAS	School does offer tenure to teachers, and this teacher does have tenure. (D)

SCHOOL CHARACTERISTICS [b]

A. Student characteristics

PROP WHITE [c]	Proportion of the student body that is white. ($\times 100$)
ST VERBAL	Mean verbal score for participating twelfth-grade students, as a proportion of answers given correctly. ($\times 100$)
CLRM/ST	Classrooms per student. ($\times 100$)
# STUDENTS	Number of students in school.
ATTEND 93%+	Attendance is 93 percent or better in this school. (D)
ATTEND < 93%	Attendance less than 93 percent in this school. (D)
DRPOUTS 20%+	Twenty percent or more of the tenth-grade boy students drop out of school by the twelfth grade. (D)
DRPOUTS 10–19%	Between 10 and 19 percent of the tenth-grade boy students drop out of school by the twelfth grade. (D)
DRPOUTS 0–9%	Less than 10 percent of the tenth-grade boy students drop out of school by the twelfth grade. (D)

B. Curriculum related

SCHL CLASS: A	School classification: academic. (D)
SCHL CLASS: C	School classification: comprehensive. (D)
SCHL CLASS: S	School classification: specialized (vocational, technical school). (D)
LABS	Number of separate laboratories for science courses. (D)
PROP GRADS/ COLL [c]	Proportion of high school graduates who enter college. ($\times 100$)

Table 2.1 • *(continued)*

SLOW LRN AUTO	Automatic promotion of slow learners. (D)
SLOW LRN NOT	Slow learners are promoted on the basis of their scholastic performance. (D)
REMED RDG NONE	No remedial reading program is available in this school. (D)
REMED RDG 0–4%	Less than 5 percent of the student body participates in a remedial reading program. (D)
REMED RDG 5%+	Five percent or more of the student body participates in a remedial reading program. (D)
ADV CUR I YES	(Advanced Curriculum) This school offers accelerated courses. (D)
ADV CUR I NO	This school does not offer accelerated courses. (D)
ST ASSGN FULL DS	Any student who lives in the school district may attend this school. (D)
ST ASSGN NOT	Only students living in a particular geographic region or who fulfill other requirements may attend this school. (D)

C. Neighborhood related

LOC RURAL	School location: rural. (D)
LOC RES SUB	School location: residential suburb. (D)
LOC SM TOWN	School location: small town. (D)
LOC IND SUB	School location: industrial suburb or small city. (D)
LOC LG CTY RES	School location: residential section of a large city. (D)
LOC INNER CTY	School location: inner city. (D)
TRANSFERS < 10%	Less than 10 percent of the student body consists of transfer students. (D)
TRANSFERS 10%+	Ten percent or more of the student body consists of transfer students. (D)
NW HIST RECENT	The first nonwhite student entered this school within the last five years. (D)
NW HIST NOT	The first nonwhite student entered this school more than five years ago, or there are no nonwhite students presently in this school. (D)
FREE LUNCH 0%	No students receive a free lunch in this school. (D)
FREE LUNCH 1–9%	Between 1 and 9 percent of the student body receives a free lunch in this school. (D)
FREE LUNCH 10%+	Ten percent or more of the student body receives a free lunch in this school. (D)

Table 2.1 · *(continued)*

D. Geographic

REGION I	Schools in Maine, New Hampshire, Vermont, Massachusetts, Rhode Island, Connecticut. (D)
REGION II	Schools in New York, New Jersey, Pennsylvania, Maryland, Delaware, D.C. (D)
REGION III	Schools in Indiana, Michigan, Ohio, Illinois, Wisconsin. (D)
REGION IV	Schools in Iowa, Kansas, Minnesota, Missouri, Nebraska, North Dakota, South Dakota. (D)
REGION V	Schools in Alabama, Arkansas, Florida, Georgia, Kentucky, Louisiana, Mississippi, North Carolina, South Carolina, Tennessee, Virginia, West Virginia. (D)
REGION VI	Schools in Arizona, New Mexico, Oklahoma, Texas. (D)
REGION VII	Schools in Alaska, California, Colorado, Hawaii, Idaho, Montana, Nevada, Oregon, Utah, Washington, Wyoming. (D)

a. All teacher variables from teacher questionnaire, except T EXAMS (from principal questionnaire).

b. All school and student variables from principal questionnaire, except ST VERBAL (from student questionnaire—see text).

c. Original data were in interval form. Values of interval midpoints assigned to individuals. Open-ended salary midpoint estimated by fitting Pareto distribution to upper tail of salary distribution over all subsamples.

space, summary statistics are presented for males only, since sample statistics of females within each race class are similar to their male counterparts. Notice that white teachers tend to be in better-quality schools than black teachers. Also notice the extent of student–teacher segregation.[6]

6. We attempted to reduce the statistical dimensions of the problem by using principal components from the correlation matrix of school characteristics variables. However, the attempt was not successful. There are 26 school characteristics variables. The first principal component (for white males, using only clean data) accounted for 10 percent of the variance, and the first 13 principal components accounted for only 75 percent of the variance. Further, the weights assigned to these components did not lend themselves to systematic interpretation.

Table 2.2 • Sample means and standard deviations: White and black male teachers.

Variable	White male		Black male	
	Mean	Std. Dev.	Mean	Std. Dev.
TCHR INCOME	7599.137	2247.059	5798.520	1586.586
EDUCATION < BA	0.027	0.161	0.021	0.143
EDUCATION BA	0.095	0.293	0.182	0.385
EDUCATION BA+	0.407	0.491	0.515	0.499
EDUCATION MA	0.096	0.294	0.077	0.266
EDUCATION MA+	—	—	—	—
EXP 0–4 YRS	0.339	0.473	0.334	0.471
EXP 5–9 YRS	0.254	0.435	0.250	0.432
EXP 10–19 YRS	0.252	0.434	0.293	0.455
EXP 20+ YRS	—	—	—	—
EXP THS SC 0–4	0.546	0.497	0.511	0.499
EXP THS SC 5–9	0.222	0.414	0.239	0.426
EXP THS SC 10–19	0.178	0.381	0.221	0.414
EXP THS SC 20+	—	—	—	—
T AGE	37.528	10.800	36.394	9.683
TCH ASSN MMBR	0.931	0.253	0.950	0.218
TCHR ASSN NOT	—	—	—	—
T VERBAL LOW	0.023	0.147	0.169	0.368
T VERBAL MID −	0.082	0.272	0.266	0.439
T VERBAL MID +	0.366	0.477	0.397	0.486
T VERBAL HIGH	—	—	—	—
T EXAMS YES	0.186	0.389	0.333	0.471
T EXAMS NO	—	—	—	—
HOW ASSGN SELF	0.705	0.453	0.562	0.493
HOW ASSGN OTHER	—	—	—	—
CAR COM PERM	0.891	0.311	0.824	0.380
CAR COM TEMP	—	—	—	—
TENURE NO SYS	0.198	0.398	0.504	0.499
TENURE LACKS	0.284	0.450	0.185	0.387
TENURE HAS	—	—	—	—
PROP WHITE (×100)	80.763	24.777	8.589	23.217
ST VERBAL (×100)	58.201	9.244	34.045	10.544
CLRM/ST	0.040	0.013	0.038	0.012
# STUDENTS	1524.7	1020.3	1045.3	721.8
ATTEND 93%+	0.778	0.415	0.469	0.499
ATTEND < 93%	—	—	—	—

Table 2.2 • *(continued)*

Variable	White male		Black male	
	Mean	Std. Dev.	Mean	Std. Dev.
DRPOUTS 20%+	0.092	0.281	0.152	0.350
DRPOUTS 10–19%	0.159	0.347	0.198	0.386
DRPOUTS 0–9%	—	—	—	—
SCHL CLASS: A	0.185	0.388	0.323	0.468
SCHL CLASS: C	—	—	—	—
SCHL CLASS: S	0.065	0.247	0.097	0.297
LABS	2.893	0.363	2.561	0.784
PROP GRADS/COLL (×100)	44.5	19.8	28.9	17.5
SLOW LRN AUTO	0.119	0.311	0.111	0.306
SLOW LRN NOT	—	—	—	—
REMED RDG NONE	—	—	—	—
REMED RDG 0–4%	0.316	0.463	0.294	0.453
REMED RDG 5%+	0.535	0.497	0.379	0.483
ADV CUR I YES	0.445	0.497	0.234	0.423
ADV CUR I NO	—	—	—	—
ST ASSGN FULL DS	0.461	0.499	0.399	0.490
ST ASSGN NOT	—	—	—	—
LOC RURAL	0.133	0.333	0.244	0.429
LOC RES SUB	0.174	0.376	0.052	0.223
LOC SM TOWN	0.125	0.325	0.152	0.359
LOC IND SUB	0.202	0.397	0.291	0.454
LOC LG CTY RES	0.198	0.396	0.148	0.355
LOC INNER CTY	—	—	—	—
TRANSFERS < 10%	0.810	0.390	0.915	0.273
TRANSFERS 10%+	—	—	—	—
NW HIST RECENT	0.157	0.358	0.093	0.284
NW HIST NOT	—	—	—	—
FREE LUNCH 0%	0.379	0.484	0.189	0.390
FREE LUNCH 1–9%	0.536	0.497	0.476	0.497
FREE LUNCH 10%+	—	—	—	—
REGION I	—	—	—	—
REGION II	0.308	0.462	0.087	0.281
REGION III	0.186	0.390	0.044	0.205
REGION IV	0.055	0.228	0.015	0.122
REGION V	0.150	0.357	0.687	0.469
REGION VI	0.058	0.234	0.132	0.337
REGION VII	0.181	0.385	0.032	0.175

Information on worker characteristics in the EEOS sample is at least as good as that used in other studies of wage determination (e.g., from the decennial census samples) and is better than most. Aside from the usual education, age, and general experience variables, we have information on job-specific experience, screening (use of teacher exams—really a school characteristic), and a crude measure of teacher ability from a short, self-administered "test" in the teacher questionnaire. The tenure and unionism variables are self-explanatory (though existence of a tenure system could be thought of as a school rather than a teacher characteristic). Unfortunately we only have information on teacher association membership and not on whether the school was covered by a collective agreement. The assignment variable, in conjunction with specific school experience, is included to capture in part the fact that low seniority teachers in large city systems often have restricted choices among available schools. The career variable, though contrary to the above objective criteria, is included to pick off some unobserved quality components, under the general hypothesis that individuals earning large rents tend to protect their positions through harder work and greater dedication. Finally, we have considered the teacher's major subject in college and subject matter of courses taught. They had virtually no additional explanatory power and their inclusion did not affect the other results. Consequently, they are not included in this report. Measures of college quality were not available.

An outstanding feature of the data, not found in most other sources, is extensive proxies for working conditions in the form of student and school characteristics. Aside from the usual regional dummies, school variables roughly can be classified into three types: directly measured school and student variables, variables indexing school differences in curriculum content, and variables which, for lack of a better term, might serve as indicators of perceived "hazards." Needless to say, many variables overlap these boundaries.

(a) *Direct measures of student characteristics.* Racial composition and student ability variables are of course crucial to the analysis. We could have used mean mathematics score as an index of ability, though it, as well as any other measure derived from the student test, is highly correlated with verbal score. Dropout and attendance variables are correlated with other aspects of student motivation. In addition, dropouts help correct for potential selectivity bias in the student ability measure: the test was administered to twelfth-grade students whereas teachers in the sample taught tenth- through twelfth-grade students. We expect teachers to exhibit preferences for able, well-motivated students. Classrooms per student is highly correlated with teacher–student ratio and is used because it contains less measurement error. Finally, teachers may have preferences for school size per se, measured by number of students. However, school size may also be related to the extent of teacher specialization, in which case it corrects for some otherwise unmeasured difference in teacher quality.

(b) *Curriculum-related variables.* In general, these variables represent a mixture of otherwise unmeasured teacher quality components, through differences in work content and the presence of specialized teacher skill, and of student characteristics. However, the proportions between taste and skill factors are unknown and separate effects cannot be identified. Specialized schools, labs, proportion of graduates in college, and presence of advanced curriculum courses are related to utility bearing "good" attributes of students and also to the presence of specialized skills commanding premiums in the market: the two effects on wage rates tend to work in opposite directions. Treatment of slow learners and remedial reading programs also demand special skills of teachers, but perhaps are associated with negatively valued ("bad") aspects of students: the two effects tend to work in the same direction. The student assignment variable is a crude proxy for student homogeneity. If all students in the district can attend the school, it is likely to have a less homogeneous student body than if all students originate in a particular neighborhood. Other things equal, more homogeneity leads to greater division of labor and higher specialization of teacher function.

(c) *Neighborhood-related variables.* These are meant to index several nonacademic aspects of students, related to discipline and student motivation; and also to quality and "climate" of neighborhoods in which schools are located. Transfers measure neighborhood stability, nonwhite history indexes recent racial tension in both school and neighborhood, and free lunches are a crude proxy for neighborhood poverty and income. If names and exact locations of schools had been revealed, it would be possible to match schools with census tract neighborhood statistics. But it is necessary to make do with what is available, even though census matching would have been preferable in some respects. Inclusion of urban–rural location is standard practice in wage studies and the school location variables used here are slightly more detailed than usual.

While our data are better than most, it is apparent they leave something to be desired. Direct teacher quality measures particularly are less than ideal. Therefore, in interpreting results, readers must bear in mind that unmeasured teacher quality effects may be spread out over many of the school characteristics variables. Unmeasured teacher quality components are likely to be positively correlated with "good" school and student attributes, and at least there is strong presumption about the sign of the bias, if not about its magnitude.[7]

4. Estimation

Least-squares estimates of $w(t, s)$ by sex and race class are presented in Tables 2.3 and 2.4. Table 2.3 includes teacher characteristics listed in Table 2.1 plus regional dummies, but only one school characteristic—percentage white student body. Table 2.4 includes all variables listed in Table 2.1. Before examining details, a few estimation problems must be discussed.

First, the functional form used is reasonably "free" because most independent variables are in dummy form. However, it arbitrarily assumes independence between the incremental impact of any variable and levels of all other variables. Use of log wage as a dependent variable instead of the wage itself forces an equally arbitrary independence of percentage impact effects. Limited examination of the second form revealed estimated effects at sample means to be close to those in the tables and the matter has not been pursued further.

Second, recall all sample information was used to compute covariances underlying the estimates in Tables 2.3 and 2.4. A uniform reduction of degrees of freedom does not result, because sample response rates are slightly different for each independent variable. The t-statistics reported in Tables 2.3 and 2.4 were computed as if there were no nonresponses (recall assignment of appropriate means to missing data). We have not bothered to go through the tedium of making adjustments, since the number of observations is large and reported t-statistics must be only trivially overstated.

7. Greenberg and McCall (1973) found evidence of positive correlation between teacher and student quality within school systems with uniform salary schedules. That study and this one are highly complementary.

Table 2.3 • Wage-characteristics function estimates: Limited specification. (*t*-statistic below regression coefficient.)

| | Regression coefficients | | | |
| | White | | Black | |
Independent variables	Male	Female	Male	Female
Teacher characteristics				
EDUCATION < BA	−948.54	−1047.93	−766.47	−961.52
	(−7.68)	(−6.14)	(−3.58)	(−3.57)
EDUCATION BA	−1102.99	−1134.50	−1069.56	−745.65
	(−14.09)	(−17.33)	(−9.47)	(−7.76)
EDUCATION BA+	−1018.79	−1090.60	−831.18	745.36
	(−21.77)	(−22.84)	(−10.03)	(−10.52)
EDUCATION MA	−377.47	−606.27	−138.51	−203.18
	(−5.43)	(−7.80)	(−1.12)	(−1.95)
EDUCATION > MA	—	—	—	—
EXP 0–4 YRS	−2244.81	−1507.27	−992.89	−1114.67
	(−20.01)	(−15.60)	(−5.52)	(−7.53)
EXP 5–9 YRS	−1459.14	−919.84	−576.47	−505.12
	(−14.52)	(−11.08)	(−3.54)	(−3.92)
EXP 10–19 YRS	−447.83	−317.75	12.99	−28.95
	(−4.79)	(−4.24)	(0.08)	(−0.25)
EXP 20+ YRS	—	—	—	—
EXP THS SC 0–4	−80.93	−514.76	−87.92	−10.34
	(−0.98)	(−6.89)	(−0.71)	(−0.10)
EXP THS SC 5–9	−18.24	−333.90	−169.56	−105.40
	(−0.22)	(−4.76)	(−1.39)	(−1.05)
EXP THS SC 10–19	291.33	−78.45	−161.85	−52.76
	(3.49)	(−1.12)	(−1.23)	(−0.52)
EXP THS SC 20+	—	—	—	—
T AGE	0.88	−8.00	10.41	9.39
	(0.28)	(−3.26)	(1.97)	(2.13)
TCH ASSN MMBR	202.05	208.10	133.99	138.50
	(2.68)	(3.05)	(1.00)	(1.30)
TCHR ASSN NOT	—	—	—	—
T VERBAL LOW	−224.82	−451.14	−290.77	−351.98
	(−1.73)	(−2.56)	(−2.79)	(−4.18)
T VERBAL MID−	−147.83	25.04	−328.63	−325.35
	(−2.05)	(0.28)	(−3.55)	(−4.40)

Table 2.3 • *(continued)*

Independent variables	Regression coefficients			
	White		Black	
	Male	Female	Male	Female
T VERBAL MID+	−140.73 (−3.41)	−103.30 (−2.54)	−194.03 (−2.27)	−116.81 (−1.72)
T VERBAL HIGH	—	—	—	—
HOW ASSGN SELF	−3.43 (−0.08)	−36.85 (−0.96)	−140.35 (−2.39)	−26.20 (−0.52)
HOW ASSGN OTHER	—	—	—	—
CAR COM PERM	175.39 (2.81)	247.45 (5.53)	111.83 (1.42)	−46.30 (−0.73)
CAR COM TEMP	—	—	—	—
TENURE NO SYS	−661.20 (−10.63)	−708.96 (−12.77)	−630.36 (−8.29)	−554.22 (−8.49)
TENURE LACKS	−645.56 (−12.12)	−588.54 (−11.94)	−506.44 (−5.66)	−326.52 (−4.41)
TENURE HAS	—	—	—	—
School characteristics				
PROP WHITE (×100)	−7.27 (−8.95)	−5.41 (−7.04)	2.68 (1.67)	1.05 (0.69)
Geographic				
REGION I	—	—	—	—
REGION II	758.09 (8.93)	618.86 (7.20)	419.61 (0.82)	724.28 (2.13)
REGION III	484.78 (5.47)	209.66 (2.33)	215.31 (0.41)	354.51 (0.99)
REGION IV	−122.52 (−1.07)	−300.18 (−2.65)	322.58 (0.58)	262.03 (0.68)
REGION V	−1032.92 (−10.99)	−1338.97 (−15.33)	−1092.83 (−2.12)	−1289.39 (−3.68)
REGION VI	−527.66 (−4.61)	−779.80 (−7.14)	−338.44 (−0.65)	−679.67 (−1.90)
REGION VII	1117.95 (12.53)	1042.67 (11.30)	1327.99 (2.54)	1229.07 (3.32)

Table 2.3 • *(continued)*

| Independent variables | Regression coefficients | | | |
| | White | | Black | |
	Male	Female	Male	Female
Constant	9681.04	9473.61	7824.69	7502.87
R^2	0.62	0.66	0.63	0.67
Std. Error	1383.59	1179.09	978.64	897.72
No. of Obs.	5454.00	4491.00	1202.00	1422.00

Finally, a matter of greater substance has been investigated. The regression model underlying the tables is $w_{ij} = w(t_{ij}, s_j) + u_{ij}$, where i indexes teachers, j indexes schools, and u_{ij} is a random variable. Thus, it bears a resemblance to variance-components models. The difference is that we have a host of real "school effect" indicators. However, a question naturally arises as to how much of total school effects are captured by measured school characteristics, s_j. If some schools systematically pay more or less to all their teachers for reasons unrelated to measured school characteristics, residuals are $u_{ij} = v_j + e_{ij}$, where v_j is the unmeasured school effect. While least-squares parameter estimates are unbiased in any event, least-squares-estimated sampling variances are biased downward in proportion to the ratio of the variance of v_j to total residual variance. How large is var (v_j)? Unfortunately a straightforward answer is not easily provided because we have an unbalanced classification (different numbers of teachers in each school) and standard variance-component methods in the econometric literature are not applicable. Methods do exist for unbalanced schemes, but are computationally complex. Moreover, computational complexity is intensified by the large mass of data and variables to be processed. Therefore, we opted for a second-best procedure that should indicate the magnitude of the problem.[8]

---

8. We are indebted to G. S. Maddala for suggesting this procedure.

Table 2.4 • Wage-characteristics function estimates: Full specification.
(*t*-statistic below regression coefficient.)

| | Regression coefficients | | | |
| | White | | Black | |
Independent variables	Male	Female	Male	Female
Teacher Characteristics				
EDUCATION < BA	−799.77	−1113.28	−794.43	−1021.85
	(−6.86)	(−6.85)	(−3.88)	(−4.06)
EDUCATION BA	−856.87	−931.55	−983.58	−669.69
	(−11.65)	(−15.09)	(−8.97)	(−7.45)
EDUCATION BA+	−811.12	−947.83	−760.44	−689.89
	(−18.34)	(−21.07)	(−9.43)	(−10.42)
EDUCATION MA	−282.23	−509.38	22.71	−184.57
	(−4.37)	(−7.02)	(0.19)	(−1.90)
EDUCATION > MA	—	—	—	—
EXP 0–4 YRS	−2245.12	−1592.70	−1017.66	−1119.13
	(−21.55)	(−17.64)	(−5.90)	(−8.12)
EXP 5–9 YRS	−1495.74	−973.59	−598.09	−539.66
	(−16.02)	(−12.54)	(−3.84)	(−4.51)
EXP 10–19 YRS	−493.98	−359.74	26.76	−119.80
	(−5.69)	(−5.14)	(0.18)	(−1.12)
EXP 20+ YRS	—	—	—	—
EXP THS SC 0–4	−135.02	−497.40	−220.99	−124.04
	(−1.75)	(−7.08)	(−1.87)	(−1.31)
EXP THS SC 5–9	−57.28	−331.31	−222.60	−150.71
	(−0.77)	(−5.04)	(−1.91)	(−1.62)
EXP THS SC 10–19	326.16	−40.23	−197.63	24.30
	(4.21)	(−0.61)	(−1.57)	(0.25)
EXP THS SC 20+	—	—	—	—
T AGE	−1.95	−7.74	7.10	5.40
	(−0.67)	(−3.37)	(1.39)	(1.31)
TCH ASSN MMBR	303.45	304.69	47.83	247.47
	(4.33)	(4.75)	(0.37)	(2.49)
TCHR ASSN NOT	—	—	—	—
T VERBAL LOW	−138.05	−558.72	−156.50	−200.45
	(−1.14)	(−3.41)	(−1.54)	(−2.50)

Table 2.4 • *(continued)*

Independent variables	Regression coefficients			
	White		Black	
	Male	Female	Male	Female
T VERBAL MID−	−74.97 (−1.12)	23.05 (0.28)	−177.15 (−1.95)	−150.14 (−2.14)
T VERBAL MID+	−75.69 (−1.97)	−67.79 (−1.78)	−94.49 (−1.14)	−30.23 (−0.47)
T VERBAL HIGH	—	—	—	—
T EXAMS YES	244.31 (4.07)	79.09 (1.44)	−132.27 (−1.78)	47.61 (0.80)
T EXAMS NO	—	—	—	—
HOW ASSGN SELF	107.08 (2.61)	34.14 (0.92)	−73.51 (−1.28)	37.36 (0.79)
HOW ASSGN OTHER	—	—	—	—
CAR COM PERM	168.21 (2.91)	230.22 (5.49)	171.41 (2.27)	−6.31 (−0.10)
CAR COM TEMP	—	—	—	—
TENURE NO SYS	−512.93 (−8.52)	−560.60 (−10.29)	−524.71 (−6.60)	−370.09 (−5.59)
TENURE LACKS	−626.02 (−12.63)	−580.51 (−12.61)	−493.25 (−5.65)	−351.67 (−5.02)
TENURE HAS	—	—	—	—
School Characteristics				
A. Students				
PROP WHITE (×100)	1.74 (1.59)	1.31 (1.33)	−3.81 (−1.80)	−3.15 (−1.69)
ST VERBAL (×100)	−23.76 (−6.23)	−11.08 (−3.21)	20.78 (3.56)	20.46 (4.75)
CLRM/ST (×100)	21.29 (1.18)	−26.40 (−1.50)	109.94 (3.82)	−6.29 (−0.26)
# STUDENTS	0.25 (8.11)	0.22 (7.43)	0.33 (5.33)	0.01 (0.38)
ATTEND 93%+	−88.96 (−1.61)	−142.20 (−2.71)	−30.27 (−0.48)	6.86 (0.13)

Table 2.4 • *(continued)*

Independent variables	Regression coefficients			
	White		Black	
	Male	Female	Male	Female
ATTEND < 93%	—	—	—	—
DRPOUTS 20%+	179.74 (2.35)	142.01 (2.02)	−25.06 (−0.27)	−1.18 (−0.01)
DRPOUTS 10–19%	16.57 (0.29)	−95.60 (−1.77)	−182.46 (−2.36)	−162.04 (−2.49)
DRPOUTS 0–9	—	—	—	—
B. Curriculum				
SCHL CLASS: A	26.44 (0.51)	−63.53 (−1.42)	−157.20 (−2.26)	−107.21 (−1.87)
SCHL CLASS: C	—	—	—	—
SCHL CLASS: S	688.68 (7.73)	786.04 (7.52)	22.38 (0.20)	277.20 (3.26)
LABS	−9.29 (−0.17)	−202.66 (−3.95)	−153.87 (−3.73)	−23.95 (−0.75)
PROP GRADS/COLL (×100)	14.66 (10.50)	6.60 (4.96)	3.19 (1.52)	2.05 (1.25)
SLOW LRN AUTO	−288.94 (−4.71)	−251.02 (−4.31)	−16.24 (−0.16)	−27.78 (−0.33)
SLOW LRN NOT	—	—	—	—
REMED RDG NONE	—	—	—	—
REMED RDG 0–4%	158.43 (2.66)	118.81 (2.23)	131.36 (1.76)	186.45 (3.04)
REMED RDG 5%+	215.62 (3.62)	144.21 (2.70)	84.13 (1.14)	28.20 (0.44)
ADV CUR I YES	93.12 (2.11)	54.04 (1.32)	46.33 (0.57)	18.47 (0.28)
ADV CUR I NO	—	—	—	—
ST ASSGN FULL DS	−184.15 (−4.33)	−146.07 (−3.57)	−218.22 (−3.51)	−307.94 (−6.01)
ST ASSGN NOT	—	—	—	—

Table 2.4 • *(continued)*

	Regression coefficients			
	White		Black	
Independent variables	Male	Female	Male	Female
C. Neighborhood				
LOC RURAL	110.53 (1.26)	170.92 (2.02)	59.65 (0.42)	−380.07 (−3.38)
LOC RES SUB	645.86 (8.65)	520.70 (7.12)	−63.81 (−0.37)	−623.04 (−4.46)
LOC SM TOWN	−57.88 (−0.65)	−55.25 (−0.66)	−134.80 (−0.90)	−624.11 (−5.34)
LOC IND SUB	−31.40 (−0.43)	3.99 (0.05)	−202.61 (−1.66)	−506.93 (−5.24)
LOC LG CTY RES	15.11 (0.24)	173.97 (2.79)	−13.64 (−0.10)	−300.29 (−2.89)
LOC INNER CTY	—	—	—	—
TRANSFERS < 10%	−308.77 (−6.10)	−247.41 (−5.03)	−329.87 (−2.77)	−376.09 (−3.63)
TRANSFERS 10%+	—	—	—	—
NW HIST RECENT	247.64 (4.06)	202.53 (3.85)	−81.56 (−0.66)	232.36 (2.01)
NW HIST NOT	—	—	—	—
FREE LUNCH 0%	−318.30 (−3.92)	−104.31 (−1.27)	37.57 (0.41)	−278.54 (−3.70)
FREE LUNCH 1–9%	−204.91 (−2.60)	−83.42 (−1.08)	21.80 (0.30)	−187.03 (−3.27)
FREE LUNCH 10%	—	—	—	—
D. Geographic				
REGION I	—	—	—	—
REGION II	626.46 (7.42)	447.30 (5.20)	569.33 (1.14)	760.75 (2.34)
REGION III	552.65 (6.19)	161.43 (1.79)	397.88 (0.77)	201.13 (0.59)
REGION IV	−91.35 (−0.81)	−332.35 (−3.01)	415.34 (0.75)	−0.82 (−0.00)

Table 2.4 • *(continued)*

| | *White* | | *Black* | |
| | Male | Female | Male | Female |
Independent variables				
REGION V	−1070.28	−1379.68	−492.58	−1045.04
	(−11.11)	(−15.58)	(−0.96)	(−3.15)
REGION VI	−461.07	−728.55	165.88	−363.49
	(−4.11)	(−6.85)	(0.32)	(−1.08)
REGION VII	1069.09	955.45	1289.65	1188.27
	(11.61)	(10.23)	(2.46)	(3.32)
Constant	9268.90	9597.01	6718.85	7441.01
R^2	0.68	0.71	0.67	0.73
Std. Error	1280.91	1097.12	928.79	828.36
No. of Obs.	5454.00	4491.00	1202.00	1422.00

The method consists of two steps. With some assumptions, it is possible to estimate the entire population of school effects using separate dummies for every school and ignoring all sample school characteristics information. That is estimate

$$w_{ij} = At_{ij} + \sum \delta_j D_j. \tag{9}$$

Regression coefficients **A** are within-school individual teacher effects. D_j is a dummy variable for each school, and δ_j estimates all cross-school effects whatever their source.[9] Now regress estimated values of δ_j on all measured school characteristics, s_j. If residual variance at the second-step regression is small, use of s_j in Tables 2.3 and 2.4 captures most of the school effects and estimated sampling variances reported in the tables are not seriously biased.

---

9. Notice that separate school dummies cannot simply be added to $w(t_{ij}, s_j) + u_{ij}$ to estimate the v_j's, because s_j and the school dummies are perfectly collinear. In fact, this collinearity implies that regression coefficients in Tables 2.3 and 2.4 are certain linear combinations of A and δ_j in eq. (9). But regression coefficients in (9) cannot be inferred from those in the tables.

The method was implemented for 4,455 clean observations on white male teachers and 420 schools. **A** was estimated from within-school covariances and δ_j was estimated by subtracting At_j from w_j, where w_j is the mean wage in the jth school and t_j is the vector of mean teacher characteristics in the jth school.[10] The second-step regression was weighted by the square root of the number of teachers in each school. Second-stage regression coefficients of δ on **s** were broadly similar to those reported in Table 2.4, and the R^2 statistic was about 0.7. Hence there appear to be some omitted school effects underlying estimates of Tables 2.3 and 2.4, and the t-statistics reported there probably are biased upward. However, use of measured s_j picks off most of the school effects and the resulting bias must not be very important.

5. Interpretation of Results

5.1 Teacher Characteristics

Tables 2.3 and 2.4 indicate teacher characteristic effects are insensitive to school characteristic specifications. Most coefficients have the usual signs and it is unnecessary to dwell at length on them. Notice that the general experience gradient is much larger than the school-specific experience gradient, as might be expected for teacher's skills. Further, the white male experience gradient is slightly larger than that of white females and much larger than that of black males and females. These results are similar to those usually obtained from census data. The measure of teacher ability tends to work in the expected direction, but is certainly not a very powerful explanatory variable. Teacher association membership has a small effect (about 5 percent as a ratio to mean salary), but the estimate may be confounded with effects of tenure, which has a significantly larger impact. Tenure also renders screening more profitable and may borrow from the teacher exam effect.

---

10. A difficulty with the whole variance components analogy for the present problem is the problematical assumption of equality of within-school and between-school teacher effects. Remember, schools choose among teachers partially on the basis of interrelationships between endowed student characteristics and potential teacher productivity in the educational production function, and endowments are far from uniform across schools.

Regional effects are an important source of wage variation and follow the usual pattern, highest in the West and lowest in the South.

5.2 School Characteristics

Table 2.3 specifies only one student characteristic in s_j, the percentage of white students in the school. Taken at face value, the estimate suggests the preference of white teachers for white students and perhaps a mild preference of black teachers for black students, both at the appropriate margin. Toder (1971) has made comparable estimates for Massachusetts teachers in 1968, using similar variables to those in Table 2.3. His estimate is about $25 per percentage point black students (a $2,500 differential in going from all white to all black) and, though considerably larger than the $5 to $7 estimate for white teachers in Table 2.3, is in the same general ballpark as ours.

Sample means in Table 2.2 show white teachers work in considerably better schools than black teachers. Do Table 2.3 estimates measure discrimination or is racial composition serving as a proxy for equalizing differences on other school characteristics associated with race? Estimates of school characteristic effects in Table 2.4 shed some light on this question.

Consider estimates for whites first. A step regression routine was followed in arriving at the numbers in Table 2.4. Two experiments were carried out. In the first, all teacher characteristics, regional dummies, and student racial composition were forced into the regression at the initial step (Table 2.3). As other students and school characteristics entered the regression according to the conventional algorithm, explanatory power and estimated point effects of student racial composition shrank at each successive step until it stabilized at its Table 2.4 value very near the last step. Indeed, it shrank a bit too much and reversed sign. However, the final coefficient is trivial in magnitude and certainly not significantly different from zero. In the second experiment, only teacher characteristics and regional dummies were forced into the regression at the initial step. The racial composition variable entered at a very late stage, if at all (on a low tolerance level), seeming to indicate it is not as "important" in some sense as most other school characteristics.

Perhaps the most interesting variable for shifts in Table 2.4 is the measure of student ability (ST VERBAL). The estimates suggest that white teachers value student quality very highly and accept significant reductions in pay for the privilege of teaching good students. Converting the coefficient to standard form transforms the estimate to about $240 per standard deviation unit (of the raw score) for white males and about $110 per standard deviation unit for females. This result cannot be explained by unmeasured teacher-quality variables proxied by verbal score. Results for dropouts and attendance are consistent with this same interpretation, and cannot be explained away by appealing to unmeasured quality components.

The general neighborhood hazard indicators—transfers, recent nonwhite history, and free lunches—all work in the expected direction. Again, unmeasured teacher-quality effects cannot account for these estimates. Of curriculum-related variables, teacher-quality components appear to dominate taste factors for most, with the possible exceptions of laboratory facilities and remedial reading. The student assignment effect is not inconsistent with teacher distaste for student heterogeneity. Small support is given by the fact that when the within-school variance of ST VERBAL was added to the regression (not reported) its coefficient was consistently positive, though insignificantly different from zero.

There is little evidence of preference for class size in Table 2.4, and most size effects are attributable to size of school rather than class size. When the number of students is omitted from the regression, classrooms per student takes on the expected negative sign, with a high *t*-ratio. Number of students also borrows heavily from school location variables (rural, etc.), which, not unexpectedly, also become much more important explanatory variables when student size is omitted. As is, school location variables do not have much explanatory power for white teachers and there is no evidence of an inner-city differential after taking account of all other neighborhood and school variables. The large residential suburb variable is unexpected, but note this was a period of increasing relative demand for suburban teachers, as borne out by 1960 and 1970 census figures on residential patterns in metropolitan areas.

Now consider the results for black teachers. Here again the stepped regression experiments reversed initial and final signs of student race effects, but they were of trivial magnitude at each step. Both curriculum and neighborhood effects are similar to those of whites. Curiously, neighborhood variables have much more explanatory power for black females than for black males. There is a significant inner-city differential for black females, and systematic intraregion location effects for black males. General neighborhood variable effects for black females are practically identical to those of white males, while effects for black males are nil.

The most striking features of the results for black teachers are sign reversals for student ability and dropouts compared with white teachers. The estimates have an obvious utility explanation that is difficult to accept. They also could be due to a differential pattern of omitted teacher quality effects, but that too is difficult to accept. After all, the fundamental reason we expect omitted teacher-quality effects to be positively correlated with good student and school attributes is a presumption of strong complementarity between teacher quality and student quality in the educational production function.[11] Why should such technical relationships differ between whites and blacks?

There is only one other possibility. It could be true that racial composition and other school characteristics are so collinear that distinguishing between race and other characteristics is virtually impossible.[12] The numbers in Table 2.2 are suggestive in that regard. As a further check, weighted regressions of the proportion of white students in each school on all other student characteristics were computed for each race–sex class of teacher. R^2 statistics from these regressions were 0.58 for white male teachers, 0.54 for white females, 0.69 for black males, and 0.66 for black females.[13] Further, patterns of partial correlations between student racial composition and other school characteristics were similar for each teacher class and had the obvious signs (e.g., positive between proportion white and student verbal score, etc.) for the most part. Thus it is clear that schools tend to be stratified by racial composition and other school and student characteristics, and lack of identification is a distinct possibility.[14]

---

11. There is no direct evidence on this issue, but plenty of casual evidence is available. For example, if the presumption were not true, the five top-rated economics departments wouldn't look much different from the top thirty.

12. Systematic racial income differences, student–teacher quality complementarity, parental own-race preferences, and perhaps complementarities among student abilities in educational production are sufficient conditions for such stratification to occur.

13. R^2 statistics for both these regressions and those in Tables 2.3 and 2.4 are spuriously inflated due to the fact that both dependent variables were in interval form in the original data.

14. In terms of marginal condition (1) on teacher choice discussed above, the presence of independent constraints on s_j means the *partial* derivative of $w(t, s)$ with respect to any single attribute does not exist. The range of choice is restricted to a space of lesser dimensionality defined on certain combinations of the s variables.

Table 2.5 • Analysis of salary differentials.

	White			Black		
	Male	Female	F/M	Male	Female	F/M
Mean salary	7599	6631	87.26	5798	5506	94.95
Mean, male struct.	7599	7234	95.19	5798	5850	100.89
Mean, female struct.	7007	6631	94.63	5436	5506	101.28
	Male			Female		
	Male	Female	B/W	Male	Female	B/W
Mean salary	7599	5798	76.30	6631	5506	83.03
Mean, white struct.	7599	6825	89.81	6631	6100	92.00
Mean, black struct.	7379	5798	78.58	6682	5506	82.40

Source: Computed from Table 2.4.

However, the case is not airtight. First, collinearity is more serious for black teachers than for white teachers. While independent directions of choice in the space of school characteristics are restricted, there is still plenty of room for some independent choices, especially for white teachers. Moreover, if all school characteristics are so highly interrelated, why is racial composition consistently knocked out of the regression by the other variables, rather than vice versa? Finally, it is still difficult to resolve all the similarities between white and black teachers for neighborhood and curriculum effects on the basis of this kind of argument. Whatever, it is difficult to see how the issue can be completely settled on the basis of present data.

5.3 Race–Sex Effects

Standardized wage comparisons between race and sex of teachers are shown in Table 2.5. Write the regressions in Table 2.4 as $w = a^{kl}X$, where $\mathbf{a}$ is a vector of regression coefficients, $\mathbf{X}$ is the vector of teacher and school variables, k indexes race, and l indexes sex. Standardizing gross wage differences for differences in characteristics amounts to computing $(a^{1l} - a^{2l})\bar{X}$, $(a^{kl} - a^{kl})\bar{X}$, and so on, where $\bar{X}$ is an arbitrary "standard" value of teacher and student characteristics. Columns one and two of the first row in each panel in Table 2.5 list group sample mean salaries. Corresponding columns of row two show what the comparison group would have earned if they had the same mean characteristics ($\bar{X}$) as the base group. Computations using comparison group means rather than base group means are shown in row three. Entries in the third column give gross and standard wage ratios.

A gross salary differential between white male and female teachers of 13 percent is reduced to about 5 percent at a common set of characteristics. Put differently, white male and female differences in teacher and student characteristics account for about 60 percent of the gross salary differential. For black teachers, differences in student and teacher characteristics account for all of the gross difference, and no residual remains. There is little evidence of discrimination against females in this data, not a surprising result considering what everybody knows about the occupation. Both gross and residual differentials are larger for black–white comparisons. A gross male difference of about 25 percent is narrowed to somewhere between 10 and 20 percent and a gross female differential of about 20 percent is at most narrowed to 8 percent on account of structural differences. Again, qualifications regarding unmeasured quality variations apply to all these computations.

6. Conclusions

Considerable evidence has been presented to support the fact that equalizing wage differentials on working conditions are important sources of teacher wage variation. Neighborhood and teacher segregation, and stratification of students according to racial composition and other school and student attributes, raises difficult issues of identifying the separate effects of pure racial attitudes of teachers and preferences for student ability and other school attributes. But whatever the precise causes of pay differentials, they are an important source of the real cost differences of educating different students.

Coefficients of variation computed at mean teacher characteristics over various schools, and their characteristics in each subsample, were computed to summarize the practical importance of equalizing differences. Coefficients of variation across schools in each subsample were remarkably uniform at about 15 percent. In dollar terms, the range of variation (highest minus lowest) among schools exceeded $4,000 in each teacher class. A substantial portion of wage variation is due to geographic differences in school location. When subsample mean regional distributions are included as part of "standard" teacher characteristics, coefficients of variation fall to approximately 7.5 percent and the range of standard teacher pay differences across schools also falls to somewhere in the neighborhood of $2,500. These are still substantial real cost differences.

Finally, the economic analysis underlying the estimates underscores their limitations for answering the question of how much additional salary is necessary for white teachers to teach in black schools and, similarly, for black teachers in white schools. It should be clear from the previous discussion that we are confronted with a variant of the index number problem. Consider the imputations $p^{kl} = b^{kl} \Delta \bar{s}^l$, where b^{kl} are estimated school characteristic regression effects in Table 2.4 for teachers of race k and sex l, and $\Delta \bar{s}^l$ are black–white differences in mean school characteristics for each sex. The estimates p^{klL} can be interpreted as incremental prices for white and black teachers to swap each other's average school characteristics, "holding constant" all teacher characteristics.

A necessary condition for p^{kl} to provide exact answers to the question posed is that teachers (within race–sex classes) have identical preferences for school characteristics. For only in that case are estimated wage differences equalizing for all teachers everywhere in the sample space. When teachers are not identical, economic rents must exist in the market and optimal location in school characteristics space only requires equality between marginal prices and marginal subjective values. Thus regression estimates b^{kl} in Table 2.4 provide information only about the marginal subjective valuations, not average valuations.

However, the imputed prices p^{kl} provide an internal consistency check of the model. Notice there is nothing in the computations guaranteeing p^{kl} to be positive. A revealed preference type of argument suggests that p^{kl} must be positive or else there would be a clear gain for teachers to move to more preferred locations. Furthermore, when preferences are convex, p^{kl} must estimate the minimum amount necessary for the average teacher to exchange school characteristics by $\Delta \bar{s}^l$ if teacher preferences are not identical. Therefore p^{kl} must be a lower bound to the numbers we seek. When all school characteristics except geographic region are included in $\Delta \bar{s}^l$, we estimate at least $105 additional salary is required for the average white male teacher to accept average black male teacher school characteristics. The corresponding estimate of p^{kl} for average black male teachers to accept average white male teacher school characteristics is at least \$500. Corresponding estimates for white and black females are \$90 and \$300, respectively. When curriculum related school characteristics are omitted from $\Delta \bar{s}^l$, on the grounds they mostly proxy teacher quality, estimates are at least \$430 and \$300 for white and black males and at least \$150 and \$300 for white and black females. The positivity of the imputations is consistent with the revealed preferences of teachers for working conditions, and represents strong indirect conformation of the model design. We hope to improve on these numbers at a later date.

References

Becker, G. S. 1957. *The economics of discrimination* (University of Chicago Press, Chicago).

Friedman, M., and S. Kuznets. 1954. *Income from independent professional practice* (NBER, New York).

Greenberg, D., and J. McCall. 1973. Analysis of the educational personnel system. Rand Reports R-1071-HEW and R-1270-HEW.

Levin, H. M. undated. Recruiting teachers for large city school, mimeo.

Rosen, S. 1974. Hedonic prices and implicit markets: Product differentiation in pure competition. *Journal of Political Economy.*

Tiebout, C. 1956. The pure theory of local government expenditure. *Journal of Political Economy.*

Toder, E. 1971. The distribution of public school teachers by race and income class in an urban metropolitan area. Ph.D. dissertation (University of Rochester, Rochester, N.Y.).

3

The Value of Saving a Life: Evidence from the Labor Market

RICHARD THALER

SHERWIN ROSEN

1. Introduction

Lively controversy has centered in recent years on the methodology for evaluating life-saving on government projects and in public policy. It is now well understood that valuation should be carried out in terms of a proper set of compensating variations, on a par with benefit measures used in other areas of project evaluation. To put it plainly, the value of a life is the amount members of society are willing to pay to save one. It is clear that most previously devised measures relate in a very imperfect way, if at all, to the conceptually appropriate measure.[1] However, in view of recent and prospective legislation on product and industrial safety standards, some new estimates are sorely needed.

This paper presents a range of rather conservative estimates for one important component of life value: the demand price for a person's own safety. Estimates are obtained by answering the question, "How much will a person pay to reduce the probability of his own death by a 'small' amount?" Another component of life value is the amount other people (family and friends) are willing to pay to save the life of a particular

This research was partially funded by a grant from the National Institute of Education. Martin J. Bailey, Victor Fuchs, Jack Hirshleifer, and Paul Taubman provided helpful comments on an initial draft.

From *Household Production and Consumption,* ed. Nestor J. Terleckyj, NBER-Studies in Income and Wealth, vol. 40 (New York: Columbia University Press, 1975) 265–298. Copyright © 1976 by the National Bureau of Economic Research, Inc. All rights reserved.

1. See Schelling (1998), Usher (1972), and especially Mishan (1971) and the references therein.

individual. This second component is ignored. As a matter of course, a new conceptual framework for analyzing this problem is offered. We believe our model will be valuable for other investigations in this and related areas.

The usual methodology of preference revelation from observed behavior in demand theory is the most natural way of approaching the problem. Two types of behavior are relevant in this connection. First, individuals voluntarily undertake many risks of death and injury that are not inherent in their everyday situation, and, which could be avoided through expenditure of their own resources.[2] Suppose a person is observed taking a known incremental risk that could be removed by spending one dollar. Then the implicit value of avoiding the additional risk must be something less than one dollar or else it would not have been observed. For example, many people would not purchase automobile seat belts if they were not mandatory. Further, when installation was required, many individuals did not use them, or at least that was so prior to the tied installation of ignition locks and warning buzzers. Some people make a point of crossing streets in the middle of the block rather than at corners, most do not completely fireproof their homes, and so forth. While these and other examples provide scattered evidence on death and injury risk evaluation, it appears doubtful whether they can be systematized enough to yield very convincing evidence on the matter. The second kind of behavior is observed in the labor market in conjunction with risky jobs. Analysis of those data is pursued here.

Our method follows up Adam Smith's ancient suggestion that individuals must be induced to take risky jobs through a set of compensating differences in wage rates. Here the evidence is highly systematic and the data are good. Different work situations exhibit vastly different work-related probabilities of death and injury. Moreover, lots of data are available on wages in these jobs, on the personal characteristics of people who work at them, and on the industrial and technical characteristics of firms who offer them. Further, parties who voluntarily face such risks daily and as a major part of their lives, or production processes, have a special interest in obtaining reliable and objective information about the nature of the risks involved. This is especially true of very risky jobs. Finally, we have uncovered a new source of genuine actuarial data

---

2. Such an approach is suggested by Bailey (1968) and Fromm (1968).

on death rates in risky occupations that is superior to other existing data sources and that until now has not been used for estimation.

Smith's theory has been familiar to economists for almost two hundred years and, in fact, forms the basis for the best recent inquiries into the economics of safety.[3] Yet very little effort has gone into empirical implementation of the idea. Some people have been hostile to it, asserting—without proof—that forces producing observed wage variation are so varied and complex as to preclude isolating the effect of risk. As will be demonstrated below, Smith's logic suggests that the labor market can be viewed as providing a mechanism for implicit trading in risk (and in other aspects of on-the-job consumption) with the degree of risk (and other job attributes) varying from one job to another. It certainly is not clear why price determination in such markets should be more complex than in any other markets where tied sales occur, such as the housing market. Indeed, the hedonic reconstruction of demand theory suggests that tied sales and package deals of product "characteristics" are the rule and not the exception in virtually all market exchange. Moreover, estimates presented below belie the assertion that partial effects of job risk on wage rates cannot be observed.

Given that risk-wage differentials can be estimated, how are the estimates to be interpreted, and how do they relate to the demand price for safety? Existence of a systematic, observable relationship between job risk and wage rates means that it is possible to impute a set of implicit marginal prices for various levels of risk. Like other prices, the imputations result from intersections of demand and supply functions. In the present case, there are supplies of people willing to work at risk jobs and demands for people to fill them. Alternatively, workers can be viewed as demanding on-the-job safety and firms can be regarded as supplying it.

Difficulties of interpretation arise from two sources. Individuals have different attitudes toward risk bearing and/or different physical capacities to cope with risky situations. In addition, it is not necessarily true that observed risks are completely and technologically fixed in various occupations and production processes. For example, changing TV tower light bulbs on top of the World Trade Building in New York is inherently more risky than changing light bulbs inside the offices of that

3. For example, see Calabresi (1972).

building. However, it is conceivable to think of ways in which the first job could be made safer, though at some real cost. Whether, in general, firms find it in their interest to make safety-enhancing expenditures, and in what amounts, depends on weighing the costs of providing additional safety to workers against prospective returns. Costs are incurred from installing and maintaining safety devices and returns come in the form of lower wage payments and a smaller wage bill. How can it be known whether observed risk-wage relationships reflect mainly marginal costs of producing safety—the supply of job safety—rather than the demand for it?

This question raises fundamental and familiar issues of identification. Its resolution in terms of job attributes (or in terms of goods attributes in the hedonic view of demand, for that matter) requires a framework of analysis slightly altered from the usual one. The identification problem is resolved on a conceptual level in the following sections, where the nature of equilibrium in the implicit market for job risk is examined in some detail.[4] We show how the observations relate to underlying distributions of worker attitudes toward risk and to the structure of safety technology and particular production processes. The extent to which inferences about the demand for safety can be unscrambled from wage and risk observations quite naturally follows from this exercise. Data, estimates, and interpretation of the results are presented subsequently.

2. The Market for Job Safety

As noted above, the theory of equalizing differences suggests labor market transactions can be treated as tied sales. Workers sell their labor, but at the same time purchase nonmonetary and psychic aspects of their jobs. Firms purchase labor, but also sell nonmonetary aspects of work. Thus firms are joint producers: some output is sold on products markets and other output is sold to workers in conjunction with labor-service rentals. For purposes of exposition, we concentrate on one nonmonetary aspect of jobs, namely the risks of injury and death to which they give rise. The model can easily be extended to several attributes such as free lunches, good labor relations, prospects for on-

---

4. In fact, the model is an empirical application of a general model suggested by Rosen (1974).

the-job learning and the like, but the resulting complexity would detract from the main point.

For purposes of analyzing demand for job safety, it is sufficient to consider a market for productively and personally homogeneous workers. Assume worker attitudes toward death and injury risk are independent of their exogenously acquired skills. Workers in this market all have the same skill and personal characteristics, though tastes for job risk bearing generally differ among them. Workers are productively homogeneous, and the only distinguishing characteristic of jobs is the amount of death and injury risk associated with each of them.[5] Jobs exhibiting the same risks are identical, and, by assumption, the personal identity of particular employers and employees is irrelevant to the problem. Job risk itself is a multidimensional concept and requires, at least, a distinction between deaths and injury probabilities, on the one hand, and various levels of injury severity, on the other. Again, in line with our aim at simplification, represent job risk by a univariate index p. Further, let p denote the probability of a "standard accident." Then each job is perfectly described by a particular value of p on the unit interval.

Equilibrium in the job market is characterized by a *function $W(p)$*, yielding the wage rate associated with each value of p. In fact $W(p)$ is a functional generalization of Smith's equalizing differences concept. Given an equilibrium function $W(p)$, each worker chooses an optimal value of p by comparing psychic costs of increased risk with monetary returns in the form of higher wages. This assumes, of course, that workers are risk averse and $W(p)$ is increasing in p. Operationally, optimal choice is achieved through each worker applying for a job offering the desired degree of risk (p). Firms decide what risks their jobs contain by comparing costs of providing additional safety with

---

5. The reader should note that analysis of worker job choice is confined to people with identical personal characteristics. The point is tricky and will be considered again below. For now, the following example will have to do. Suppose clumsy and careless persons have large negative externalities in risky settings involving groups of workers. Then a set of equalizing differences must arise on worker characteristics (one of which is "carelessness") that are not independent of risk. Costs of employing a careless worker exceed the costs of employing a careful one, and the latter must be paid less than the former. Employers attempt to internalize these externalities by choosing employees with the optimal packages of personal characteristics. It is as if there are separate risk markets for workers with each bundle of personal characteristics, and the present analysis of worker choice is confined to only one of those markets.

returns in the form of lower wage payments, and are constrained by their basic underlying technologies. $W(p)$ is an equilibrium function when the number of workers applying for jobs at each value of risk equals the number of jobs offered at each risk. Therefore, $W(p)$ serves as an equilibrating device for matching or marrying off workers and firms, the same role that prices play in standard markets.

Analysis of optimal choices of workers and firms gives an intuitive picture of the mechanism generating the observations on risk and prices (the function $W(p)$). Both decisions are considered in turn. We have sometimes found it convenient to think in terms of supply of workers to risky jobs and firms' demands for job risk, rather than the obverse concepts of workers' demand for job safety and firms' supply of it: safety is the negative of risk.

3. An Example

A good starting point for our analysis is the essay by Walter Oi (1973). Some fundamental aspects of the problem and our basic methodology are well illustrated by proving a variant of Oi's main result in very simple fashion and going on from there.

Again, suppose all job risk involves standard injuries and can be represented by work time lost and, consequently, by earnings lost. Deaths and "pain and suffering" due to injuries are ignored for the time being. Adopting this simplification, injuries can be measured in monetary equivalents: a proportion of the wage permanently lost, say, kW, where k is an exogenously determined constant and $0 < k < 1$. Workers choose jobs offering injury probability p, basing decisions on maximization of expected utility. Let $U(Y)$ represent some worker's utility function, where Y is the prospect of certain income. Assume risk aversion: $U' > 0$ and $U'' < 0$. Assume a perfect insurance market: the cost of insurance equals its actuarial value, with no additional load factor, and workers choosing jobs offering injury probability p can purchase insurance at price $p/(1 - p)$ per dollar coverage. Both workers and insurance companies know the true probabilities and there is no moral hazard. Let I denote the amount of insurance purchased. Expected utility is given by

$$E = (1 - p)U[W(p) - \frac{p}{1 - p}I] + pU[(1 - k)W(p) + I], \qquad (1)$$

where $W - [p/(1-p)]I$ is net income if an accident does not occur, and $W(1-k) + I$ is income if it does. The worker chooses p and I to maximize E.

Consider optimal amounts of insurance coverage first, conditional on an arbitrary value of p. Differentiate E with respect to I, set the result to zero, and simplify to obtain

$$U'(W - \frac{p}{1-p}I) = U'[W(1-k) + I] \qquad (2)$$

or equalization of marginal utility in both states of the world. In that losses are converted into monetary equivalents and U is strictly increasing in its argument, condition (2) can be realized only if incomes in both states of the world are equated. That is, (2) implies $I = (1-p)kW$. Substituting this result into equation (1) and simplifying gives

$$E = U[(I - pk)W(p)]. \qquad (3)$$

The problem has been converted to optimal choice of p, conditional on prior optimization of insurance coverage.

Define an *acceptance wage* θ as the payment necessary to make the worker indifferent to jobs offering alternative risks, again conditioned on purchasing optimal insurance coverage for each risk. The acceptance wage is defined for a constant expected utility index E, and with recourse to (3) implicitly is defined by

$$E = U[\theta(p, E{:}k)(1 - pk)]. \qquad (4)$$

Invert equation 4

$$\theta(p, E{:}k) = U^{-1}(E)/(1 - pk) \equiv f(E)/(1 - pk). \qquad (5)$$

Equation (5) defines a family of indifference curves in the earnings/risk (θ, p) plane such that the compensated (utility held constant) acceptance wage is increasing in risk at an increasing rate: The marginal rate of substitution between job risk and money is positive and increasing. Differentiating the log of (5) with respect to p shows that the relative marginal acceptance wage, $\frac{1}{\theta}\frac{\partial\theta}{\partial p} = k/(1 - pk)$, depends only on risk, and k is independent of E. In other words, relative marginal acceptance wages are the same for all workers, independently of workers' degrees of risk aversion. This is due to the presence of perfect insurance so that full coverage is rational.

The fact that the function $\dfrac{1}{\theta}\dfrac{\partial\theta}{\partial p}$ is equal for all workers yields some arbitrage restrictions on observable wage/risk relationships in the market. Arbitrage mandates the restriction $W'(p)/W(p) = \dfrac{1}{\theta(p, E)} \cdot \dfrac{\partial\theta(p, E)}{\partial p}$ for every possible value of p. For proof, assume to the contrary that at some value of p, say p^*, $W'(p^*)/W(p^*) > \dfrac{1}{\theta(p^*, E)} \cdot \dfrac{\partial\theta(p^*, E)}{\partial p}$. Then everybody currently working at a job with risk p^* could improve themselves by applying for jobs involving slightly higher risk. Additional wages on higher-risk jobs exceed relative marginal valuations of them and expected utility must rise from taking slightly larger risks. Jobs such as p^* are unfilled, and relative wages have to change in an obvious way to induce people to apply for them. Exactly the opposite logic applies when the inequality goes in the other direction. In that case, it is also not rational for anyone to apply for any job offering risk p^*. Jobs offering smaller risks yield larger expected utility, and $W'(p^*)/W(p^*)$ must increase if p^* type jobs are to be filled. Therefore $W'(p)/W(p) = \dfrac{1}{\theta}\dfrac{\partial\theta}{\partial p}$ must hold for all p, and the observed market wage-risk function must satisfy $W'(p)/W(p) = k/(1 - pk)$. This market equilibrium condition can be integrated to yield

$$W(p) = C/(1 - pk). \tag{6}$$

In (6), C is a constant of integration, determined by the side condition that total quantity of labor supplied to the market equals total demand for it. Only if market observations lie along an approximately semilog function such as (6) can the labor market be in equilibrium in this simple example.

The problem considered above reveals the basic essentials of Smith's theory. In this case, wage differentials are exactly equalizing everywhere, both at the margin and on the average, and wage differences only reflect actuarial differences in risk between jobs. To see this, note that expected earning is $(1 - p)W(p) + p(1 - k)W(p)$, which, from (6), equals C: expected earnings is constant across all jobs, independent of job risk and the distribution of risk aversion in the labor force. Following the general "free lunch theorem," such a distinct and strong result comes from strong assumptions. Perfect insurance implies all risk-averse workers act as expected income maximizers and induces them to act alike, independently of their degree of risk aversion. The result would not have been true had we allowed for pain and suffering, imperfect insurance (nonzero load and hence incomplete coverage), or interpersonal differences in physical capacities to cope with job risk.[6] Equalizing wage-risk relationships depends on the demand for workers, as well as on the supply of them, in those cases, as well be spelled out below.

It is important to note differences between compensation and earnings before turning to a more general formulation of the problem. The two are related by an identity: compensation ≡ earnings + fringe benefits. Fringe benefits were ignored above. Had they been included (employers "pay" insurance premiums), no systematic relationship between earnings and risk would have occurred. However, the relationship between compensation and risk would have been described by (6). Insurance fringes act like a tax that is completely "backward shifted" and nominal earnings fall by the amount of the benefit. Workers always pay these costs, whether or not they nominally do so. Therefore, since earnings before fringe benefits and insurance premiums stand in a fixed relationship to each other (the insurance premium is pkW), differences in compensation serve to equalize the market, not differences in net earnings. For example, workmen's compensation is a force making for uniformity in net wage rates across jobs with alternative risks, so long as benefit schedules reflect true monetary (and psychic) losses and the amount of insurance is no more than workers would buy voluntarily. Henceforth the words "wage" and "compensation" will be used interchangeably.

---

6. Suppose realized risks in a given situation differ from person to person for exogenous reasons and that personal characteristics (e.g., sense of balance) involve no externalities. Also, in line with footnote 5, assume equalizing difference functions for job risk $W(p)$ and personal characteristics are independent of each other in the relevant sense. Differences in real risks can be handled in the example by specifying a distribution on k across workers. Then the arbitrage-everywhere argument breaks down because all workers cannot be indifferent to all jobs. Even in the presence of perfect insurance, relative marginal acceptance wages depend on k and are not equal for everyone. Obviously those individuals for whom k is small apply for the riskier jobs.

4. Supply Price of Job Risk

Now the assumptions of perfect insurance and the absence of pain and suffering are relaxed. Only two states of the world were distinguished in the example above, accident–no accident. Taking account of alternative levels of injury severity requires introducing N possible states. For example, N might be 4, a value of 1 indexing no accident, 2 indexing "minor" accidents, 3 "nonminor," nondeath accidents, and 4 indexing death. Demarcation between states 2 and 3 or any other boundaries along the injury-severity continuum are achieved through the use of dummy variable splits on an index such as workdays lost. For instance days lost greater than zero but less than some number D_1 correspond to state 2, days lost between D_1 and D_2 correspond to state 3, and so forth. Finer distinctions (and more states) can be made by combining workdays-lost severity indexes and the physical nature of accidents, such as loss of limb, impairment of hearing and so on.

Conceptually, pain and suffering are represented by different-state utility functions depending on the states themselves. For example, suppose losses for states n through $n + m$ can be converted into monetary equivalents. Then the n through $n + m$ state utility functions are of the same functional form as utility associated with the no-accident state. All other states have utility functions specific to themselves measured in such a way as to be conformable with expected utility axioms.[7]

In general, each possible job is described by an $N - 1$ component vector of probabilities $(p_2, p_3, \ldots, p_N)$ with p_i indexing the probability of state i. [The no-accident probability is ignored because it can be inferred from all the other probabilities: $p_1 = 1 - \prod_{j=2}^{N} p_j$, assuming independence.] In other words, each job is perfectly described by a bundle of different accident probabilities, with the package varying from one job to another. Jobs are associated with a multivariate function. $W(p_2, \ldots, p_N)$, giving the market wage for alternative bundles of job risk. Workers maximize expected utility over all states subject to the equalizing difference function $W(p_2, \ldots, p_N)$. Each worker chooses an optimal p-vector and applies for the job offering those probabilities.

---

7. See Hirshleifer (1965).

We shall not attempt to present a completely general treatment of the problem. Discussion is specialized to two states for purposes of illustration. State 1 represents no accident; and state 2, accidents resulting in death. Workers either survive their jobs or they don't, certainly two mutually exclusive events! Each job is associated with a number p, now indexing the probability of death. The market reveals an equalizing difference function $W(p)$ giving compensation as a function of death risk. $W'(p)$ is positive, and other restrictions will be put on it later. Insurance is available at market price $\lambda p/(1 - p)$ per dollar of coverage, with $\lambda \geq 1$. The load factor is $(\lambda - 1)$.

Assume a concave utility function $U(Y)$ for the life state as before, choosing the origin so that $U(0) = 0$. The utility (bequest) function for the death state is $\psi(Y)$, also concave with $\psi(0) = 0$. For obvious reasons, U and ψ are restricted to obey the inequality $U(Y) > \psi(Y)$ for all common values of Y. The worker chooses p and I to maximize

$$E = (1 - p)U[W(p) + y - \frac{\lambda p}{1 - p}I] + p\psi(y + I), \qquad (7)$$

where y is nonlabor income. $W + y - [\lambda p/(1 - p)]I$ is income if the worker lives and $y + I$ is beneficiaries' income if he dies. Assuming E is strictly concave in p and I, necessary and sufficient conditions for a maximum are

$$E_I = -p(\lambda U' - \psi') = 0$$

$$E_p = -U + \psi + (1 - p)U'[W' - \lambda I/(1 - p)^2] = 0. \qquad (8)$$

Equations (8) jointly determine optimal values of p and I. Notice that it is no longer true that marginal utilities in both states are equal. Even if they were (i.e., if $\lambda = 1$), equality would not imply equal incomes in both states, because U' and ψ' are not identical functions. Hence the arbitrage argument used in the example above no longer applies because people with alternative utility functions behave differently.

Conditions (8) are not very informative in and of themselves unless functional forms are specified for U and ψ. In the absence of that, a very general picture of equilibrium is obtained by going the route described in the section above. Again define an acceptance wage θ as the amount of money the worker would willingly accept to work on jobs of different risks at a constant utility index, conditioned on optimal purchase of insurance. Then $\theta(p, E{:}y, \lambda)$ is defined implicitly by solving for θ and I in terms of E, y and λ from

$$E = (1 - p)U[\theta + y - \frac{\lambda p}{1 - p}I] + p\psi(y + 1)$$

$$0 = \lambda U'\{\theta + y - [\lambda p/(1 - p)]I\} - \psi'(y + I). \qquad (9)$$

The following properties of θ can be derived from the implicit function theorem[8]

$$\theta_p > 0, \quad \theta_{pp} > 0. \qquad (i)$$

The marginal acceptance wage is positive and increasing in risk, θ_p is the expected-utility compensated supply price to risky jobs and is rising because of risk aversion, imperfect insurance, and pain and suffering (U is not the same as ψ). Property (i) is crucial to what follows.[9]

$$\theta_E > 0, \quad \theta_y \overset{\bullet}{<} -1. \qquad (ii)$$

The acceptance wage is increasing in expected utility and decreasing in nonlabor income at any given risk. Moreover, an additional dollar of nonlabor income lowers the acceptance wage (utility held constant) by more than a dollar. The reason for the latter is that additional dollars of nonlabor income increase utility in both states, thereby reducing optimal amounts of insurance and payments of insurance premiums in the life state.

$$\theta_{pE} > 0, \quad \theta_{py} < 0, \quad \theta_{p\lambda} > 0. \qquad (iii)$$

The marginal acceptance wage increases at higher levels of welfare: the better off a person is, the larger the monetary inducement necessary to coax him into a higher risk job. On the other hand, marginal acceptance wages decrease as nonlabor income rises (utility "held constant") for

---

8. These results can easily be checked by the reader. Take care always to treat θ *and* I as dependent variables and p, E, y, and λ as independent variables in the differentiation.

9. It is conceivable that no insurance is purchased if strict concavity in (7) is not assumed. Suppose marginal utility of bequests rapidly approach zero after some dollar value. A husband might want to leave his wife with at least $100,000 if he dies, but bequest dollars in excess of 100,000 do not yield much additional utility. It may be rational for him not to purchase insurance if his nonlabor wealth is in the neighborhood of $100,000. Even in such cases, the fundamental convexity property of indifference curves in Figure 3.1 below still applies.

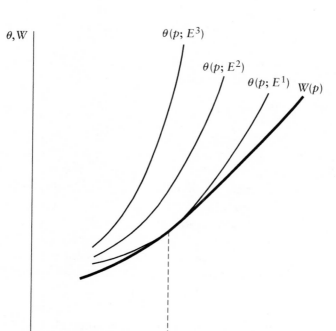

Figure 3.1 • Worker equilibrium

reasons stated under property (ii). Finally, increasing λ renders risk bearing more expensive and increases its reservation price.

Risk/earnings indifference curves $\theta(p; E, y)$ for a worker with some fixed amount of nonlabor income are shown in Figure 3.1. Labels $E_1, E_2, \ldots$, are in ascending order of expected utility, from property (ii). Convexity follows from property (i). Notice that the slopes of the indifference curves rise along a vertical line, a result of property (iii).

The heavy line labeled $W(p)$ represents risk/earnings opportunities or the market equalizing-difference wage function.[10] As usual, optimum choice of p (represented by p^* in the figure) occurs where the budget line and an adjoining indifference curve have a common tangent. Clearly, the curvature of $\theta(p)$ and $W(p)$ must stand in a proper relationship to

---

10. As shown by example in the preceding section, there is no reason for $W(p)$ to be linear in p. The budget constraint can be distinctly nonlinear.

each other if the solution is to be unique and interior, as is true in the assumption of strict concavity of (7).

Three empirically meaningful propositions emerge from properties (i)–(iii) and the equilibrium condition in Figure 3.1.[11]

Proposition I: Job safety is a normal good.

This statement needs careful interpretation and qualification. Consider the following parameterization of the budget: $W(p) = A + BV(p)$, where $V(p)$ is an increasing function of p and A and B are parameters. The statement holds true for changes in A. For example, let A increase. The budget line rises parallel to its initial position and expected utility also rises. But property (iiia) implies marginal acceptance wages rise too. Hence risk falls and the worker chooses a safer job.[12] Changes in A are analogous to pure income effects in demand theory. The statement does not hold for changes in B. An increase in B results in a negative income effect (on risk), but a positive substitution effect (on risk) in that increasing marginal earnings on riskier jobs makes risk bearing more attractive. The net outcome is unpredictable without further specification.

Proposition II: Job safety is positively related to the price of insurance.

This is an immediate consequence of (iiic). Decreasing the insurance load factor makes risk bearing cheaper, everywhere decreasing marginal rates of substitution between money and risk. More risk necessarily is purchased.

Proposition III: Job safety is not necessarily normal with respect to property income.

This nonintuitive result can be motivated in part as follows. Increasing nonlabor income provides a kind of self-insurance against the death state, since nonlabor income (willed to one's heirs) is not at risk in the labor market. This reduces needs for market insurance and makes risk

---

11. These statements are easy to prove analytically. Differentiate equations (8) and exploit second-order conditions for a maximum, as usual.

12. Some casual evidence is relevant here. Secularly increasing job safety in the United States has been accompanied by a trend of rising real wages. No doubt improvements in safety technology have decreased the price of safety as well.

bearing less expensive, a kind of substitution effect. However, increasing y also increases expected utility and has the effect of increasing the marginal acceptance wage for any incremental risk, a kind of income effect. The two effects work against each other. Mechanically, the result comes from properties (iib), (iiia) and (iiib). An additional dollar of nonlabor income shifts the entire indifference map downward by more than a dollar (iib) and also reduces marginal rates of substitution for given expected utility measures (iiib). However, marginal valuation of risk is increasing in expected utility (iiia) and marginal rates of substitution still increase along any vertical line in Figure 3.1. The first effect is a force making for increased risk, while the second works in the opposite direction. Curiously, it can be shown analytically that risk is necessarily inferior in nonlabor income when the insurance load is zero (i.e., $\lambda = 1$). Evidently, when the price of insurance exceeds its actuarial value there is a possibility for the kind of substitution effect described above to dominate the real income effect, tantamount to a type of risk preference.

5. Equalizing Differences and Supply Prices

The discussion above shows that worker choice is characterized by two equilibrium conditions: $W(p) = \theta(p, E)$ and $W'(p) = \partial\theta/\partial p$, two equations in two unknowns, p and E. Workers differ in their attitudes toward risk, bequest motives, and nonlabor income. Consequently there is a distribution of acceptance wage functions in the market. those with less risk aversion have smaller marginal acceptance wages (i.e., smaller values of $\partial\theta/\partial p$) and lower reservation prices to risky jobs. The opposite might be true of people with many dependents or with high degrees of risk aversion in the accident state. Whatever the source of interpersonal differences, workers with lower marginal acceptance wages work on riskier jobs.

A picture of market equilibrium on the supply side of the market is shown in Figure 3.2. Ignore the curves labeled ϕ^j for the moment. $W(p)$ is the equalizing difference function as in Figure 3.1. Two workers are shown in Figure 3.2, one with acceptance wage θ^1 and the other with θ^2. $(\partial\theta^1/\partial p) > (\partial\theta^2/\partial p)$ and worker 2 is employed on a riskier job, since safety is not as valuable to him. The picture may be generalized. Add more workers and fill in all points on the $W(p)$ line. It is apparent that $W(p)$ is the lower envelope of a family of acceptance wage functions depending on the joint distribution of y, U, and ψ across workers.

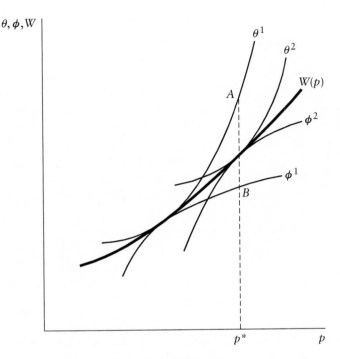

Figure 3.2 • Market equilibrium

$W(p)$ is observed, while the functions θ^i are not. However, evaluate the derivative of the equalizing wage difference function at some value of p, say p^*. Then, from the equilibrium conditions, $W'(p^*) = \partial\theta^i(p^*, E^*)/\partial p$ for workers finding p^* optimal, and $W'(p^*)$ identifies the marginal acceptance wage for such workers. Therefore, $W'(p^*)$ identifies $\partial\theta^i/\partial p$. $W'(p^*)$ estimates how much money is necessary to induce a person into accepting a small incremental risk. Alternatively, it estimates how much the person will pay to reduce risk by a small amount, exactly the number we seek.

The empirical work reported below uses data from very risky jobs, on the average perhaps as much as five times more risky than most jobs in the U.S. economy. It must be true that individuals working on such jobs have lower reservation supply prices and consequently smaller demand prices for safety than the average worker. The point is illustrated in Figure 3.2. Evaluating W' at p^* provides the correct estimate for person 2, but is an underestimate for person 1. The price the latter is willing to pay for safety at p^* is given by the slope of his acceptance wage function evaluated at p^*, the slope of θ_1 at the point marked A in Figure 3.2. It follows from the fact that compensated supply functions to risky jobs are rising (i.e., acceptance wage functions are convex) that $\partial\theta^1(p^*, E^*)/\partial p$ exceeds $W'(p^*)$. Most people in the labor force do not work on risky jobs. Therefore, use of data on very risky jobs understates average demand prices for safety at the observed risk levels in our sample. This justifies our initial assertion that the estimates below are conservative and probably biased downward when extrapolated to the population as a whole.

6. Demand Price for Job Risk

It was demonstrated above that $W'(p)$ identifies supply price of risk at the relevant margin. That conclusion was reached independently of demand considerations. We now consider a very simple model of demand prices and firm decisions in order to complete the model. It will hardly be shocking to discover that $W'(p)$ also identifies demand price for risk at some margin.

Accidents are an unpleasant, though in part avoidable, by-product of production. This fact of life (or of death!) can be represented analytically by a joint production function $F(s, p, L) = 0$ for some firm, where x is marketable output, p is the accident rate, and L is labor input. Inputs other than labor are ignored, p can be a vector of state accident probabilities as mentioned above. However, to simplify, collapse it into a univariate index denoting the probability of death. Invert F and assume the following properties for $x = g(p, L)$: (i) $g_L > 0$ and $g_{LL} < 0$. Labor has positive and diminishing marginal product. (ii) $g_{Lp} < 0$. Safety increases the marginal product of labor. (iii) $g_p > 0$ for $0 \le p < \bar{p}$, $g_p \gtrless 0$ for $p \ge \bar{p}$, where $\bar{p}$ is some "large," technically determined constant, and $g_{pp} < 0$. The assumptions on g_p are best explained by noting that they imply that the transformation locus between output (x) and safety ($1 - p$) is negatively inclined, except possibly at very low levels of safety. Accidents are "productive," at least up to a certain point, and can be avoided only by changing the organization of production within the firm away from marketable output and toward accident prevention. The assumption on g_{pp} means the transformation function is concave.

The production function $g(p, L)$ has been written so that safety is, in effect, produced internally by the firm. Safety devices (such as guard rails and hard hats) can also be purchased and installed externally. Let $G(1 - p)$ represent the cost of externally provided safety (converted to an annual flow), with G' and $G'' > 0$. The latter means installation activities are subject to increasing costs, though that is not strictly necessary to what follows.

The firm maximizes profit Π with respect to L and p

$$\Pi = g(p, L) - W'(p)L - G(1 - p), \tag{10}$$

where the price of x has been normalized at unity. Again $W(p)$ represents the competitive wage that must be paid for alternative levels of risk. Necessary conditions for a maximum are

$$g_p + G' = W'(p)L$$
$$g_L = W(p). \tag{11}$$

Labor is hired up to the point where its wage and marginal product are equal. Marginal costs of risk are the additional market wage payments necessary to attract workers to riskier jobs. Marginal benefits come in the form of additional market output and cost savings from installing fewer safety devices. Second-order conditions require certain curvature restrictions on $W(p)$ as will be shown.

Symmetrically with the treatment above, define an *offer* function ϕ as the amount the firm willingly pays the optimal number of workers at alternative levels of risk and constant profit. With recourse to the definition of profit and the marginal condition on labor, $\phi(p, \Pi)$ is defined implicitly by

$$\phi = [g(p, L) - G(1 - p) - \Pi]/L$$
$$\phi = g_L(p, L). \tag{12}$$

Clearly $\partial \phi / \partial p$ is the compensated demand price for risk. Differentiating (12) [again, always treat ϕ and L as dependent variables, and Π and p as independent variables]

$$\partial \phi / \partial \Pi = -1/L$$
$$\partial \phi / \partial p = (g_p + G')/L$$
$$\frac{\partial^2 \phi}{\partial p^2} = \left[(g_{pp} - G'')g_{LL} - (\phi_p - g_{Lp}^2) \right] / L g_{LL} \gtreqless 0.$$

The marginal demand price for risk is positive. However, even the common assumption of concavity of the production function does not guarantee that the compensated demand schedule is negatively inclined: $\partial^2\phi/\partial p^2$ can be positive.

The offer function $\phi(p, \Pi)$ defines a family of indifference curves in money and risk, one member of which is shown in Figure 3.2. ϕ^1 refers to one firm and ϕ^2 refers to another firm, possibly in a different industry and in any case, with a different technology than firm 1. The diagram assumes $\partial^2\phi/\partial p^2 < 0$, which is not necessarily true. Equilibrium of each firm is characterized by tangency between the market availabilities function $W(p)$ and the lowest possible constant-profit indifference curve (profit increases as ϕ decreases at any level of risk, since $\partial\phi/\partial\Pi < 0$). W'' must exceed $\partial^2\phi/\partial p^2$ at the point of tangency for an interior maximum.

Similarly to the case of worker choice, $W'(p) = \partial\phi/\partial p$ at equilibrium, and $W(p)$ represents an upper envelope of the distribution of offer functions in the market. The family of offer functions depends on the nature of production functions in various firms and industries and on corresponding distributions of industrial safety technology. In any event $W'(p^*)$ also identifies $\partial\phi^i(p^*, \Pi^*)/\partial p$, where firm i is one that has chosen p^* optimally. Using the same logic as above, $W'(p^*)$ overestimates the average supply price of safety (again, at p^*) if p^* is a very risky job. This is easily seen in Figure 3.2, since the slope of $\partial\phi^1/\partial p$ at point B necessarily is smaller than the slope of $\partial\phi^2/\partial p$ evaluated at the same level of job risk.[13]

7. Market Equilibrium: Summary

It will be useful to summarize results of the model so far.

(a) The observable wage-risk relation represents a double envelope function: it is the lower boundary of a set of acceptance wage functions and the upper boundary of a set of offer wage functions. Marriages between jobs and applicants at each level of risk are represented by common tangents of appropriate acceptance wage and offer wage functions.

---

13. Suppose L is exogenous. Then the offer function is defined by the first equation in 12, and it is easy to show that increased values of L reduce demand price for risk ($\phi_{pL} < 0$), providing incentives to offer safer jobs. Increasing incentives toward job safety vary directly with establishment size because of larger cost savings from lower wage rates. It is well known that accident rates decline with establishment size, at least after some minimum size. Accident rates also tend to be low in very small establishments as well, so this cannot be the entire story.

(b) The envelope property in (a) implies that the derivatives of observed risk-wage differentials (evaluated at each level of risk) identify *marginal* supply and demand prices of workers and firms choosing those particular job risks.

(c) Supply price of risk (equivalently, demand price for safety) identified in (b) from very risky jobs underestimates the average supply price in the labor force for those risks, since people choosing risky jobs have a comparative advantage at job risk bearing. Similarly, demand price for risk (supply price of safety) identified from very risky jobs overestimates the average demand price for most firms in the economy, since firms offering risky jobs have a comparative disadvantage at producing safety.

(d) The numbers identified in (b) represent single points on compensated supply and demand functions, not the functions themselves. Use of such numbers for evaluation overestimates consumer surplus of finite increases in safety because workers' compensated demand schedules for safety are negatively inclined.

8. Equilibrium and Worker Characteristics

A very simple demand model has been specified above, and it may be too simple. Recall the production function has been written $x = g(p, L)$, where L is labor and p is risk. But what is labor?[14] Our data contain indicators of personal productivity such as education and work experience. Suppose there are m such indicators, denoted by a vector $c = (c_1, \ldots, c_m)$. Of course, sample wages vary with worker characteristics as well as with job risk. Let $W(p, c)$ represent the market wage-risk–characteristics equalizing difference function. Writing the production function for a firm as we did implies that firms act as if there exists a single index of labor input, $L = f(c_1, \ldots, c_m)$ defined independently of job risk. If so, the production function must be separable in c and p. This is also a sufficient condition for separability of $W(p, c)$ as well. Suppose $W(p, c)$ is additive in p and c: $W(p, c) = V(p) + T(c)$. Hence, firms care only about total amounts of "skill" they employ (i.e., L) independently of how skills come packaged in people and also independently of job

---

14. The reader may be thinking, "What is risk?" The two questions are very much related. See below.

risks to which their employees are subjected. In effect, it means that packages of worker characteristics can be untied. For example, firms might be indifferent between a worker with 8 years of schooling and 10 years of experience and another with 12 years of school and 3 years of experience, or between workers with other combinations of these characteristics.

The real issue under discussion here involves how many interactions to allow in the risk and characteristics wage-explaining regression. At one extreme is the possibility for a universal implicit market for risk, independent of worker personal productivities (no interactions). At the other extreme are separate implicit markets for all possible combinations of personal characteristics (complete interactions). The former case corresponds to the firm choice model sketched above. Yet there is a distinct possibility that risk affects productivity in a nonhomogeneous manner with respect to various productivity indicators. Then some interactions are required. In general, the market reveals implicit prices for both risk and worker characteristics. All prices are determined simultaneously and cannot be separated.[15] and the firm choice model sketched above must refer to a single type of worker (c held constant).

If there is no interaction in production between worker characteristics and safety, only one risk premium for each value of risk appears in the market. Furthermore, the risk-wage function is independent of any further interaction between worker characteristics and attitudes toward risk. Differences in worker characteristics (age, marital status, and so on) that result in different acceptance wage functions simply help identify which workers accept riskier jobs. On the other hand, if there are interactions in production, differential risk premiums according to personal characteristics generally appear, so long as the preferred characteristics are in sufficiently scarce supply. If these characteristics are not in short supply, only those workers with preferred attributes work on risky jobs and no differential risk premium need arise in the market. Finally, if differential risk premiums exist, $W(p)$ in Figures 3.1 and 3.2

---

15. In part, firm decisions can be handled formally as follows. The production function is $x = h(p, c_1, \ldots, c_m) = h(p, c)$. Profit is $h(p, c) - W(p, c)$, maximized over p and c. The firm organizes production taking account of factor supplies (i.e., $W(p, c)$), designing jobs and their risks and determining a set of worker-characteristics requirements. Workers not meeting requirements are not hired by the firm. Now define a joint offer-requirements function $\zeta(p, c, \Pi)$, indicating offer prices for alternative risk-characteristics requirements at constant profit, and compare the resulting indifference surfaces in (money, p, c) space with market availabilities $W(p, c)$.

becomes a family of curves $W(p, c)$, one for each value of c, as was noted above (see footnote 5).

The issue is rather thorny, but an example will clarify it. Consider the regression model

$$W = a_0 + a_1 p + a_2(pz) + \text{ random error}, \qquad (13)$$

where W is observed wages, p is risk, z is worker age, and the a's are regression coefficients. The pure effect of age, higher-order terms in p, and all other explanatory variables are impounded in the constant term a_0 for purposes of this discussion.

Age presumably affects worker's acceptance wages. Young workers risk entire lifetimes of future consumption in taking high-risk jobs and have far more to lose than their older counterparts. Supply price to risky jobs should fall with age on that account. Further, a typical individual may become more or less risk averse over his lifetime, inducing shifts in acceptance wage functions over the life cycle. Job risk should be systematically related to age for both reasons. However, variations of this variety are completely captured by movements along the observed risk-wage function (taking account of possible effects of age on a_0) and there is no role here for extra marginal effects of age on risk premiums per se. Look at Figure 3.1. The changes under consideration are represented by systematic variations in money-risk preferences, resulting in moving points of tangency between a life-cycle shifting acceptance wage function and a fixed-risk, market opportunities function. Movements along $W(p)$ should not be confused with shifts in it, and all such changes are already counted in the pure risk coefficient a_1.

Age can affect risk premiums only insofar as it reflects unmeasured characteristics whose productivities are affected by differential risk. Exposure to risky situations makes some people far less effective agents of production than others. They not only accomplish less work of their own, but also impose extra costs on others. Both effects have to reduce wage rates of these persons if they are observed working at risky jobs. Such wage differentials serve as compensation for additional costs firms incur in employing them. For example, "nerves of steel" is a scarce factor, but steely nerves capture rents only in risky situations. Good balance is valuable to ironworkers on building sites but not to desk clerks, and so forth. In the present case, young workers on the average have speedier reflexes than older ones and have faster reactions to potential accidents. But older workers have had more exposure and experience with job risk, and experience and quick reflexes probably are substitutes. Hence the effect of age on productivity in the presence of risk is uncertain, though we might expect the reflex effect to dominate, by and large, for workers past some age that varies across occupations.

Whatever the interactions between risk differentials and personal characteristics, the analysis underlying Figure 3.1 still applies. The marginal effect of risk on wages evaluated at the person's exogenously determined characteristics estimates supply price for risk or demand price for safety. It also estimates firms' supply price of safety to workers with those characteristics. It is certainly possible, however, that observed risk differentials vary with worker attributes.

9. The Data

Empirical implementation of the model requires information on earnings of individuals, job risks they face, and their personal and job-related characteristics. It involves augmenting standard wage equations with job-risk measures. Many cross-sectional sources of earnings data are available and we have chosen one of them, the 1967 Survey of Economic Opportunity (SEO). The (SEO) survey was designed to heavily represent low-income populations and our sample is restricted to an extract of the data, consisting of a random sample of 9,488 representative households in the U.S. population. Of these observations, the sample was further reduced to adult male heads of households. The SEO data provides information on personal and industrial characteristics and labor force activities of individuals. It also lists individuals' industry of employment and occupation.

The standard source of data on industrial hazards is published by the Bureau of Labor Statistics (BLS) in conjunction with compliance and experience surveys under the Workmen's Compensation Act. These data give accidental death and injury rates for 4-digit SIC industry codes on an annual basis. Unfortunately, the BLS death and injury data cannot be adequately matched to individuals and is unsuitable for the purposes of this study. For example, it is possible to assign the BLS average death and injury indexes (by industry) to individuals in the SEO tape because the individual's industrial attachment is known. However, using the death and injury statistics in that manner implies introducing a huge component of measurement error for individuals, because job risks in each industry are not uniform across occupations. Hence, any estimates of the risk premium obtained in this way will probably be biased.

Luckily, another data source was discovered which does not suffer from the aggregation problems inherent in published BLS sources. The data used here come from the 1967 Occupation Study of the Society of Actuaries. The purpose of the 1967 study was to measure *extra* risks associated with some very hazardous occupations and the study was based on a sample of insurance company records covering 3,252,262 policy years of workers' experience over the period 1955–1964. The data were tabulated on a combined industry and occupational basis, and can be matched directly to individuals on the SEO sample, using Census categories contained in the latter. The matching procedure yielded 37 occupations on about 900 individuals. The occupations and their sample actuarial risks are listed in Table 3.1. Of course, it would be quite rash to assert that the actuarial data overcome all matching difficulties, because Table 3.1 shows that the actuarial classifications are rather broad. However, they are far more narrowly defined than the BLS data. We are extremely confident that the degree of measurement error in attributing risks to SEO individuals using the actuarial data is perhaps as much as an order of magnitude smaller than would be true had we matched with BLS risk data—especially for individuals working on very risky jobs, such as most of those in Table 3.1. In other words, the actuarial study simply provides the best data that are available for estimating risk premiums in the labor market.[16]

The actuarial data have one other very good feature. An expected number of deaths was estimated in each occupation, based on the age distribution of persons in the sample records and standard life tables. Expected deaths were then subtracted from actual deaths and the result normalized to yield an *extra* deaths per thousand policy years statistic (those numbers are multiplied by 100 in Table 3.1). Hence the numbers in Table 3.1 are net of normal age-specific death experience and measure extra death risk associated with occupations. These statistics reflect genuine occupational hazards that may cumulate with time spent in the

---

16. After this study was completed, we discovered a paper by R. Smith (1973), who used the BLS hazard data. At an earlier stage of our research, and before discovering the Actuaries Study, we too experimented with BLS data. Our results were very similar to Smith's. However, in view of the measurement error, we believe that Smith's very strong conclusions about the workings of the labor market are totally unwarranted and that his estimates must surely be seriously biased.

Table 3.1 • Sample occupations and risks

Occupation	Risk [a]	Occupation	Risk [a]
Fishermen	19	Truck drivers	98
Foresters	22	Bartenders	176
Teamsters	114	Cooks	132
Lumbermen	256	Firemen	44
Mine operatives	176	Guards, watchmen, and doorkeepers	267
Metal filers, grinders, and polishers	41	Marshals, constables, sheriffs, and bailiffs	181
Boilermakers	230	Police and detectives	78
Cranemen and derrickmen	147	Longshoremen and stevedores	101
Factory painters	81	Actors	73
Other painters	46	Railroad conductors	203
Electricians	93	Ships' officers	156
Railroad brakemen	88	Hucksters and peddlers	76
Structural ironworkers	204	Linemen and servicemen	2
Locomotive firemen	186	Road machine operators	103
Power plant operatives	6	Elevator operators	188
Sailors and deckhands	163	Laundry operatives	126
Sawyers	133	Waiters	134
Switchmen	152		
Taxicab drivers	182		

Source: Society of Actuaries.

a. Units of measure are extra deaths per 100,000 policy years. To convert to the probability of an extra death per year on each job multiply by 0.00001.

profession. To see how risky these jobs are, note that the mean value in Table 3.1 is approximately 100. In probability terms, this amounts to an extra 1 in 1,000 probability of death. The probability of death from the 1967 life table for white males 35 years of age was 2 in 1,000. Thus, though the probabilities are small in absolute terms, they are very large relative to the risks most people incur in the ordinary course of their lives.

A less attractive feature of the actuarial risk data is that they only include death rates. Separate indexes for death and nondeath accidents would be preferable, but nondeath accident statistics comparable to those in Table 3.1 are not available. We must rest content with the knowledge that death rates and injury rates in the BLS industry data are highly correlated, and there is no reason for that not to be true in our data as well.

Several earnings measures are available from SEO data. We have experimented with all of them and settled on the weekly wage, because it probably is measured most accurately. We would prefer to use a measure of total compensation, but the value of fringe benefits are not available on the SEO tape or any other data set on individuals known to us. This omission must reduce the observed risk differential, again pointing toward conservative estimates. The extent of bias depends on the size of the load factor and the importance of pain and suffering, as well as on the precise differences between life (U) and bequest (ψ) utility functions. In any event, the average amount of life insurance provided in fringe benefits is not very large, and this source of bias must be rather small.

10. Estimation

Our goal is to estimate the equalizing difference function $W(p, c)$. Four types of independent variables are used to control for factors determining wage rates other than job risk. These are the content of the c variables. The first set controls for regional and urban-nonurban wage differentials. The second set measures individuals' personal characteristics, including age, education, family size (or marital status), and race. The square of age and education can be included to allow for nonlinearities. The third set controls for other characteristics of the job, including unionization, dummy variables for manufacturing and service industries, and three major occupational dummy variables, one for operatives (OC1), another for service workers (OC2), and a third for laborers (OC3). Socioeconomic status (SES) was used at one stage instead of the occupational dummies as a crude measure of other nonpecuniary aspects of work. SES is an index number based on occupation, education, and income, and it might capture some other types of equalizing differences, though it was not constructed for that purpose.

Means and standard deviations of all variables are shown in Table 3.2. Note that the sample includes a much higher proportion of union members than obtains in the labor force generally. Sample mean

Table 3.2 • Summary statistics

Variable	Mean	Standard deviation
Dummy variables[a]		
Urban	.69	.46
Northeast	.28	.45
South	.29	.45
West	.17	.38
Family size exceeds 2	.76	.42
Manufacturing industry	.24	.42
Service industry	.58	.49
Worker is white	.90	.30
Worker is employed full time	.98	.10
Worker belongs to union	.45	.49
Worker is married	.92	.26
Occupation is operative	.27	.44
Occupation is service	.45	.49
Occupation is laborer	.22	.42
Continuous variables		
Age (years)	41.8	11.3
Education (years)	10.11	2.73
Weeks worked in 1966	49.4	5.4
Hours worked last week	44.9	11.6
Risk (probability $\times$ 10^5)	109.8	67.6
Weekly wage (week prior to survey)	$132.65	50.80

a. Mean is proportion in sample with designated characteristic. The number of observations is 907.

earnings on an annual basis is about $6,600 ($= 132 \times 50$), which is a bit less than average earnings among male manufacturing workers during this period.

Regression planes have been fitted by least squares, using arithmetic values of earnings as the dependent variable; and alternatively, using the log of earnings as the dependent variable. The arithmetic results are shown in Table 3.3. Results using the log of earnings are reported in Table 3.4 and are very similar to the arithmetic results when evaluated at sample means.

Table 3.3 • Regression estimates of $W(p, c)$: Linear form

Independent variable	Equation 1	Equation 2	Equation 3	Equation 4
Risk	.0352 (.0210)	.0520 (.0219)	.100 (.108)	.0410 (.102)
Risk × age	—	—	−.0019 (.0018)	−.0030 (.0019)
Risk × married	—	—	.0791 (.0380)	.0701 (.0412)
Risk × union	—	—	.0808 (.040)	.0869 (.042)
Risk × white	—	—	−.118 (.072)	—
Urban	13.80 (4.2)	15.71 (2.95)	17.0 (3.0)	17.0 (3.2)
Northeast	−3.71 (3.65)	−4.29 (3.67)	−4.27 (3.63)	−4.92 (3.83)
South	−8.86 (3.70)	−8.90 (3.74)	−10.5 (3.72)	−8.18 (3.97)
West	9.13 (4.13)	10.30 (4.18)	9.57 (4.12)	9.50 (4.37)
Age	3.89 (0.80)	3.81 (0.83)	3.83 (0.82)	3.78 (0.87)
(Age)^2	−.0479 (.0092)	−.0468 (.0097)	−.0442 (.010)	−.0415 (.011)
Education	3.40 (0.55)	3.27 (2.40)	4.13 (2.39)	4.81 (2.80)
(Education)^2	—	−.021 (.128)	−.0237 (.128)	−.042 (.148)
Manufacturing industry	—	—	−13.0 (4.3)	−14.7 (4.62)
Service industry	—	—	−9.45 (3.95)	−10.9 (4.24)
White	22.92 (4.53)	22.93 (4.50)	37.7 (9.6)	—
Family size > 2	—	—	.400 (3.57)	2.10 (3.89)

Table 3.3 • *(continued)*

Independent variable	Equation 1	Equation 2	Equation 3	Equation 4
Union	25.5 (3.25)	27.16 (3.23)	15.9 (5.4)	15.39 (5.72)
Full-time	−1.63 (12.9)	−.86 (12.6)	−1.16 (12.6)	.45 (15.0)
Hours worked	1.50 (.12)	1.41 (.12)	1.47 (.123)	1.44 (.129)
Occupation 1: operative	−18.7 (9.2)	—	−13.9 (3.24)	−13.5 (3.51)
Occupation 2: service worker	−24.6 (9.5)	—	−18.1 (4.66)	−19.9 (5.05)
Occupation 3: laborer	−25.0 (13.4)	—	—	—
SES 1	—	4.68 (5.17)	—	—
SES 2	—	−17.17 (3.34)	—	—
SES 3	—	−20.69 (5.53)	—	—
R^2	.41	.41	.42	.39
No. of obs.	907	907	907	813
Sample	All	All	All	White only

Note: The dependent variable is the weekly wage rate. The SES index has been converted to dummy variables. Standard errors are in parentheses.

The first two columns in Table 3.3 give alternative estimates of $W(p, c)$ on the strong assumption of no interactions. All the non-risk variables are assumed to simply shift the wage-risk relationship, leaving its slope intact. Regression coefficients of almost all characteristics variables have expected signs found in most other studies, and most are statistically significant. Further discussion is unwarranted here.

Table 3.4 • Regression estimates of $W(p, c)$: Semilog linear form

Independent variable	Equation 1	Equation 2	Equation 3	Equation 4
Risk	.000206 (.000167)	.000286 (.000174)	.000943 (.000856)	.000108 (.000782)
Age × risk	—	—	−.000022 (.000014)	−.000032 (.000015)
Married × risk	—	—	.000969 (.000301)	.000907 (.000316)
Union × risk	—	—	.000823 (.000315)	.000895 (.000320)
Race × risk	—	—	−.001312 (.000572)	—
Urban	.114 (.033)	.132 (.024)	.144 (.023)	.135 (.024)
Northeast	−.00357 (.00289)	−.00573 (.0291)	−.00904 (.0288)	−.0131 (.0292)
South	−.0632 (.0293)	−.0568 (.0298)	−.0729 (.0295)	−.0459 (.0304)
West	.0857 (.0327)	.0974 (.0332)	.0933 (.0327)	.0855 (.0334)
Age	.0381 (.0063)	.0385 (.0065)	.0390 (.0065)	.0380 (.0067)
$(Age)^2$	−.000469 (.000073)	−.000475 (.000077)	−.000450 (.000078)	−.000419 (.000081)
Manufacturing industry	—	—	−.0790 (.0340)	−.0888 (.0353)
Service industry	—	—	−.0758 (.0314)	−.0922 (.0324)
Education	.0332 (.00436)	.0531 (.0190)	.0623 (.0189)	.0613 (.0215)
$(Education)^2$	—	−.00129 (.00101)	−.00147 (.00102)	−.00133 (.00113)
White	.228 (.036)	.228 (.036)	.389 (.076)	—
Family size > 2	—	−.00204 (.0274)	−.0194 (.0283)	−.00220 (.0297)

Table 3.4 • *(continued)*

Independent variable	Equation 1	Equation 2	Equation 3	Equation 4
Union	.203 (.026)	.214 (.025)	.108 (.043)	.0997 (.0437)
Full-time	.275 (.103)	.303 (.101)	.284 (.100)	.340 (.115)
Hours worked	.0113 (.00096)	.0105 (.00095)	.0109 (.00098)	.0101 (.00099)
Occupation 1: operative	−.0885 (.0728)	—	−.105 (.026)	−.101 (.027)
Occupation 2: service worker	−.126 (.075)	—	−.110 (.037)	−.124 (.039)
Occupation 3: laborer	−.218 (.106)	—	—	—
SES 1	—	.0152 (.0411)	—	—
SES 2	—	−.128 (.026)	—	—
SES 3	—	−.194 (.042)	—	—
R^2	.47	.46	.48	.43
No. of obs.	907	907	907	813

Note: The dependent variable is the log of the weekly wage rate. The SES index has been converted to dummy variables. Standard errors are in parentheses.

The theory requires the wage-risk function to be positively inclined, and that is certainly the case on the appropriate one-tailed test of significance (see equations 1 and 2 in Table 3.3. [It is interesting to note that the simple correlation between risk and wage (not shown) is negative in these data.] (Risk)^2 was also entered in the regression but was not significant. We are not trying to argue here that $W(p, c)$ is linear in p, since most of the results using log W as dependent variable in Table 3.4 are at least as good as those in Table 3.3. The data simply do not provide enough resolution on functional form to make a choice. The implied *t*-statistic on risk is larger when SES is used in place of occupation (equation 2, Table 3.3), though the point estimates are not very different. First, consider the point estimate 0.0352 obtained from equation 1 of Table 3.3. The risk variable has been scaled by 10^5 for computational purposes and the estimate 0.0352 implies that jobs with extra risks of 0.001 (a value near the sample mean) pay $3.52 per week more than jobs with no risk. This amounts to about $176 per year, and the slope of the regression on a yearly basis is $176,000 ($= .0352 \times 50 \times 10^5$). Recall that the slope of the wage-risk relation $W'(p)$ estimates the implicit supply and demand price to risky jobs. To interpret the result, think in terms of the following conceptual experiment. Suppose 1,000 men are employed on a job entailing an extra death risk of .001 per year. Then, on average, one man out of the 1,000 will die during the year. The regression indicates that each man would be willing to work for $176 per less if the extra death probability were reduced from .001 to .0. Hence, they would together pay $176,000 to eliminate that death: the value of the life saved must be $176,000. Furthermore, it must also be true that those firms actually offering jobs involving .001 extra death probabilities must have to spend more than $176,000 to reduce the death probability to zero, because there is a clear-cut gain from risk reduction if costs were less than that amount.

Use of SES dummies instead of occupational dummies increases the point estimate of the risk variable to .0520, with virtually no change in its standard error. Going through the same argument as above implies a value of life of $260,000. Though the *t*-statistic is larger in equation 2 than in equation 1 of Table 3.3, we are not prepared to accept equation 2 as a necessarily better specification because of some reservations on the meaning of the SES variable. Corresponding estimates in Table 3.4 evaluated at the sample mean wage range somewhat smaller than those in Table 3.3. Equation 1 of Table 3.4 implies a point estimate of $136,000 ($= .000206 \times 132 \times 50 \times 10^5$), while equation 2 implies an estimate of $189,000 ($= .000286 \times 50 \times 132 \times 10^5$). Further, standard errors of risk coefficients are slightly larger in Table 3.4. Nevertheless, the estimates lie in a reasonably narrow range of about $2000,000 \pm $60,000.

Equation 3 in Tables 3.3 and Table 3.4 shows the results of limited interactions between risk and some of the other characteristics. Limitations on sample size forced a simple cross-product specification, rather than separate regressions on corresponding data cells. Risk is crossed with age, union membership, marital status and race in equation 3. As explained earlier, cross-product terms do not reflect differences in individual's utility functions. Instead they represent differences in the locus of opportunities available to them, due to differential ability to work in risky situations.

A. Age

To reiterate our example above, age is likely to cut two ways on risky jobs. Young workers lack caution and experience, but have superior reflexes and recuperative ability. Our hypothesis was that physical deterioration of skills would eventually dominate and the results seem to be consistent with it. The age-risk cross-product term is negative though not significant and firms offer older workers smaller risk premiums than younger workers. Evidently younger workers are more productive in risky situations. However, the estimate may also reflect measurement error.[17]

B. Marital Status

There is also some evidence that marital status affects risk premiums. Of course we expect married workers to have a higher supply price to risky jobs than unmarried workers, because they have more dependents. Again, this should induce married workers to apply for less risky jobs, other things being equal, and not change the observed risk premium. The fact that marital status increases the risk premium must mean that when married workers do in fact take risky jobs they are more productive at working on them. Exactly how such differential productivity arises is difficult to say, though we conjecture that married

---

17. There is a possibility that the negative regression coefficient reflects measurement error. Older workers may be heavily weighted in the low-risk end of each occupation and our risk measures may overstate the real risks they face. If $W(p)$ is truly increasing, earnings are lower for older workers appearing to work on riskier jobs in our data than they really do. We know age-specific extra-risk data must be available on the work sheets of the actuarial study, because the published statistics have been age adjusted in the manner described above. Unfortunately we were unable to obtain the raw data.

workers might on the average be more careful and cautious than the nonmarried.

C. Unionism

Unionism also increases the risk premium. Here the market is restricted, and unions might collect their rents through higher risk premiums rather than by other means. It is possible that lack of free entry into these markets renders the typical union member more risk averse than would be true in free markets, forcing firms to pay higher risk premiums in order to entice unwilling union members to work on the riskier jobs. Again, we cannot rule out the hypothesis that unionism and its resulting "industrial discipline" make workers more productive on risky jobs.

D. Race

The relationship between race and risk premiums is very complex. The white-risk cross-product term is negative (and not significant at conventional levels), but the results are not easy to interpret. For one thing, we know from other studies that nonwhites tend to be loaded in the low-wage end of occupational job classifications. Notice again that the occupations in Table 3.1 may be too broadly defined for detecting racial differences. If nonwhites tend to be highly represented in the riskier subcategories of each classification, our risk index is measured erroneously for them. This in itself would tend to produce the result found in Tables 3.3 and 3.4 and cross-terms would reflect measurement error in the data. The coefficient suggests that nonwhites receive higher risk premiums than whites, but it may simply be the case that they work at even more risky jobs than our data say they do (again, assuming $W'(p) > 0$). Alternative hypotheses are also available. (1) Nonwhites may be better workers in risky situations than whites. For example, we know that a large fraction of structural ironworkers are nonwhite, and it is said that these individuals have an unusual sense of balance compared with most people in the population. (2) There may be less discrimination against nonwhites in risky jobs than in less risky ones.

To get around possible measurement errors, we reran the regression excluding nonwhites from the sample. The result is shown by equation 4 in Table 3.3, and previous conclusions regarding other variables are hardly affected.[18]

11. Conclusion

We have estimated marginal valuations of safety for a select group of individuals in 1967. All qualifications surrounding our estimates have been given in the text and there is no need to repeat them here.[19] Certainly this study indicates feasibility of the method, the usual caveats about data quality notwithstanding. Are the estimates reasonable? We are unaware of similar studies with which to compare our results. However an example suggested by Bailey (1968) may be informative in this regard, and also illustrates how the estimates can be used.

The National Safety Council estimates that highway deaths would be reduced by about 10,000 per year if all automobile users wore lap safety belts. Assuming that the estimate is correct, seat belts reduce the probability of dying in an automobile accident from about 25 per hundred thousand (25×10^{-5}) per year to about 20 per hundred thousand per year (20×10^{-5}). Using the risk coefficient in equation 1 of Table 3.3 we estimate that the *average person in our sample* would be willing to pay *at least* $8.80 per year (in 1967 dollars) for a seat belt for himself. The cost of seat belts includes not only the purchase price and installation costs, but also costs associated with use, including bother and time spent buckling and unbuckling, so that it is easily within the realm of possibility that decisions not to purchase seat belts prior to

---

18. Computation of the marginal risk premium under the cross-product specification must be made at specific values of the interactive variables (age, race, and so on) because $W'(p)$ is then a function of those variables. A little experimentation with equations 3 and 4 of Tables 3.3 and 3.4 shows that the imputations vary a great deal, depending on the point in the sample at which they are made. Indeed, some of these imputations are actually negative (e.g., older white nonunion, nonmarried individuals), which may indicate an undesirable restriction of the function form or measurement error and not necessarily a model defect. We have not imposed any nonnegative restrictions on the estimates. Further, the possibilities of measurement error extensively pointed out at several points in the text preclude too much massaging of the data. Hence we regard the cross-product results as suggestive only.

19. These issues are discussed in greater depth in chapter 1 of Thaler (1974).

the law were rational. We can make some more back-of-the-envelope calculations. How much would the time and bother costs (of individuals in our sample) have to be to justify not using seat belts even after they are mandatory? The sample mean hourly wage was about $3.50. Using that as an estimate of the value of time, time spent buckling and unbuckling would have to be about 2.5 hours per year to cost as much as $8.80. Assuming 500 trips per year, this amounts to about 18 seconds per trip in time-equivalent costs of using seat belts, a much smaller number than Bailey assumed. We leave it to the reader to experiment with other possibilities.

References

Bailey, M. J. "Comment on T. C. Schelling's Paper." In S. B. Chase, ed., *Problems in Public Expenditure*. Washington, D.C.: Brookings Institution, 1968.

Calabresi, G. *The Costs of Accidents: A Legal and Economic Analysis*. New Haven: Yale University Press, 1970.

Fromm, G. "Civil Aviation Expenditures." In R. Dorfman, ed., *Measuring Benefits of Government Investments*. Washington, D.C.: Brookings Institution, 1965.

Hirshleifer, J. "Investment Decision under Uncertainty: Choice Theoretic Approaches." *Quarterly Journal of Economics* 79 (November 1965): 509–536.

Mishan, E. "Evaluation of Life and Limb: A Theoretical Approach." *Journal of Political Economy* 79 (July/August 1970): 687–705.

Oi, W. "An Essay on Workmen's Compensation and Industrial Safety." In *Supplemental Studies for the National Commission on State Workmen's Compensation Laws*, vol. 1, pp. 41–106, 1973.

Rosen, S. "Hedonic Prices and Implicit Markets: Product differentiation in Pure Competition." *Journal of Political Economy* 82 (January/February 1974): 34–55.

Schelling, T. C. "The Life You Save May Be Your Own." In S. B. Chase, ed., *Problems in Public Expenditure*. Washington, D.C.: Brookings Institution, 1968.

Smith, R. S. "Compensating Wage Differentials and Hazardous Work." Technical Analysis Paper no. 5, Office of Evaluation, Department of Labor, August, 1973.

Thaler, R. "The Value of Saving a Life: A Market Estimate." Ph.D. Dissertation, University of Rochester, 1974.

Usher, D. "An Imputation to the Measure of Economic Growth for Changes in Life Expectancy." In Milton Moss, ed., *The Measurement of Economic and Social Performance*, New York: NBER, 1973.

4

Learning and Experience
in the Labor Market

I. Introduction

The importance of formal education for economic growth and development and individual well-being is well established (e.g., see [6]). Yet
much evidence suggests that a large fraction of directly marketable skills
possessed by individuals are not acquired from formal schooling, but
rather from work experience [11]. Clearly, "education" is not produced
only in schools and learning does not cease after graduation. Instead,
it is economical to transfer its location to the market; for after some
point learning and work are complementary, and knowledge is more
efficiently acquired in conjunction with work experience rather than
in school. It is self-evident that work-connected learning is extremely
widespread and characterizes almost all labor market activities and at
every level of formal education. This paper attempts to model the role
of the labor market in the transmission and acquisition of marketable
skills and knowledge.

The main feature of the model lies in a theoretical construction of an
implicit market for learning opportunities, the major outlines of which
are set forth in Section II. The analytical consequences of this specification are spelled out in Section III, where both demand and supply
of learning opportunities are considered, as well as the nature of market equilibrium. Some details of the analysis are elaborated in Section
IV and the implications of the model for the problem of occupational
discrimination against minority groups are presented in Section V. Con-

I have benefited from discussions with James W. Friedman at an early stage of this
research, and from comments by Glen Cain on an initial draft. Financial assistance from
the Carnegie Commission on Higher Education and the Office of Economic Opportunity
to the National Bureau of Economic Research is gratefully acknowledged.

From *Journal of Human Resources* 7, no. 3 (1972): 326–342. © 1972. Reprinted
from the *Journal of Human Resources* by permission of the University of Wisconsin
Press.

clusions are contained in Section VI. To focus attention on essential features and to stress fundamental economic issues, only the simplest possible cases are discussed. I hope to show that the analytical structure presented here provides a conceptual framework for an economic theory of occupational mobility and also for the determination of age-earnings profiles of workers. Moreover, the model suggests an explicit mechanism by which income and occupational patterns evolve over the course of working life.

II. Nature of the Market

In this work, embodies knowledge or skill is treated at a kind of capital that has market rental value. Hence, learning represents the rate of change of knowledge or capital and is therefore an investment.[1] The fundamental hypothesis is that *individuals learn from their working experience*. Firms supply learning opportunities in the form of different types of work-learning activities, and to that extent engage in a kind of joint-production, for learning is a by-product of market goods production. But provision of learning options is not costless, since productive resources must be diverted away from current production and toward (largely informal) "teaching" and learning. Hence, firms will not provide such opportunities unless they are reimbursed. This is accomplished by, in effect, selling jobs to workers. Workers demand learning opportunities and are willing to pay for them since their marketable skill or knowledge and subsequent income are increased.

   Learning characteristics of work activities are central to the analysis, and the problem can be viewed in terms of supply and demand for jobs: Markets for learning opportunities have operational content through their connection with the job market, since work and learning are complementary. Now, the market for jobs is the dual of the market for labor services, and the two are related by a set of wage differentials

---

1. Following Becker's [2] distinction, knowledge can either be specific to the firm or have general market value. In this paper, all knowledge is assumed to have general market value. As will be seen, the model is an extension and generalization of the analysis of Becker [2][4] and Ben-Porath [5]. Firm-specific knowledge has rather different implications and has been treated elsewhere [12][13].

making jobs display equal net advantage at the margin. Labor market contracts are tied-sales, determining both exchange of labor services and the nature of work, where the latter includes opportunities for investment or learning. Competitive markets establish premiums on jobs offering greater human investment value, depending on the costs to firms of providing them and the distributions of worker ability, motivation, and other characteristics.

The nature of the market is such that workers have their choice among all-or-nothing bargains or "package deals," in which they simultaneously sell the services of their skills and "purchase" a job offering a fixed opportunity to learn. By the same token, firms purchase services of skills and at the same time "sell" jobs offering learning possibilities. The labor market provides a broad range of choice in these matters, for different kinds of work activities offer a wide variety of learning opportunities. Thus it is possible to analyze optimum accumulation of knowledge over working life by applying the theories of capital accumulation (e.g., see [7]) and of equalizing wage differences [8].

Before examining rational choices in such a market in detail, one possible mechanical difficulty must be clarified. The difference between the market rental of a worker's existing skill and his actual wage is the shadow or implicit *price* he pays for learning. It is also gross revenue to the firm providing a learning opportunity to him. Prices for jobs could be either explicit or implicit, but the distinction is of no analytical importance. In the former case, workers would be paid in proportion to the services of their skill (if any) and remit a sum back to the employer in exchange for learning. In the latter case, which tends to characterize actual transactions, investment costs are simply subtracted from gross pay and no explicit price need be quoted. The price is revealed in the form of wage differences between jobs. In either case, both net revenues of firms and opportunity costs to workers are the same, and there is no need to distinguish between the two in the analysis.[2]

---

2. Explicit payments were common in nineteenth-century apprenticeship. If services of skills sold by workers is less than the cost of a learning opportunity, net income is negative and implicit payments are not possible. It may be surmised that growth of formal schooling raised the value of skills at the time of entry into the labor force, making implicit prices practical. Aside from the fact of transactions cost avoidance, implicit payments dominate the current market, probably due to income tax advantages.

III. The Model

This section specifies an elementary model of the market for learning opportunities. Demand and supply are considered in turn.

Demand for Investment Opportunities

Let h index capital or skill possessed by an individual, the services of which can be sold on a competitive market at (implicit) rental price R. Suppose workers enter the labor force at "age" 0 and have a fixed length of working life N. Hence, "age" is shorthand for length of working experience. Finally, assume workers can borrow or lend on a perfect capital market at interest rate r. These assumptions serve to illustrate some basic points, without altering the substance of the argument, and will be partially relaxed later on.

To begin: Suppose there exist two kinds of jobs or work activities. Job 1 gives a worker the opportunity to acquire knowledge at rate k_1, and job 0 entitles him to acquire nothing. That is, k_1 indexes the maximum learning potential of job 1 per "period." Let P_1 denote market price (explicit or implicit) or total expenditure incurred by a worker if job 1 is chosen. Then earnings y_j of worker j on job 1 is given by $y_j = Rh_j - P_1$, where Rh_j is total value of services the worker sells to his employer, and P_1 is the purchase flow price of the job (which is a market price and the same for all workers). If a job of type 0 is chosen, income is Rh_j, since nothing is purchased in that activity. Which job should the worker choose? To answer the question, note that the value of an additional unit of skill is the discounted future marginal value of embodied knowledge, or the stock demand price of skill, and let n denote age. Then,[3]

$$q(n) = \int_0^{N-n} Re^{-rt}\, dt = (R/r)[1 - e^{-r(N-n)}]. \tag{1}$$

The term $q(n)$ is a declining function of age, n, since there is less time available to capitalize future returns as retirement approaches. Suppose

---

3. More generally, $q(n) = \int_0^{N-n} R(t) \exp[-\int_0^t r(\tau)d_\tau]\, dt$, where $R(t)$ and $r(t)$ are rental prices and interest rates at time t in the future. The special case (1) is chosen for expository convenience and to obtain explicit results, but the major features of the model hold for the more general form.

worker j actually obtains k_{1j} units of knowledge per period from job 1 (with $k_{1j} \leq k_1$). Then the unit cost to him of learning k_{1j} units is (P_1/k_{1j}). It is worthwhile to apply for the job so long as unit return, q, exceeds unit cost, P_1/k_{1j}. Hence, job 1 will be chosen if $k_{1j}q > P_1$, and the worker will receive a surplus, or economic rent. If the inequality is reversed, job 0 is preferred, for then investment costs exceed returns. Only by choosing in this manner is lifetime income or human wealth maximized. Assume for the moment that learning capacity on the job, k_{1j}, is constant over a worker's lifetime. Then it is possible for the inequality $k_{1j}q > P_1$ to be reversed at some point in the worker's lifetime, for q is large at younger ages and decreases to zero as n approaches N. Define a critical age, n_{ij}^*, as the value for which $k_{1j}q(n_1^*) = P_1$ for worker j. Then, using (1)

$$n_{1j}^* = N + (1/r) \ln \left[1 - (P_1/k_{1j})(r/R) \right]. \tag{2}$$

n_{1j}^* is in fact the "investment period" in this case. If $n_j < n_{1j}^*$, investment cost is less than return, while if $n_j > n_{1j}^*$, cost exceeds return. Hence, it is optimal to work at job 1 up to the critical age n_{1j}^* and then to *switch* to job 0 from that age onward. The worker's capital or skill grows at rate k_{1j} while on job 1 and income grows at rate Rk_{1j} during that period. At the switch point, n_{1j}^*, skill and income reach a steady plateau for the remainder of working life. Thus, even this extraordinarily simple model is consistent with the major distinguishing characteristic of observed age-income profiles, that earnings rise at a rapid rate during the early years of working life and then level off [9].[4]

Market demand for job 1 is found by varying the price P_1 and calculating the number of workers applying for it. To illustrate, suppose all workers are alike in all respects other than age and have identical capacity for learning ($k_{1j} = k_1$ for all j). Then the distribution function of q in the market (across workers) is uniquely determined by the age distribution of workers in the market, $f(n)\,dn$. The distribution of demand price, $g(q)\,dq$, is a transformation of the age distribution $f(n)$, given the functional relation between q and n in (1). Demand is found

---

4. The periodic payment P_1 ceases at age n_{1j}^* imparting discontinuity to the age-earnings profile at that point. Note that depreciation and obsolescence of skills have been ignored. Their inclusion yields no analytical difficulties, but would imply that earnings actually fall at later ages. See [14] for an attempt to estimate depreciation-obsolescence on human capital.

by identifying those for whom demand price, q, exceeds "supply price," P_1/k_1. For example, suppose workers are exponentially distributed by age, $f(n) = Ae^{\beta^n}$, where A is a normalizing constant. Then,[5]

$$g(q)\,dq = f\,[n(q)]\,|\partial n/\partial q|\,dq$$
$$= \beta e^{\beta N}(1 - e^{\beta N})\,[1 - (r/R)q]^{-(1+\beta/r)} \quad 0 \le q \le \bar{q},$$

where $\bar{q}$ is the maximum value of q, $(R/r)[1 - e^{rN}]$. The fraction of workers applying for type 1 jobs is denoted by Θ_1, and

$$\Theta_1 = \int_{P_1/k_1}^{\bar{q}} g(q)\,dq = (A/\beta)e^{-\beta N}\{e^{\beta N} - [1 - (r/R)(P_1/k_1)]^{-\beta/r}\}$$

$(1 - \Theta_1)$ is the fraction applying for job 0. Multiplying Θ_1 by the total number of workers in the labor market expresses demand in terms of numbers rather than as a fraction. Straightforward differentiation reveals that $\partial\Theta_1/\partial P_1 < 0$: demand is downward sloping, as usual. As P_1 falls, all who previously applied for the job still find it advantageous to do so, while those whose demand prices for human capital were lower are now attracted to it. Furthermore, $\partial\Theta_1/\partial r < 0$ and $\partial\Theta_1/\partial N > 0$. Decreases in r and increases in R or N all raise the marginal value of embodied knowledge at any age, rendering investment more profitable, increasing the investment period, and increasing the demand for job 1. Of course the elasticity of demand depends on the distribution of q. In general, whatever the age distribution, demand is more elastic throughout most of its range the smaller the variance of $g(q)$, for in such cases any given change in P_1 is likely to have a greater impact on individuals at the margin of indifference between jobs 1 and 0 than if $g(q)$ is more diffused.

This elementary model shows that the nature of tie-in contracts relating work and investment is such that individuals specialize their efforts in particular work activities at different points in their lives. To generalize somewhat, consider a case where there are three work activities. Job 2 gives it holder a chance to learn at most k_2 units of

---

5. Rearrange (1) to express n as a function of q: $n = N + (1/r)[\ln(1 - (r/R)q)]$. Then $\left|\dfrac{\partial n}{\partial q}\right| = \dfrac{1}{R}\left[\dfrac{1}{1 - (r/R)q}\right]$. The absolute value is necessary to reflect the change in order of integration, in that q attains its minimum when n is at its maximum, and conversely. Assuming k_{1j} identical across workers simplifies matters. If k_{1j} has some variance, it is necessary to deal with the joint distribution of k_{1j} and n (see below).

knowledge ($k_2 > k_1$), while jobs 1 and 0 are defined as above. Assume $k_{2j} > k_{1j}$ for worker j, and, again, that learning capacity is constant over working life. If worker j chooses among the three alternatives in such a way as to maximize lifetime income or wealth, he chooses the job that maximizes annual rent or the value of his knowledge. If the worker is n years of age, this rent is $[P_2 - k_{2j}q(n)]$ if job 2 is chosen, where P_2 is the market price of the job. If job 1 is chosen rent is $[P_1 - k_{1j}q(n)]$. He is indifferent between jobs if rents are equal. Let s_j represent a critical value of demand price (q) at which equality of rent between jobs 1 and 2 occurs for worker j. Then,

$$s_j = (P_2 - P_1)/(k_{2j} - k_{1j}),$$

which has a ready interpretation as the marginal cost of purchasing ($k_{2j} - k_{1j}$) more units of skill on job 2 compared with k_{1j} units on job 1. Now, if $q(n) > s_j$, the marginal value of k_{2j} units of knowledge exceeds its marginal cost and job 2 is chosen, for rents are highest there. A transfer point occurs at age n_{2j}^*, defined implicitly by $q(n_{2j}^*) = s_j$, at which the worker switches to either job 1 or 0. At that point, P_1/k_{1j} is the marginal cost of accumulating knowledge at rate k_{1j} at activity 1 compared with nothing at activity 0. If $P_1/k_{1j} \geq s_j$, it is clearly not worthwhile to invest in job 1, for job 2 gas greater learning content and dominates job 1 at every point in time. In such a case, the worker switches to job 0 at age n_{2j}^*. On the other hand, if $P_1/k_{1j} < s_j$, he switches to job 1 at age n_{2j}^* and remains there up to a second critical age n_{1j}^* at which rent is zero, transferring to job 0 as before. For a worker progressing through the entire job sequence, skill grows at rate k_{2j} between ages 0 and n_{2j}^* and at rate k_{1j} between ages n_{2j}^* and n_{1j}^*. Income rises at rate Rk_{2j} and Rk_{1j} in these intervals, respectively, reaching a plateau after n_{1j}^*. Therefore, income grows at a decreasing rate with work experience and age-earnings profiles are rendered more concave compared with the previous two-job case.[6] Note that this is true even though no aging or depreciation phenomena have entered into the model.

6. Assuming all individuals are alike so that $s_j = s$ and $k_{1j} = k_j$, the fraction of workers applying for job 2 is $\Theta_2 = \int_2^{\bar{q}} g(q)\, dq$ if $s < \bar{q}$ and $\Theta_2 = 0.0$ if $s \geq \bar{q}$, where $\bar{q}$ is the highest value of q in the market (at $n = 0$). The fraction applying for job 1 is $\Theta_1 = \int_{P_1/k_1}^s g(q)\, dq$ if $P_1/K_1 < s$ and $\Theta_1 = 0.0$ if $P_1/k_1 \geq s$.

The condition $P_1/k_{1j} < s_j$ if job 1 is ever to be chosen amounts to a requirement that marginal cost of learning or investment to a worker be increasing. This must be so, for demand price q at any age is independent of knowledge previously accumulated. Hence investment demand at any age is infinitely elastic, and decreasing marginal cost would always imply dominance of the investment opportunity offering the highest real investment. That distinct unit prices for the same good (i.e., learning) can exist in the market is a result of all-or-nothing bargains and specialization in the labor market. Tie-in contracts imply that different learning possibilities are in a sense different "commodities." Workers must devote all their efforts to one work activity or another and arbitrage is not possible, since knowledge is embodied in human agents of production and not freely transferable to others.

It is now possible to sketch a more general model. The labor market provides a great variety of work-learning activities. Imagine that there are indefinitely many possibilities arranged along a continuum with respect to learning potential, again indexed by k, ranging from $k = 0$ to some upper limit $\bar{k}$. Market equilibrium establishes a most likely implicit or shadow *price function $P(k)$* in the form of equalizing wage differences between work activities exhibiting different learning possibilities, and relating learning content to its cost. Let the actual amount of learning by worker j be an increasing function of learning potential, k. For example, suppose $kh_j/dt = k_j = (1/\gamma_j)k$ where γ_j is a constant for worker j. Then earnings of a person n years of age and possessing $h_j(n)$ units of skill is given by

$$y_j(n) = Rh_k(n) - P(\gamma_j k_j) \tag{3}$$

or gross earnings, Rh_j, minus opportunity costs $P(\gamma_j k_j)$ [equals $P(k)$] of purchasing option k. Equation (3) is an income generating function that defines a tradeoff or transformation schedule between current income y_j and investment k_j. If a large value of investment is chosen, much current income is foregone, but future tradeoffs are shifted outward to a greater extent. Clearly, $P'(k) > 0$: marginal cost of learning is positive. On the assumption that $P''(k) > 0$ (increasing marginal cost), the tradeoff or transformation function is concave. The worker chooses a sequence of jobs—or an optimum function $k(n)$ over his lifetime to maximize human wealth. It is the function $k(n)$ that is associated with "occupational" mobility over working life. The problem is to maximize

$$W_j \int_0^N \left[Rh_j(t) - P(\gamma_j k_j(t)) \right] e^{-rt} \, dt$$

subject to an initial stock of knowledge $h_j(0)$ obtained from formal schooling and other sources. Optimization requires choice of a sequence of work activities, or a function $k(n)$, such that at any age n

$$\gamma_j P'(k) = R/r \left[1 - e^{-r(N-n)} \right], \, 0 \le n \le N \tag{4}$$

The term on the left of equation (4) is marginal (stock) cost of investment, and the term on the right is discounted marginal return.[7] Hence, optimality requires P' to be large at the time of entry into the labor force and to decrease over time. Therefore, high values of k—large learning opportunities—are chosen at first and diminish with age. Earnings rise at a decreasing rate with age, consistent with observed data. Moreover, an important implication of the analysis is that workers progress through a "hierarchy" of jobs with lesser learning content over time and as their skill accumulates.[8] For example, M.D.s go through long periods of internship and residencies before entering full-time practice. Young lawyers write briefs for established law firms in order to learn

---

7. On the present assumption that $dh/dt = \gamma k$, condition (4) is derived by applying the Euler condition to the definition of W_j and integrating. (4) assumes that the individual accumulates over his entire lifetime, which will be the case if $\lim_{k \to 0} P'(k) = 0$. If $\lim_{k \to 0} P'(k) > 0$, there will be an age $N^* < N$ after which marginal cost of learning exceeds marginal return, and no accumulation will occur from N^* onward. In such a case, N^* replaces N in (4). If obsolescence-depreciation occurs at rate δ, the rate of interest (r) in equation (4) is replaced by ($r + \delta$).

8. Assuming learning capacity to be constant over working life greatly simplifies exposition, since the maximization problem can be solved as a sequence of independent "one-period" problems. More generally, it is to be expected that the capacity to learn depends not only on the learning option chosen, but also on prior knowledge. That is, write $dh/dt = \psi(k, h)$. Now learning not only has value due to future rentals but also because it enhances future learning capacity. The problem is no longer time independent, because present choices affect constraints available for future choices. A solution for the general case (including obsolescence and depreciation) is found in [14]. For present purposes, it is sufficient to point out that the general nature of the solution is similar to the simpler case considered here: accumulation is more rapid at younger ages, and workers choose jobs with lesser learning opportunities with age. Cases where learning capacity diminishes with age [e.g., let $\gamma = \gamma(n)$ with $\gamma' > 0$] are easily handled, since the time-independence feature is preserved, and they do not alter the essential characteristics of the solution, as the reader can easily verify.

their "trade." New Ph.D.s begin their careers as postdoctoral fellows and instructors and gradually rise to higher ranks. Skilled craftsmen learn their crafts by first observing others as apprentices and helpers. Evidently such processes are characteristic of practically all working activities.

Supply of Investment Opportunities

As noted above, supply of investment opportunities derives from the fact that provision of opportunities to learn is not free. Costly inputs must be allocated away from current physical production and toward teaching and learning, resulting in foregone market output. Supplying learning-type jobs requires allocating the time of skilled workers toward (informal) instruction rather than toward marketable output, wasted output of "students" due to mistakes necessarily incurred in the learning process, additional wear and tear on physical capital and machinery, etc. Thus the problem is one of joint-production or, more generally, multiproducts. As usual, supply price depends on rates of transformation between learning opportunities and physical product.

Again beginning with the simplest case, reconsider the two-job example. Let s denote physical product and let the firm have two production alternatives. (a) All workers can be hired at type 0 jobs and only produce x according to a production function (with the usual properties)

$$x = G(H, Z), \tag{5}$$

where H is total skill employed and Z is other inputs. (b) The firm can supply jobs of type 0 and 1 to product both x *and* investment opportunities. Index the latter by k_1. In this case the production function might be

$$x = \alpha G(H, Z) \quad m_1 = vx, \tag{6}$$

where m_1 is the number of type 1 jobs offered and α and v are fixed parameters. For every unit of x produced under this arrangement, workers in type 1 jobs receive the chance to acquire k_1 units of skill per period. Evidently, $\alpha < 1$, or otherwise alternative (b) dominates (a), for more of both x and type 1 jobs could be produced with the same total resources. If $\alpha < 1$, more x is produced under (5) with given inputs than under (6), but alternative (6) also produces learning opportunities. The marginal rate of transformation between x and m_1, T, implicit in the two alternatives is given by $T = (1 - \alpha)/\alpha v$. For every unit of x produced with (5), only α units are produced with (6). Hence, $(1 - \alpha)$ units of x are given up if technique (6) is chosen. However, (6) also yields αv "units" of m_1, or αv opportunities to learn k_1 units of skill. Now revenue is maximized by choosing (5) or (6) according as $[(P_1/k_1)/P_x] \gtrless T$, where P_x is the market price of x and P_1 is the market price of the learning opportunity. Hence, T is the minimum supply price of type 1 jobs. If alternative (5) turns out to be optimal, profit maximization requires marginal value products of H and Z ($P_x G_H$ and $P_x G_z$) to be set equal to unit prices R and P_z, respectively. However, if (6) is optimal, marginal conditions are $(P_x + P_1)\alpha G_H = R$ and $(P_x + P_1)\alpha G_z = P_z$, since marginal revenue now equals P_x plus the value of the investment opportunity provided with each unit of x, P_1. Marginal value products with respect to x alone ($P_x \alpha G_H$ and $P_z \alpha G_z$) exceed marginal factor cost [2] [15] in order to cover expenses due to provision of learning opportunities, in this pure joint-product specification.

The market supply function for type 1 jobs depends on the joint distribution of T and firm size in the labor market, on a par with demand. If all firms are alike and have identical values of T, supply is elastic and market price is $P_1 = T$. More generally, some variance in T across firms is to be expected. Some firms in an industry may be more efficient at producing learning opportunities and have lower values of T. Interindustry differences in productive efficiency as well as product price differences are also to be expected. All these factors produce variance in supply prices across firms, rendering market supply upward sloping with respect to price, as usual: When P_1 rises, all firms who found it advantageous to offer type 1 jobs at lower prices still do so, while additional firms are induced to enter the market.

Toward generalization, suppose a firm can produce x along with v different types of work activities or jobs, arranged in ascending order with respect to learning potential. Job 0 offers no learning opportunity, job 1 offers k_1 units, job 2 offers k_2 units, and so on. $k_{v-1} > \ldots > k_2 > k_1$. Let m_1 denote the number of workers employed in job type i and specify a total (minimum) cost function for the multiple products $(s, k_1, \ldots, k_v)$

$$C = C(x, m_1, \ldots, m_v), \tag{7}$$

with marginal costs $\partial C/\partial x$ and $\partial C/\partial m_j$ positive and increasing. The marginal rate of transformation, T_i, between x and m_i is given by $(\partial C/\partial m_i)/(\partial C/\partial x)$. To establish properties of (7), appeal to the law of diminishing return. Consider T_i evaluated at a point where $m_1 = m_2 = \ldots = m_v$. Then it must surely be the case that at that point $T_1 < T_2 < \ldots < T_v$. That is marginal cost of providing learning opportunities in terms of x foregone rises with k_i, the magnitude of the opportunity. To produce a given increase in learning undoubtedly requires increasingly greater resources devoted to teaching and learning as learning potential rises. The "teacher/student" ratio rises with k_i, implying ever-increasing physical output foregone and rising supply price (at any given level of jobs provided) with respect to k_j. As more time of skilled workers is devoted toward instruction and supervision of students, work interruptions, less possible specialization of work effort, and generally diminishing returns suggest that output foregone will rise at an increasing rate. Hence, it is likely that the market supply price of jobs rises with learning potential. Therefore, the nature of the production process itself gives rise to a market price function $P(k)$ that displays increasing marginal cost, as required for the worker's decision problem.

The firm chooses to offer particular work activities by comparing T_i with relative market prices $(P_1/k_1)/P_x$. It is, of course, not necessary that the firm find it advantageous to provide *all* jobs. For the ones it does provide, the condition for optimality (assuming interior solutions) is $T_i = (P_1/k_1)/P_x$, for only then is total revenue from all outputs maximized. A condition for a positive number of jobs of type i to be provided is that $T_i(m_i = 0)$, or the marginal rate of transformation between x and job i evaluated at zero jobs of type i, be less than $(P_i/k_i)/P_x$. If this condition is not met, marginal cost of job i (relative to marginal cost of x) exceeds relative marginal revenue at all possible values of m_i and it is not rational to provide jobs of type i.

In any event, the interaction of worker demand for skills and the supply of learning opportunities by firms implies a very interesting dynamic process within firms, in which workers move from one type of work activity to another over their working lives. For example, if a firm provides the entire range of jobs, workers will be hired into jobs offering high values of k or investment potential and go through a series of "promotions" to successively lower values of k as their skill and knowledge accumulates. Some workers will progress through the entire sequence within the firm. If more workers are hired at entry-type jobs than there are spaces for further up the hierarchy, some workers will not be promoted and will seek jobs offering their desired level of k elsewhere. If the firm finds it advantageous not to provide certain work-learning activities at current market prices, workers employed by the firm who are desirous of such positions will leave and seek them elsewhere. Workers who reach their desired maximum level of skill (in light of investment opportunities and costs) may stay with the firm, working at type 0 jobs, or go to other firms and work at them, depending on their availability. A wide variety of intra- and interfirm transfers are possible.[9] These phenomena are so characteristic of observed labor market behavior that further comment is unnecessary.

IV. Further Analysis

Some additional properties of the model can be obtained by examining the consequences of differences in learning capacity among individuals and of capital market imperfections. Both affect job choice and income patterns in predictable ways.

Differences in learning capacity imply differences in k_{ij} among workers. If k_{ij} is large, worker j obtains more units of skill from job i than if k_{ij} is small. There is no reason to expect individuals at any given level of schooling to possess equal capacity for learning, for some workers are more "able" than others. Furthermore, differences in k_{ij} may be systematically associated with differences in formal schooling. School not only gives students higher skill at the time of entry into the labor force $[h_j(0)]$, but may also increase their ability to learn. Indeed, most major courses of study in the liberal arts do not apparently produce any directly marketable skills at the undergraduate level. Instead, students acquire patterns of thought and behavior that make learning specific

---

9. Considerable simplicity has been achieved by considering only one, homogeneous type of skill in the analysis. A promising future development might be to include "skill requirements" in work-learning activity combinations. In effect, the amount learned from a particular activity would depend on the *path* by which the worker arrived there. A related idea in the case of formal school has been discussed by Weisbrod [19]. Though such modifications would add more "realism" (and a great deal of complexity) to the analysis, it is clear that major features remain intact. It is worth stressing that the sequential and "hierarchical" nature of the evolution of skills and jobs over working life has been derived in the present model without imposing any sequential restrictions on the problem whatsoever!

tasks easier and allow them to be more "flexible" in adapting to new situations (see [14]). That is, workers with higher levels of schooling may be more efficient learners.[10]

Variations in learning capacity produce corresponding and opposite variations in real costs of learning and thereby alter incentives to accumulate knowledge and skill. For example, reconsider the case where $k_{ij} = (1/\gamma_j)k_i$, so that the actual learning per period is proportionality differs among workers. Then the marginal cost to worker j of learning $(1/\gamma_i)(k_i - k_{i-1})$ more units of actual knowledge or skill on job i compared with job $i - 1$ is

$$s_{ij} = \gamma_j(P_i - P_{i-1})/(k_i - k_{i-1})$$

Since market prices and maximum learning potential are the same for everyone, marginal cost of a given real investment decreases with $(1/\gamma)$. Hence, at given demand prices individuals with greater learning capacity (smaller γ) choose jobs with greater learning potential, for the additional cost of doing so is more than offset by the greater value of knowledge obtained. Economic incentives induce more "able" workers to learn more and to accumulate knowledge more rapidly than the less "able." Earnings rise more rapidly with work experience and lifetime wealth is correspondingly greater. Earnings across individuals tend to "fan out" with work experience, consistent with observed age-earnings profiles [9] [11].

The analysis is similar if there are interest rate differences among workers, except that demand price, q, is affected rather than real supply price. If some workers have cheaper access to financial markets than others, the discounted value of knowledge is higher for them. They have incentives to accumulate more and at more rapid rates than others. Workers forced to borrow at high rates of interest cannot afford to undertake work activities offering superior investment value. Moreover, they cannot invest as much on the ones that are open to them, for the pay-back period on investment must be increased sufficiently to make investment profitable at higher rates of interest. Consequently, their age-earnings profiles are flatter and peak earlier than others (cf. [4]).

---

10. Whether schooling only serves as a filter or certification device in this process, or whether it is a real producer of knowledge and ability to learn is immaterial for present purposes.

An extremely important implication of the analysis should be noted at this point. Anything producing differences among individuals in learning capacity or financial cost can result in cases where some workers do not participate at all in certain job markets. The market can very well establish equilibrium prices on the total opportunity package of some jobs that is high enough to literally price those with low values of $(1/\gamma)$ or higher interest rates out of the market. All workers for whom s_{ij} exceeds demand price at any age never find it advantageous to apply for job i. The optimum transfer point for such workers occurs at age zero, as it were. They are intramarginal with respect to job i all their lives, essentially forming a noncompeting group. Among other things, the model generates the possibility of "secondary labor markets" (e.g., see [10]) so often found in recent discussions of poverty and discrimination. To elaborate, note that if prices of jobs are implicit, a worker will not be hired at job i if the value of skills he has to sell, Rh, does not exceed purchase price, P_i. For example, the effect of a minimum wage is to put a ceiling on the range of learning opportunities to workers. Suppose a worker enters the market with skills having slightly greater value than the minimum wage. Then the most he can pay for learning is $Rh - MW$, where MW is the ("annual") minimum wage. Then he can only be hired at jobs selling at low implicit prices and having minimal learning content. His range of choice is severely constrained and guarantees a relatively flat lifetime income pattern. This argues for a lower minimum wage for younger workers than for more experienced workers.

V. Occupational Discrimination

It is well known that a significant fraction of total income differences between whites and nonwhites in the United States is due to the fact that a much larger portion of nonwhite workers are employed in lower-skilled occupations (e.g., see [18]). Why should discrimination take the form of occupational restrictions in addition to outright wage discrimination regardless of occupation? This observation is troublesome for economic analysis, and various ad hoc explanations have been put forth to explain it. For example, it is often asserted in the popular press and elsewhere that various occupations are by convention or tradition more or less closed to certain minority groups, and also that white employers conspire to reduce occupational mobility and maintain nonwhites at low levels of skill to increase their won (relative) income. Whatever the merits of these arguments, once it is recognized that occupations or jobs provide opportunities to learn and that these opportunities are available at some price, it is possible to analyze the problem in economic terms (see [1] [3] [17]). In fact, discrimination can take place on either side of work-learning bargains.

Wage Discrimination

For the sake of argument, divide the labor into two groups, A and B. Suppose employers on balance act as if the marginal product of skill embodied in A exceeds that of the same real skills embodied in B. Then, market rental prices R_a and R_b will differ, with $R_a > R_b$. The effect is to reduce capital demand prices of skill to members of group B at every age, dulling B's incentives to acquire it. At any age they choose work activities offering lesser possibilities for learning and capital accumulation and tend to work at them for shorter periods of time. Human wealth of B is thereby rendered even relatively smaller than any differences in market rental values. Age-income profiles of B are flatter and do not rise as rapidly at any age compared with those of A. In fact, there is evidence that relative white-nonwhite income differences rise with age at every level of formal schooling [16], as predicted by the model.

Discrimination in the Job Market

Firms may discriminate against some groups in the provision of learning opportunities. They may act as if demand prices for jobs by members of group A exceed those of group B. Reasons for discrimination of this sort are not difficult to enumerate. Movement or progression through a series of work activities with learning content typically places a worker in a position of greater supervisory control and responsibility over workers at lower levels. Managers or others with this type of responsibility may simply exhibit prejudice and resent sharing their prerogatives with members of a disfavored group. Also, managers may feel that real (or imagined) productivity of other workers is impaired if they are supervised by members of such groups, discrimination arising from workers further on down the hierarchy. Such processes tend to produce self-selection, in which firms are segregated and in which managers are indifferent about such matters. The extent of discrimination then depends on how many possibilities for integration exist, and casual evidence suggests these are small.

The consequence of discrimination of this sort is to raise the supply price function $P(k)$ to members of groups to which discrimination applies. Again, economic forces impel them to choose jobs offering smaller opportunities to learn and to work at them for shorter periods of time, causing age-earnings profiles to be flatter. In view of the above, it is also likely that discrimination renders $P'(k)$ higher for these groups, thereby reinforcing incentives to make these choices. There is evidence that discrimination against nonwhites rises with level of formal schooling [16], consistent with the joint hypothesis that $P'(k)$ is higher for nonwhites than for whites and that formal schooling makes its recipients more efficient at learning in the labor market.[11]

A Policy Implication

An interesting policy conclusion emerging from the analysis is the potential efficacy of wage subsidy training programs in increasing the income and economic status of the nonwhite poor. Wage subsidies increase the cost to employers of job discrimination and should result in less discrimination being practiced in the provision of jobs with learning content. It also gets around restrictions and ceilings on job choice imposed by minimum wage legislation and other wage rigidities. At the same time, subsidies reduce supply prices of skills to nonwhites and induce greater accumulation of marketable skills and knowledge, raising age-earnings toward equality with comparable white workers.

VI. Conclusion

This paper has examined lifetime income and job choice based on the construct of a market for learning opportunities. Different work activities offer alternative opportunities to learn and accumulate valuable skills as a by-product of work experience. Provision of jobs offering

---

11. An alternative hypothesis is that the quality of schooling received by nonwhites (in the sense of $1/\gamma$, above) is on balance lower than that obtained by whites. This has the same effect on income patterns as outright discrimination in the market for learning.

greater learning opportunities by firms requires increasingly greater output foregone, or rising supply price. Market equilibrium establishes equality between supply and demand for learning options in the form of equalizing wage differences between work activities offering greater or lesser amounts. Given market prices, maximization of lifetime wealth is a problem of optimum capital accumulation and implies choice of an optimum sequence or progression of work activities over working life, that simultaneously determines both earnings and occupational patterns of workers over their lifetimes. It has been shown that the relation between earnings and work experience depends on the real costs of providing learning options and the distribution of workers ability and education, initial capital endowments access to capital markets, labor market restrictions and discrimination, and rental values on knowledge or skills.

For some problems, the model suggests that it may be fruitful to view labor market contracts as essentially involving implicit forward contracts for future income. Jobs with a "future" really carry with them an implied pattern of lifetime work activity and income. In this sense, the labor market can be viewed as a mechanism for "trading" in lifetime incomes and wealth.

References

1. Arrow, K. J. "Some Models of Racial Discrimination in Labor Markets." Rand Corporation, RM-6253-RC, 1971.

2. Becker, G. S. *Human Capital*. New York: Columbia University Press, 1964.

3. ───── *The Economics of Discrimination*. Chicago: University of Chicago Press, 1957.

4. ───── *Human Capital and the Personal Distribution of Income*, W. S. Woytinsky Lecture no. 1, University of Michigan, 1967.

5. Ben-Porath, Y. "The Production of Human Capital and the Life Cycle of Earnings." *Journal of Political Economy* (1967).

6. Bowman, M. J., Debeauvais, M., Komarov, V. E., and Vaizey, J., eds, *Readings in the Economics of Education*. New York: UNESCO, 1968.

7. Dorfman, R. "An Economic Interpretation of Optimal Control Theory." *American Economic Review* (1969).

8. Friedman, M., and Kuznets, S. *Income from Independent Professional Practice*. New York: National Bureau of Economic Research, 1945.

9. Hanoch, G. "An Economic Analysis of Earnings and Schooling." *Journal of Human Resources* (1967).

10. Piore, M. J. "On-the-Job Training in the Dual Labor Market." In *Public-Private Manpower Policies*, eds. A. R. Weber et al. Madison: Industrial Relations Research Association, 1969.

11. Mincer, J. "Schooling, Age, and Earnings." New York: National Bureau of Economic Research, 1971.

12. Rosen, S. "Learning by Experience as Joint Production." *Quarterly Journal of Economics* (1972).

13. ———— "Some Externalities in Program Evaluation." In *Proceedings of the Conference on the Evaluation of the Impact of Manpower Programs*, ed. M. Borus (forthcoming).

14. ———— "Knowledge, Obsolescence, and Income." In *Education, Income, and Human Behavior*, ed. T. Juster, NBER (forthcoming).

15. Thompson, E. A. "Nonpecuniary Rewards and the Aggregate Production Function." *Review of Economics and Statistics* (1970).

16. Thurow, L. C. *Poverty and Discrimination*. Washington: Brookings, 1969.

17. Welch, F. "Labor Market Discrimination." *Journal of Political Economy* (1967).

18. Wolstetter, A., and Coleman, S. "Racial Disparities in Income." Rand Corporation, R-578-OEO, 1971.

19. Weisbrod, B. A. "Education and Investment in Human Capital." *Journal of Political Economy* (1962).

PART II

The Division of Labor and Human Capital

5
Substitution and Division of Labour

Introduction

Recent advances in production theory and in computer technology now make it possible to estimate complex production relationships involving many inputs. Yet the theory remains somewhat cavalier about its primitives, particularly the definition of labour inputs. In what follows, the theory of optimum assignment and comparative advantage is used to analyse the structure of work activities within firms. A job is defined as a collection of production tasks assigned to the worker who holds it, but the packaging of work activities into bundles is itself the endogenous outcome of economic decisions.

How do the requirements of technology and the distribution of worker skills interact to determine which work activities are selected and bundled into observed job assignments and occupations? Furthermore, how are different members of the labour force allocated to them and what are the characteristics of the match between job attributes and worker talents? Section I is addressed mainly to the first question and Section II mainly to the second. As will be seen, the division of labour corresponding to the optimum assignment determines marginal rates of substitution between certain workers or between certain work activities. The observable elasticities of substitution so implied are not necessarily inherent in the production technology, but rather are "swept out" of the distribution of skills as optimum work assignments respond to final demand and factor supply conditions. Thus the division of labour in part determines the nature and extent of product and factor substitutions in the economy.

I am especially indebted to Robert Lucas, Daniel MacFadden, Michael Mussa, Kamran Noman, and Robert Willis for many helpful discussions and criticism, to a referee who commented on an earlier version, and to the National Science Foundation and the U.S. Social Security Administration for financial support. Any shortcomings are my own responsibility.

From *Economica* 45 (August 1978): 235–250.

I. Indirect Production Functions

A basic result on the optimum division of labour and derived factor substitution is most easily obtained in the context of a simple engineering production function with fixed coefficients. Capital is ignored without apology, in what follows. The technology is given by

$$x = \min \left(\frac{T_1}{\alpha_1}, \frac{T_2}{\alpha_2}, \ldots, \frac{T_n}{\alpha_n} \right) \tag{1}$$

where x is output, T_1 is a production activity (input), and α_i is the input requirement per unit output. For example (1) might be the engineering production function for the proverbial pin factory. Then (T_i) represents steps in the production process, such as drawing the wire, sharpening the points, and so forth. Each T_i is associated with an independent "task," and a collection of tasks, a partition of (T_i), constitutes a job.

Let there be m types of workers. Workers of type j are described by a skill or capacity vector $(t_{1j}, t_{2j}, \ldots, t_{nj})$, $j = 1, \ldots, m$. t_{ij} indicates the maximum amount of task i obtainable from a worker of type j when the task is pursued full time. Assume that output in each activity is proportional to the time devoted to it, with no interactions if the worker's time is divided among several activities. Then a worker is completely described by the value of (t_j). Comparing workers i and j, worker i will be said to have a comparative advantage in task h relative to task k if $t_{hi}/t_{ki} > t_{hj}/t_{kj}$. Equivalently, worker j has a comparative advantage in task k. Comparative advantage is assumed to exist in all tasks and among all types; that is,

$$t_{hi}/t_{ki} \neq t_{hj}/t_{kj} \tag{2}$$

for all pairs (h, k) and (i, j).

The problem is to find the assignment of workers to production activities that maximizes output. The solution consists of two steps. First, calculate all the possible assignments that maximize activity levels attainable from a given labour force. This defines a "task possibility set," as it were. Second, maximize output relative to the efficient set.

A familiar 2×2 example illustrates the method. In Figure 5.1 there are two activities, T_1 and T_2, and two workers, A and B. The straight lines with intercepts (t_{2A}, t_{1A}) and (T_{2B}, t_{1B}) depict the capacity vectors, and are drawn under the assumption that A has a comparative advan-

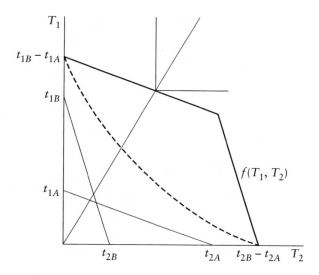

Figure 5.1

tage in T_2 and B in T_1. The efficient assignments or "task possibility frontier" is labelled $f(T_1, T_2)$ and has two facets: B is completely specialized to T_1 and A is engaged in both activities along the upper edge, due to B's comparative advantage in T_1; A and B are completely specialized at the corner; while A is specialized to T_2 and B's time is divided between both activities along the lower edge. All assignments other than $f(T_1, T_2)$ sacrifice activity levels. The case where A and B act as independent agents of production is of particular interest. Since the engineering technology dictates the use of activities in fixed proportions, the autarky total frontier is the sum of A's and B's independent allocations along arbitrary rays through the origin. It is shown by the curve and is inefficient because comparative advantage is not exploited. The gain from forming a production team and dividing up the work according to comparative advantage is measured by the distance between the efficient and autarky frontiers along a ray with slope α_2/α_1. The optimum assignment produces a kind of multiplicative effect or superadditivity. This interaction captures the fundamental notion of complementarity (in the sense of a positive cross partial derivative) in production, and leads to imperfect substitution between worker types A and B in the team.

More generally, consider the problem of allocating workers to tasks to maximize

$$x = \min\left(\sum_j T_{1j}/\alpha_1, \sum_j T_{2j}/\alpha_2, \ldots, \sum_j T_{nj}/\alpha_n\right) \tag{3}$$

subject to

$$T_{1j}/t_{1j} + T_{2j}/t_{2j} + \cdots + T_{nj}/t_{nj} \leq N_j, \quad j = 1, 2, \ldots, m \tag{4}$$

where N_j is the number of workers of type j available and (4) translates the capacity vectors into total activity constraints. By the envelope theorem there exist nonnegative multipliers $(q_1, \ldots, 1_m)$ and a quasi-concave function $x = F(N_1, N_2, \ldots, N_m)$ such that

$$x = F(N_1, \ldots, N_m) \equiv \max_{T_{ij}} \left\{ \min\left(\sum_j T_{1j}/\alpha_1, \ldots, \sum_j T_{nj}/\alpha_n\right) \right.$$
$$\left. + \sum_j q_j \left(N_j - \sum_j T_{ij}/t_{ij}\right) \right\}. \tag{5}$$

The function $F(N)$ is an efficient "indirect" production function of the neoclassical type. Its derivatives when defined satisfy $\partial x/\partial N_i = q_i$ and represent induced marginal products of worker types. It is quasi-concave so the isoquants are convex. The theorem holds for any n and m, not necessarily of the same dimension, but obviously gains considerable interest when the number of activities (n) greatly exceeds the number of types of workers (m), because it provides a natural aggregation into a factor space of much smaller dimension than equation (1). The remainder of this section treats the case $n > m$ in more detail.

The conceptual experiment that maps out the indirect production function involves assigning members of a given workforce to maximize production activities, then varying the numbers of workers of each type and efficiently reassigning them along the way to maintain a fixed level of output. The first part of this general class of allocation problems has been studied by McKenzie (1954), Jones (1961), and Whitin (1953) to analyse world production in international trade. For the problem at hand, the set of efficient assignments for a given labour force is found by solving an artificial maximum problem (cf. Dorfman, Samuelson, and Solow, 1958). Define a set of shadow prices for production activities (p_i), which in context are conveniently thought of as piece rates; and maximize the value of production activities subject to the capacities of each type of worker. That is, maximize

$$V = \sum \sum p_i T_{ij} \qquad (6)$$

subject to

$$\sum_i T_{ij}/t_{ij} \leq N_j, \quad j = 1, \ldots, m. \qquad (7)$$

The dual problem requires choosing shadow prices on worker types (w_j) such that

$$V = \min_{wj} \sum w_j N_j \qquad (8)$$

subject to

$$w_j/t_{ij} \geq p_i u, \quad i = 1, \ldots, n \quad \text{and} \quad j = 1, \ldots, m \qquad (9)$$

where w_j has the natural interpretation of the wage rate of worker type j_i. Expression (6) maximizes the value of work effort, while (8) minimizes the cost of labour.

Solution algorithms for (6) and (8) are well known. However, it is instructive to consider in detail the one case where an analytic solution is available, for it reveals the internal structure of (5) and the nature of derived factor substitution most clearly. In particular, great simplification is achieved when $m = 2$ because production tasks can be naturally ordered by comparative advantage. Let $j = A, B$ and $i = 1, 2, \ldots, n$ with $n > 2$. Then activities can be ordered on the index i such that

$$t_{1A}/t_{1B} > t_{2A}/t_{2B} > \ldots > t_{nA}/t_{nB} \qquad (10)$$

with strict inequalities following from assumption (2). When $m = 2$, the two constraints of (7) imply that two of the constraints in (9) must be binding at the minimum labour cost assignment. Therefore there are n^2 possible assignments. n of the basic solutions assign members of A and B to the same activity:

$$w_A = t_{iA} P_i \quad \text{and} \quad w_B = t_{iB} P_i \qquad (11)$$

with inequality for the rest. (11) applies when p_i is very large relative to the other shadow prices. In addition there are $(n - 1)$ basic solutions involving noncongruent activities T_i and T_j. Here elementary manipulation of (9) and (10) show that assignments follow comparative advantage, with

$$w_A = t_{iA} p_i \quad \text{and} \quad w_B = t_{jB} p_j \quad \text{for} \quad i < j \tag{12}$$

and inequality for the rest. (11) and (12) together correspond to all the specialization points of the efficient frontier illustrated by Figure 5.1, and all other points in the efficient set are linear combinations of them.

It is now possible to derive the unit isoquant of (5). Actually, it is slightly more convenient to derive its dual, the factor price frontier. One more constraint is necessary however, because (6) and (7) do not incorporate the restriction that all activities must be operated at nonzero levels to produce positive output. The constraint is obtained from the fact that the firm produces only if there is nonnegative profit, or if

$$p_1 T_1 + p_2 T_2 + \cdots + p_n T_n \leq px$$

where p is the price of output and $T_k = \sum T_{kj}$. Normalize p at unity, divide through by x and substitute the input-output coefficients from (1) to obtain the restriction

$$p_1 \alpha_1 + p_2 \alpha_2 + \cdots + p_n \alpha_n \leq 1. \tag{13}$$

Suppose sufficient numbers of workers of each type are available to produce a unit of output. Then the efficient programme partitions (i) in such a way that members of group A are assigned to activities $(1, 2, \ldots, k)$ and members of group B are assigned to $(k + 1, k + 2, \ldots, n)$ and also possibly to k, for some $k \geq 0$. Members of both groups will be found to have a comparative advantage in all tasks to which they are optimally assigned relative to all those on which they are optimally not assigned. a simple example illustrates the argument. Assume that B's are nonoptimally assigned to 1. $j, j + 1, \ldots, n$, with $j > 2$. Now consider reassigning a full-time equivalent B from 1 to j along with a sufficient amount of A's time from j to 1 to maintain activity level 1, The amount of A required for this manoeuvre is t_{1B}/t_{1A}, since that is the rate of substitution between A and B on the first activity. The change in activity level j is therefore $t_{jB} - (t_{1B}/t_{1A}) t_{jA} = t_{jA}\{(t_{jB}/t_{jA}) - (t_{1B}/t_{1A})\}$, which is strictly positive from the ordering in (10). Thus if unit output was produced before the reassignment, some workers were redundant, and so it goes.

Alternatively, (8) and (9) determine shadow wage rates w_A and w_B for given factor supplies N_A and N_B. The marginal cost to the firm of producing activity level j with an A is w_A/t_{jA} and is w_V/t_{jB} if it is produced with a B. A or B are optimally assigned to j according to the cost-minimization criteria $w_A/t_{jA} \gtrless w_B/t_{jB}$ or $w_A/w_B \gtrless t_{jA}/t_{jB}$. Therefore, the A's are assigned to all activities for which their comparative advantage exceeds the relative shadow price of workers and similarly for the B's. However, there may be one activity for which the comparative advantage ratio just equals the shadow price ratio, in which case A and B are both assigned to that activity (this corresponds to a solution on a facet rather than a corner of the task possibility frontier). In any case, they can share no more than one task for a solution to (8), and equalities (11), (12) and the requirement that $x > 0$ imply

$$w_A = t_{1A}p_1 = \cdots = t_{kA}p_k, \qquad w_A \geq t_{k+1A}p_{k+1},$$
$$\text{and} \quad w_A > t_{1A}p_1 \quad \text{for} \quad l > k+1 \qquad (14)$$
$$w_B = t_{k+1B}p_{k+1} = \cdots = t_{nB}p_n, \qquad w_B \geq t_{kB}p_k$$
$$\text{and} \quad w_B > t_{lA}p_l \quad \text{for} \quad l < k.$$

Substituting the equalities of (14) into (13) yields

$$w_A \left(\frac{\alpha_1}{t_{1A}} + \cdots + \frac{\alpha_k}{t_{kA}} \right) + w_B \left(\frac{\alpha_{k+1}}{t_{k+1B}} + \cdots + \frac{\alpha_n}{t_{nB}} \right) \leq 1 \qquad (15)$$

for all values of k.

Inequalities (15) establish the factor price possibility set and its extreme points define the factor price frontier, $g(w_A, w_B) = 0$. An example in which $n = 5$ is shown in Figure 5.2. Since flats of the factor price frontier correspond to corners of the unit isoquant and vice versa, the unit isoquant is a piecewise linear function consisting of n-connected line segments, as shown in Figure 5.3. Successive pairwise comparisons of the equalities in (15) reveals that the corners of $g(w_A, w_B)$ lie along the ordered rays (from highest to lowest) $w_A/w_B = t_{kA}/t_{kB}$, $k = 1, \ldots, n$, which in turn are equal to marginal rates of substitution along linear segments of the unit isoquant. The isoquant always cuts

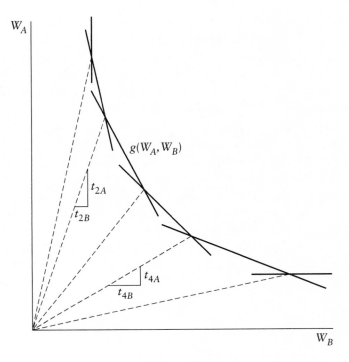

Figure 5.2

both axes. For example, the A's must be assigned to all work activities if no B's are present. When a few B's become available it pays to specialize them in task T_n, for they have the greatest comparative advantage there. Type A workers may still be engaged in all tasks, but as more B's are added they ultimately can replace all of the A'a time on task n. At the specialization point corresponding to the first corner of the isoquant, the A's are found on tasks $T_1, \ldots, T_{n-1}$ and the B's only on task T_n. The addition of still more B's allows their encroachment into task T_{n-1}, for which they have the next largest comparative advantage and for which the A's have the next smallest comparative disadvantage. In that segment the A's and B's have task T_{n-1} in common, until again the B's are sufficiently numerous to replace all of the A's time allocated to T_{n-1}. At that point the A's occupy $T_1, \ldots, T_{n-2}$ and B's occupy T_n, T_{n-1}, and so forth. The commonality of the task in each

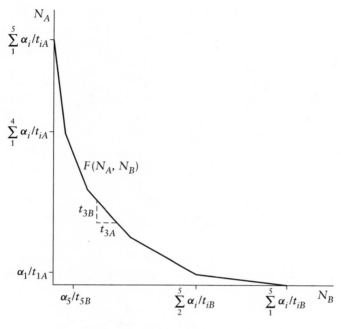

Figure 5.3

segment determines the marginal rate of substitution between N_A and N_B there.

The derivation of the factor price frontier shows that the indirect production function is supported by a price system. But it is supported by a competitive labour market as well. For example, a worker of type j chooses T_{iA} in the market to maximize income w_j with

$$w_j = p_1 T_{1j} + p_2 T_{2j} + \cdots + p_n T_{nj} \tag{16}$$

and is constrained by capacities

$$T_{1j}/t_{1j} + T_{2j}/t_{2j} + \cdots + T_{nj}/t_{nj} \leq 1 \tag{17}$$

and has exactly the same solution as (6) and (7): the market solution is efficient. Further, market arbitrage must make wage and piece rate payments equivalent in this problem. The market solution also satisfies (14), and the market piece rates are determined by the gradient of the efficient task possibility frontier. Therefore, variations in factor supplies N_A and N_B set relative market wage rates w_A/w_B equal to the marginal rate of substitution, and variations in factor supplies trace out the indirect production function.

In summary, the partition of (T_j) into "territories" and the bundling of tasks into job packages is responsive to *per capita* worker endowments and to total factor supplies. The boundary of the partition occurs at a marginal task common to both types of workers, and relative efficiencies on that task fix the marginal rate of substitution between worker types there. Moreover, observed substitution around a corner is determined by a measure of "distance" between skill endowments for example, in Figure 5.3 by the ratio $(t_{k+1A}/t_{kA}) \div (t_{k+1B}/t_{kB})$. Substitution of one kind of worker for another is more difficult the more dissimilar they are.

This last point warrants elaboration. As an approximation, imagine a continuum of tasks on an index s defined over $[0, 1]$ (this concept has been employed in trade theory by Dornbusch, Fischer, and Samuelson, 1977). Workers' skill endowments and input requirements are described by continuous (assumed twice differentiable) functions $t_j(s)$ and $\alpha(s)$. Define $r(s) = t_A(s)/t_B(s)$ and choose s such that $r'(s) < 0$. The efficient assignment is readily extended to a continuum: there is a marginal task ρ that divides the spectrum s such that it is optimal to assign $0 < s < \rho$ to the A's and $\rho < s < 1$ to the B's. Consequently the unit isoquant is defined parametrically by

$$(N_A/x) = \int_0^\rho \{\alpha(s)/t_A(s)\} \; ds = \theta(\rho)$$

$$(N_B/x) = \int_0^1 \{\alpha(s)/t_B(s)\} \; ds = \phi(\rho) \tag{18}$$

where t_j/α measures worker skills in "efficiency units" and its inverse is the worker demand per unit of output. The marginal rate of substitution at ρ is

$$d(N_A/x)/d(N_B/x) = \theta'(\rho)/\phi'(\rho) = -t_B(\rho)/t_A(\rho) = -1/r(\rho)$$

and the elasticity of substitution $\sigma(\rho)$ at ρ is

$$\sigma(\rho) \equiv \frac{d \ln(N_A/s)/(N_B/S)}{d \ln(-r)} = \left(\frac{\alpha/t_A}{N_A} + \frac{\alpha/t_B}{N_B} \right) /(t_A'/t_A - t_B'/t_B) \tag{19}$$

where all arguments of (19) are evaluated at ρ, and the expressions $(\alpha/t_j)/N_j$ are ratios of marginal to total demand for labour of type j at ρ. Substitution is inversely related to the gradient $-d \ln\{t_A(\rho)/t_B(\rho)\}/d\rho$, from (19). Apart from scale, the more similar are worker's relative talents near task ρ, the larger the elasticity of substitution there.

Expressions (18) show explicitly how the efficiency-skill endowment functions $t_j(s)/\alpha(s)$ determine the empirical form of the production function. Conversely, a given production function implies endowment functions that are consistent with it. For example, what forms of $t_A(s)/\alpha(s)$ and $t_B(s)/\alpha(s)$ imply that $F(N_A, N_B)$ has a constant elasticity of substitution? The answer is easily obtained. Normalize $\alpha(s) = 1$, substitute the expression for σ in (19) into $\sigma(\rho) = \sigma$ and differentiate with respect to ρ to obtain the restrictions

$$t_j''/t_j' = \sigma(t_j'/t_j) \qquad \text{for all } \rho, \quad j = A, B.$$

Integrating twice and obtaining boundary conditions from the fact that σ is constant for all values of ρ gives, for $\sigma > 1$.

$$t_A(s)/\alpha(s) = 1/(c_a s)^{1/\sigma - 1}$$
$$t_B(s)/\alpha(s) 1/\{c_b(1 - s)\}^{1/\sigma - 1} \tag{20}$$

where c_a and c_b are positive constants (the global CES with $\sigma \leq 1$ is inadmissible because $F(0, N_B)$ or $F(N_A, 0)$ are nonzero). In (20) the relative difficulty of tasks is increasing in s for the A's, but is decreasing in s for the B's. Further, neither group has an absolute advantage in all tasks. It is interesting to note that neither restriction is consistent with a hierarchical ranking of workers along a single ability scale.

As a practical matter, this analysis suggests difficulties in using some of the official job and occupational classifications for the study of productivity and factor demand. A job is not an invariant classification, since its boundaries are endogenously determined by the economic environment itself, and price–quantity variations across observations need not be generated by a common underlying structure. For example, the apparatus is useful for clarifying the meaning of international differences in technology. It is plausible that there exist no differences in engineering technology across countries, yet the (indirect) production function may appear to be different between them. The often observed fact that a factory in one country is more productive than its identical twin in another country can arise because work assignments embodied in the design of capital are optimal for one labour force and not for another owing to differences in the distribution of worker skills and comparative advantage.

A foundation for a structural indirect production function is best built upon groupings of workers according to comparative advantage and productive capabilities, perhaps on the basis of socioeconomic characteristics rather than on job classifications. Even so, comparative advantage implies imperfect substitution between groups. For example, the fact that different skills are accumulated with work experience suggests imperfect substitution among age cohorts in the labour force, and implies that greater relative factor supplies in a large birth cohort can haunt all of its members for their lifetimes. The same phenomenon helps explain why alternative vintages of graduates in the professions fare indifferently when output demand conditions change. It also incorporates the common managerial practice of skill bumping by seniority associated with business cycles (see Reder, 1962): so long as layoffs are not proportional across worker types, short-run employment declines change the partition of the set of tasks optimally assigned to those remaining employed, amounting to a kind of short-run substitution effect. Finally, insofar as educational classifications index differential worker capacities, the analysis suggests how education enters production and provides a link between supply-dominated theories of human capital accumulation and less well studied demands for them. Here imperfect substitution implies that fixed weighted indexes of aggregate educational input often used for measuring total factor productivity may be subject to substantial index number bias. A more subtle difficulty arises if relative capacities indexed by school completion levels change over time. Equiproportionate increases in capacities shrink the unit isoquant uniformly towards the origin, but all other kinds of changes alter it nonhomogeneously. The former appear in the measurements as neutral technical change and the latter as biased technical change, even though the engineering technology may remain unaltered.

II. Selection and Income Distribution

The other extreme case, where the number of worker types is much larger than the number of tasks, provides some interesting parallels with Section I. It is also more convenient for studying the role of demand conditions, income distribution and the characteristics of job-worker matching in the labour market.

To begin, return to the efficient frontier of Figure 5.1. The presence of a third type of person, C, with comparative advantage somewhere between that of A and B adds a third facet of slope t_{2C}/t_{1C} to the frontier. Adding still more types fills in the corners and has the effect of smoothing $f(T_1, T_2)$. Its limiting behaviour is found by making use of the fact established above that free choice and competitive markets assign people efficiently. Select a person at random with some fixed capacities (t_1, t_2). The solution to (16) and (17) shows that the worker maximizes income by devoting full time to activity 2 or to activity 1 according to $t_2/t_1 \gtrless p_1/p_2$, and is indifferent between the two if the productivity ratio equals the market price ratio. Given an arbitrary market relative price $\lambda = p_1/p_2$, all workers whose value of t_2/t_1 exceeds λ are optimally assigned to activity 2 and voluntarily choose it; all those with comparative advantage less than λ should be assigned to activity 1 and also find it in their own interests to choose it; while those for whom $\lambda = t_2/t_1$ are arbitrarily distributed to either activity or to both of them.

Again, there is a convenient ordering by comparative advantage, but this time it refers to workers rather than to tasks. Instead of partitioning the spectrum of tasks, the efficient solution partitions the set of worker types and establishes commonality of tasks for marginal workers at its boundary. Define a continuous index u on (0, 1) and twice differentiable functions $t_i(u)$ and $\beta(u)$ representing productivity of worker type u on activity i and the number of workers of that type. The index u is chosen in such a way that $R(u) \equiv t_2(u)/t_1(u)$ and $R'(u) \geq 0$. Therefore the efficient frontier is defined parametrically by

$$T_1(\lambda) = \int_0^\lambda t_2(u)\beta(u)\,du$$
$$T_2(\lambda) = \int_\lambda^1 t_1(u)\beta(u)\,du$$

(21)

and its slope is determined by the productivity ratio of the marginal worker: $dT_2/dT_1 = -t_2(\lambda)/t_1(\lambda)$. Furthermore, $d\ln\{-(dT_2/dT_1)\} = R'/R > 0$ so that $f(T_1, T_2)$ is concave. Defining the elasticity of transformation $\tau(\lambda)$ symmetrically with the elasticity of substitution yields

$$\tau = \beta(t_2/T_2 \div t_1/T_1)/(R'/R)$$

(22)

where all the arguments of (22) are evaluated at λ. The curvature of $f(T_1, T_2)$ depends on both the diversity of relative productivity in the working population and the number of workers of each type. Again, the less diversity, the larger is τ. For example, the efficient frontier is a straight line if everyone is identical (apart from scale), with slope equal to the population ratio t_2^*/t_1^*. Just as in Section I, each specification of $t_i(u)$ and $\beta(u)$ implies a specific transformation function, and vice versa.

It was tempting in Section I to (loosely) identify the spectrum s with the difficulty of tasks. In this case u is more closely associated with worker talents and abilities, as an equivalent derivation in terms of a distributional argument makes clear. Each worker's skills are described by a point in the (t_1, t_2) plane, and if m is very large the *potential* market supply of skills is a continuous distribution function $M\xi(t_1, t_2)$. M is the number of workers and $\xi(t_1, t_2)$ is a probability density indicating the proportion of workers in a neighbourhood of (t_1, t_2). Picture the probability contours of ξ in the (t_1, t_2) plane, cut by a ray $t_2 = \mu t_1$. Since all workers with skills below the ray devote full time to activity 1 and all persons above it devote full time to activity 2, the activity possibility frontier is defined parametrically by the conditional expectations

$$T_1 = M \int_0^\infty \int_0^{\mu t_1} t_1 \xi(t_1, t_2)\, dt_1\, dt_2 = \zeta(\mu)$$

$$T_2 = M \int_0^\infty \int_{\mu t_1}^\infty t_2 \xi(t_1, t_2)\, dt_1\, dt_2 = \eta(\mu).$$

(23)

The efficient frontier $f(T_1, T_2)$ is swept out of the distribution $M\xi(t_1, t_2)$ as μ varies from zero (everyone choosing T_1) to infinity (everyone choosing T_1). Differentiating (23),

$$dT_1/d\mu = M \int_0^\infty t_1^2 \xi(t_1, \mu t_1)\, dt_1 = \zeta'(\mu)$$

$$dT_2/d\mu = M \int_0^\infty -\mu t_1^2 \xi(t_1, \mu t_1)\, dt_1 = \eta'(\mu)$$

(24)

and

$$dT_1/dT_2 = \eta(\mu)/\xi(\mu) = -\mu.$$

(25)

The slope of the efficient frontier is the price ratio, equal to the comparative advantage ratio for the marginal worker, as in (21). Differentiating (25) shows that $f(F_1, T_2)$ is concave and that τ is related to the moments of ξ, though the precise relationships are very difficult to establish because market selection truncates the distribution of productivity in each activity. However, τ tends to be large if ξ concentrates large probability in a small area of the plane (measured, say, by the generalized variance). The limiting case of identical relative talent discussed above is equivalent to complete concentration of ξ on a ray with slope t_2^*/t_1^*.

A result analogous to the indirect production function is available here, but refers to production possibilities in the economy. Construction of the production possibility set with two goods X_1 and X_2 and technologies

$$X_1 = \min(T_1/\alpha_{11}, T_2/\alpha_{12}) \quad X_2 = \min(T_1/\alpha_{21}, T_2/\alpha_{22})$$

is illustrated in Figure 5.4. The production frontier is smooth and all factors are fully employed in spite of the fact that the output technologies admit no substitution. This result is reminiscent of the surprising example in Houthakker (1975) (see also the extensive elaborations by Johansen, 1972, and Sato, 1975) of well-behaved macro-structures that seem to have lives of their own, bearing little resemblance to their microfoundations, but arising from underlying distributional phenomena. Human diversity is the crux of the matter in all these examples. In this case it implies rising supply price of production activities, which translates to rising relative supply price of outputs. Thus substitution

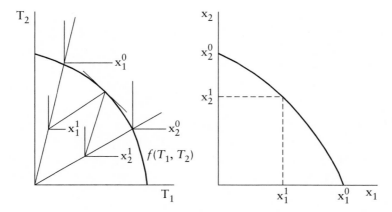

Figure 5.4

in the micro-technology or substitution in input technologies due to population heterogeneity are seen to have very similar implications.

Figure 5.4 shows explicitly how final demand conditions influence the division of labour among activities and their valuations. The total activity vectors corresponding to each feasible division of output sum to a point on $f(T_1, T_2)$ and the slope of $f(T_1, T_2)$ determines both the marginal worker and the relative market price ratio p_1/p_2: any other relative price would not call forth the division of labour necessary to support that division of output. The same principle extends to any finite n. For prices so determined a worker's income prospects in the ith activity are given by $y_i = p_i t_i$, which provide a basis for transforming the density of individual productivities $\xi(t_1, \ldots, t_n)$ into a density of *potential* income $\psi(y_1, \ldots, y_n)$. The realized personal distribution of income is related to ψ by the fact that workers choose activities to maximize their incomes. Let $h^i(y_i)$ denote the fraction of the labour force with income y_i who choose activity i. $h^i(y_i)$ is conditioned on the fact that people actually found in the ith activity could do no better elsewhere. That is (cf. Houthakker, 1975)

$$h^i(y_i) = \Pr\{y_i | y_i = \max(y_1, \ldots, y_n)\}$$
$$= \int_0^{y_i} \cdots \int_0^{y_i} \psi(y_1, \ldots, y_n) \prod_{i \neq k} dy_k.$$

Therefore the fraction of people with income y or less in activity i is

$$\int_0^y h^i(y_i)\, dy_i$$

and the cumulative density for the observed personal distribution of income in the economy is

$$\sum_i \int_0^y h^i(y_i)\, dy_i. \tag{26}$$

The derivation of $f(T_1, T_2)$ and Figure 5.4 show that final demand conditions affect observed income distributions and their influence appears through the presence of market clearing prices $p_1, \ldots, p_n$ as parameters of the potential income density ψ and hence of the functions $h^i(y_i)$ in (26).

This kind of statistical model was first stated by Roy (1951), who elaborated the supply mechanism (see also Sattinger, 1975, and related work by Tinbergen, 1959). It has been extended to a more general demand and supply setting here. The main lesson is that observed earnings distributions are truncations of the distribution of potential earnings. Individuals observed in each activity are selected into them by comparative advantage and therefore are not random samples of the whole population. The nature and extent of these selection effects depends on the moments of the distribution of potential earnings, which in turn are jointly determined by the moments of underlying skill distributions among various work activities embodies in members of the labour force (ξ) and by the valuations that the market places on these skills as derived from the demand for output (p). Large negative covariances of potential earnings across activities tend to induce skewness in the overall distribution of income, because workers observed in each activity tend to be more productive in them than the population at large: there is small probability of observing those from the lower tail of the marginal productivity distribution in any given activity since they are likely to have a much better opportunity somewhere else. On the other hand, large positive covariances tends to result in hierarchical sorting, with the most productive people found in the most remunerative activities, the next most productive found in the next most remunerative activities and so forth. In either case (not only the latter) inferences from observed data about income prospects available to those not found in any given activity can be subject to considerable bias because of nonrandom sorting. (Gronau, 1974; Lewis, 1974; Maddala, 1976; and Heckman, 1976 discuss this in other contexts, and Willis and Rosen, 1977, present some empirical evidence closely related to the subject of this paper.)

A latent variable interpretation of the underlying skill distribution (Mandelbrot, 1962) lends another perspective to the worker-job matching problem. Consider the linear statistical model

$$t_i = b_{oi} + b_{1i}Z_1 + b_{2i}Z_2 + \cdots + b_{vi}Z_u + \delta_i, \quad i = 1, \ldots, n \quad (27)$$

where Z is a vector of latent factors, b_i is a vector of factor loadings common to the ith activity and δ_i are independent activity-specific factors. Each worker is described by a point in the space of Z plus a random drawing from the joint distribution of δ. General equilibrium in the economy determines prices p as described above, and potential earnings in the ith activity are

$$y_i = p_i t_i = p_i b_{oi} + p_i b_{1i} z_1 + \cdots + p_i b_{vi} z_v + p_i \delta_i. \quad (28)$$

Equation (27) is similar to a "production function," with the marginal productivity (possibly nonpositive) of each factor varying from activity to activity. These functions transform the joint distribution of (Z, δ) to the productivity density ξ used above, and similarly for (28) and ψ. Ignoring the specific factors for a moment, the factor space Z may be partitioned into n acceptance regions in which $y_i = \max(y_1, \ldots, y_n)$ in region i. These regions are convex polyhedra and are completely determined by the loadings in (28). The polyhedra are cones if the constant terms $p_i b_{oi}$ in (27) or (28) are zero. (For the homogeneous case of $v = 2$, the acceptance regions would be defined by $n - 1$ lines through the origin plus the coordinate axes of the (Z_1, Z_2) plane and are found in a manner very similar to the construction of Figure 5.2.) In any case, all individuals choosing the same activity would tend to have Z characteristics within well-defined limits, with due allowance for noise from δ. The highly stratified outcome mentioned above would be likely if the relations in (28) were all positively loaded on a single factor, such as the usual interpretation of "general ability," in which case the acceptance regions are ordered partitions of a line. But that is too restrictive: most skills depend not so much on a single kind of ability as on combinations of them. Some characteristics and talents have zero or negative values for certain kinds of skills, or it may be that there are natural negative correlations among talents in human populations. Then the very notion of *hierarchical* sorting between workers and activities has little if any meaning. Nevertheless, sorting there will be, and workers in each activity will tend to have similar characteristics.

It is interesting to compare this approach to a "characteristic approach," wherein workers are considered to be fixed bundles of attributes (e.g., "strength" and "intelligence") which are themselves treated as factors of production (Welch, 1969). Then groups of workers are perfect substitutes for each other according to the fixed packages of attributes embodied in each group and a simple arbitrage argument establishes unique implicit market prices for characteristics depending on the total amounts available in the economy. A worker's income is simply the product of those prices times his embodied attributes. There is no tendency for systematic sorting of the labour force in that kind of world because any total attribute requirement can be obtained in the market by an infinite number of alternative linear combinations of worker types: there is no economic rent in earnings except the scale of a worker's characteristics. In contrast, the difference between marginal and average in this model generates economic rents that are signals for nonrandom assignment and sorting of workers to jobs. There is no unique market price for each attribute, but a value that varies among activities—see (28); because firms care about the amount of useful work performed, not about characteristics per se. Worker-job sorting and selection is too obvious and important an empirical phenomena to be ignored.

III. Conclusion

The main purpose of this essay has been to show how the division of labour inherent in the internal organization of work activities determines some observable substitution possibilities in production. Of course there is a considerable distance between what has been offered here and a complete theory; but substitution is such an important feature of economic life that continued efforts to explain it seem worthwhile.

Engineering technologies with fixed coefficients have been used only to focus most sharply on the contribution of the division of labour to observed substitution. It is not difficult to incorporate smooth technologies of the neoclassical type into the analysis. Further, Section II generalizes fairly easily to multidimensional cases, because the device of describing skill endowments by distribution functions captures the essence of the ordering property crucial to Section I without being quite so dependent upon it. Extending the results in Section I to more than two factors, beyond the mere statement of the envelope property—which always applies—is another matter. There is no counterpart to the distributional specification of Section II. Bilateral comparisons always result in a comparative advantage ordering, but multilateral comparisons do not without further assumptions. One possibility is to order tasks by their "intrinsic difficulty," in which case it is conceivable, but still improbable, that the optimal partition of the spectrum assigns each group to occupy contiguous territories along the line as in Section I, but with two commonalities instead of one. This is the only case where it is easy to keep track of the margins, but it is perhaps too restrictive to be of great interest.

The rules of the game that have been followed also rule out many interesting possibilities that are more difficult to analyse. First, the effect of scale on the division of labour (Stigler, 1951) plays no role here because of constant returns assumptions and the absence of indivisibilities. Second, in many labour markets there seem to be important empirical consequences of the nature of the match between different workers in the same firm that have been ignored above. The observed sorting of specific kinds of workers to specific firms in the same industry can be rationalized in many ways (see Rosen, 1974, for one possibility based on consumption aspects of the work environment); but technical task externalities and indivisibilities impose real limitations on the ability of the price system described above to achieve efficient asignments. If the price system is incomplete there is a role for entrepreneurial activity of assembling an optimal work force. Introducing such factors lead the analysis toward the economic theory of marriage (Becker, 1974) and questions of assortive matching among workers. Finally, the distribution of skills has been treated as exogenously determined. It remains to be seen how personal investments in the acquisition of skills affect the division of labour and derived factor and product substitution.

References

Becker, G. (1974). A theory of marriage. In *The Economics of the Family* (T. W. Schultz, ed.), Chicago: University of Chicago Press.

Dorfman, R., Samuelson, P., and Solow, R. (1958). *Linear Programming and Economic Analysis*. New York: McGraw-Hill.

Dornbusch, R., Fischer, S., and Samuelson, P. (1977). Comparative advantage, trade, and payments in a Ricardian model with a continuum of goods, *American Economic Review, 67,* 823–839.

Gronau, R. (1974). Wage comparison—a selectivity bias. *Journal of Political Economy, 82,* 1119–1143.

Heckman, J. (1976). *The Common Structure of Statistical Models of Truncation, Sample Selection, and Limited Dependent Variables.* University of Chicago.

Houthakker, H. (1955). Pareto distributions and the Cobb-Douglas production function in demand analysis. *Review of Economic Studies, 23,* 27–31.

——— (1975). The size distribution of labor incomes derived from the distribution of aptitudes. In *Econometrics and Economic Theory: Essays in Honor of Jan Tinbergen.* (W. Sellekaerts, ed.), 177–187 New York: Macmillan.

Johansen, L. (1972). *Production Functions.* Amsterdam: North Holland.

Jones, R. (19161). Comparative advantage and the theory of tariffs: a multi-country, multi-commodity model. *Review of Economic Studies, 28*, 161–175.

Lewis, H. G. (1974). Comments on selectivity biases in wage comparisons. *Journal of Political Economy, 82*, 1145–1155.

McKenzie, L. W. (1954). Specialization and efficiency in world production. *Review of Economic Studies, 21*, 165–180.

Maddala, G. S. (1976). *Self-Selectivity Problems in Econometric Models.* University of Florida.

Mandelbrot, B. (1962). Paretian distributions and income maximization. *Quarterly Journal of Economics, 76*, 57–85.

Reder, M. (1962). Wage differentials: theory and measurement. In *Aspects of Labor Economics.* Princeton: University Press and NBER.

Rosen, S. (1974). Hedonic prices and implicit markets: product differentiation in pure competition. *Journal of Political Economy, 82*, 34–55.

Roy, A. D. (1951). Some thoughts on the distribution of earnings. *Oxford Economic Papers* (n.s.) *3*, 135–146.

Sato, K. (1975). *Production Functions and Aggregation.* Amsterdam: North-Holland.

Sattinger, M. (1975). Comparative advantage and the distribution of earnings and abilities. *Econometrica, 43*, 455–468.

Stigler, G. (1951). The division of labor is limited by the extent of the market. *Journal of Political Economy, 59*, 185–193.

Tinbergen, J. (1959). On the theory of income distribution. In *Selected Papers.* Amsterdam: North-Holland.

Welch, F. (1969). A linear synthesis of skill distributions. *Journal of Human Resources, 4*, 311–327.

Whitin, T. (1953). Classical theory, Graham's theory and linear programming in international trade. *Quarterly Journal of Economics, 67*, 520–544.

Willis, R. and Rosen, S. (1977). *Education and Self Selection.* Washington: National Bureau of Economic Research.

6

Education and
Self-Selection

ROBERT J. WILLIS

SHERWIN ROSEN

I. Introduction

In this paper we specify and estimate a model of the demand for college education derived from its effect on expected lifetime earnings compared with its cost. Attention is focused on specifying the role of earnings expectations in the derived demand for schooling; these are found to be empirically important determinants of the decision to attend college. In addition to including financial incentives, the model allows for a host of selectivity or sorting effects in the data that are related to "ability bias," family effects, and tastes that have occupied other researchers. Background and motivation are presented in Section II. The structure of the model, a variant of a simultaneous-equations problem involving discrete choices, is presented in Section III. The estimates, based on data from the NBER-Thorndike sample, appear in Section IV. Some implications and conclusions are found in Section V.

II. Nature of the Problem

Estimates of rates of return to education have been controversial because they are based on ex post realizations and need not reflect struc-

---

Thanks are due to Sean Becketti for excellent research assistance, to Lung Fei Lee for advice on statistical issues, and to Richard Layard and W. M. Gorman for criticism of and initial draft. This research was supported by the National Science Foundation and the National Bureau of Economic Research, but this is not an official NBER publication. The order of the authors' names was selected by a random device.

From *Journal of Political Economy* 87, no. 5, pt. 2 (1979): S7–S35. © 1979 by The University of Chicago.

tural parameters necessary for correct predictions. For example, it is well understood that college and high school graduates may have different abilities so that income forgone during college by the former is not necessarily equal to observed earnings of the latter. Our objective here is twofold. One is to estimate life earnings conditioned on actual school choices that are purged of selection bias. The other is to determine the extent to which alternative earnings prospects, as distinct from family background and financial constraints, influence the decision to attend college.

One would need to go no further than straightforward comparisons of earnings outcomes among school classes for structural rate of return estimates if educational wage differentials were everywhere equalizing on the direct, opportunity, and interest costs of schooling. For then the supplies of graduates (or "demands" for each level of education) would be nearly elastic at the equalizing wage differentials, and the distribution of human wealth would be approximately independent of the distribution of schooling.[1] However, recent evidence on the structure of life earnings based on panel data strongly rejects this as a serious possibility. Total variance of earnings among people of the same sex, race, education, and market experience is very large, and more than two-thirds of it is attributable to unobserved components or person-specific effects that probably persist over much of the life cycle.[2] The panel evidence therefore suggests that supply elasticities are substantially less than completely elastic at unique wage differentials and that there are inframarginal "ability rents." Put in another way, observed rates of return are not wholly supply determined and depend on interactions with relative demands for graduates as well.

A natural approach has been to incorporate measures of ability into the statistical analysis, either directly or as indicators of unobserved factors, in order to, in effect, impute ability rent. But merely partitioning

1. The equalizing difference model originates with Friedman and Kuznets (1945). Jacob Mincer (1974) has developed it most completely in recent years.

2. See Lillard and Willis (1978) for additional detail and confirmation of these remarks. Related studies have reached similar conclusions, e.g., Weiss and Lillard (1978). Of course, it is conceivable, but unlikely, that educational wage differentials are exactly equalizing for each individual, although considerable lifetime inequality exists among individuals. This possibility is rejected in the empirical findings presented below.

observed earnings into schooling and ability components does not use any of the restrictions imposed on the data by a school-stopping rule, and that decision embodies all the economic content of the problem. Some of that additional structure is incorporated here.

Economic theories of education, be they of the human-capital or signaling varieties, are based on the principle of maximum capital value: schooling is pursued to the point where its marginal (private) internal rate of return equals the rate of interest. It is easy to show that this leads to a recursive econometric model in which (i) schooling is related to a person's ability and family background, and (ii) earnings are related to "prior" school decisions and ability. Earnings gains attributable to education do not appear explicitly in the schooling equation. Instead, the cost-benefit basis of the decision is embedded in cross-equation restrictions on the overall model, because the earnings equation is a constraint for the maximum problem that determines education attainment.[3] There are many estimates of recursive models in the literature, but very few have tested the economic (wealth-maximizing) hypothesis.[4]

We begin with the assumption of marked heterogeneity and diversity in the population, as in the unobserved-component approach to panel data. Costs and benefits of alternative school-completion levels are assumed to be randomly distributed among people according to their capacities to finance education, tastes, perceptions, expectations, and an array of talents that affect performance in work activities associated with differing levels of schooling. Some of these things are observed, while others are unobserved. Individuals are sorted into educational classes according to the interaction of a selection criterion

---

3. The basic model is discussed in Becker (1975). See Rosen (1977) for an elaboration of this argument and a survey of the relevant literature. Blaug (1976) also stresses the need for estimating structural demand for schooling relationships, and Griliches (1977) discusses the difficulty of doing so in conventional models. Part of Griliches's discussion is pursued in Griliches, Hall, and Hausman (1977). The model elaborated here is conceptually distinct from that work, though some of the statistical techniques are similar. A similar remark applies to the work of Kenny, Lee, Maddala, and Trost (in press).

4. There is aggregate-time-series evidence that earnings are important determinants of professional school enrollment (see Freeman [1971] and numerous subsequent studies by the same author); but there is virtually no micro evidence even though such data have been most often studied in the human-capital and signaling frameworks.

(such as maximum present value) and the underlying joint distribution of tastes, talents, expectations, and parental wealth. The selection rule partitions the underlying joint density into a corresponding realized educational distribution. The supply function of graduates at any level of schooling is "swept out" of the joint taste, talent, parental wealth distribution as increased wage differentials enlarge the subset of the partition relevant for that class.

Let Y_{ij} represent the potential lifetime earnings of person i if schooling level j is chosen, X_i a vector of observed talent or ability indicators of person i, and τ_i and unobserved talent component relevant for person i. Similarly, split family-background and taste effects into an observed vector Z_i and an unobserved component ω_i. Let V_{ij} denote the value of choosing school level j for person i. Then a general school-selection model is:

$$Y_{ij} = y_j(X_i, \tau_i), \quad j = 1, \ldots, n; \tag{1}$$

$$V_{ij} = g(y_j, Z_i, \omega_i); \tag{2}$$

$$i \text{ belongs to } j \text{ if } V_{ij} = \max(V_{i1}, \ldots, V_{in}); \tag{3}$$

and

$$(\tau, \omega) \sim F(\tau, \omega). \tag{4}$$

Equation (1) shows how potential earnings in any given classification vary with talent and ability.[5] The earnings function differs among school classes because work activities associated with alternative levels of education make use of different combinations of talent. Equation (2) translates the earnings stream from choice j into a scalar such as present value and is conditioned on family background to reflect tastes and financial barriers to extending schooling. Equation (3) is the selection rule: the person chooses the classification that maximizes value and is observed in one and only one of the n possibilities open to him. Equation (4) closes the model with a specification of the distribution

---

5. Actually, expository convenience dictates a more restrictive formulation than is necessary. The X and Z need not be orthogonal. They may have some elements in common, but identification requires that they not have all elements in common (see below).

of unobservables. Since observed assignments of individuals to schooling classes are selected on (X, Z, τ, ω), earnings observed in each class may be nonrandom samples of population potential earnings, because those with larger net benefits in the class have a higher probability of being observed in it.

This formulation is suggested by the theory of comparative advantage.[6] It allows for a rather eclectic view of the role of talent in determining observed outcomes, since the X's may affect earning capacity differently at different levels of schooling (see eq. [1]) and covariances among the unobservables are unrestricted. Indeed, there may be negative covariance among talent components. For example, plumbers (high school graduates) may have very limited potential as highly schooled lawyers, but by the same token lawyers may have much lower potential as plumbers than those who actually end up choosing that kind of work. This contrasts with the one-factor ability-as-IQ specifications in the literature which assume that the best lawyers would also be the best plumbers and would imply strictly hierarchical sorting in the absence of financial constraints. In effect an IQ-ability model constrains the unobserved ability components to have large positive covariances— an assumption that is probably erroneous and is not necessary for our methods. Note also that population mean "rates of return" among alternative schooling levels have no significance as guides to the social or private profitability of investments in schooling. For example, a random member of the population might achieve a negative return from an engineering degree, yet those with appropriate talents who choose engineering will obtain a return on the time and money costs of their training which is at least equal to the rate of interest.

There are difficult estimation problems associated with selectivity models. In brief, the unobservables impose distinct limits on the amount of structural information that can be inferred from realized assignments in the data. For example, it would be very desirable to know the marginal distribution of talents in (4), since it would then be possible to construct the socially efficient assignment of individuals to school classes, defined as the one that maximizes overall human wealth. Then

---

6. Roy (1951) gives a surprisingly modern and rigorous treatment of a selection problem based on the theory of comparative advantage. See Rosen (1978) for extensions and elaboration on this class of problems. Heckman (1976), Lee (1976), and Maddala (1977) develop the appropriate estimation theory.

the deadweight losses due to capital market imperfections could be computed by comparing optimal with observed assignments. However, the marginal density is not itself identified, since unobserved financial constraints and talent jointly determine observed outcomes. These issues will be made precise shortly, but, roughly speaking, we do not necessarily know if a person chose college education because he had talent for it or because he was wealthy. What can and will be done is to map out the joint effects of the unobservables embedded in the actual demand curve for college attendance, which embodies all constraints inherent in the actual market but which nevertheless is a valid structural basis for prediction. Selectivity or ability bias in unadjusted rate of return computations that do not take account of the sorting by talent inherent in observed assignments can also be computed.

A few limitations to these methods must be noted at the outset. It is crucial to the spirit of the model, based as it is on human diversity, that few covariance restrictions be placed on the distribution of unobservables. This practically mandates the assumption of joint normality, since no other nonindependent multivariate distribution offers anything close to similar computational advantages. While the general selection rule specified below is likely to emerge from a broad class of economic models of school choice, it is not known how sensitive the results are to the normality assumptions. In addition, nonindependence forces some aggregation in the number of choices considered for computational feasibility, even though the statistical theory can be worked out for any finite number.[7] This rules out of consideration other selection aspects of the problem that should be considered, such as choice of school quality.[8] All people in our sample have at least a high school education, and we have chosen a dichotomous split between choice of high

---

7. The problem is that the aggregates are sums of distributions that are themselves truncated and selected. Therefore the distributions underlying the aggregate assignments are not necessarily normal. We are unaware of any systematic analysis of this kind of aggregation problem.

8. Methods such as conditional logit have been designed to handle high-dimensional classifications (McFadden 1973) but require independence and other (homogeneity) restrictions that are not tenable for this problem. Hausman and Wise (1978) have worked out computational methods on general normal assumptions for three choices. Note also that maximum likelihood methods are available, but are extremely expensive because multiple integrals must be evaluated. Hence we follow the literature in using consistent estimators.

school and more than high school (college attendance). Some internal diagnostic tests help check on the validity of this aggregation. Experiments with a college completion or more classification, compared with a high school graduation or some college classification, yielded results very similar to those reported below.

III. The Model

Specification of the econometric model is tailored to the data at our disposal. More details will be given below, but at this point the important feature is that earnings are observed at two points in the life cycle for each person, one point soon after entrance into the labor market and another point some 20 years later. The earnings stream is parameterized into a simple geometric growth process to motivate the decision rule. This is a reasonable approximation to actual life earnings patterns for the period spanned by the data. Two levels of schooling are considered, labeled level A (for more than high school) and level B (for high school).

If person i chooses A, the expected earnings stream is

$$
\begin{aligned}
y_{ai}(t) &= 0, & 0 < t \leq S, \\
y_{ai}(t) &= \bar{y}_{ai}\exp[g_{ai}(t - S)], & S \leq t < \infty,
\end{aligned}
\tag{5}
$$

where S is the incremental schooling period associated with A over B and $t - S$ is market experience. If alternative B is chosen, the expected earnings stream is

$$
y_{bi}(t) = \bar{y}_{bi}\exp(g_{bi}t), \qquad 0 \leq t < \infty.
\tag{6}
$$

Thus earnings prospects of each person in the sample are characterized by four parameters: initial earnings and rates of growth in each of the two alternatives. Diversity is represented by a random distribution of the vector $(\bar{y}_a, g_a, \bar{y}_b, g_b)$ among the population.[9]

---

9. Wise (1975), Lazear (1976), and Zabalza (1977) have used initial earnings and growth of earnings to study life earnings patterns. The distribution of potential earnings and growth is not constrained in our model, thus, e.g., allowing the possibility that $\bar{y}_a$ and g_a are negatively correlated (and similarly for $\bar{y}_b$ and g_b), as in Mincer (1974). On this see Hause (1977).

Equations (5) and (6) yield convenient expressions for present values. Assume an infinite horizon, a constant rate of discount for each person, r_i, with $r_i > g_{ai}, g_{bi}$, and ignore direct costs of school. Then the present value of earnings is

$$V_{ai} = \int_g^\infty y_{ai}(t) \exp(-r_i t)\, dt = [\bar{y}_{ai}/(r_i - g_{ai})] \exp(-r_i S) \qquad (7)$$

if A is chosen and

$$V_{bi} = \int_0^\infty y_{bi}(t) \exp(-r_i t)\, dt = \bar{y}_{bi}/(r_i - g_{bi}) \qquad (8)$$

if B is chosen. These are likely to be good approximations, since the consequences of ignoring finite life discount corrections and nonlinearities in earnings paths toward the end of the life cycle are lightly weighted for nonnegligible values of r.

Selection Rule

Assume that person i chooses A if $V_{ai} > V_{bi}$ and chooses B if $V_{ai} \le V_{bi}$. Define $I_i = \ln(V_{ai}/V_{bi})$. Substitution from (5) to (8) yields $I_i = \ln \bar{y}_{ai} - \ln \bar{y}_{bi} - r_i S - \ln(r_i - g_{ai}) + \ln(r_i - g_{bi})$. A Taylor series approximation to the nonlinear terms around their population mean values $(\bar{g}_a, \bar{g}_b, \bar{r})$ yields

$$I_i = \alpha_0 + \alpha_1(\ln \bar{y}_{ai} - \ln \bar{y}_{bi}) + \alpha_2 g_{ai} + \alpha_3 g_{bi} + \alpha_4 r_i, \qquad (9)$$

with

$$\begin{aligned} &\alpha_1 = 1, \\ &\alpha_2 = \partial I/\partial g_a = 1/(\bar{r} - g_a) > 0, \\ &\alpha_3 = \partial I/\partial g_b = -1/(\bar{r} - \bar{g}_b) < 0, \\ &\alpha_4 = -[S + (\bar{g}_a - \bar{g}_b)/(\bar{r} - \bar{g}_a)(\bar{r} - \bar{g}_b)]. \end{aligned} \qquad (10)$$

Hence the selection criteria are

$$\begin{aligned} \Pr\ (\text{choose A}) &= \Pr(V_a > V_b) = \Pr(I > 0), \\ \Pr\ (\text{choose B}) &= \Pr(V_a \le V_b) = \Pr(I \le 0). \end{aligned} \qquad (11)$$

Earnings and Discount Functions

Let X_i represent a set of measured characteristics that influence a person's lifetime earnings potential, and let $u_{1i}, \ldots, u_{4i}$ denote permanent person-specific unobserved components reflecting unmeasured factors influencing earnings potential.[10] Specify structural (in the sense of population) earnings equations of the form

$$\ln \bar{y}_{ai} = X_i \beta_a + u_{1i},$$
$$g_{ai} = X_i \gamma_a + u_{2i} \tag{12}$$

if A is chosen and

$$\ln \bar{y}_{bi} = X_i \beta_b + u_{3i},$$
$$g_{bi} = X_i \gamma_b + u_{4i} \tag{13}$$

if B is chosen. The variables on the left-hand sides of (12) and (13) are to be interpreted as the individual's expectation of initial earnings and growth rates at the time the choice is made. In order to obtain consistent estimates of $(\beta_a, \gamma_a, \beta_b, \gamma_b)$ from data on realizations it is assumed that expectations were unbiased. Hence forecast errors are assumed to be independently normally distributed, with zero means.

Let Z_i denote another vector of observed variables that influence the schooling decision through their effect on the discount rate. Then

$$r_i = Z_i \delta + u_{5i}, \tag{14}$$

where u_5 is a permanent unobserved component influencing financial barriers to school choice. The vector (u_j) is assumed to be jointly normal, with zero means and variance-covariance matrix $\Sigma = [\sigma_{ij}]$. The Σ is unrestricted.

Reduced Form

The structural model is (9), (12), (13), and (14). A reduced form of the selection rule is obtained by substituting (12)–(14) into (9):

$$I = \alpha_0 + X[\alpha_1(\beta_a - \beta_b) + \alpha_2\gamma_a + \alpha_3\gamma_b] + \alpha_4 Z\delta + \alpha_1(u_1 - u_3)$$
$$+ \alpha_2 u_2 + \alpha_3 u_3 + \alpha_5 u_5 \tag{15}$$
$$= W\pi - \epsilon,$$

---

10. The τ's of Section II are related to $(u_i, \ldots, u_4)$ by a set of implicit prices that vary across school classifications, as in Mandelbrot (1960). See Rosen (1978) for the logic of why these differences in valuation can be sustained indefinitely and cannot be arbitraged.

with $W = [X, Z]$ and $-\epsilon = \alpha_1(u_1 - u_3) + \alpha_2 u_2 + \alpha_3 u_4 + \alpha_5 u_5$. Thus an observationally equivalent statement to (9) and (11) is

$$\text{Pr (A is observed)} = \Pr(W\pi > \epsilon) = F\left(\frac{W\pi}{\sigma_\epsilon}\right), \qquad (16)$$

where $F(\cdot)$ is the standard normal c.d.f. Equation (16) is a probit function determining sample selection into categories A or B, to be estimated from observed data.[11]

Selection Bias and Earnings Functions

The decision rule selects people into observed classes according to largest expected present value. Hence the earnings actually observed in each group are not random samples of the population, but are truncated nonrandom samples instead. The resulting bias in observed means may be calculated as follows. Note that Pr [observing $y_a(t)$] $\Pr(I > 0) = \Pr(W\pi > \epsilon)$. Therefore, from (12), $E(\ln \bar{y}_a | I > 0) = X\beta_a + E(u_1 | W\pi > \epsilon)$. Define $\rho_1 = \rho(u_1/\sigma_1, \epsilon/\sigma_\epsilon) = \sigma_{1\epsilon}/\sigma_1\sigma_\epsilon$. Then $E(\ln \bar{y}_a | I > 0) = X\beta_a + \sigma_1\rho_1 E(\epsilon/\sigma_\epsilon | \epsilon/\sigma_\epsilon < W\pi/\sigma_\epsilon) = X\beta_a + \sigma_1\rho_1[-f(W\pi/\sigma_\epsilon)/F(W\pi/\sigma_\epsilon)]$, where F is the cumulative normal density and f is its p.d.f. Define

$$\lambda_a = -f(W\pi/\sigma_\epsilon)/F(W\pi/\sigma_\epsilon) \qquad (17)$$

as the truncated mean (with truncation point $W\pi/\sigma_\epsilon$) of the normal density due to selection. Making use of the definition of ρ_1 and λ_a yields

$$E(\ln \bar{y}_a | I > 0) = X\beta_a + \frac{\sigma_{1\epsilon}}{\sigma_\epsilon}\lambda_a. \qquad (18)$$

A parallel argument for g_a, $\bar{y}_b$, and g_b yields

$$E(g_a | I > 0) = X\gamma_a + \frac{\sigma_{2\epsilon}}{\sigma_\epsilon}\lambda_a, \qquad (19)$$

$$E(\ln \bar{y}_b | I \leq 0) = X\beta_b + \frac{\sigma_{3\epsilon}}{\sigma_\epsilon}\lambda_b, \qquad (20)$$

---

11. For completeness, $-\epsilon$ should be redefined to take account of deviations between realizations and expectations at the time school decisions were made. Thus, let $\ln \bar{Y}_{ai} = \ln \bar{y}_{ai} + v_{1i}$, where $\bar{Y}_{ai}$ is realized initial earnings, $\bar{y}_{ai}$ is expected initial earnings, and v_{1i} is normally distributed forecast error. Similarly, forecast errors v_{2i}, v_{3i}, and v_{4i} are defined for g_{ai}, $\ln \bar{y}_{bi}$, and g_{bi}. Then the complete definition of $-\epsilon$ is obtained from replacing u_{ji} with $(u_{ji} + v_{ji})$, $j = 1, \ldots, 4$, in (15). Clearly this has no operational significance for the model, given the assumption of unbiased expectations.

and

$$E(g_b | I \le 0) = X\gamma_b + \frac{\sigma_{4\epsilon}}{\sigma_\epsilon} \lambda_b, \tag{21}$$

with

$$\lambda_b = E\left(\epsilon/\sigma_\epsilon \,\middle|\, \frac{\epsilon}{\sigma_\epsilon} > \frac{W\pi}{\sigma_\epsilon}\right) = f(W\pi/\sigma_\epsilon)/[1 - F(W\pi/\sigma_\epsilon)] \tag{22}$$

and

$$\sigma_{k\epsilon} = -[\alpha_1(\sigma_{1k} - \sigma_{3k}) + \alpha_2\sigma_{2k} + \alpha_3\sigma_{4k} + \alpha_5\sigma_{5k}], \quad k = 1, \ldots, 4. \tag{23}$$

Note from (17) that $\lambda_a \le 0$. Therefore the observed (conditional) means of initial earnings and rates of growth among persons in A are greater or less than their population means as $\sigma_{1\epsilon}$ and $\sigma_{2\epsilon} \gtrless 0$, from (18) and (19). Conversely, $\lambda_b \ge 0$ (see [22]), and there is positive or negative selection bias in initial earnings and growth rates for people observed in class B according to $\sigma_{3\epsilon}$ (and $\sigma_{4\epsilon}$) $\gtrless 0$. Since σ_{ij} is unrestricted, $\sigma_{k\epsilon}$ is also unrestricted, and selection bias can go in either way. In particular, it is possible that the bias is positive in both groups, consistent with the comparative-advantage argument sketched above. Positive bias in A and negative bias in B would be consistent with a singe-factor (hierarchical) interpretation of ability. Of course, neither finding yields a definitive "ability" interpretation because of the presence of expectational errors and financial factors (σ_{5k}) in (23): the assignments are based on talent, expectations, and wealth, not on talent alone.

Estimation

Consider the following regressions applied to observed data:

$$\begin{aligned}
\ln \bar{y}_a &= X\beta_a + \beta_a^*\lambda_a + \eta_1, \\
g_a &= X\gamma_a + \gamma_a^*\lambda_a + \eta_2, \\
\ln \bar{y}_b &= X\beta_b + \beta_b^*\lambda_b + \eta_3, \\
g_b &= X\gamma_b + \gamma_b^*\lambda_b + \eta_4.
\end{aligned} \tag{24}$$

Equations (18)–(21) suggest that β_a^* estimates $\sigma_{1\epsilon}/\sigma_\epsilon$, γ_a^* estimates $\sigma_{2\epsilon}/\sigma_\epsilon$, and so on. Including λ_a or λ_b in the regressions along with X corrects for truncation and selectivity bias, and $E(\eta_{ij}) = 0$ for $j = 1, \ldots, 4$. In addition, $E(\eta_{ij}^2)$ is heteroskedastic (see below), because the observations are truncated and at different points for different people. Equation (24) cannot be implemented directly because λ_a and λ_b are not known. However, it can be shown[12] that consistent estimates of (24) are obtained by replacing λ_a and λ_b with their values predicted from the reduced-form probit equation (16). These values are

$$\hat{\lambda}_{ai} = -f(W_i\widehat{\pi/\sigma_\epsilon})/F(W_i\widehat{\pi/\sigma_\epsilon}),$$
$$\hat{\lambda}_{bi} = f(W_i\widehat{\pi/\sigma_\epsilon})/[1 - F(W_i\widehat{\pi/\sigma_\epsilon})] \tag{25}$$

and are entered as least-squares regressors along with X_i. Estimation of (24) with λ_i replaced by $\hat{\lambda}_i$ corrects for selectivity bias in the observations. What is more interesting for the economic theory of educational choice is that these estimates provide a basis for estimating the structural selection rule or structural probit function (9) and (11). The structural probit is

$$\text{Pr (choose A)} = \text{Pr}\{[\alpha_0 + \alpha_1(\ln \bar{y}_a - \ln \bar{y}_b) + \alpha_2 g_a$$
$$+ \alpha_3 g_b + \alpha_4 Z\delta]/\sigma_\epsilon > \epsilon/\sigma_\epsilon\}, \tag{26}$$

from (9), (11), and (14). Use the consistent estimates of structural earnings and growth described above to predict earnings gains for each person in the sample according to

$$\ln (\widehat{\bar{y}_{ai}/\bar{y}_{bi}}) = X_i(\hat{\beta}_a - \hat{\beta}_b),$$
$$\hat{g}_{ai} = X_i\hat{\gamma}_a, \tag{27}$$
$$\hat{g}_{bi} = X_i\hat{\gamma}_b,$$

where $\hat{\beta}$ and $\hat{\gamma}$ are estimated by the method above.[13] These predicted values are inserted into (26) and estimated by the usual probit method to test the economic restrictions (10).[14]

---

12. See Heckman (1976) and Lee (1976).

13. This method is due to Lee (1978), who used it to study unionization status. Our model differs somewhat in that there is more than one structural equation in each classification.

14. Heckman (1976) and Lee (1977) show that OLS estimates of the standard errors of $\beta_a, \gamma_a, \beta_b, \gamma_b$ in (24) are biased if $\sigma_{k\epsilon}/\sigma_\epsilon \neq 0$ when estimated values of λ_b are used in place of their true values. Lee also shows that the usual estimates of standard errors for the structural probit (26) are biased when estimated values of $\ln(\bar{y}_a/\bar{y}_b)$, g_a, and g_b are used in place of their true values and derives exact asymptotic distributions for these parameters. We use Lee's (1977) results to compute consistent estimates of standard errors below.

Other Tests

Alternative estimates are available to serve as an internal consistency check on the model. In particular, the model can be specified using the observed level of earnings at time $\bar{t}$ and earnings growth instead of initial earnings. From (5) and (6) it follows that

$$\ln y_a(\bar{t}) = X_t(\beta_a + \gamma_a \bar{t}) + u_1 + \bar{t}u_2,$$
$$\ln y_b(\bar{t}) = X_t(\beta_b + \gamma_b \bar{t}) + u_3 + \bar{t}u_4. \tag{28}$$

Substitute for the level equations in (12) and (13) and this model also can be estimated as described above. However, now the structural probit is of the form

$$\Pr \ (A \text{ is chosen}) = \Pr(\{\theta_0 + \theta_1[\ln y_a(t) - \ln y_b(t)]$$
$$+ \theta_2 g_a + \theta_3 g_b\} + \theta_4 r/\sigma_\epsilon > \epsilon/\sigma_\epsilon). \tag{29}$$

Since $\ln y_a(\bar{t}) - \ln y_b(\bar{t}) = \ln \bar{y}_a - \ln \bar{y}_b + (g_a - g_b)\bar{t} - g_a S$, the following restrictions are implied:

$$\theta_1 = \alpha_1,$$
$$(\bar{t} - S)\theta_1 + \theta_2 + \alpha_2, \tag{30}$$
$$-\bar{t}\theta_1 + \theta_3 + \alpha_3.$$

Hence we have a check on the validity of the model. Of course, its main validation is the power to predict behavior and assignments on independent data.

Identification

Two natural questions regarding identification arise in this model.

1. Estimation of the selection rule or structural probit equation is possible only if the vectors X and Z have elements that are not in common. If X and Z are identical, the predicted values of $\ln \bar{y}_a - \ln \bar{y}_b$, g_a, and g_b are colinear with the other explanatory variables in (26), and its estimation is precluded. Note, however, that even if X and Z are identical, the reduced-form probit (16) is estimable, and it still may be possible to estimate initial earnings and growth-rate equations and selection bias. The reason is that, although the $\hat{\lambda}$ corrections in (24) are functions of the same variables that enter the $X\beta$ or $X\gamma$ parts of these equations, they are nonlinear functions of the measured variables. Structural earnings equations might be identified off the nonlinearity, though in any

particular application there may be insufficient nonlinearity, though in any particular application there may be insufficient nonlinearity if the range of variation in $W\pi$ (see [15]) is not large enough.[15]

In the general discussion of Section II, X was tentatively associated with measured abilities and Z with measured financial constraints (and tastes), corresponding to the Beckerian distinction between factors that shift the marginal rate of return to investment schedule and those that shift the marginal supply of funds schedule. Evidently, if one takes a sufficiently broad view of human investment and in particular of the role of child care in the new home economics, easy distinctions between the content of X and of Z become increasingly difficult, if not impossible, to make. If X and Z are indistinguishable, the economic theory of school choice has no empirical content. In the empirical work below a very strong dichotomy with no commonalities is maintained: X is specified as a vector of ability indicators and Z as a vector of family-background variables. This hypothesis is maintained for two reasons. First, it provides a test of the theory in its strongest form. Certainly if the theory is rejected in this form there is little hope for it. Second, there have been no systematic attempts to find empirical counterparts for the things that shift marginal rate of return and marginal cost of fund schedules that cause different people to choose different amounts of schooling. The validity of the theory rests on the possibility of actually being able to find an operational set of indicators, and this distinction is the most straightforward possibility.

---

15. Heckman (1979) raises some subtle issues regarding specification error in selection models. Elements of Z may be incorrectly specified in X and can be statistically significant in least-squares regressions because of truncation. Conversely, coefficients on selection-bias variables λ_a and λ_b can be significant because variables are incorrectly attributed to selection when they more properly belong directly in X. E.g., some might argue that family background belongs in structural earnings equations and our selectivity effects work (see below) because family background comes in the back door through its indirect effect on $\hat{\lambda}$. However, a reversal of the argument suggests that family-background variables might have significant estimated direct effects on earnings merely because they work through selection and resulting truncation. There is no statistically satisfactory way of resolving this problem. In any event, we cannot be "agnostic" about specification because both the economic and statistical theories require certain nontestable zero identifying restrictions. The problem is even more complicated in the present context because the theory is based on unobserved talent and financial constraint shifters and must have observable counterparts to be operational. Evidently choice among alternative specifications ultimately must rest on predictive performance outside the sample.

Given resolution of problem 1, not all parameters in the model can be estimated. Some are overidentified and some are underidentified. The selectivity-bias-corrected structural earnings equations (24) directly estimate β_a, β_b, γ_a, γ_b, and the structural probit (26) provides estimates of $(\alpha_1/\sigma_\epsilon, \alpha_2/\sigma_\epsilon, \alpha_3/\sigma_\epsilon, \alpha_4\delta/\sigma_\epsilon)$. Furthermore, from the approximations in (10), the coefficient on $\ln(\bar{y}_a/\bar{y}_b)$ in (26) estimates $1/\sigma_\epsilon$ (given that $\alpha_1 = 1$), so that it is possible to estimate population average real rates of interest. In addition, there are 15 parameters in the unobserved-component variance-covariance matrix Σ. Following a development similar to the one leading to (18)–(21), it can be shown that the variances of residuals in (24) are

$$\text{var}(\eta_{ij}) = \sigma_{jj} + \frac{\sigma_{j\epsilon}}{\sigma_\epsilon}\left(\frac{W_i\pi}{\sigma_\epsilon}\lambda_{ai} - \lambda_{ai}^2\right), j = 1, 2;$$

$$\text{var}(\eta_{ij}) = \sigma_{ij} + \frac{\sigma_{j\epsilon}}{\sigma_\epsilon}\left(\frac{W_i\pi}{\sigma_\epsilon}\lambda_{bi} - \lambda_{bi}^2\right), j = 3, 4. \tag{31}$$

Similar expressions hold for covariances between η_{i1} and η_{i2} and between η_{i3} and η_{i4}. Hence it is possible to estimate the own-population variances σ_{jj} for $j = 1, \ldots, 4$, two within-group covariances, and four covariances $\sigma_{j\epsilon}$ for $j = 1, \ldots, 4$. These, along with the estimate of σ_ϵ, provide only 11 statistics to estimate 15 parameters. Evidently all the covariance terms in Σ cannot be estimated without additional zero or other restrictions because we never observe the path not taken. This is the basis for the statement above that deadweight losses from assignments based jointly on wealth and talent rather than on talent alone cannot be imputed. The demand function for college attendance implicit in (26) reflects the joint density of talent, wealth, tastes, and expectations, and their separate effects cannot be disentangled.

IV. Estimation

The model has been estimated on a sample of 3,611 respondents to the NBER-Thorndike-Hagen survey of 1968–71.[16] These data refer to male World War II veterans who applied for the army air corps.

---

16. These data have been extensively analyzed by other investigators, especially Taubman (1975), who also discovered them. For complete documentation see NBER (1973).

They do not come from a random sample of the population, since the military screening criteria were based on certain aspects of ability and physical fitness. Therefore it is not possible to extrapolate these results to the population at large. However, the sample's advantages more than compensate for this. First, it covers more than 20 years of labor-market experience, far longer than any other panel of comparable size and most appropriate for measuring lifetime earnings effects of educational choice as the theory requires. Second, it contains extensive information on family background and talent. While several other panels are as good on family background, virtually none compare in their range of talent and ability indicators most appropriate to the theory of comparative advantage.

The sample actually used is a subset of 5,085 total respondents. Forty-two observations were dropped for not responding to the age question, another 480 persons were deleted because they were pilots, had extended military service, or did not report both initial ($\bar{y}$) and latest ($y[\bar{t}]$) earnings required for structural estimation. Definitions of variables are given in Appendix 6A. Individuals were put into two categories: group A represents those who entered college and group B those who stopped school after high school graduation. Not all members of group A completed college, and a substantial fraction completed more than a college education. They are labeled "college attendees" hereafter. Descriptive statistics appear in Table 6.1. Notice that more than 75 percent of the sample chose to attend college for some period, reflecting the unusual ability distribution in the sample and eligibility for a liberal school subsidy (the GI Bill). However, the presence of the GI Bill is common to both college attendees and high school graduates.

There are some obvious differences between the two groups. Both mean and relative variance of earnings in both years are smaller for high school graduates, as tends to be true in other samples. In addition, high school graduates had smaller earnings growth over the period, had more siblings and were lower in birth order than college attendees, and were more likely to have taken vocational training in high school. Their fathers had less schooling and were more likely to be blue-collar workers as well. Four ability measures have been chosen for analysis, out of some 16 indicators available in the data. Math and reading scores are related to IQ type of ability (in fact, it is known that math score is highly correlated with IQ score in these data), while the other two are more associated with manual skills. The four together

Table 6.1 • Descriptive statistics

Variable	High School (Group B)		More than High School (Group A)	
	Mean	SD	Mean	SD
Father's ED	8.671	2.966	10.26	3.623
Father's ED^2	83.99	55.53	118.4	78.09
DK ED	.0999	. . .	.0464	. . .
Manager	.3628	. . .	.4954	. . .
Clerk	.1239	. . .	.1450	. . .
Foreman	.2238	. . .	.1695	. . .
Unskilled	.1492	. . .	.0819	. . .
Farmer	.1062	. . .	.0720	. . .
DK job	.0177	. . .	.0124	. . .
Catholic	.2933	. . .	.2138	. . .
Jew	.0405	. . .	.0617	. . .
Old sibs	1.143	1.634	.9035	1.383
Young sibs	.9381	1.486	.8138	1.266
Mother works				
Full 5	.0468	. . .	.0486	. . .
Part 5	.0392	. . .	.0504	. . .
None 5	.7168	. . .	.7507	. . .
Full 14	.0822	. . .	.0936	. . .
Part 14	.0708	. . .	.0851	. . .
None 14	.6384	. . .	.6713	. . .
H.S. shop	.2592	. . .	.0908	. . .
Read	20.57	10.17	24.06	11.63
NR read	.0291	. . .	.0128	. . .
Mech	59.24	18.27	58.88	18.96
NR mech	.0025	. . .	0	. . .
Math	18.13	11.82	28.94	17.17
NR math	.0683	. . .	.0188	. . .
Dext	50.04	9.359	50.68	9.811
NR dext	0	. . .	.0071	. . .
Exp	29.33	2.439	24.54	2.907
Exp^2	866.1	147.1	610.4	147.4
S13–15	. . .	. . .	.3106	. . .

Table 6.1 • *(continued)*

Variable	High School (Group B)		More than High School (Group A)	
	Mean	SD	Mean	SD
S16	...	...	.3993	...
S20	...	...	.0823	...
Year 48	46.62	1.584	48.05	1.869
Year 69	69.11	.3691	69.08	.3437
ln $\bar{y}$	8.635	.4107	8.526	.3871
ln $y(\bar{t})$	9.326	.4573	9.639	.4904
g	.0309	.0251	.0535	.0283
λ_a	−1.2870	.2873	−.3193	.2256
λ_b	.4666	.3763	1.605	.5212
No. observations	791		2820	

Note: Variables are defined in Appendix 6A.

seem well suited to the comparative-advantage logic underlying the formulation of the model. High school graduates tend to score lower in the math and reading-comprehension tests, about the same in manual dexterity, and somewhat better on mechanical ability. In line with the previous discussion, all ability measures in Table 6.1 are assigned to X, while the family-background measures—reflecting financial constraints, tastes, and perceptions—are assigned to Z. Experience, school-completion dummies (for group A), and year of reported earnings are used exclusively as controls in structural earnings equations.

The first columns in Table 6.2 present estimated coefficients and asymptotic t-statistics of the reduced-form probit selection into group A—equation (16). These effects more or less parallel the summary of Table 6.1 given above. Math score has a particularly strong positive effect and mechanical score a strong negative effect on the college attendance decision. The effect of mother's working is somewhat unexpected. Mother's home time when the respondent was 5 years old or younger has virtually no effect on college attendance, whereas the respondent was more likely to go to college if his mother worked when

Table 6.2 • College selection rules—Probit analysis

Variable	Reduced Form (16) Coeff.	t	Structure (26) Coeff.	t	Structure (29) Coeff.	t
Constant	.0485	.20	.1512	.22	.1030	.17
Background						
Father's ED	−.0145	−.41	−.0168	−.54	−.0152	−.49
Father's ED^2	.0037	2.05	.0038	2.26	.0037	2.26
DK ED	−.4059	−3.96	−.3924	−2.79	−.4001	−2.91
Manager	.1897	2.17	.1825	2.13	.1871	2.21
Clerk	.0556	.54	.0561	.59	.0554	.59
Foreman	.0182	.19	.0210	.23	.0200	.22
Unskilled	−.0910	−.85	−.0948	−.89	−.0928	−.87
Farmer	−.2039	−2.12	−.2256	−2.27	−.2094	−2.14
DK job	−.0413	−.19	−.0629	−.29	−.0609	−.28
Catholic	−.1144	−1.91	−.0982	−1.51	−.1083	−1.66
Jew	−.0293	−.23	.0143	.12	−.0158	−.14
Old sibs	−.0162	−.93	−.0162	−.93	−.0161	−.93
Young sibs	.0122	.63	.0096	.49	.0112	.57
Mother works						
Full 5	.1039	.66	.1168	.81	.1104	.76
Part 5	.2179	1.42	.2106	1.52	.2156	1.56
None 5	.0655	.63	.0677	.65	.0661	.64
Full 14	.2898	2.29	.2884	2.30	.2888	2.33
Part 14	.2709	2.20	.2768	2.02	.2693	2.03
None 14	.1980	1.91	.1990	1.92	.1966	1.92
H.S. shop	−.4411	−6.14	−.4397	−3.74	−.4379	−3.90
Ability						
Read	.0047	1.67	. . .	. . .	. . .	. . .
NR read	−.2575	−1.41	. . .	. . .	. . .	. . .
Mech	−.0070	−4.29	. . .	. . .	. . .	. . .
NR mech	−3.0236	−1.04	. . .	. . .	. . .	. . .
Math	.0244	12.34	. . .	. . .	. . .	. . .
NR math	−.7539	−5.75	. . .	. . .	. . .	. . .
Dext	.0019	.72	. . .	. . .	. . .	. . .
NR dext	2.2797	.47	. . .	. . .	. . .	. . .

Table 6.2 • *(continued)*

Variable	Reduced Form (16)		Structure (26)		Structure (29)	
	Coeff.	t	Coeff.	t	Coeff.	t
Earnings						
$\ln(\bar{y}_n/\bar{y}_b)$	...	...	5.1486	2.25	...	...
g_a	...	...	138.3850	1.83	7.6632	.11
g_b	...	...	−44.2697	−1.28	71.8981	2.34
$\ln y_a(t)/y_b(t)$	...	...	...	...	5.1501	2.57
Observations	3611		3611		3611	
Limit observations	791		791		791	
Nonlimit observations	2820		2820		2820	
−2 ln (likelihood ratio)	579.5		568.8		576.6	
χ^2 degree freedom	28		23		23	

Note: t is asymptotic *t*-statistic; DK: Don't know, dummy variable; NR: No response, dummy variable; other variables are defined in Appendix 6A.

he was 6–14 years of age. This is more supportive of market investment through relaxation of financial constraints than of home investments in kind.[17]

Structural estimates of earnings and growth equations corrected for selection are found in Table 6.3. These are somewhat different from the typical earnings equations found in the literature, because they include a much sparser set of regressors. For example, we know respondents' unemployment experience, weeks worked, weeks ill, marital status, and so forth but have not included them in the regressions. The logic of this lies in the model itself: at the time the college attendance decision was made, there is no reason to expect that respondents knew the outcomes of such variables. It is more in the spirit of the choice framework of

17. Recall that female labor-force participation during the war increased. The normalized category for mother's work classifications is nonresponse. We do not know how many did not respond because no mother was in the home.

Table 6.3 • Structural earnings estimates: Equations (24) and (28), OLS

Regressor	$\ln \bar{y}_a$ (1)	$\ln \bar{y}_b$ (2)	g_a (3)	g_b (4)	$\ln y_a(\bar{t})$ (5)	$\ln y_a(\bar{t})$ (6)
	Dependent variable					
Constant	8.7124 (16.51)	2.8901 (1.37)	.1261 (3.90)	.2517 (2.11)	10.3370 (5.52)	7.5328 (2.08)
Read	.0009 (1.21)	−.0019 (−1.17)	.0001 (1.11)	.0003 (3.20)	.0027 (2.80)	.0057 (3.28)
NR read	.0791 (1.24)	.0506 (.58)	−.0034 (−.76)	−.0046 (−.89)	.0033 (.04)	−.0402 (−.42)
Mech	−.0002 (−.48)	−.0005 (−.54)	−.0001 (−2.16)	−.0001 (−1.13)	−.0021 (−3.59)	−.0017 (−1.73)
NR mech	. . .	.1969 (.69)	. . .	.0002 (.01)	. . .	.2196 (.68)
Math	.0015 (2.02)	−.0013 (.74)	.0001 (1.18)	−.0000 (−.20)	.0030 (3.31)	−.0019 (−1.00)
NR math	−.1087 (−1.94)	.0562 (.83)	.0015 (.38)	.0006 (.15)	−.0877 (−1.24)	.0712 (.96)
Dext	.0008 (1.03)	−.0019 (−1.21)	−.0000 (−.78)	.0003 (2.77)	.0002 (.16)	.0036 (2.19)
NR dext	.0751 (.28)	. . .	−.0004 (−.02)	. . .	.1466 (.43)	. . .
Exp	−.0523 (−1.49)	.4260 (3.10)	−.0028 (−1.11)	−.0154 (−1.93)	−.0129 (−.29)	.0776 (.53)
Exp^2	.0015 (2.22)	−.0067 (−2.95)	.0000 (.21)	.0002 (1.82)	−.0000 (−.01)	−.0012 (−.49)
Year 48	−.0020 (−.48)	−.0156 (−1.72)	. . .	. . .	. . .	. . .
Year 69	. . .	. . .	. . .	. . .	−.0067 (−.26)	.0039 (.09)
S13–15	.1288 (5.15)	. . .	−.0062 (−3.49)	. . .	.0168 (.52)	. . .
S16	.0760 (3.82)	. . .	.0026 (1.79)	. . .	.1095 (4.26)	. . .
S20	.1318 (4.10)	. . .	.0049 (2.13)	. . .	.2560 (6.15)	. . .

Table 6.3 • *(continued)*

Regressor	$\ln \bar{y}_a$ (1)	$\ln \bar{y}_b$ (2)	g_a (3)	g_b (4)	$\ln y_a(\bar{t})$ (5)	$\ln y_a(\bar{t})$ (6)
	Dependent variable					
λ_a	−.1069 (−3.21)	...	.0058 (2.45)	...	.0206 (.49)	...
λ_b	...	−.0558 (−.66)	...	.0118 (2.39)	...	.2267 (2.48)
R^2	.0750	.0439	.1578	.0513	.0740	.0358

Note: NR: No response, dummy variable; other variables are defined in Appendix 6A; t-values are shown in parentheses.

the model to allow these "current" events to be captured indirectly via their correlations with included variables in order to estimate expected or anticipated values relevant to the structural probit.[18] The problem is more difficult in the case of school-completion differences among members of group A in Table 6.3 and, in truth, raises an unresolvable aggregation problem. The anticipations argument above suggests that school-completion differences within group A may not enter the earnings equations, so that included variables pick up average completion experience in the sample. Alternatively, it can be argued that the level of schooling achieved within group A should be controlled by including school-completion dummies. This latter specification is reported in Table 6.3 and is the one used to estimate the structural probit in Table 6.2. Of course we do not switch on the school-completion dummies to estimate the earnings advantages of college attendance, since that would clearly stack the deck in favor of finding strong financial effects. Earnings and structural probit equations were also estimated with school dummied deleted, and the results were very similar to those reported here. However, it is clear that this issue only can

---

18. A related and thorough discussion of this issue appears in Hanoch (1967), to which the reader is referred. It has not escaped our attention that current variables such as hours of work and unemployment experience might serve as indicators of an unobserved "taste for leisure" component, but we have not experimented with that possibility.

be resolved by going into a more disaggregated model with multiple classifications.

With the exception of experience, most of the variables have little effect on initial earnings in either A or B (see cols. 1 and 2 of Table 6.3).[19] Experience effects are the strongest and are known to be most important at early and late stages of career patterns, facts borne out in these data since experience has little effect on later (surveyed around 1969) earnings. The ability measure that has the largest effect on initial earnings is math score for college attendees. Ability indicators are more important for earnings growth (cols. 3 and 4) and later earnings (cols. 4 and 5). Dexterity and reading scores have positive effects on g_b and $y_b(\bar{t})$, while math and reading scores have positive effects on $\ln y_a(\bar{t})$ but exhibit much weaker effects on earnings growth. Interestingly enough, the effect on mechanical score is negative in all cases, raising obvious questions about what it is that this test supposedly measures (recall, however, the sample truncation on high-ability military personnel). Even so, it seems to have a more important negative effect for members of group A. This, along with the results for dexterity and math scores, lends support to the comparative-advantage hypothesis.

Selectivity biases are particularly interesting in that regard. The coefficients of λ_b show no selectivity bias for initial earnings of high school graduates, but positive bias for growth rates. Therefore, observed earnings patterns of high school graduates show higher rates of growth compared with the pattern that would have been observed for the average member of this sample had he chosen not to continue school. On the other hand, the coefficients of λ_a show positive selection bias for initial earnings of college attendees and negative bias for earnings growth. The latter is due to the fact that there are no selection effects for late earnings. Thus the observed earnings pattern among members of group A is everywhere higher than the population mean pattern would have been and converges toward the population mean late earnings level. *Posi-*

---

19. Initial earnings is recall data from the 1955 Thorndike survey and refers to a period as much as 9 years prior to that survey date. Late earnings is closer to the NBER survey date and probably has less recall error in it. The low R^2 statistics in Table 6.3 are due to the fact at we are looking at within-group variation, whereas most results in the literature get a lot of mileage out of current variables and explanation of between-group mean variation. It is also worth noting that the standard errors in the earnings and growth equations computed from the exact asymptotic distribution reported in the table are virtually identical with those estimated by OLS.

tive selection among both A and B also lends support to comparative advantage.

The most novel empirical results are the structural probit estimates in Table 6.2, which show how anticipated earnings gains affect the decision to attend college. The predicted earnings variables are statistically significant except for g_b in (26) and g_a in (29).[20] More striking, however, is the agreement of the sign patterns predicted by the theory (see eq. [10] and recall that the structural probit coefficients are normalized by σ_ϵ, from [26] and [29]). The model passes two internal consistency checks. The first is restriction (30). Working backward to normalized α estimates from directly estimated θ's in column 5 of Table 6.2 yields[21] a predicted (α/σ_ϵ) vector of (5.15, 155.90, −52.68), which is similar to the direct estimates in column 3 of (5.15, 138.39, −44.27). Working forward from actual estimates of normalized α to predicted estimates of θ gives prediction (5.15, 37.04, 80.31), compared with actual (5.15, 7.66, 71.90). These comparisons probably would not be so close if the two-parameter approximation to earnings patterns in (5) and (6) was not reasonably good. Second, equations (15) and (26) indicate that estimated coefficients on the Z variables in structural and reduced-form probits should be the same. Direct comparison of coefficients of Z in Table 6.2 shows extremely close similarity of $\alpha_4\delta$ in all three equations. In sum, the results give direct, internally consistent evidence on the validity of the economic theory of the demand for schooling derived

---

20. Recall (n. 14) that the t-statistics for the structural probit in Table 6.2 are based on consistent estimates of the standard errors, as suggested by Lee (1977). The t-statistics on background variables are not very different from the biased values computed by a standard probit algorithm. However, the t-statistics on the predicted earnings and growth variables are substantially reduced when corrected for bias; e.g., the standard probit estimates of t-values for $\ln(\bar{y}_a/\bar{y}_b)$, g_a, and g_b in (26) are (10.8, 8.15, −4.81), compared with the unbiased values of (2.25, 1.83, −1.28) in Table 6.2.

21. There are two ways of estimating $\bar{t}$ and $(\bar{t} - S)$ for these computations. First, a direct estimate of $\bar{t} - S$ is obtained as the difference between average year of 1969 job and average year of initial job for members of group A in Table 6.1. A direct estimate of $\bar{t}$ is the average difference between 1969 job and initial job for members of group B. However, an independent estimate of S is the average years of schooling among members of group A minus 12.0. Hence another estimate of $(\bar{t} - S)$ is the direct estimate of $(\bar{t} - S)$ minus the direct estimate of S; and another estimate of $(\bar{t} - S)$ is the direct estimate of $\bar{t}$ minus the direct estimate of S. The two estimates for each parameter were averaged for purposes of these checks. They are 24.19 for $\bar{t}$ and 19.68 for $(\bar{t} - S)$.

from its (private) investment value. The economic hypothesis cannot be rejected.

V. Conclusions

The structural probit estimates of Table 6.2 support the economic hypothesis that expected gains in life earnings influence the decision to attend college. They also show important effects of financial constraints and tastes working through family-background indicators, a finding in common with most other studies of school choice.[22] Availability of the GI Bill might well be expected to dull the observed monetary effects, but they remain strong enough to persist for a significant fraction of the sample.

The estimates also show positive sorting or positive selection bias in observed earnings of both high school graduates and college attendees. To be clear about the implications of these results it is necessary to distinguish between the effects of measured abilities and unmeasured components on earnings prospects in A or B. The selection results refer to unmeasured components of variance. If we examine a subpopulation of persons with given measured abilities (i.e., with the same values of X in [12] and [13]), the empirical results on selectivity imply that those persons who stopped schooling after high school had better prospects as high school graduates than the average member of that subpopulation and that those who continued on to college also had better prospects there than the average member of the subpopulation. That is, the average earnings at most points in the life cycle of persons with given measured characteristics who actually chose B exceeded what earnings would have been for those persons (with the same characteristics) who chose A instead. Conversely, average earnings for those who actually chose A were greater than what earnings would have been for measurably similar people who actually chose B had they continued their schooling instead. This is a much different picture than emerges from the usual discussions of ability bias in

---

22. See Radner and Miller (1970) and Kohn, Manski, and Mundel (1976) for logit models of college choice. These models contain more detail in personal and college attributes but do not make any attempt to assess the effects of anticipated earnings in college attendance decisions. See Abowd (1977) for another approach to the selection problem focusing on school quality.

the literature, based on hierarchical or one-factor ability considerations. The one-factor model implies that persons who would do better than average in A would also do better than average in B. That is, positive selectivity bias in B cannot occur int he strict hierarchical model.[23]

The most attractive and simplest interpretation is the theory of comparative advantage, because hierarchical assignments are not observed. While the results are consistent with comparative advantage, they do not prove the case because life-persistent luck and random extraneous opportunities could have played just as important roles in the observed assignments as differential talents did. For all we know, those who decided to stop school after high school may have married the boss's daughter instead, or made better career connections in the military, and so forth. The important point is that their prospects in B were higher than average.

As noted above, the population average rate of discount, $\bar{r}$, is an identifiable statistic in the model. Estimates are obtained by applying restriction (10) to the estimates in Table 6.2. Maintain the hypothesis that $\alpha_1 = 1$. Then the estimated coefficient of $\ln(\bar{y}_a/\bar{y}_b)$ in Table 6.2 estimates $(1/\sigma_\epsilon)$, from equation (26). Since all the equations of the structural probit are normed by σ_ϵ this estimate provides a basis for estimating the population parameters in (10).

Straightforward computations using the structural probit estimates (26) in Table 6.2 yield

$$\begin{aligned}(\bar{r} - \bar{g}_a) &= .0372, \\ (\bar{r} - \bar{g}_b) &= .1163.\end{aligned} \tag{32}$$

Estimates of $\bar{g}_a$ and $\bar{g}_b$ are necessary to impute values of $\bar{r}$, and a slight ambiguity arises because the growth rates are functions of measured characteristics (see [12] and [13]). For illustrative purposes we use the

---

23. It should be emphasized that the special nature of this sample makes it impossible to extrapolate this result to the entire population. The reason is that the selection criteria for sample eligibility were established by entrance requirements into the army and our sample is a subset of those who volunteered for the air corps. It is possible to conceive of systematic truncation and selection rules by the military that would support the comparative-advantage argument in this subset, even though roughly hierarchical talents and positive correlations among alternative income prospects might well characterize the population at large.

overall sample mean values of characteristics (the X's) to impute $\bar{g}_a$ and $\bar{g}_b$ from the structural earnings in Table 6.3, purged of selectivity bias. The average person in the sample would have obtained growth rates $\bar{g}_a = .0591$ and $\bar{g}_b = .0262$ in A and B, respectively. The population mean discount rate, $\bar{r}$, is overidentified. The first equation of (32) yields an estimate of $\bar{r} = .0963$, while the second gives $\bar{r} = .1425$. Two more estimates of $\bar{r}$ are implied by the structural probit that uses the late earnings difference rather than the initial earnings differences. These are $\bar{r} = .0981$ and $\bar{r} = .1240$. Even if the precise derivation and specification of the model in Section III strain the reader's credulity, it is nonetheless clear that the structural specification is consistent with more casual derivations, and the estimated sign patterns in the structural probit, if not the precise restrictions among coefficients, would be predicted by virtually any economic model.

The positivity of earnings selection effects in both groups also implies that selection bias in simple rate of return estimates could go in either direction. The following procedure gives a rough and ready indication in this sample. First the two-parameterization of earnings in (5) and (6) implies that the average internal rate of return, i, is estimated by $\ln(y_a/y_b) + \ln(i - g_b) - \ln(i - g_a) - iS = 0$, where i is the rate of discount that equates average present values. Using sample mean values of $\bar{y}_a, \bar{y}_b, g_a,$ and g_b in Table 6.1 and a schooling increment of 4.11 years yields a simple unadjusted rate of return of $i = 9.0$ percent. This is comparable to the statistic usually presented in rate of return studies that make no allowance for differential ability between high school and college graduates. Several adjustments must be made to this number, however. First, correcting for selectivity alone yields an adjusted mean rate of return of $i = 9.8$ percent, which is actually larger, not smaller, than the observed mean rate of return. The 9.8 percent figure is obtained by subtracting the selectivity bias corrections from the observed sample means of $\bar{y}_a, \bar{y}_b, g_a,$ and g_b and in principle could be larger or smaller than the unadjusted figure due to positive selection in both A and B. It does not make any allowance for differential measured ability effects between the two groups. A more meaningful computation in the context of the model is to use measured abilities and the parameters of the corrected earnings and growth-rate functions to answer the following question: what is the expected rate of return to college of the typical person who chose A as compared to the expected rate of return of the typical person who chose B? This is a "standardized" comparison:

the rates of return differ between the typical A person and the typical B person because their measured abilities differ and because the values of these abilities (the regression coefficients in Table 6.3) differ in A or B. Assuming that persons with the average characteristics of those who chose B would have exhibited the same values of experience and initial year of earnings as those who actually chose A and vice versa, the average rate of return for persons of type A is 9.9 percent, while the average is 9.3 percent for persons of type B. Thus those who actually chose A had measured abilities that were more valuable in A than did those who actually chose B.

Predictions

The model passes the test of empirical verification of its structural restrictions. How well does it do in predicting assignments on independent data? The sample used is not a random drawing of the U.S. population and for this reason cannot be extrapolated to the population at large. However, only a subset of the NBER-Thorndike-Hagen sample was used to estimate it, and the remaining remnant is more likely to be a suitable group for prediction purposes. The remnant refers to those who did not report initial earnings. For this reason it may not be a random sample of the relevant population either. And while there is no reason to suppose that the censoring of initial earnings was systematically related to the selection mechanism of the model, it should be noted that a somewhat smaller proportion of these individuals (66 percent of them) chose to attend college than in the sample used for structural estimation.

One indirect test of the model's predictive content has been calculated. Fist, the reduced-form probit was reestimated for the remnant, which does not involve extrapolations, since the sample selection between A and B and the content of $W = [X, Z]$ is known for these people. Results appear in Appendix 6B. While there is some conformity with Table 6.2, there are also many differences between reduced-form estimates in the two samples. In short, family-background coefficients are not too stable.

The second experiment involves an extrapolation. Both initial earnings differences and growth rates were predicted for members of the remnant sample from the structural earnings estimates of Table 6.3 and then used to reestimate the structural probit of this group (no t-statistics are reported for structural probit coefficients because of the large expense of doing so). The results also appear in Appendix 6B. The sign reversals on family-background indicators carry over to these estimates too, though the coefficients and signs of the Z variables in the structural estimates are very close to those found in the reduced-form estimates in Appendix 6B. However, the coefficients on the earnings differences and growth rates for the remnant sample are very close to those estimated for the original sample of Table 6.2.

Enrollment Functions

Perhaps the simplest and most useful summary of the results is obtained from the demand function for college attendance implicit in the structural probit estimates. Recalling the definition of the index function in (9), the probability of attending college is given by Pr (A is chosen) $= F(I/\sigma_\epsilon)$, where F is the standard normal c.d.f. Let m denote the size of the relevant population, and let N represent the number choosing to attend college. Then the number enrolled in college is given by

$$N = mF(I/\sigma_\epsilon). \tag{33}$$

This would be equivalent to a supply function of graduates were it not for the aggregation involved in group A. The supply of graduates is somewhat different since we do not know how long people outside the sample would stay in school. The normality assumptions imply that the enrollment function (33) follows the cumulative normal curve. It therefore has zero elasticity at its extremes and positive elasticities in between. The major point of interest here is responsiveness of enrollments to earnings opportunities near the sample mean. From the definitions of present value in Section III, note that dln (V_a/V_b)/dln $(\bar{y}_a/\bar{y}_b) = 1$. A 1 percent change in relative initial earnings changes relative capital values by 1 percent. To clarify a possible point of confusion on this conceptual experiment, dln $(\bar{y}_a/\bar{y}_b)$ represents a permanent—not a transitory—change in lifetime prospects, because it increases relative differences between potential earnings in A compared with B not only initially but forevermore (see [5] and [6]). Differentiating (33) yields an elasticity formula

$$\text{dln } N/\text{dln } (\bar{y}_a/\bar{y}_b) = [F'(I/\sigma_\epsilon)(\alpha_1/\sigma_\epsilon)]/F(I/\sigma_\epsilon),$$

where I/σ_ϵ is evaluated at the desired sample proportion. For example, the elasticity evaluated at a sample proportion of .5 (half in A and half in B) is 4.1. On the other hand, the initial earnings elasticity at the observed sample proportion is 1.94, still a substantial response given the presence of marked diversity in the population. By way of comparison, an increment of father's education of 1.59 years (the difference in means of father's schooling between groups in Table 6.1) elicits a relative response of .0337.

Appendix 6A: Definitions of Variables for Tables

Father's ED	Father's years of school. Nonresponse assigned mean.
Father's ED^2	Square of Father's ED.
DK ED	Dummy variable: 1 if respondent did not know father's education.
Manager	Dummy variable: 1 if father was a businessman, manager, or professional.
Clerk	Dummy variable: 1 if father had white-collar occupation other than those in management.
Foreman	Dummy variable: 1 if father was a foreman, supervisor, or skilled craftsman.
Unskilled	Dummy variable: 1 if father was semiskilled operative or unskilled laborer.
Farmer	Dummy variable: 1 if father was a farmer.
DK job	Dummy variable: 1 if respondent did not know father's occupation.
Catholic	Dummy variable: 1 if respondent is Catholic.
Jew	Dummy variable: 1 if respondent is Jewish.
Old sibs	Number of older siblings.
Young sibs	Number of younger siblings.
Mother works:	
Full 5	Dummy variable: 1 if mother worked full time when respondent was less than 6 years of age.
Part 5	Dummy variable: 1 if mother worked part time when respondent was less than 6 years of age.
None 5	Dummy variable: 1 if mother did not work when respondent was less than 6 years of age.
Full 14	Dummy variable: 1 if mother worked full time when respondent was 6–14 years of age.

Mother works:

Part 14	Dummy variable: 1 if mother worked part time when respondent was 6–14 years of age.
None 14	Dummy variable: 1 if mother did not work when respondent was 6–14 years of age.
H.S. shop	Dummy variable: 1 if respondent majored in vocational courses in high school.
Read	Raw score on college undergraduate level reading comprehension test. Continuous variable, nonrespondents assigned mean.
NR read	Dummy variable: 1 if reading score not reported.
Mech	Raw score on pictorial representation of mechanical problem test. Continuous variable, nonrespondents assigned mean.
NR mech	Dummy variable: 1 if mechanical score not reported.
Math	Raw score on mathematics test (performance in advanced arithmetic, algebra, and trigonometry). Continuous variable, nonrespondents assigned mean.
NR math	Dummy variable: 1 if math score not reported.
Dext	Score on test of finger dexterity. Continuous variable, nonrespondents assigned mean.
NR dext	Dummy variable: 1 if dexterity score not reported.
Exp	Continuous variable: Age − Schooling − 6.
Exp^2	Square of Exp.
S13–15	Dummy variable: 1 if respondent received 13–15 years of school.
S16	Dummy variable: 1 if respondent received 16 years of school.
S20	Dummy variable: 1 if respondent received 20 or more years of school.
Year 48	Year in which initial postwar earnings are reported. Continuous variable.
Year 69	Year in which earnings at time of NBER survey are reported. Continuous variable.
$\ln \bar{y}$	Log of earnings on first job after finishing school, in 1967 prices.
$\ln y(t)$	Log of earnings at time of NBER survey in 1967 prices.
g	(ln earn 69 − ln earn 48) ÷ (Year 69 − Year 48) percentage rate of growth between the two observations.
λ_a	See equation (17), based on estimates in Table 6.2, column 1.
λ_b	See equation (22), based on estimates in Table 6.2, column 1.

Appendix 6B

College selection rules—Probit analysis (independent subsample of individuals with no report on initial earnings)

Variable	Reduced Form (16) Coefficient	*t*	Structure (26) Coefficient	Structure (29) Coefficient
Constant	−.4424	−.986	−.1170	−.1514
Background				
Father's ED	−.0183	.27	.0131	.0123
Father's ED^2	.0020	.61	.0023	.0023
DK ED	−.2645	−1.69	−.2548	−.2608
Manager	.2009	1.50	.1689	.1768
Clerk	.1664	.92	.1523	.1490
Foreman	−.1276	−.83	−.1359	−.1369
Unskilled	−.3118	−1.79	−.3298	.3260
Farmer	.1353	.75	.1174	−.1332
DK job	−.3515	−1.04	−.3133	−.3426
Catholic	−.0887	−.80	−.0847	−.1024
Jew	−.2169	−.95	−.1879	−.2159
Old sibs	.0335	1.02	.0343	.0336
Young sibs	.0191	.56	.0170	.0176
Mother works				
Full 5	−.6039	−2.06	−.6080	−.6080
Part 5	−.0470	−.18	−.0409	−.0351
None 5	−.0200	−.11	−.0345	−.0248
Full 14	.1656	.67	.1747	.1764
Part 14	−.1248	−.58	−.1258	−.1310
None 14	−.0581	−.31	−.0360	.0448
H.S. shop	−.5387	−3.95	−.5436	−.5395
Ability				
Read	.0056	1.07	...	...
NR read	.2393	.74	...	...
Mech	−.0480	−1.64	...	...
NR mech	...	...	...	
Math	.0251	6.80	...	...
NR math	−.4775	−2.15	...	...
Dext	.0050	1.03	...	...
NR dext	...	...	...	...

Appendix 6B • *(continued)*

Variable	Reduced Form (16) Coefficient	*t*	Structure (26) Coefficient	Structure (29) Coefficient
Earnings				
$\ln(\bar{y}_a/\bar{y}_b)$	...	...	4.9674	...
g_a	...	...	122.1460	−1.8761
g_b	...	...	−34.8393	76.4555
$\ln y_a(t)/y_b(t)$	...	...	...	4.8837
Observations	952		952	952
Limit observations	321		321	321
Nonlimit observations	631		631	631
−2 ln (likelihood ratio)	184.446		179.419	184.446
χ^2 degree freedom	...		...	...

Note: *t* is asymptotic *t*-statistic; DK: Don't know, dummy variable; NR: No response, dummy variable; other variables are defined in Appendix 6A.

References

Abowd, John M. "An Econometric Model of the U.S. Market for Higher Education." Ph.D. dissertation, Univ. Chicago, 1977.

Becker, Gary S. *Human Capital.* 2d ed. New York: Nat. Bur. Econ. Res., 1975.

Blaug, Mark. "The Empirical Status of Human Capital Theory: A Slightly Jaundiced Survey." *J. Econ. Literature* 14 (September 1976): 827–55.

Freeman, Richard. *The Market for College Trained Manpower: A Study in the Economics of Career Choice.* Cambridge, Mass.: Harvard Univ. Press, 1971.

Friedman, Milton, and Kuznets, Simon. *Income from Independent Professional Practice.* New York: Nat. Bur. Econ. Res., 1945.

Griliches, Zvi. "Estimating the Returns to Schooling: Some Econometric Problems." *Econometrica* 45 (January 1977): 1–22.

Griliches, Zvi; Hall, B.; and Hausman, Jerry. "Missing Data and Self-Selection in Large Panels." Discussion Paper no. 573, Harvard Inst. Econ. Res., 1977.

Hanoch, Giora. "An Economic Analysis of Earnings and Schooling." *J. Human Resources* 2, no. 3 (1967): 310–29.

Hause, J. "The Fine Structure of Earnings and the On-the-Job-Training Hypothesis." Mimeographed. Univ. Minnesota, 1977.

Hausman, Jerry, and Wise, D. "A Conditional Probit Model for Qualitative Choice. *Econometrica* 46 (March 1978): 403–26.

Heckman, James J. "The Common Structure of Statistical Models of Truncation, Sample Selection and Limited Dependent Variables and a Simple Estimator for Such Models." *Ann. Econ. and Soc. Measurement* 5 (Fall 1976): 475–92.

———— "Sample Selection Bias as a Specification Error." In *Female Labor Supply: Theory and Estimation,* edited by J. P. Smith. Princeton, N.J.: Princeton Univ. Press, 1979.

Kenny, L.; Lee, L.; Maddala, G. S.; and Trost, R. "Returns to College Education: An Investigation of Self-Selection Bias in Project Talent Data." *Internat. Econ. Rev.* (in press).

Kohn, M. G.; Manski, C. F.; and Mundel, D. S. "An Empirical Investigation of Factors Which Influence College-going Behavior." *Ann. Econ. and Soc. Measurement* 5 (Fall 1976): 391–420.

Lazear, Edward. "Age, Experience and Wage Growth." *A.E.R.* 66 (September 1976): 548–58.

Lee, Lung Fei. "Estimation of Limited Dependent Variables Models by Two-Stage Methods." Ph.D. dissertation, Univ. Rochester, 1976.

———— "On the Asymptotic Distributions of Some Two-Stage Consistent Estimators: Unionism and Wage Rates Revisited." Mimeographed. Univ. Minnesota, 1977.

———— "Unionism and Wage Rates: A Simultaneous Equations Model with Qualitative and Limited Dependent Variables." *Internat. Econ. Rev.* 19 (June 1978): 415–33.

Lillard, L., and Willis, Robert. "Dynamic Aspects of Earnings Mobility." *Econometrica* 46, no. 5 (1978): 985–1012.

McFadden, D. "Conditional Logit Analysis of Qualitative Choice Behavior." In *Frontiers in Econometrics,* edited by P. Zarembka. New York: Academic Press, 1973.

Maddala, G. S. "Self-Selectivity Problems in Econometric Models." In *Applications in Statistics,* edited by P. R. Krishnaia. Amsterdam, North-Holland, 1977.

Mandelbrot, Benoit. "Paretian Distributions and Income Maximization." *Q.J.E.* 76 (February 1960): 57–85.

Mincer, Jacob. *Schooling, Experience and Earnings.* New York: Nat. Bur. Econ. Res., 1974.

National Bureau of Economic Research. "The Comprehensive NBER-TH Tape Documentation." Mimeographed. March 1973.

Radner, Roy, and Miller, L. S. "Demand and Supply in U.S. Higher Education." *A.E.R.* 60 (May 1970): 326–34.

Rosen, Sherwin. "Human Capital: Relations between Education and Earnings." In *Frontiers of Quantitative Economics,* edited by Michael D. Intriligator. Vol. 3*B*. Amsterdam, North-Holland, 1977.

———— "Substitution and Division of Labour." *Economica* 45 (August 1978): 235–50.

Roy, Andrew D. "Some Thoughts on the Distribution of Earnings." *Oxford Econ. Papers,* n.s. 3 (June 1951): 135–46.

Taubman, Paul. *Sources of Inequality of Earnings.* Amsterdam: North-Holland, 1975.

Weiss, Yoram, and Lillard, Lee A. "Experience, Vintage, and Time Effects in the Growth of Earnings: American Scientists, 1960–1970." *J.P.E.* 86, no. 3 (June 1978): 427–47.

Wise, D. "Academic Achievement and Job Performance." *A.E.R.* 65 (June 1975): 350–66.

Zabalza, A. "The Determinants of Teacher Supply." Mimeographed. London School Econ., 1977.

7

Specialization and Human Capital

It is no accident that Smith begins *The Wealth of Nations* with a discussion of the division of labor. The enormous productivity and complexity of modern economies are in good measure attributable to specialization. It is the sine qua non of decentralization and coordination of economic activity through trade, and economics would be a very dull subject without it. This is so basic that it is largely taken for granted now. The gains from labor market specialization that arise from different endowments and the principle of comparative advantage (or, in modern labor economics terminology, from heterogeneity and selection [Rosen 1978]) have been understood since Babbage (1832). Yet Smith himself minimized the role of endowed differences. Instead, he concentrated on factors that are regarded today as cases of increasing returns.[1] The purpose of this note is to point out that incentives for specialization are promoted by another type of increasing return to human capital accumulation.

The return to investment in a particular skill is increasing in its subsequent rate of utilization because investment costs are independent of how acquired skills are employed. This element of fixed costs of investment makes it advantageous to specialize investment resources to a narrow band of skills and employ them as intensively as possible. Increasing returns to utilization are the main private incentives for specialization.

The argument is illustrated for two skills, k_1 and k_2. Human capital augments the efficiency of a person's time in each activity. Let t_i represent

I am indebted to Jose Scheinkman, Robert Topel, and Robert Barro for helpful discussions and to the National Science Foundation for financial support.

From *Journal of Labor Economics* 1, no. 1 (1983): 43–49. © 1983 by The University of Chicago. All rights reserved.

1. The list includes improved dexterity of workers, avoidance of setup costs, and a greater pace of labor-saving innovations. Rosenberg (1976) also attributes to Smith the idea that specialization results in larger gains through enhanced personal reputation, but that too rests on an informational scale economy.

the amount of time allocated to skill i. Then the amount of useful work a person supplies to activity i is $t_i k_i$, measured in efficiency units. Imagine competitive labor markets under stationary conditions which establish efficiency wage rates in each skill. Let w_i denote these wages discounted to present value. Then the worker's gross human capital value in Activity i is $w_i t_i k_i$.

It is always something of a nuisance to formulate workable representations of human capital investment costs. Since those issues are well known and divert attention away from the main point, abstract from life-cycle considerations and represent investment costs by a convex function $C(k_1, k_2)$. Assume strictly increasing marginal costs of investment in each skill: $C_{ii} > 0$. Notice that the subsequent utilization rate of skills t_i is not an argument of the cost function. That is the fundamental source of increasing returns to specialization.

Ignoring labor supply decisions, a worker with one unit of available market time has human capital value of

$$V = w_1 k_1 t + w_2 k_2 (1 - t) - C(k_1, k_2). \tag{1}$$

The worker chooses k_1, k_2, and t to maximize V. The utilization decision t adds a new dimension to this problem, which has been rarely analyzed explicitly.[2] First-order conditions for a maximum of (1) subject to the constraints $k_i \geq 0, 0 \leq t \leq 1$, are

$$(w_1 k_1 - w_2 k_2) \cdot t = 0, \tag{2}$$

$$(w_2 k_2 - w_1 k_1) \cdot (1 - t) = 0, \tag{3}$$

$$(w_i t_i - C_i) \cdot k_i = 0, \quad i = 1, 2. \tag{4}$$

There are two general classes of solutions to this problem. The worker either invests in both skills and allocates some time to each or goes to a corner and invests all time and money in k_1 or k_2.

2. Two recent exceptions are Becker (1981) and Barzel and Yu (1981). Analysis of the connection between specialization and economic development reached its zenith in the 1920s (Young 1928) and has been inexplicably ignored since then. The scale economy to utilization has its counterpart in nonhuman capital investment decisions and is related to so-called volume effects (Alchian 1958). Long production runs increase the return to capital-intensive production methods and are analogous to the utilization effects noted here.

What are the conditions under which the solution is interior or at a corner? Assume, provisionally, that the solution is interior and the worker invests in both. Then by (2) or (3) the marginal value of a unit of time spent on each skill must be equalized, and relative investment is constrained by

$$k_1 = (w_2/w_1)k_2 \equiv \gamma k_2. \tag{5}$$

Letting V^{12} denote the value of (1) when the worker invests in both skills and noting that $w_1 k_1 = w_2 k_2$ in this case, by (2) or (3),

$$V^{12}(k) = w_2 k - C(\gamma k, k) = w_1 k - C(k, k/\gamma). \tag{6}$$

On the other hand, if the worker specializes in k_1, then $t = 1$, $k_2 = 0$, and (1) becomes

$$V^1(k) = w_1 k - C(k, 0); \tag{7}$$

and if the worker specializes in k_2 it becomes

$$V^2(k) = w_2 k - C(0, k). \tag{8}$$

All of these expressions are functions of a single variable, k. Therefore, whatever the optimal value of k happens to be, specialization is optimal if either $V^{12}(k) - V^1(k) < 0$ or $V^{12}(k) - V^2(k) < 0$ for all conceivable values of k. Subtracting (7) and (8) from (6), sufficient conditions for specialization to be the best course of action are

$$C(\gamma k, k) - C(0, k) > 0 \tag{9}$$

$$C(k, k/\gamma) - C(k, 0) > 0 \tag{10}$$

for all values of k.

For example, suppose there is no interaction in costs: $C(k_1, k_2) = C^1(k_1) + C^2(k_2)$, with $C^i(0) = 0$. Then

$$V^{12}(k) - V^2(k) = -C^1(\gamma k) \tag{11}$$

$$V^{12}(k) - V^1(k) = -C^2(k/\gamma). \tag{12}$$

Both of these expressions are negative so long as $k > 0$. Therefore specialization is always optimal in this case. This conclusion follows for *every* separable function, no matter how rapidly marginal costs increase with investment. Intuitively, it might be thought that suffi-ciently increasing marginal cost tends to spread the optimal investment

around, but that is not true. The reason lies in the optimal allocation of time. If the worker invests in both skills, (2) and (3) imply
that time is always allocated to make the imputed full gross values
of capital, $w_i k_i$, equal in both uses. Therefore, by going to a corner the worker does not lose any value and saves costs by eliminating investment in one activity. Since this argument holds for every
value of k satisfying (2) or (3), specialization necessarily is the best
choice.

Consequently, nonspecialization occurs only when costs are non-
separable. Expending the cost terms in (9) and (10) in Taylor's series around $(0, 0)$ and substituting into the appropriate expressions
yields

$$V^{12}(k) - V^1(k) = -C_2 \cdot (k/\gamma) - C_{12} \cdot (k^2/\gamma)$$
$$- (C_{22}/2)(k/\gamma)^2 \tag{13}$$

$$V^{12}(k) - V^2(k) = -C_1 \cdot (\gamma k) - (C_{11}/2)(\gamma k)^2$$
$$- C_{12} \cdot \gamma k^2, \tag{14}$$

where C_i and C_{ij} are evaluated somewhere between $(0, 0)$ and $(\gamma k, k)$
or $(k, k/\gamma)$. Marginal cost of investing is nondecreasing, so (13) and
(14) prove that specialization is always optimal if $C_{12} > 0$: investing
in one skill increases the marginal cost of investing in the other and
reinforces the argument for the separable case. It can be optimal to invest
in both skills only if $C_{12} < 0$, when investment in one skill decreases the
cost of investing in the other and there is an economy of scope. Even
so, the interaction must be sufficiently large to overcome the effects of
increasing marginal costs.

The breadth of this result is somewhat greater than the specific
example. With separability, specialization is optimal even if the return to investment in skill i is a strictly convex function of k_i—for
example, $w_i f(k_i) t_i$, with $f' > 0$ and $f'' < 0$—because the decision to
specialize rests only on the optimality of time allocation at a given
level of investment and not on the level of investment itself. Thus both
diminishing marginal return and increasing marginal cost of investment, so long as they are independent across activities, imply specialization. It is also obvious that positive productivity interactions tend

to promote nonspecialization, whereas a negative interaction promotes specialization.[3]

The results are sensitive to the assumption that productivity of each skill is linear in utilization and that costs are independent of utilization. Activity-specific fatigue or boredom implies diminishing marginal productivity of time in each activity and may induce nonspecialization even if costs and returns are independent or noncomplementary across skills. Furthermore, if costs could somehow be scaled in proportion to utilization—for example, $C(t_1k_1, t_2k_2)$ rather than $C(k_1, k_2)$—the increasing return character of investment vanishes and incentives for specialization disappear.

There is an old saying that it does not pay to purchase a hammer to drive a single nail. Only if a sufficiently small hammer were available to accomplish the task would it be advantageous to do so. Like hammers, indivisibilities make it impossible for human capital to be scaled down in this way. In effect, the equivalent of a small hammer is produced by hiring a person to drive the nail. That person drives many other nails as well. It pays someone to acquire a specific skill and associated nonhuman capital, and sell his services to many people whose demand for them is very small relative to their own resources. Specialization and trade maximize both the social and the private returns to human capital accumulation because utilization of costly skills is pushed to the limit. Hence specialization and the production of comparative advantage through human capital accumulation is an efficient social use of resources, even if all people are inherently identical and goods production functions exhibit constant returns to scale. Nonconvexities in human capital investment technology produce this result.[4]

---

3. Thus suppose gross return takes the form of joint production $F(t_1k_1, t_2k_2)$. One skill assists the other if $F_{12} > 0$ and is detrimental if $F_{12} < 0$. Notice that sufficiently large investment costs may still lead to specialization even if $F_{12} > 0$, if the loss of productivity through lack of coordination among skills is offset by cost savings from specialization. A coordination skill might be expected to arise under these circumstances. In the case of a firm it is management.

4. In standard trade theory there are no gains from trade if everyone is equally endowed and there are constant returns to scale. The "new" international trade (Krugman 1981) stresses the effects of increasing returns on trade patterns, though the rationale is substantially different than here.

An interesting special case of this principle is illustrated by differential human capital investment incentives between men and women (Mincer and Polachek 1974) and the division of labor within households more generally (Becker 1981). In those cases inherent comparative advantage is reinforced by specific skill acquisition. However, the point has significantly greater generality to virtually all human capital investment, even in the absence of inherent differences among people. It may be the main reason why trade occurs at all.

The trend toward greater specialization and division of labor with economic progress is in part explained by increasing indivisibilities of human capital investments. Technical change and the development of new knowledge increase the amount, complexity, and productivity of skills available to be acquired and increase fixed elements of investment costs that are independent of utilization. This is one reason why the rate of return to education does not fall with economic development and why education is a more desirable investment in advanced economies than in undeveloped ones.

Cross-sectional differences in specialization within a country must be explained in terms of an interaction between the size of the relevant market and diminishing marginal productivity of time in any activity. For example, a physician in a sparsely populated area has sharply diminishing returns to utilization of specialized skills because there is insufficient business to occupy his full-time attention. A more general type of practice is optimal under those circumstances. Practicing in a larger and more densely populated area generates enough business to maintain full utilization of a single skill. Then specialization is optimal. There is also an interaction between specialization and total investment. The nonspecialist has lesser incentives to invest in each of his portfolio of skills than the specialist because the average return is smaller. Therefore worker productivity is smaller on average when specialization is not feasible.

Market constraints on utilization of individual capacities must arise from transport (transactions) costs that limit the size of a person's market. This is not consistent with the technical definition of competition, that there are no constraints on individual supply at prevailing prices. Pure competition is not sustainable when specialization is constrained by market size, but noncompetitive elements are bounded by potential entry of other nonspecialists. Therefore, greater division of labor is itself a manifestation of increasing competition in the labor market.

References

Alchian, A. "Costs and Outputs." In *The Allocation of Economic Resources,* edited by M. Abramovitz et al. Stanford, Calif.: Stanford University Press, 1958.

Babbage, C. *On the Economy of Machinery and Manufactures.* London: Charles Knight, 1832.

Barzel, Y., and Yu, B. T. "The Interdependence between the Accumulation of Human Capital and Its Utilization." Unpublished paper, University of Washington, 1981.

Becker, G. S. *A Treatise on the Family.* Cambridge, Mass.: Harvard University Press, 1981.

Krugman, P. R. "Intraindustry Specialization and the Gains from Trade." *Journal of Political Economy* 89, no. 5 (October 1981): 959–73.

Mincer, J., and Polachek, S. "Family Investments in Human Capital: Earnings of Women." *Journal of Political Economy* 82, no. 2, pt. 2 (March 1974): S76–S108.

Rosen, S. "Substitution and Division of Labor." *Economica* 45, no. 2 (August 1978): 861–68.

Rosenberg, N. "Another Advantage of the Division of Labor." *Journal of Political Economy* 84, no. 4 (August 1976): 861–67.

Smith, Adam. *The Wealth of Nations.* New York: Modern Library, 1937.

Young, A. A. "Increasing Returns and Economic Progress." *Economic Journal* 38, no. 6 (December 1928): 527–42.

PART III

Diversity and the
Distribution of Income

8

The Economics of Superstars

The phenomenon of Superstars, wherein relatively small numbers of people earn enormous amounts of money and dominate the activities in which they engage, seems to be increasingly important in the modern world. While some may argue that it is all an illusion of world inflation, its currency may be signaling a deeper issue.[1] Realizing that world inflation may command the title, if not the content of this paper, quickly to the scrap heap, I have found no better term to describe the phenomenon. In certain kinds of economic activity there is concentration of output among a few individuals, marked skewness in the associated distributions of income, and very large rewards at the top.

Confidentiality laws and other difficulties make it virtually impossible to obtain systematic data in this field. However, consider the following.

(i) Informed opinion places the number of full-time comedians in the United States at approximately two hundred. This is perhaps a smaller number than were employed in vaudevillian days, though it hardly can be maintained that the demand for (intended) comic relief is in a state of secular decline. Some of the more popular performers today earn extraordinary sums, particularly those appearing on television. The capacity for television to produce high incomes is also manifest in the enormous salaries paid to network news broadcasters.

(ii) The market for classical music has never been larger than it is now, yet the number of full-time soloists on any given instrument is also on the order of only a few hundred (and much smaller for instruments other than voice, violin, and piano). Performers of first

---

I am indebted to the National Science Foundation for financial support, and to Gary Becker, David Friedman, Robert J. Gordon, Michael Mussa, Edward Prescott, and George Stigler for helpful discussion and comments.

From *American Economic Review* 71, no. 5 (December 1981): 845–848.

1. That escalation is not confined to wars and prices is established by the fact that Stars would have sufficed not long ago. Academics have a certain fondness for Giants, while businessmen prefer Kings. Obviously there is a fair bit of substitution among all these terms in depicting related data in different contexts.

rank comprise a limited handful out of these small totals and have very large incomes. There are also known to be substantial differences in income between them and those in the second rank, even though most consumers would have difficulty detecting more than minor differences in a "blind" hearing.

(iii) Switching to more familiar territory, sales of elementary textbooks in economics are concentrated on a group of best-sellers, though there exists a large number of very good and highly substitutable alternatives in the market (the apparent inexhaustible supply of authors willing to gamble on breaking into the select group is one of the reasons why so many are available). A small number of graduate schools account for a large fraction of Ph.D.s. A relatively small number of researchers account for a large fraction of citations and perhaps even articles written.

Countless other examples from the worlds of sports, arts and letters, and show business will be well known to readers. Still others can be found in several of the professions. There are two common elements in all of them: first, a close connection between personal reward and the size of one's own market; and second, a strong tendency for both market size and reward to be skewed toward the most talented people in the activity. True, standard theory suggests that those who sell more generally earn more. But that principle applies as well to shoemakers as to rock musicians, so something more is involved. In fact the competitive model is virtually silent about any special role played by either the size of the total market or the amount of it controlled by any single person, because products are assumed to be undifferentiated and one seller's products are assumed to be as good as those of any other. The elusive quality of "box office appeal," the ability to attract an audience and generate a large volume of transactions, is the issue that must be confronted. Recognition that one's personal market scale is important in the theory of income distribution has a long history, but the idea has not been developed very extensively in the literature.[2] I hope to fill in some of the gaps in what follows.

---

2. Albert Rees is a good introduction to the size distribution of income. The selectivity effects of differential talent and comparative advantage on the skew in income distributions are spelled out in my 1978 article, also see the references there. Melvin Reder's survey touches some of the issues raised here. Of course social scientists and statisticians have had a long-standing fascination with rank-size relationships, as perusal of the many entries in the *Encyclopedia of the Social Sciences* will attest.

The analytical framework used is a special type of assignment problem, the marriage of buyers to sellers, including the assignment of audiences to performers, of students to textbooks, patients to doctors, and so forth. Rest assured that prospective impresarios will receive no guidance here on what makes for box office appeal, sometimes said to involve a combination of talent and charisma in uncertain proportions. In the formal model all that is taken for granted and represented by a single factor rather than by two, an index, q labeled talent or quality. The distribution of talent is assumed to be fixed in the population of potential sellers and costlessly observable to all economic agents. Let p be the price of a unit of service (for example, a performance, a record, a visit, etc.) and let m be the size of the market, the number of "tickets" sold by a given seller. Then an overall market equilibrium is a pair of functions $p(q)$ and $m(q)$ indicating price and market size of sellers of every observable talent and a domain of q such that: (a) all sellers maximize profit and cannot earn larger amounts in other activities, and (b) all buyers maximize utility and cannot improve themselves by purchasing from another seller.

Properties of sellers' maximum net revenue functions, $R(q)$, will have special interest. Specifically, convexity of this function describes much of the observable consequences of Superstars. Since $R(q)$ is the transformation that takes the distribution of talent to the distribution of rewards, convexity implies that the income distribution is stretched out in its right-hand tail compared with the distribution of talent. Hence a genuine behavioral economic explanation is provided for differential skew between the distributions of income and talent, a problem that has been an interesting and important preoccupation of the literature on income distribution down through the years.[3] Convexity of $R(q)$ literally means that small differences in talent become magnified in larger earnings differences, with great magnification if the earnings-talent gradient increases sharply near the top of the scale.

---

3. Few economic behavioral models exist in the literature. On this see Harold Lydall. Jacob Mincer has shown that investment can produce skewness through the force of discounting, and established that as an important source of skewness empirically. Learning is not treated here because those issues are well understood, whereas the assignment problem has received little attention. Some recent works, but with different focus and emphasis than is discussed here, are Gary Becker (1973), David Grubb, and Michael Sattinger.

This magnification effect is characteristic of the phenomenon under consideration.

Convexity of returns and the extra skew it imparts to the distribution of earnings can be sustained by imperfect substitution among different sellers, which is one of the hallmarks of the types of activities where Superstars are encountered. Lesser talent often is a poor substitute for greater talent. The worse it is the larger the sustainable rent accruing to higher-quality sellers, because demand for the better sellers increases more than proportionately: hearing a succession of mediocre singers does not add up to a single outstanding performance. If a surgeon is 10 percent more successful in saving lives than his fellows, most people would be willing to pay more than a 10 percent premium for his services. A company involved in a $30 million lawsuit is rash to scrimp on the legal talent it engages.

Imperfect substitution alone implies convexity and provides a very general explanation of skewed earnings distributions which applies to myriad economic service activities. However, preferences alone are incapable of explaining the other aspect of the Superstar phenomenon, the marked concentration of output on those few sellers who have the most talent. This second feature is best explained by technology rather than by tastes.[4] In many instances rendering the service is described as a form of joint consumption, not dissimilar to a public good. Thus a performer or an author must put out more or less the same effort whether 10 or 1,000 people show up in the audience or buy the book. More generally, the costs of production (writing, performing, etc.) do not rise in proportion to the size of a seller's market.

The key difference between this technology and public goods is that property rights are legally assigned to the seller: there are no issues of free riding due to nonexclusion; customers are excluded if they are unwilling to pay the appropriate admission fee. The implied scale economy of joint consumption allows relatively few sellers to

---

4. Milton Friedman proposed a model based on preferences for risk taking, but did not explain why or how the market sustains the equilibrium ex post which sellers earning enormous incomes (for example, why the losers in the lottery rest content with such low incomes if they have the same talents as the winners). Issues of uncertainty that make these elements of supply more interesting are abstracted from here. A model of prizes based on effort-incentive monitoring and the principal agency relation is found in my article with Edward Lazear.

service the entire market. And fewer are needed to serve it the more capable they are. When the joint consumption technology and imperfect substitution features of preferences are combined, the possibility for talented persons to command both very large markets and very large incomes is apparent.

A theory of the assignment of buyers to sellers is required to make these ideas precise. The demand and supply structure of one such model is set forth in Sections I and II. The nature of market equilibrium and its implications for income and output distributions are discussed in Sections III and IV. Comparative static predictions of the model are sketched in Section V and conclusions appear in Section VI.

I. Structure of Demand

Imperfect substitution among quality-differentiated goods in the same product class arises from indivisibilities in the technology of consumption. No satisfactory analytical specification exists in the literature, because indivisibilities lead to nonadditivities in preference relations which are analytically intractable.[5] Yet some specific model is required to make any progress on this problem. My solution to this dilemma is to adopt a smooth quantity-quality substitution technology and introduce the indivisibility through a fixed cost of consumption per unit of quantity. Consumers' attempts to minimize consumption costs gives an extra competitive advantage to higher-quality sellers. However, it is a surprising implication of the analysis that this form of indivisibility is not crucial to the central conclusions, so that true nonadditivities would only strengthen the argument.

Assume the consumer has a well-behaved weakly separable utility function $u = u(x, g(n, z))$, where x is a composite commodity and $y = g(n, z)$ has the natural interpretation of consumption of "services" of the type in question. n is the quantity purchases, a measure of exposure to a seller, such as a patient visit, a performance, etc.; and z is the quality of each unit of exposure. Quantity-quality substitution requires that $g(\cdot)$ is increasing in both of its arguments and that $\partial^2 g / \partial n \partial z > 0$.

---

5. Some of the thorny issues of primitives in problems of product differentiation are discussed from the point of view of the theory of measurement by Manuel Trajtenberg.

This specification has the virtue of being simple, at the cost of ignoring some details and not being perfectly general. The definitions of markets are left somewhat vague: for example, for some purposes it is sufficient to think about the market for novels as a whole and for others distinguishing between mysteries, romances, and so forth is necessary. This is simply treated by allowing y to be a vector and is therefore ignored. There are several dimensions to quantity in any specific application which might be treated in a similar manner. For example, most people do not purchase more than one copy of an author's book but may buy several different books written by the same author. Or there may be preferences for variety. But these considerations are less than compelling in markets for professional services where direct personal contact between buyers and sellers is required. Preferences for variety per se cannot be treated in a quantity-quality substitution model, and since the generalization of increasing the dimensionality of exposure is clear enough in any given case, it is ignored too. It is doubtful whether the general nature of the results is greatly affected by these simplifications.

A cardinal measure of quality or talent must rely on measurement of actual outcomes. Taken to extreme, this view would define the talent distribution as the realized output or income distribution. However, that goes too far, because it ignores the fact that more talented people typically command greater cooperating resources in producing observed outcomes and it refers to all consumers as a group rather than to any one of them. The service flow y is a natural personal outcome measure in this case and is the prime candidate for scaling talent, so long as n is held constant in the imputation to obtain the right ceteris paribus conditions. Still, the measure is strongly dependent on n unless $g(n, z)$ is multiplicatively separable. To avoid ambiguity I restrict $g(n, z)$ to the form $zf(n)$, so that relative talent is defined independently of n (since y is the product of a function of a function of n and another function of z, talent can always be rescaled to be the function of z itself, for example, if $y = f_1(z') f_2(n)$, change the scaling of z' by defining $z \equiv f_1(z')$). The properties of $f(n)$ play no important role in this analysis, so it is assumed to be linear. Therefore $y = nz$, which is the familiar efficiency units specification. This is a very strong form of substitution which obviously works in the direction of spreading sales around all qualities of sellers, not concentrating them among the top, and is a weak specification in that sense.

The cost of one unit of service of a given quality is its price $p(z)$ plus a fixed cost s. For example, if each unit requires t hours and the wage rate is w, then $s = tw$. Measuring prices in units of x, the budget constraint is

$$I = x + (p + s)n \qquad (1)$$
$$= x + [(p + s)/z]\, y = x + vy,$$

where I is full income and v is the full price of services directly implied by the multiplicative specification $y = nz$ (herein lies the analytical value of that assumption).

Marginal conditions for consumer choice are

$$u_y/u_x = dp(z)/dz \qquad \text{for } z; \qquad (2)$$
$$u_y/u_x = (p + s)/z \qquad \text{for } n.$$

Combining these two, choice of z solves

$$dp/dz = p'(z) = (p + s)/z. \qquad (3)$$

Choice of n follows from the requirements that the marginal rate of substitution between y and x equals the relative marginal cost $v = (p + s)z$. The schedule $p(z)$ is the same for all buyers. It maps the talent of a seller into the unit price charged for that quality of service. Therefore optimal choice of z in (3) depends only on s and not on the form of the utility function under the separability assumption. Condition (3) balances larger direct costs of greater talent against larger indirect costs of greater quantity and lesser talent. For example, customers with larger s prefer more talented sellers to economize on consumption time in this specification. Finally, all effects of intensity of preferences are absorbed in choice of the quantity consumed, given the optimum value of z determined by condition (3).

Because it plays an important role in the analysis below, suppose the equality in (3) held for all possible values of z, not just for one of them. Evidently that occurs only if $p(z)$ happens to follow a definite functional form; the one satisfying (3) interpreted as a differential equation for all z. Integrating and simplifying equation (3) yields

$$p(z) = vz - s. \qquad (4)$$

The full price v is the constant of integration, since $v = (p + s)/z$ by definition. If market prices line up as in (4), the consumer is indifferent among all values of z that appear on the market, since (3) is an identity. Therefore (4) must be a price-talent indifference curve, an equalizing difference function, showing the maximum amount the customer is willing to pay for alternative values of z at a given utility index. The larger is v, the smaller the utility index. Finally, if (4) does in fact hold true in the market, too, then both equations in (2) reduce to $u_y/u_x = v$, so that y is uniquely determined for the consumer even though z and n are not.

II. Structure of Supply: External and Internal Diseconomies

The economic activities under consideration invariably involve direct contact of buyers with the seller in one way or another. If a competitive market was ever impersonal, this surely is not it. The seller's choice of market size (volume of transactions) amounts to determining the number of contacts to make with buyers. In many cases the technology admits a certain kind of duplication in which the seller delivers services to many buyers simultaneously, as a form of joint consumption. Once the author tells his tale to the publisher, it can be duplicated in writing as many times as desired. A performer appearing on television literally clones his performance to whoever happens to tune in. The services rendered by any seller become more like a kind of public good the more nearly the technology allows perfect duplication at constant cost.

Just as it is difficult to find practical examples of pure public goods in public finance, so too it is difficult to find them here. In fact services of this type are analogous to local public goods, due to ultimate limitations on joint consumption economies. To the extent that the technology is subject to congestion, that is, to external diseconomies of scale, the required analytical apparatus is the theory of clubs rather than the theory of pure public goods.[6] These external diseconomies reflect a type of degradation of services a seller supplies to each of his customers as

---

6. That a doctor's patients or a performer's fans might be considered as a club has intuitive plausibility. The original reference in the theory of public finance is James Buchanan. Eitan Berglas and Berglas and David Pines present elegant developments of that model.

the number of contacts expands. There are two fundamental reasons for this.

First, in cases where duplication is possible, market expansion ultimately requires using inferior techniques to render the service. It is preferable to hear concerts in a hall of moderate size rather than in Yankee Stadium. Recordings are a superior way of reaching a large audience, but are inferior in quality to live performances with smaller audiences. Furthermore, many of the activities in question involve certain creative elements so the ultimate negative impact of market sizes sometimes can be interpreted as the effect of overexposure and repetition.

Second, the analysis should not be constrained to only those activities where some form of cloning is possible. The general model also applies to cases of one-on-one buyer-seller contact, as is true of professional services. Here the negative effects of personal market scale are caused by limitations on the seller's time. As a doctor's patient load increases, the amount of direct contact time available to any person decreases, waiting time between appointments and in the office increases, and so forth. Nevertheless patients may be willing to trade off service time against quality of service per unit time.

In both cases the quality of service z that appears in consumers' preferences is itself produced by both the quality and the size of the market of the seller with whom transactions occur: $z = h(q, m)$, where q is an index of seller talent or quality and $m = m(q)$ is the total number of units sold by a seller of type q. The arguments above imply $\partial z/\partial q = h_q > 0$ and $\partial z/\partial m = h_m \leq 0$. Furthermore, I assume that $h_{qm} \geq 0$: superior talent stands out and does not deteriorate so rapidly with market size as inferior talent does. The importance of this assumption will emerge later on.

Preferences are structured on service flows, which in turn depend upon q and m. Therefore $p = p(q, m)$ is the unit price charged by a seller of quality q selling m units. Competition in the market for services implies that the *function* $p(q, m)$ is taken as given by a seller. This market is competitive even though a seller affects the unit price charged by choosing m. The reason for competition in markets of this type is that each seller is closely constrained by other sellers offering similar services. Though sellers of different quality are imperfectly substitutable with each other, the extent of substitution decreases with distance. In the limit very close neighbors are virtually perfect substitutes. Assume there is a regular distribution of talent in the population $\phi(q) \, dq$. Then potential substitution is generated both by the density ϕ in the neighborhood dq of q and by degradation through larger market size of better-quality sellers some distance above q, and the opposite for those some distance below q.

In addition to market-size effects on demand, the other factor influencing the output decision is direct cost of production. Let $C(m)$ be out-of-pocket costs of producing m units, with $C' \geq 0$ and $C'' \geq 0$. There are nondecreasing (marginal) costs of production—internal diseconomies—for the usual reasons, including the fact that here the seller must work harder as m increases. Assume also that all sellers have opportunity cost K of working in this sector compared with the next best alternative, with K independent of q.

A seller of type q chooses $m(q)$ to maximize net revenue

$$R(q) = p(q, m)m - C(m). \tag{5}$$

Therefore $m(q)$ is chosen to satisfy

$$mp_m(q, m) + p(q, m) - C'(m) = 0 \tag{6}$$

so long as

$$2p_m + mp_{mm} - C'' < 0 \tag{7}$$

and R exceeds K. Equation (6) determines the intensive margin. If $R(q)$ is monotone in q, then free entry determines an extensive margin as well; the value of q, denoted q_1, which satisfies both $R(q_1) = K$ and (7) simultaneously.

In context a more elaborate return specification decomposes the internal margin above into two additional components, one being the size of each act of joint consumption, m_1, and the other being the number of such acts, m_2. In that case the revenue function is

$$m_2 \left[m_1 p(q, m_1, m_2) - C_1(m_1) \right] - C_2(m_2) \tag{8}$$

where $m_1 p - C_1$ are the "gate" receipts for each event and $C_2(m_2)$ is the cost of increasing the number of events. This avoids some of the dimensionality or units ambiguities in (5), as noted in Section I. If all external diseconomies reside in m_1 alone and not m_2 (so that $p = p(q, m_1)$), then (8) and (5) have very similar implications; only the diseconomy associated with each event is somewhat overcome by expanding their number in formulation (8). This carries over to a case where the external diseconomy of m_2 is small. Otherwise, precise results depend on whether the effect on performance services of m_1 are stronger than those of m_2 and on their interaction. It is simplest to merely think of m in (5) as the product of m_1 and m_2, in those cases where this type of decomposition is applicable.

III. Market Equilibrium

A complete, closed market solution is available if all buyers have the same fixed cost s, though possibly different marginal rates of substitution between y and x. In that case it is possible to aggregate total services in a single market, with a unique implicit market price v which contains all the relevant information and acts as a "sufficient statistic." The unit price p charged by a seller of type q is then constrained to follow (4) independent of market supply conditions. Though n and z are not uniquely determined for any consumer, each one has a regular demand function for services y which depends only upon v. These demands in turn can be summed across consumers to obtain the total market demand for services $\sum y \equiv Y^d = F(v)$. Since consumers are indifferent between n and z, the composition of services between qualities and quantities are determined completely by sellers, who maximize profit according to condition (6). Individual supply choices may be aggregated too, this time by integrating the optimum value of zm, the total services a seller supplies to the market, over those values of q which are actually found in the market, weighted by the number of sellers of type $q, \phi(q)$. This sum represents total services supplied to the market, $Y^s = G(v)$. The intersection of supply and demand determines v itself. Given this equilibrium, the internal cross-section price, output, and income distributional structure may be examined in detail.

To find the supply decision of each seller at a given value of v, substitute $z = h(q, m)$ into the equalizing difference function (4). Applying (6) and (7) yields

$$vmh_m(q, m) + vh(q, m) - s - C'(m) = 0 \tag{9}$$

$$2vh_m + vmh_{mm} - C'' < 0. \tag{10}$$

Differentiate (9) with respect to q:

$$\partial m / \partial q = -v \left(h_q + mh_{qm} \right) / \left(2vh_m + vmh_{mm} - C'' \right) > 0. \tag{11}$$

Market size increases with q if $h_{qm} > 0$. Next differentiate net revenue $R(q)$ in (5) with respect to q, at its maximized value. By the envelope property

$$R'(q) = vmh_q > 0. \tag{12}$$

Net revenue is monotonically increasing in talent, since $h_q > 0$. Finally, differentiate (12) with respect to q and simplify to obtain

$$R''(q) = v\left(h_q + mh_{qm}\right)(\partial m/\partial q) + vmh_{qq}, \tag{13}$$

where $\partial m/\partial q$ is defined by equation (11). So long as h_{qq} is not sufficiently negative, reward is convex in q.

The market supply of services is easily calculated. Let $m(q; v)$ be the solution to (9). Then the amount of service supplied to the market by a seller of equality q is $h(q, m(q; v))m(q; v)$ and the total amount supplied to the market by all active sellers is

$$Y^s(v) = \int_{q_l(v)}^{\infty} h(q, m(q; v))(q; v)\phi(q)\, dq,$$

where $q_l(v)$ is the extensive margin. Differentiate with respect to v:

$$dY^s/dv = -h(q_l, m')m'\phi(q_l)(dq_l/dv)$$
$$+ \int_{q_l}^{\infty} h\left[1 + \frac{m}{h}\left(\frac{\partial h}{\partial m}\right)\right]\left(\frac{\partial m}{\partial v}\right)\phi(q)\, dq,$$

where $m' = m(q_l; v)$. Condition (9) implies that $1 + (m/h)h_m$ is positive. Therefore the second (integral) term in dY/dv is positive. The fact that R is increasing in both q and v from (12) implies that $dq_l/dv < 0$, so that the first term is positive as well. Hence there is rising supply price in the service market. It is obvious from Section I that there is falling demand price for services, so a conventional equilibrium is obtained and v is uniquely determined.

A. Internal Diseconomies

The cross-section structure of the market equilibrium is most easily established in the case where there are no effects of a seller's market size on service quality.[7] In that case m is not an argument of $h(\cdot)$ and talent is scaled so that $z = h(q) = q$. Now the model has a Ricardian flavor, with differential rent sustained by talent induced product differentiation.

Since $z \equiv q$ the unit price charged by sellers of talent q is increasing linearly in q at rate v, from (4); and since price is higher for the better sellers and cost conditions no less favorable, more talented sellers produce more and have larger markets.[8] Application of (11) to this case yields $\partial m/\partial q = v/C'' > 0$. From (12), $R'(q) = vm > 0$, and $R''(q) = v^2/C'' > 0$, from (13). Not only does rent reward increase in talent, but marginal rent reward increases in talent as well. $R(q)$ is convex because both price and quantity increase in q. To see the powerful force of convexity in producing skewness, consider an example where $s = 0$ and $C(m)$ is quadratic. Then $m \propto vq$ and both price and quantity increase linearly in q. Therefore, revenue increases in the square of q. In fact $R \propto v^2 q^2 /2$. A person who is twice as talented as another earns four times more money in this example.[9]

This case is important in showing that the tendency toward skewed rewards arising from convexity of revenues holds under very general circumstances: individuals who, by virtue of superior talent and ability in an activity, can sell their services for higher prices have strong incentives to produce more so long as costs are not perfectly correlated with talent. The increase in both price and quantity with quality implies that talent has a multiplicative effect on reward. It is surprising that the tendency toward skewed rewards is not necessarily dependent on indivisibilities and occurs in the linear efficiency-units case, perhaps the weakest possible specification. However, no relative skew is implied in

---

7. This version of the model has a strong family resemblance to a class of problems previously considered in my 1974 article.

8. Throughout this paper I make the usual club theory assumptions and ignore indivisibilities requiring as integer number of sellers. This can be problematic when the number of sellers is very small, and raises well-known problems in industrial organization about which I have nothing to contribute. The magnitude of the rent of the lowest rent seller (extensive margin) is the issue. That must be sufficiently small for this analysis to apply.

9. The two functions $m(q)$ and $R(q)$ are the transforms from the distribution of ability to the distribution of output and reward. Inverting and computing the Jacobians, the distribution of output is $(1/v)\phi(m/v)$, the same form as the distribution of talent because $m(q)$ is linear. The distribution of rent is $(v(8R)^{1/2})\phi((2R/v)^{1/2})$, which is skewed to the right relative to ϕ.

the distribution of output in this case because there are no interactive effects in that dimension of the problem.

B. Pure Joint Consumption

The effect of scale economy on seller concentration is strikingly seen in the extreme case when internal and external diseconomies vanish, when $C(m) \equiv 0$ (nonzero constant marginal costs will do also) and $h_m \equiv 0$, so $z = h(q) = q$. Then there literally is public goods technology and a single seller service s the total market in equilibrium. That person is the most talented of all potential sellers. Even though there is one seller, essentially competitive market conditions are maintained by threats of potential entry.

Let $N = N(p, q)$ denote the total market demand for quantity at price p and talent q. If there were several potential sellers of the same talent, only one of them is required to provide the service efficiently, so $m \equiv N$. This is seen in Figure 8.1. Free entry implies that total revenue pN must be driven down to opportunity cost K in equilibrium. This equation, $pN = K$, is the rectangular hyperbola in Figure 8.1. It is competitive supply price. Market equilibrium occurs where demand intersects supply from above. Suppose the seller were to charge price p_1. Then the value of sales exceeds K and rents are nonzero.

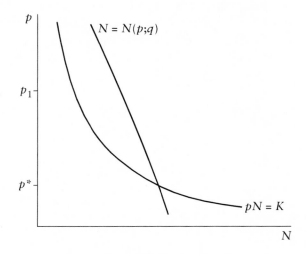

Figure 8.1

Therefore another seller would enter and charge a slightly lower price, attracting all business away from the initial seller. By continuation, price must be driven down in equilibrium to p^*, rents are driven to zero, there is one seller and potential entry maintains that situation indefinitely.

What happens when sellers have different talents? The demand function facing a more able seller is different from the one in Figure (8.1) because q is an argument of demand, $N(p, q)$. Whether N_q is positive or negative, less talented sellers are driven out of the market. To see this, note that $R(q) = p \cdot N(p, q)$ in this case. Therefore

$$R'(q) = N\,[1 + (p/N)\partial N/\partial p]\,\partial p/\partial q + p(\partial N/\partial q). \qquad (14)$$

Given the structure of demand above, equation (4) implies that $\partial p/\partial q = v$. Furthermore, it is easy to show that the price and quality elasticities of demand for quantities are related to the full price elasticity of services as follows:

$$(p/N)\partial N/\partial p = \theta(v/Y)\partial Y/\partial v,$$
$$(q/N)\partial N/\partial q = -\,[1 + (v/Y)\partial Y/\partial v]\,,$$

where $\theta = p/(p + s)$ is the share of full price accounted for by nonfixed costs and $Y = \sum y$ with the sum extending over individual consumers. The quality elasticity of demand for quantity is negative if the full price elasticity of demand for services is inelastic. Substituting these relations into (14) and simplifying yields

$$R'(q) = Nv(1 - \theta) > 0. \qquad (15)$$

Consider the following two cases.

(i) Assume $\phi(q)$ is dense on the interval $[q_0, q]$, where q_0 is the least talented and q the most talented potential seller. Equation (15) shows that R is increasing in both q and v. For a given value of v all sellers for whom $R(q) - K > 0$ would choose to enter and, since $R' > 0$, they must be selected from the upper tail of $\phi(q)$. But in equilibrium there is only one seller. Therefore v must adjust so that $R(\bar{q}) - K = 0$ and all people for whom $q < \bar{q}$ rationally choose the alternative occupation. There is no rent in equilibrium when ϕ is dense even though there is a single seller, because someone is waiting in the wings who is imperceptibly different from that supplier.

230 • Markets and Diversity

(ii) Assume $\phi(q)$ basically the same as before, with the addition of outlier q^* a finite distance ϵ above $\bar{q}: q^* = \bar{q} + \epsilon$. The Superstar is perceptibly different from the closest rival and earns rent on this unique talent. Now it is q^* who supplies the service. Equilibrium v must be slightly smaller than in case (i) so that people for whom $q \leq \bar{q}$ choose not to compete. q^* charges price $p^* = vq^* - s$ (see equation (4)), whereas $\bar{q}$ would charge $\bar{p} = v\bar{q} - s$. The price differential $p^* - \bar{p} = v\epsilon$ is the unit rent accruing to q^*. This is a small number if ϵ is small. Yet the total rent received by q^* is $Nv\epsilon$, which can be very large if N is large. Though unit rent is limited by the equalizing difference (4) and the supply (distance) of close competitors, scale economies can make total rent very large in equilibrium.[10]

C. External Diseconomies

External diseconomies support a nondegenerate equilibrium distribution of sellers. The spatial structure of the market is illustrated in Figure 8.1. Given the market full price v, prices charged by sellers of different talent must satisfy (4) and $z = h(q, m)$. Therefore a seller of talent q must solve the following constrained maximum problem:

$$\max_{m} \left[pm - C(m) \right] \tag{16}$$

$$\text{subject to} \quad p = vh(q, m) - s.$$

To examine the pure effect of externalities assume no internal diseconomies, $C(m) \equiv 0$. Two families of curves are shown in Figure 8.2, one corresponding to the objective function, and the other to the constraint at alternative values of q. A seller of given talent q_1 is constrained by both consumer preferences and sellers of other talents to charge prices along the curve-marked $vh(q_1, m) - s$; seller q_2 is constrained by the presence of q_1 and others to operate along $vh(q_2m) - s$, etc. The iso-revenue curves are rectangular hyperbolas. Points of tangency between the two represent the solution to (9) and (10) or to (16) for each value

---

10. The equilibrium concept used in this particular example is the same as the notion of sustainability in natural monopoly. The equilibrium in Figure 8.1 is inefficient. This inefficiency vanishes when the externality is bounded sufficiently by either internal or external diseconomies. Those bounds are implicitly assumed in all other portions of this paper.

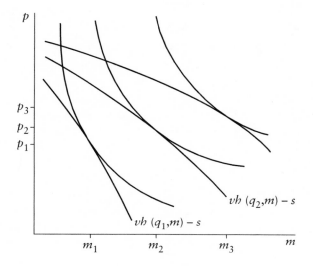

$vh\,(q_2,m) - s$

$vh\,(q_1,m) - s$

m_1 m_2 m_3 m

Figure 8.2

of q. Thus q_1 charges price p_1 and has a market size m_1; q_2 charges p_2 and sells m_2 units, etc.

The importance of the crowding condition $h_{qm} > 0$ is now apparent. Since the services produced by more talented sellers are less contaminated by crowding, the quantity-price gradient grows as talent increases. Therefore the better sellers can and do handle much larger crowds in equilibrium. Equation (11) demonstrates that the market size gradient increases with q when h_{qm} is positive. To see what effect this has on prices, differentiate the constraint in (16) with respect to q:

$$dp/dq = vh_q + vh_m(\partial m/\partial q). \qquad (17)$$

The first term is positive, but the second is negative if $\partial m/\partial q > 0$, which it must be if $h_{qm} > 0$. The extra crowding and dilution of unit service of high-quality sellers constrains unit prices from rising with quality as much as they would without it. Figure (8.2) shows market size increasing with quality to a much larger extent than the price-quality gradient. It is definitely not irrational for better sellers to have a great deal of business, but prices that are not much higher than those with lesser talents. The market may impel them to act that way, to become relatively "crowded out" in equilibrium.

With only internal diseconomies, the multiplicative effect of both positive price and quantity gradients with respect to quality implies convexity of the return function $R(q)$. In this case the quantity gradient tends to be larger and the price gradient tends to be smaller. Nevertheless, there are strong forces working toward convexity. Substitute (11) into (13) to obtain

$$R''(q) = -v^2(h_q + mh_{qm})^2/(2vh_m + vmh_{qm} - C'') + vmh_{qq} \qquad (18)$$

Since the first term in (18) is positive, $R(q)$ is convex so long as h_{qq} is not sufficiently negative. In fact, given the caveat about h_{qq}, $R''(q) > 0$ independent of the sign of h_{qm}. When $h_{qm} < 0$ the constraint functions in Figure 8.2 become steeper as q increases, tending to stretch out the equilibrium price-quality gradient and to compress the quantity-quality gradient, just the opposite of the case where $h_{qm} > 0$. Symmetry of the reward function in p and m implies similarity of $R(q)$ in either case.

The effects of external diseconomies are illustrated by the following example. Let $z = h(q, m) = q - a(q/m)^{-b}$ where a and b are constants. Here adulteration depends on the talent-audience ratio and the unadulterated service satisfies $z = h(q, 0) = q$. Assuming $s = 0$, it is readily verified that $p(q)$ is proportional to q, $m(q)$ to $q^{1+1/b}$ and $R(q)$ to $q^{2+1/b}$. Suppose $b = 1$. Then p is linear in q, m is quadratic in q, and R is a cubic in q. A seller that is twice as talented has a market that is four times larger and earns eight times more money. If $b = 1/2$ market size grows with the cube of talent and incomes by powers of four: a seller who is twice as talented earns sixteen times more, but only charges prices that are twice as large.[11]

---

11. Notice that with imperfect information the effect of a reputation and fixed costs creates a type of scale economy which broadens the scope of this result. If two scholars write on the same subject, the one with the better track record is much more likely to be read and subsequently cited. Similarly, a firm with a fine reputation is more likely to get the business than one that is of unknown quality. While a reputation has many of the elements of a public good, the analogy is not quite complete because this discussion ignores the dynamics of how reputations are established. An "epidemic model" is an intriguing possibility.

IV. Heterogeneous Consumers

Consumer differences in intensity of demand for services are unrestricted in Section III, though much use is made of the assumption that s is identical among them. How should the equilibrium be described when s is distributed in the population of customers? That analysis is more complex because there is no longer a single equilibrium market price for services, v, that summarizes all the information. Nevertheless, differences in s imply restrictions on market outcomes that actually strengthen the qualitative results. I do not attempt a full analysis here, but the reason is that the market assignment of customers to sellers may force the relationship between p and z to be convex. Therefore the more talented sellers receive even greater rents and service even larger markets than when p is linear in z as in (4).

That $p(z)$ must be convex can be sketched as follows. Figure 8.3 shows the equalizing difference function (4) for two types of customers, s_1 and s_2, at alternative values of v. Each line represents the willingness to pay for z at a given utility index. At the same value of v the functions are parallel and s_1 type consumers outbid s_2 types at all values of z. In equilibrium the relevant v (the negative of the utility index) for type s_2 must exceed that for type s_1. Otherwise the former group would not purchase the service at all. Consequently the observed market relation

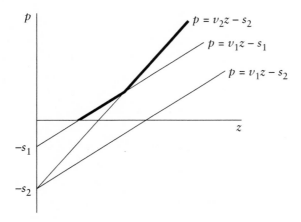

Figure 8.3

234 •   *Markets and Diversity*

must be the envelope of functions such as $p = v_q z - s_1$ and $p = v_2 z - s_2$, the heavier curve in Figure 8.3. The envelope is convex. Evidently the main features of the analysis above hold for each linear piece of $p(z)$ in Figure 8.3. There are, however, additional implications of sorting between segments. First, the more talented sellers gravitate to that segment of the market with the largest value of v, precisely the reason why the convexity implications of the previous analysis are strengthened. Second, consumers with smaller values of s buy from less talented sellers. This is quantity-quality substitution at work: buyers with smaller values of s find quantity relatively cheaper and economize on quality, while those with large values of s demand greater quality and economize on quantity. Adding more types of consumers smooths the locus of equilibrium points in Figure 8.3 without affecting the general principles.[12]

V. Comparative Statics

Since Section IV indicated that the qualitative results are not affected, it is convenient to exploit the assumption of common s in the consuming population. Demand and supply shifts are considered in turn.

A. Demand Shifts

An increase in the number of consumers or in the intensity of their demands for y increases the market demand for services. Market equilibrium price v rises due to rising supply price. Hence unit prices, $p(q)$, of all sellers increase. Since $R(q)$ increases everywhere, less talented people enter. At the same time, existing sellers expand their scales of operations. Though average quality of sellers falls, all previous entrants earn larger rents than before, and the largest increases accrue to the most talented persons (see the effect of v in equation (13) or (18)). Therefore the distribution of reward becomes more skewed than before.

---

12. Reder points out that the market is less concentrated if there are differences of opinion on who is the most talented. This raises subtle questions of the definition of markets that remain to be solved. An approximate solution in the analysis here is to adjust the density of $\phi(q)$: if several sellers are thought by different customers to have the same value of q, that is nearly the same as more mass in ϕ at that value.

The important practical implication is that it is monetarily advantageous to operate in a larger overall market; and it is increasingly advantageous the more talented on is. No wonder that the best economists tend to be theorists and methodologists rather than narrow field specialists, that the best artists sell their work in the great markets of New York and Paris, not Cincinnati, or that the best writers are connected with the primary literary centers such as New York or London. The best doctors, lawyers, and professional athletes should be found more frequently in larger cities. For a given place in the distribution of talent, it is more lucrative to be a violinist than an accordianist, a heavyweight than a flyweight, a rock musician than a folk singer, a tennis player than a bowler, or a writer of elementary texts rather than of monographs.

B. Supply Shifts

The interesting experiments are changes in internal and external diseconomies. Lesser diseconomies increase the market supply of services, reduce the equilibrium value of v, and make consumers better off. The effects on the distributions of talents and rents are less obvious and are complicated by the presence of two opposing forces: the reduction in v lowers unit prices of all sellers, tending to decrease individual output and reward; whereas the reduction in costs or congestion tends to increase them. The balance between the two depends on the elasticity of demand for services.

If demand for services is sufficiently elastic, then cost-reducing effects swamp the decline in unit prices and rents of sellers increase. The rent-talent gradient increases as well and there is greater concentration in the distribution of rewards among the most talented. A reduction in the internal diseconomy induces entry at the extensive margin, and the average seller becomes less talented. However, a reduction of the external diseconomy, if large enough, can actually reduce the number of sellers, kicking out the less talented and increasing the average quality of those remaining. If demand is inelastic, then the number of sellers declines and, since those leaving are selected from the lower tail, the average remaining talent rises. Effects on the return function $R(q)$ are ambiguous in this case, though sufficient reductions in the costs of congestion still can imply increases in both $R(q)$ and $R'(q)$. However, that is a less likely outcome than when demand is elastic.

The practical importance of all this is related to technical changes that have increased the extent of scale economies over time in many activities. Motion pictures, radio, television, phono reproduction equipment, and other changes in communications have decreased the real price of entertainment services, but have also increased the scope of each performer's audience. The effect of radio and records on popular singers' incomes and the influence of television on the incomes of news reporters and professional athletes are good cases in point. And there are fine gradiations within these categories. Television is evidently a more effective medium for American football and basketball than it is for bowling, and incomes reflect it. Nonetheless, television has had an enormous impact on the incomes of the top bowlers, golfers, and tennis players, because their markets have expanded. The "demise" of the theater is more a complaint about competition from the larger-scale media; and incomes of the top performers in the theater, motion pictures, and television certainly are closely geared to audience size. These changes are not confined to the entertainment sector. Undoubtedly, secular changes in communications and transportation have expanded the potential market for all kinds of professional and information services, and allowed many of the top practitioners to operate at a national or even international scale. With elastic demands there is a tendency for increasing concentration of income at the top as well as greater rents for all sellers as these changes proceed over time.

C. Interactions

A change in s shifts the supply of services, not demand, even though it is a consumer parameter. This has no counterpart in standard theory. Demand is not directly affected because v embodies all relevant information for the consumption decision. Supply is shifted because s affects unit prices (see (4)). An increase in s reduces unit prices at any value of v and reduces market supply. Therefore the equilibrium service price v increases and the rent distribution is altered in favor of the more talented sellers. The less talented leave the market. Both the increase in average quality of sellers and greater concentration in rewards at the top reflect customers' substitution of quality for quantity as s rises.

Since important components of s are time and effort costs, time-series changes are correlated with consumer earnings. Therefore market demand increases at the same time that supply is reduced, resulting in an even greater increase in v and additional skew. It can even push the extensive margin down rather than up. The incentives for investments in time-saving innovations that tend to reduce s as earnings rise, for example, consumption at home, have been well remarked upon in the literature.[13]

VI. Conclusion

In discussing the general influence of economic progress on value, Alfred Marshall wrote:

> The relative fall in the incomes to be earned by moderate ability . . . is accentuated by the rise in those that are obtained by many men of extraordinary ability. There never was a time at which moderately good oil paintings sold more cheaply than now, and . . . at which first-rate paintings sold so dearly. A business man of average ability and average good fortune gets now a lower rate of profits . . . than at any previous time, while the operations, in which a man exceptionally favoured by genius and good luck can take part, are so extensive as to enable him to amass a large fortune with a rapidity hitherto unknown.
>
> The causes of this change are two; firstly, the general growth of wealth, and secondly, the development of new facilities for communication by which men, who have once attained a commanding position, are enabled to apply their constructive or speculative genius to undertakings vaster, and extending over a wider area, than ever before.
>
> It is the first cause . . . that enables some barristers to command very high fees, for a rich client whose reputation, or fortune, or both, are at stake will scarcely count any price too high to secure the services of the best man he can get: and it is this again that enables jockeys and painters and musicians of exceptional ability to get very high prices . . . But so long as the number of persons who can be reached by a human voice is strictly limited, it is not very likely that any singer will make an advance on the £10,000 said

---

13. See Becker (1965).

to have been earned in a season by Mrs. Billington at the beginning of the last century, nearly as great as that which the business leaders of the present generation have made on those of the last. (pp. 685–86)

Even adjusted for 1981 prices, Mrs. Billington must be a pale shadow beside Pavarotti.[14] Imagine her income had radio and phonograph records existed in 1801! What changes in the future will be wrought by cable, videocassettes, and home computers?

References

G. Becker. "A Theory of the Allocation of Time." *Econ. J.*, Wept. 1965, *73*, 493–508.

——— "A Theory of Marriage: Part I." *J. Polit. Econ.*, July/Aug. 1973, *81*, 813–46.

E. Berglas. "On the Theory of Clubs." *Amer. Econ. Rev. Proc.*, May 1976, *66*, 116–21.

E. Berglas and D. Pines. "Clubs as a Case of Competitive Industry with Goods of Variable Quality." Tel Aviv University, 1980.

J. M. Buchanan. "An Economic Theory of Clubs." *Economica*, Feb. 1965, *32*, 1–14.

M. Friedman. "Choice, Chance, and the Personal Distribution of Income." *J. Polit. Econ.*, Aug. 1953, *61*, 277–90.

D. Grubb. "Power and Ability in the Distribution of Earnings." Centre for Labour Economics, London School of Economics, 1980.

E. Lazear and S. Rosen. "Rank-Order Tournaments as Optimum Labor Contracts." *J. Polit. Econ.*, 1981.

Harold Lydall. *The Structure of Earnings*. Oxford 1968.

Alfred Marshall. *Principles of Economics*. 8th ed. New York: Macmillan, 1947.

---

14. The entries for Elizabeth Billington in the eleventh edition of the *Encyclopedia Britannica* and *Grove's Musical Dictionary* indicate that she earned somewhere between £10,000 and £15,000 in the 1801 season singing Italian opera in Covent Garden and Drury Land. She is reported to have had an extraordinary voice and was highly paid throughout her professional life, but there is a hint that the 1801 sum was unusual even for her. No information is given on endorsements.

Jacot Mincer. *Schooling, Experience, and Earnings.* New York: Columbia University Press, 1974.

M. Reder. "A Partial Survey of the Income Size Distribution." In Lee Soltow, ed., *Six Papers on the Size Distribution of Wealth and Income*, New York: Columbia University Press, 1969.

Albert Rees. *The Economics of Work and Pay.* New York: Harper and Row, 1973.

S. Rosen. "Hedonic Prices and Implicit Markets: Product Differentiation in Pure Competition." *J. Polit. Econ.*, Jan./Feb. 1974, *82*, 34–55.

———— "Substitution and Division of Labor." *Economica*, Aug. 1978, *45*, 235–50.

M. Sattinger. *Capital and the Distribution of Labor Earnings.* Amsterdam: North Holland, 1980.

M. Trajtenberg, "Aspects of Consumer Demand for Characteristics." Maurice Falk Institute, Jerusalem, 1979.

9

Authority, Control, and the Distribution of Earnings

1. Introduction and Summary

This article sketches a theory of the joint distribution of firm size and managerial reward generated by market assignments of personnel to hierarchical positions in firms. The model is designed to account for some well-known empirical regularities that are not readily explained by standard production theory. Specifically.

1. The distribution of firms by size within industries is skewed to the right (Quandt, 1966). Familiar manifestations of this fact are sizable concentration ratios, even in industries where competitive conditions might be expected to apply. In addition, the relative distribution of firm sizes exhibits a remarkable degree of stability over time. There is little systematic tendency for firms to gravitate toward a unique size implied by U-shaped average cost curves (Hymer and Pashigian, 1962, and references therein).

2. The distribution of earnings, both within and across firms, is also quite stable and highly skewed (Bronfenbrenner, 1971; Lydall, 1968). In fact, firm size and earnings distributions follow similar functional forms and exhibit similar general appearances. Both have large concentrations of density in their right-hand tails.

3. Earnings of top executive officers of large firms are enormous in magnitude and are positively correlated with firm size (Lewellen and Huntsman, 1970). The statistical relation between top execu-

This article was written while I was visiting the Centre for Labour Economics, LSE and later, the Hoover Institution. I am also indebted to the National Science Foundation for financial support: to Gary Becker and Robert Lucas for advice and encouragement; and to Thomas MaCurdy, Herbert Simon, Oliver Williamson, and Robert Willis for criticism of an initial draft. I alone am responsible for the contents.

From *The Bell Journal of Economics* 13, no. 2 (Autumn 1982): 311–323.

tive pay and sales is log linear and the elasticity is approximately .3, irrespective of industry and time period (Roberts, 1956; Fox, 1978).

4. Earnings within firms are closely associated with rank, that is, compensation tends to rise with positions of greater authority and control within the organization.

A technology that admits multiplicative interaction among worker productivities is necessary to explain these data. A simple recursive, hierarchical structure building on previous work by Simon (1965), Mayer (1960), Williamson (1967), Beckmann (1977), Calvo and Wellisz (1979), and Keren and Levhari (1979) is used here. Decisions at each level above the bottom of a hierarchical organization affect the environment and therefore the efficiency of labor inputs at the next lowest level (Mesarovic et al., 1970). Though the organization is only linked directly between adjacent levels, improved labor productivity at any given level has indirect effects that successively filter through all lower levels, by recursion. The magnitudes of these indirect spillovers are increasing in rank because they have farther to travel, and may be substantial at the top of a large triangular organization. Figure 9.1 depicts a three-level organization—deeper layers would be shown by adding layers to the tree. If the span of control at each level exceeds unity, the organizational structure pyramids toward the top, and slight improvements in upper-level decisions have an enormous influence on the

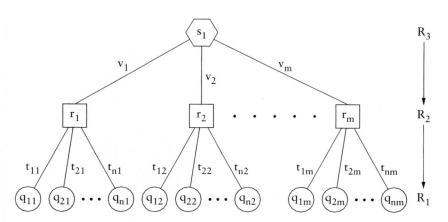

Figure 9.1

organization as a whole by affecting productivity of all lesser-ranking workers.

Considerations such as these are the intuition for assertions that compensation follows "responsibility." Yet this force alone is insufficient for a theory, because it does not make reference either to the supply of responsibility or to its allocation and distribution among positions. The job does not make the man. Indeed, the job cannot be completely defined without knowing the capabilities of the person who will fill it. The matching of authority with talent through the market, the marriage of personnel to positions, and its interaction with internal decision-making structures determine final outcomes in market equilibrium. This is a sorting or assignment problem. Its solution yields a stable distribution of firm size and structure, supported by a price system and an implied reward distribution. The joint distribution of income and output are thus seen to be generated by the same underlying assignment process. The main contribution of this work is to exhibit the interrelations among these factors in a simple and tractable equilibrium framework.[1]

Three elementary components of technology are distinguished in Figure 9.1: management, supervision, and production. Management involves discrete and indivisible choices and commands, such as which goods to produce, in what varieties and volume, and how to produce them. Supervision insures that management directives are carried through at the production level. Indivisibilities inherent in management decisions are represented analytically as a form of total factor productivity improvement and, as such, imply a strong scale economy, not unlike a public good but limited to the confines of the firm. For example, the decision of which good to produce is largely independent of scale, applying equally well to a very large enterprise as to a very small one. This force alone, therefore, promotes very large scale organizations. In fact, if the scale economy were unbounded, efficiency dictates one huge enterprise with the most efficient person managing everything.

It is the supervisory activity that congests management scale economies and produces determinate firm sizes. As specified below, super-

---

1. The model is in the spirit of Tuck (1954) and Mayer (1960). Recent, related contributions include Grubb (1980) and Waldman (1982). Miller (1980) gives the general equilibrium solution to Mayer's original problem.

vision is a strongly decreasing return activity, necessitated by loss of control as organizational size increases. As suggested by Williamson (1981) and others, fulfillment of plans requires monitoring of workers in adjacent ranks, because transactions costs raise possibilities for opportunistic behavior of subordinates and impose limitations on information transfer within the firm.[2] Diseconomies arise from imperfect substitution between a manager's own production of this activity and the use of market alternatives, and by limitations on the manager's time. While loss of control through principal-agent relationships has been studied intensively in recent years (e.g., Holmstrom, 1979), the details of that important work are ignored here, because the model is addressed to more macro, market equilibrium questions. Focus on the equilibrium sustainable distributions is well enough served by a simple effort-monitoring abstraction of a richer and more complex contracting problem at the micro level.

The combination of these two factors and the recursive technology are sufficient to explain the empirical observations. For efficiency, the scale economy of management inputs requires that the most able personnel be assigned to top-level positions in very large firms. The diseconomy of direct supervision maintains rigid bounds on the extent to which this can be accomplished and allows many firms to coexist. However, these bounds can be partially relaxed by subordinating authority through many levels in a deeper organization. Subordination through a chain of command economizes on the limited time of more talented individuals, who imperfectly "clone" themselves by transferring part of their talent to their immediate subordinates, who, in turn, transfer it to their subordinates and so on down the line. Consequently, the equilibrium assignment sorts persons with superior skills to top control positions of the largest and deepest firms, the next most talented to the top ranks of smaller and shallower firms or to lower-level positions in larger firms and so forth. Multiplicative productivity interactions render the equilibrium distribution of control and income more skewed than the underlying distribution of talent.[3]

---

2. Earlier, Williamson (1967) suggested garbling of information in longer chains of command as the ultimate constraint on the height of organizations. Keren and Levhari (1979) present a formal model to that effect.

3. A related technology is used in Rosen (1981) to explain the large concentration of output and extreme skew of income distributions in the professions, sports, arts, and entertainment services.

This article is organized as follows. Specifications of talent and technology are presented in the following section. Recursive technology allows the use of an induction-type argument, starting from the lowest ranks and working backward toward the top. The first step, a two-level firm, is analyzed in Section 3. Higher-level firms are briefly analyzed in Section 4. The scope and limitations of the model are discussed in Section 5.

2. Structure of Technology and Control

The model is specified to exploit as much of the neoclassical apparatus as possible. In a multilevel firm, output of levels below the top is regarded as intermediate product that is processed or improved by the activities of the next highest level. However, firms of different levels are allowed to coexist. Thus in Figure 9.1, a two-level organization can either sell its output to the open market and exist as an independent square and circles; or alternatively, merge with a three-rank or higher firm (represented by the whole of Figure 9.1), indirectly "selling" its output to a third-level manager whose activities increase its value. Similarly, a three-level firm can exist as an independent entity or alternatively merge into the organization of a firm with four ranks or more. Let R_j index rank: R_1 corresponds to production workers, R_2 corresponds to heads of two-rank firms or to second-line subordinates of deeper organizations, etc. (see Figure 9.1).

Beginning with the bottom two layers in Figure 9.1, let q_i denote the productivity of worker i in the production activity. It is person i's endowed skill as a worker measured in efficiency units and varies from worker to worker. Let r denote the skill of a second-line manager, also in efficiency units. This too varies from person to person. Let t_i represent the amount of monitoring or supervisory time that r allocates to q_i. With capital ignored for simplicity, the product attributable to r controlling q_i is

$$x_i = g(r)f(rt_i, q_i), \tag{1}$$

where $f(\cdot)$ has standard neoclassical curvature properties and $g'(r) \geq 0$. The total output of an R_2 operation is the sum of outputs of all workers controlled:

$$X = \sum_i x_i = g(r) \sum_i f(rt_i, q_i), \tag{2}$$

where both the index of summation and the time allocation $\{t_i\}$ are to be chosen. Equation (2) represents the output of one of the squares connected to circles in Figure 9.1.

The term $g(r)$ in (1) and (2) is the analytical representation of the quality of management decisions. It is independent of i, representing the effects of skills inherent in a command system which apply equally to all workers controlled by r. The general atmosphere effect of $g(r)$ captures the indivisibility of management-type decisions and implies a scale economy because it improves productivity of all R_i workers in the firm, irrespective of their numbers or the time allocated to them. I assume that the r skill is nonadditive and noncombinable; e.g., it is not possible to combine two mediocre managers to produce a superior one.

The first argument of $f(rt, q)$ is most conveniently interpreted as supervision and monitoring, though it admits other interpretations. I assume that r cannot jointly monitor workers, but must spend time with each one to obtain useful output. This specification also implies an indivisibility and strong nonadditivity of supervision: supervisory inputs cannot be increased by access to a supervisory market, because of shirking and free riding inherent in agency relationships. As written, (1) assumes that there are no substitutes at all for the manager's own time in checking that management commands are carried out. Introducing an imperfect market substitute for supervision, while maintaining essentiality of manager's own time, would not materially affect the analysis, but would be slightly more complicated.

The necessity for a manager to use his own time in supervision is what effectively congests the scale economy inherent in $g(r)$, because time is limited and purchasing it from others is subject to an extreme form of diminishing return. The forms of observed organizations strike a bvalance between these forces of increasing and decreasing return, conditional on technology and talents of persons available to be assigned. Finally, (1) assumes that skill r is both time-augmenting and total-factor-productivity-improving, even though they represent different production activities. It would not be difficult to specify two indivisible skills. One skill is adopted for simplicity.

A person assigned to R_3 controls the output of several R_2 persons, analogous to the locus of control exercised by an R_2 over a group of R_1 workers. If y_j is the output of a person whose talent in R_3 is s and who manages output X_j of r_j in R_2, then

$$y_j = G(s)F(sv_j, X_j), \tag{3}$$

where v_j is the amount of time s allocates to monitor X_j. The variables $G(s)$ and sv have the same interpretation for the three-level firm as $g(r)$ and rt have for the two-level firm. Total output of the R_3 firm is

$$Y = \sum_j y_j = \sum_j G(s)F(sv_j, X_j), \tag{4}$$

where again the index of summation and the time allocation $\{v_j\}$ are to be chosen. Equation (4) is represented by the hexagon connected to squares in Figure 9.1. Since the same good is produced by all firms, the X and Y notation merely differentiate firm structure and not output. fourth-, fifth-, and higher-level firms proceed along these same lines, with each controlling a collection of outputs produced at the next lowest level.[4]

The description of production possibilities is completed by a specification of factor supplies. Each person is completely described by a vector of endowed *latent* skills $(q, r, s, \ldots)$, indicating the amount of skill potentially supplied to each level of authority. Assignments are assumed to be specialized to one position only. People cannot or do not find it worthwhile to divide their time between two or more. The actual skill that is used is given by the rank to which the person is assigned, with all other skills remaining latent and unutilized. The available or potential skills in the economy overall are given by a distribution function $h(q, r, s, \ldots)dqdrds \ldots$ The number of workers is taken to be fixed, and all persons are assumed to work "full time."

For the most part, I analyze a special case in which latent skills follow a nonhomogeneous one-factor structure (ignoring rank-specific factors and details of nonnegativity constraints):

$$q = a_q + b_q \xi$$
$$r = a_r + b_r \xi$$
$$s = a_s + b_s \xi \tag{5}$$
$$\ldots,$$

where a_i and b_i are positive constants, and ξ has the natural interpretation of general ability. The distribution of ξ is given in the population by $m(\xi)d\xi$. This case is interesting because it is meaningful to

---

4. Beckmann (1977) employs a similar nested, recursive specification for production of management inputs, but ignores heterogeneity of talents and the assignment problem.

talk about undifferentiated ability and it implies rank-order sorting by ability.[5]

The assignment problem may now be stated succinctly. Find an assignment from the distribution of talents $h(\cdot)$ to ranks and firms that maximizes the total output of all persons to be assigned. This requires determining the number of firms and their internal structure, with respect to both hierarchical breadth and depth, as well as a conformable partition of the skill distribution to those skills that are actually utilized. Associated imputations (prices) sustain the equilibrium assignment. With a finite number of agents, straightforward enumeration ensures that there exists a solution, but it cannot be characterized without further restrictions. The problem becomes simple in the important special case where the functions $f(\cdot)$, $F(\cdot)$, ... exhibit constant returns to scale. That case is analyzed in detail in what follows.

3. Two-Level Firms

Economics of the Firm

Consider a firm with two ranks, where a person of talent r in R_2 controls n production workers in R_1 of talents $q_1, q_2, \ldots, q_n$. Given the quantity and quality of production labor inputs, the firm's production function is defined by the allocation of supervisory effort $\{t_i\}$ that maximizes total output:

$$
\begin{aligned}
X &= H^n(r, T, q_1, q_2, \ldots, q_n) \\
&= \max_{t_i} \left[\sum g(r) f(rt_i, q_i) + \lambda \left(T - \sum t_i \right) \right],
\end{aligned}
\tag{6}
$$

where T is total time available to person r and λ is a Lagrange multiplier. The optimal allocation equates the marginal value of time over all workers

$$
rg(r) f_1(rt_i, q_i) = \lambda, \quad i = 1, \ldots, n.
\tag{7}
$$

---

5. The one-factor model is adopted because of its precision and simplicity. It clarifies the usual discussions of ability-rank order sorting. Some empirical evidence suggests that a two-factor model, or more, is necessary to account for observed occupational selection (Willis and Rosen, 1979).

Diminishing returns ($f_{11} < 0$) and complementarity ($f_{12} > 0$) imply that more effort is allocated to the more able workers.

$H^n(\cdot)$ in (6) is found by solving the first-order conditions (7) for t_i as functions of r and q_i and substituting back into the definition of X. In general, the production function must be indexed by n, and each q_i is a separate factor of production. Therefore, the skill composition of the work force is important, because each worker's productivity depends on both the number of other workers in the firm and the precise skills embodied in each of them. This is true in spite of the fact that there are no direct interactions in production. Considerable simplification is available if $f(\cdot)$ exhibits constant returns, for then powerful results in production theory on decentralization and separability (Blackorby et al., 1978) may be used.

If $f(rt_i, q_i)$ is linearly homogeneous in its arguments, then

$$x = g(r)f(rt, q) = g(r)q\theta(rt/q) \tag{8}$$

with $\theta' > 0$ and $\theta'' < 0$. The marginal conditions for optimal time allocation are

$$rg(r)\theta'(rt_i/q_i) = \lambda, \quad i = 1, \ldots, n. \tag{9}$$

Second-order conditions are satisfied from concavity. Since r is fixed for a second-level manager, (9) implies that $t_i/q_i = k$, where k is some constant. Therefore, supervision time is allocated in proportion to production worker skill: $t_i = kq_i$. Summing across all workers,

$$T = \sum t_i = kq_1 + kq_2 + \cdots + kq_n \equiv kQ, \tag{10}$$

where $Q = \sum q_i$ is the total amount of worker skill in R_1 controlled by r. Therefore, $t_i/q_i = T/Q$. Substituting into (8) yields $x_i g(r)\theta(rT/Q)$. Since the sum of these expressions is the firm's total output, the production function of the firm is

$$X = \sum x_i = \sum q_i g(r)\theta(tT/Q) = g(r)Q\theta(rT/Q). \tag{11}$$

When $f(rt, q)$ exhibits constant returns to scale, equilibrium production depends only on the total amount of production labor controlled, not on the number of R_1 workers or on their skill composition. The enterprise production function is a perfect linear aggregator of work-specific production functions, because r allocates time in proportion to worker skill and the output at each "station" is also proportional to worker skill. Since production depends on the sum $q_1 + q_2 + \cdots + q_n$, it follows that q_i and q_j are perfect substitutes for each other within the firm; and it no longer matters who works with whom in R_1. But that is true for all values of r, so there is perfect substitution across as well as within firms. Consequently, a competitive production labor market implies a single efficiency price for Q.

There are constant returns to scale in variable inputs in (8), so in a sense there is no "loss of control" there. Nonetheless, there is loss of control, or limited span of control, at the aggregator or firm level. Equation (11) exhibits decreasing returns to Q. A fixed amount of supervision time must be spread more thinly over larger total resources. This results in diseconomies because r is a fixed factor of production. The law of variable proportions also implies diminishing returns to r in the $Q\theta(rT/Q)$ part of (11), though that might be overcome by the additional effects of r through the total factor productivity effect $g(r)$.

Imagine a competitive labor market for production skill Q which establishes an efficiency price w. If r sets up a firm, then profit is

$$\pi_r(r) = \max_Q \{ pg(r)Q\theta(Tr/Q) - wQ \}, \tag{12}$$

where p is the market price of output. Normalizing $T = 1$, the necessary and sufficient condition for a maximum of (12) is

$$g(r) \left[\theta(r/Q) - (r/Q)\theta'(r/Q) \right] = w/p. \tag{13}$$

Define $\beta = Q/r$ as the ratio of production labor controlled to talent in R_2. Given perfect quantity-quality production labor substitution, this has a natural interpretation as the *span of control* at R_2. Equation (13) shows that the span of control is an equilibrium construct that depends on talent r and the real wage, as well as technology. Define $\epsilon = rg'(r)/g(r)$ as the elasticity of $g(r)$, and σ as the elasticity of substitution between rt and q in $f(rt, q) = q\theta(rt/q)$. Comparative statics on (13) yields

$$d \ln \beta / d \ln r = \epsilon\sigma/(1 - \kappa) \geq 0 \tag{14}$$

$$d \ln Q / d \ln r = 1 + \epsilon\sigma/(1 - \kappa) \geq 1 \tag{15}$$

and, using (15) and (11),

$$d \ln X / d \ln r = 1 + \epsilon + \epsilon\sigma/(1 - \kappa) \geq 1, \tag{16}$$

where κ is the ratio of R_1 labor cost to total sales of the firm.

(14) shows that the span of control is nondecreasing in talent r. The span of control is independent of r only when $\epsilon = 0$ and $g(r)$ is a constant, a case of "pure" supervision. Note the interaction between ϵ and σ in all these expressions. For a given σ, the incremental span of control is increasing in ϵ, viz., greater economies of scale of the management activity. The span of control also increases more rapidly the larger is σ. More talented managers are more efficient users of time and economize it by employing more labor input. (15) and (16) show explicitly that greater managerial talent commands greater resources, following from complementarity between r and Q in production function (11). Moreover, the scale economy of the management activity (i.e., $\epsilon > 0$) implies that both production labor hired and output produced rise more than proportionately with r. Not only do larger firms have more capable personnel at the top, but size differences are increasingly larger than inherent differences in the quality of their managers. This force is the fundamental explanation for maintenance of a long-tailed equilibrium size distribution of firms. At the very least, the size distribution must be more skewed than the conditional distribution of top talent.

These same forces imply that R_2 reward is increasing in talent r. Using the envelope theorem on (12),

$$d \ln \pi / d \ln r = 1 + \epsilon/(1 - \kappa) \geq 1 \qquad (17)$$

(note that σ drops out of (17) by the envelope property). Again, increasing scale economies of superior management imply that reward increases more than proportionately with r. This is what maintains the observed long-tailed distribution of income at the top ranks: the distribution of reward is more skewed than the distribution of talent among R_2 personnel.[6]

The analysis so far has related span of control, firm size, and reward in R_2 to talent r. However, r is not directly observed by the analyst.

---

6. An innocuous assumption strengthens this result considerably and implies that $\pi(r)$ is a globally convex function. Differentiate (12) twice and exploit (13)–(16) to obtain

$$\pi''(r) = (rg''/g' + 2 - \kappa)X\epsilon/r^2 + (1 + r\sigma/(1 - \kappa))w\epsilon^2/r^2.$$

The only term in this expression that could possibly be negative is rg''/g', the elasticity of g'. $\pi(r)$ is strictly convex if that term is not sufficiently negative, a condition that is almost certain to be satisfied throughout most of the relevant range; e.g., convexity is implied by any positive, constant elasticity $g(r)$ function.

The problem is compounded by the fact that r is not directly revealed from the data because in equilibrium more capable people control more cooperating resources, and the correct ceteris paribus conditions are never met in any realizations of the assignment process.[7] However, the expressions above imply an equilibrium relationship between managerial reward and output that has been studied empirically. Dividing (17) by (16) yields

$$d \ln \pi / d \ln X = \frac{(1 - \kappa)(1 + \epsilon) + \kappa \epsilon}{(1 - \kappa)(1 + \epsilon) + \kappa \epsilon \sigma}. \quad (18)$$

This expression is interesting on two counts: First, its parametric derivation emphasizes that the distributions of firm size and managerial reward are the joint outcomes of the same underlying problem. This fact has been insufficiently recognized in the literature on firm size and the largely independent literature on earnings distributions. Second, (18) is readily related to observed facts. The empirical estimate of .3 suggests that: (i) management decisions are subject to atmosphere-like scale economies of the type that underlie this model—otherwise the elasticity would be unity; (ii) quality adjusted supervision time and production worker quality are good substitutes; the elasticity of substitution σ exceeds unity.

Market Equilibrium and Assignments

The market assignment of individuals to position is based on the principle of comparative advantage. Constant returns to scale in $f(rt, q)$ imply that only rank order need be determined and that complex sorting questions within ranks and firms are irrelevant (e.g., compare (6) with (11)). That is precisely the analytical advantage of that assumption. Therefore, in a world of two-rank firms, a person must ask whether it

7. That this model does not rest on empty primitives is revealed by the following operational experiment. Randomly assign different production workers to the same R_2 manager for the same period of time. Observed personal output differences measure differences in q, by (1), since r and t are fixed. Similarly, randomly assign different managers to the same worker for the same period of time. q and t are fixed in (1) in this experiment, so output differences index differences in r. The measures are nonlinear in "true" abilities, from the curvature of $f(rt, q)$. They are not unique because $f_{12} > 0$, but are uniquely ordered. Market data do not duplicate these experiments because more able managers command greater cooperating resources in the equilibrium assignment, which is not random.

is preferable to work for somebody else and use the q skill in R_1, or alternatively, to set up a firm and use the r skill in R_2. Market equilibrium defines the efficiency price for production worker skill, w, and the reward function $\pi(r)$. Ignoring nonpecuniary differences between positions, choice of position rests on which alternative yields the largest income, given market data and the latent talents possessed by each person.[8]

An analytical representation of the complete solution is readily available when endowed talents follow the one-factor representation (5), which is a case of absolute as well as comparative advantage. The content of specification (5) is most easily expressed when technology involves supervision only ($\epsilon = 0$). Then (17) implies $\pi(r) = pr$, where p is the market marginal valuation of (supervisory) talent r.[9] Let I_j denote earnings prospects at rank j. Multiplying the first expression in (5) by w and the second expression by p,

$$I_1 = wa_q + wb_q\xi$$
$$I_2 = pa_r + pb_r\xi. \tag{19}$$

The efficient choice set is represented by the upper envelope of these two lines in the (I, ξ) plane. Assuming that the two lines cross, which they must in equilibrium, the assignment of ability to rank must be hierarchical (unless the functions (19) are coincident, in which case the assignment is random). Less able people are assigned to R_1 and more able people are assigned to R_2 if the I_2 line has a smaller intercept and a larger slope than the I_1 line. In that case the unconditional variance of potential R_2 talent exceeds that of potential R_1 talent. The relationship between value productivity and ability would be "flatter" for production workers, meaning that there is less scope for ability to stand out there, that anyone can do about the same value of work in R_1, whereas talent stands out and has a larger marginal effect in R_2. Of course, the assignment remains hierarchical if R_1 exhibits larger unconditional variance, for then *it* represents the "higher" skill. In

8. This criterion of choice is also used in recent and related work by Lucas (1978), Kihlstrom and Laffont (1979), and Kanbur (1979).

9. The full equilibrium solution is easily derived when $\epsilon = 0$. Constant span of control, from (15), and linearity of X in r, from (16) imply a perfect aggregate industry production function. This combined with assignment by comparative advantage from $h(q, r)$ uniquely determines w and p. The two-level firm market equilibrium in this case is very similar to Lucas (1978) and Rosen (1978).

either case it is important to notice that the envelope of (19), call it $I(\xi)$, is a convex function. Since $I(\xi)$ is the transformation that takes the ability distribution $m(\xi)d\xi$ to the observed income distribution, the overall earnings distribution must be more skewed to the right than the underlying distribution of ability. These relations become a bit fuzzier if orthogonal activity-specific factors are allowed in (5), because strictly hierarchical rankability sorting does not occur. Nonetheless, the overall earnings distribution is skewed relative to the ability distribution.

In the empirically relevant case where $\epsilon > 0$, the first expression in (19) remains and the second expression becomes

$$I_2 = \pi(a_r + b_r\xi). \tag{20}$$

$\pi(r)$ is itself convex and the envelope appears as in Figure 9.2. Convexity of the profit function at R_2 means that there are less stringent conditions for rank-ability sorting than above. Increasing marginal return to r talent requires that the highest-ability people are assigned to R_2, irrespective of the values of a_i and b_i in (5). Increasing returns of management and increasing span of control in r and linearity of R_1 reward in

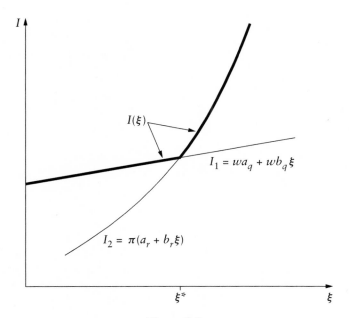

Figure 9.2

q and ξ guarantee this result.[10] The envelope function is "more" convex in this case, thereby leading to even greater relative skew in the overall observed earnings distribution.

The partition of ξ into rank order is found by maximizing the total value of output, subject to factor supply limitations. It is evident from the discussion above that with (5) all people above some critical value ξ^* are assigned to R_2 and all people below ξ^* are assigned to R_1. Total industry output is

$$\int_{\xi^*}^{\infty} g(r)Q(r)\theta(r/Q(r))m(\xi)d\xi, \tag{21}$$

where $Q(r)$ is the amount of labor controlled by r. The dependence of both r and q on ξ through (5) has been suppressed to economize on notation. The total supply of production labor, the amount to be allocated among all r_2 workers is

$$\bar{Q} = \int_{-\infty}^{\xi^*} qm(\xi)d\xi. \tag{22}$$

The market demand for production labor is the sum of each firm's demand:

$$\bar{Q}^d = \int_{\xi^*}^{\infty} Q(r)m(\xi)d\xi. \tag{23}$$

We seek a function $Q(r)$, representing the optimal allocation of production labor to each active r, and a partition ξ^* that maximizes (21) subject to the side condition that the amount of labor services to be allocated (22) is exhausted (23). That is, find $Q(r)$ and ξ^* that maximize

$$\int_{\xi^*}^{\infty} g(r)Q(r)\theta(r/Q(r))m(\xi)d\xi +$$
$$\mu\left[\int_{-\infty}^{\xi^*} qm(\xi)d\xi - \int_{\xi^*}^{\infty} Q(r)m(\xi)d\xi\right], \tag{24}$$

---

10. Convexity of I_2 and linearity of I_1 in ξ could imply that the most talented *and* the least talented people become managers, with those in between assigned to production positions (I_2 may cut I_1 twice in Figure 9.2). Those pathological cases are ignored, but are logical possibilities.

where μ is an undetermined multiplier. The Euler condition for $Q(r)$ is

$$(g(r)[\theta - (r/Q)\theta'] - \mu)m(\xi) = 0, \qquad (25)$$

and the condition for the extensive margin ξ^* is

$$X^* - Q(r^*)\mu = \mu q^*, \qquad (26)$$

where $r^* = r(\xi^*)$ is the marginal manager, $q^* = q(\xi^*)$ is the potential R_1 talent embodied in the marginal manager, and X^* is his output. Assuming $m(\xi) > 0$ over the range of ξ, (25) requires that the marginal product of labor is equalized for all observed r. Therefore, μ is the economy-wide marginal product of Q, equal to its imputed wage in equilibrium. The left-hand side of (26) is imputed profit of the marginal firm and the right-hand side is imputed opportunity cost of the marginal supervisor, what he would be worth as a worker. The partition is therefore determined by the absence of rent at the margin, as usual. It is obvious that a competitive market duplicates these conditions and maximizes output.

4. Multilevel Firms

Recursive technology and the constant returns to scale assumption make analysis of multilevel firms a straightforward generalization of what was presented in Section 3. Either a firm of a given level stands on its own and sells its output directly to the market, or it becomes a component of a higher-level organization, where its output is treated as intermediate product whose value is increased by the activities of someone at the next highest rank. Since all firms can be disassembled in this way, an additional equilibrium condition is that incomes of top managers at any rank above the bottom must be the same whether they merge into a lower-rank position in a higher-level firm or act on their own.

For example, a person of ability s in R_3 processes the output of an R_2 suborganization with micro technology

$$y_j = G(s)X_j\varphi(sv_j/X_j), \qquad (27)$$

where X_j is output of the jth r_2 component of R_3. The R_3 production function is the maximum of a sum of expressions such as (27). As before, the optimum time allocation $\{v_j\}$ is a proportionality rule in X_j and the production function aggregates nicely to $Y = \sum y_j = G(s)\bar{X}\varphi(s/\bar{X})$, where $\bar{X}$ is total R_2 output controlled by s. Since X and Y are the same product, they must be valued at the same price, p, and the marginal condition for maximum profit at R_3 is

$$G(s)\left[\varphi(s/\bar{X}) - (s/\bar{X}\varphi'(s/\bar{X})\right] = 1. \tag{28}$$

This differs slightly from the R_2 firm case because it is independent of prices. Still, $\bar{X}/s$ is naturally interpreted as the span of control and is nondecreasing in s. For that reason firm size and managerial earnings in R_3 increase more than proportionately with s, and the conclusions about relative skew and the within-level relation between size and reward remain intact.

The equilibrium assignment in the one factor specification (5) is a straightforward extension of the logic underlying Figure 9.2. Now there are some additional constraints on the isoperimetric problem (21), arising from the fact that a sufficiently large number of lesser-rank units must be available for merger into higher-level organizations. The triangular structure requires that there must be fewer (quality-adjusted) individuals at each successive rank. Otherwise, all the pieces would not fit together properly.

Perfect rank-ability sorting goes through when the level and gradient of management total factor productivity effects and/or possibilities of delegation through easier monitoring and greater time substitution are increasing in rank. Then the (I_j, ξ) loci in Figure 9.2 are increasingly convex and exhibit increasing gradients by rank order (e.g., if I_3 were added to Figure 9.2, it would cut I_2 from below and establish another margin $\xi^{**} > \xi^*$). The most talented persons are presidents of the largest firms, the next most talented are either vice presidents of larger firms or presidents of the next largest firms, etc. The least talented are found in the ranks of production workers.[11] Clearly, the envelope itself tends to skew the overall distribution of rewards to an even greater extent than in Section 3, and increasing scale economies with rank tend to produce even greater skew to the upper tail of the firm size distribution than was feasible there. To the extent that management economies play

---

11. In both this and the previous case the assignment is not so conveniently ordered if the one factor specification is dropped. However, assignment by comparative advantage applies irrespective of the form of $h(q, r, s, \ldots)$.

out at very high echelons, the envelope does not cover those organizations, placing bounds on the height and breadth of firms that appear in competitive equilibrium.

5. Qualifications, Extensions, and Conclusions

There is a common sense in which chief executive officers of large corporations exercise a great deal of economic power. This power, sometimes labeled responsibility, derives from the influence their decisions exert on the productivity of large numbers of others in the enterprise as a whole. The most capable foot soldier is not very effective if he is fighting the wrong war. Under these circumstances it pays to assign the most talented persons to positions of greatest power and influence. Though other, less talented individuals could manage these organizations, it is inefficient for them to do so. The value of output falls by more than the opportunity cost of their services in a lower-ranking position or in a smaller firm. The supporting price system is reflected in market observations by an enormous salary gradient and apparent concentration of control that persists in equilibrium. Large wage payments to superior managers in large firms are sustained by corresponding increments of productivity, rendering the observations squarely consistent with the marginal productivity theory of distribution (demand) and with the theory of rent (supply).

In focusing on total supply conditions, neoclassical production theory is better equipped to study the functional distribution of income rather than the personal distribution. Yet much of the standard apparatus can be used to illuminate questions of size distributions through a recursive technological structure, and I hope this work will stimulate others to investigate these issues more thoroughly. It is important to keep in mind a subtle methodological distinction between this type of problem and the standard theory of the firm (Viner, 1952). The firm cannot be analyzed in isolation from other production units in the economy. Rather, each person must be placed in his proper niche, and the marriage of personnel to positions and to firms must be addressed directly.

The analysis above is greatly simplified by assumptions of constant returns to scale in the monitoring technology. That leads to a perfect internal transfer pricing mechanism with complete decentralization, working backward from the bottom layers toward the top. People assigned to ranks above the bottom capitalize on their superior skills by setting up their own suborganizations and earn rents by acting as residual income recipients at each level. While this is adequate to account for the major empirical findings stated in the introduction, it should be extended to allow for true joint production and for external economies. The public goods features of some management decisions may not be fully confined to lower ranks in one's own organization, but may also spill over to those in similar or higher ranks in other firms. That extension would also lead to explicit consideration of coordination problems within organizations (Mesarovic et al., 1970) which have been ignored here. Another obvious extension is to incorporate the use of capital in the technology.[12]

The problem has been simplified by assuming that the management activity requires a fixed amount of time. However, another margin of choice can be considered, where managers allocate time to augment the productivity of management skills, but at the cost of lesser time available to supervise activities of others (Oi, 1981). It is apparent that this modification strengthens the skewness implication of the distributions of control and reward; superior managerial talent is further economized by allocating more time to improved management decisions and subordinating supervision through a longer and deeper chain of command.

There is yet another major empirical observation that cannot be treated within the limited confines of this analysis. The weight of evidence now suggests that the relationship between firm size and earnings holds true at virtually all ranks and not only at the top (Mellow, 1981). A cost of the decentralization assumptions is that rank-order alone matters and not the specific identity of firms or other personnel within the firm. This issue, as well as many other interesting questions of sorting solved by competitive labor markets can only be fully addressed

---

12. There is no loss of generality in the model above from the apparent absence of capital. Add capital to $f(\cdot)$, $F(\cdot)$ in (1), (3), . . . Given rt and q, etc., optimally assign capital to immediate subordinates. Then (1), (3), . . . can be regarded as quasi-indirect production functions where the price of capital enters as an additional argument which has been suppressed as written. The indirect functions exhibit constant returns if the direct functions have constant returns.

by a more complete representation of the marriage problem. While few results are available, Becker's (1973, 1981) analysis suggests positive assortative matching of production, supervision, and managerial talents within firms.

These considerations might be introduced into the present model in the following way. Break the linearity of supervision technology by introducing a fixed time cost of transferring monitoring time from subordinate to subordinate. More skillful persons at each level command an additional premium because they minimize lost transactions time. The value of time is greater for the more able persons at adjacent higher ranks due to complementarity, and in equilibrium they outbid less capable competitors for higher quality subordinates. This force lends greater convexity to the earnings-ability relations in Figure 9.2 (including those at the bottom) and strengthens the general conclusions regarding concentration and skewness. Superior managers would not only control more than proportionately larger resources, but would employ greater than average quality personnel within their enterprises.

Finally, further work needs to be done to link these ideas with the growing literature on principal-agent relationships, and the dynamics of mobility between ranks (Lazear and Rosen, 1981). We have hardly begun to study the mechanism by which extraordinary talents are revealed to the market and how individuals find their proper niche in the economy.

References

Becker, G. S. "A Theory of Marriage." *Journal of Political Economy*, vol. 81, no. 4 (1973).

————— *A Treatise on the Family*, Cambridge: Harvard University Press, 1981.

Beckmann, M. "Management Production Functions and the Theory of the Firm." *Journal of Economic Theory*, vol. 14, no. 1 (1077).

Blackorby, C., Primont, D. and Russel, R. R. *Duality, Separability, and Functional Structure: Theory and Applications.* Amsterdam: North-Holland, 1978.

Bronfenbrenner, M. *Income Distribution Theory.* Chicago: Aldine-Atherton, 1971.

Calvo, C. A., and Wellisz, S. "Hierarchy, Ability, and Income Distribution." *Journal of Political Economy*, vol. 87, no. 5 (1979).

Fox, H. *Top Executive Compensation (1978 Edition)*. New York: National Industrial Conference Board, 1978.

Grubb, D. "Power and Ability in the Distribution of Earnings." Centre for Labouor Economics, London School of Economics, April 1980.

Holmstrom, B. "Moral Hazard and Observability." *Bell Journal of Economics*, vol. 10, no. 1 (Spring 1979).

Hymer, A., and Pashigian, P. "Firm size and Growth." *Journal of Political Economy*, vol. 70, no. 6 (1962).

Kanbur, S. M. "Of Risk-Taking and the Personal Distribution of Income." *Journal of Political Economy*, vol. 87, no. 4 (1979).

Keren, M., and Levhari, D. "The Optimum Span of Control in a Pure Hierarchy." *Management Science*, vol. 25, no. 11 (1979).

Kihlstrom, R., and Laffont, J. J. "A General Equilibrium Theory of the Firm Based on Risk Aversion." *Journal of Political Economy*, vol. 87, no. 4 (1979).

Lazear, E., and Rosen, S. "Rank Order Tournaments as Optimum Labor Contracts." *Journal of Political Economy*, vol. 89, no. 5 (1981).

Lewellen, W. G., and Huntsman, B. "Managerial Pay and Corporate Performance." *American Economic Review*, vol. 60, no. 4 (1970).

Lucas, R. E. "On the Size Distribution of Business Firms." *Bell Journal of Economics*, vol. 9, no. 2 (Autumn 1978).

Lydall, H. *The Structure of Earnings*. London: Oxford University Press, 1968.

Mayer, T. "The Distributions of Ability and Earnings." *Review of Economics and Statistics*, vol. 42, no. 2 (1960).

Mellow, W. "Employer Size and Wages." U.S. Department of Labor, Bureau fo Labor Statistics, Office of Research and Evaluation, April 1981.

Mesarovic, M. D., Macko, D., and Takahara, Y. *Theory of Hierarchical, Multilevel Systems*. New York: Academic Press, 1970.

Miller, F. "Wages and Firm Size." University of Chicago, 1980.

Oi, W. Y. "The Fixed Employment Costs of Specialized Labor." University of Rochester, 1981.

Quandt, R. E. "On the Size Distribution of Firms." *American Economic Review*, vol. 56, no. 3 (June 1966).

Roberts, D. R. "A General Theory of Executive Compensation Based on Statiscally Tested Propositions." *Quarterly Journal of Economics*, vol. 70 (May 1956).

Rosen, S. "Substitution and Division of Labor." *Economica*, vol. 45, no. 1 (1978).

―――― "The Economics of Superstars." *American Economic Review.* vol. 71, no. 5 (December 1981).

Simon, H. *Administrative Behavior: A Study of Decision Making Processes in Administrative Organizations*, 2nd ed. New York: Free Press, 1965.

Tuck, R. H. *An Essay on the Economic Theory of Rank*. Oxford: Blackwell, 1954.

Viner, J. "Cost Curves and Supply Curves" in G. Stigler and K. Boulding, eds., *Readings in Price Theory*, Chicago: Richard D. Irwin, 1952.

Waldman, M. "Worker Allocation, Hierarchies, and the Wage Distribution." University of Pennsylvania, 1981.

Williamson, O. E. "Hierarchical Control and Optimum Firm Size." *Journal of Political Economy*, vol. 75, no. 2 (1967).

―――― "The Modern Corporation: Origins, Evolution, Attributes." *Journal of Economic Literature*, vol. 19, no. 4 (December 1981).

Willis, R., and Rosen, S. "Education and Self-Selection." *Journal of Political Economy*, vol. 87, no. 5, Pt. 2 (1978).

10

Prizes and Incentives in Elimination Tournaments

Several recent papers have clarified the problem of incentives when competitors are paid on the basis of rank or relative performance (Edward Lazear and myself, 1981; Jerry Green and Nancy Stokey, 1983; Barry Nalebuff and Joseph Stiglitz, 1984; Bengt Holmstrom, 1982; James Malcomson, 1984; Lorne Carmichael, 1983; Mary O'Keefe, W. Kip Viscusi, and Richard Zeckhauser, 1984). The main focus so far has been to examine the economic efficiency of these schemes. However, a much longer tradition in statistics views relative comparisons as an experimental design for ranking and selecting contestants. These two views are joined in this work.

I investigate the incentive properties of prizes in sequential elimination events, where rewards are increasing in survival. The inherent logic of these experiments is to determine the best contestants and promote survival of the fittest; and to maintain the "quality of play" as the game proceeds through its stages. Athletic tournaments immediately come to mind, but much broader interest in this class of problems arises from its potential application to career games, where the tournament analogy is supported (James Rosenbaum, 1984). Many organizations have a triangular structure (for example, Martin Beckmann, 1978) and most top-level managers come up through the ranks (Kevin J. Murphy, 1984). A career trajectory is, in part, the outcome of competition among peers to attain higher ranking and more remunerative positions over the life cycle. The structure of rewards influences the nature and quality of competition at each stage of the game.

I am especially indebted to Barry Nalebuff for many suggestions that greatly improved this work, to Edward Lazear, Kevin M. Murphy, David Pierce, and Nancy Stokey for advice on a number of points, and to Gary Becker, James Friedman, Sandy Grossman, and John Riley for comments on an initial draft. Robert Tamura was my research assistant. This project was supported by the National Science Foundation.
From *American Economic Review* 76, no. 4 (September 1986): 701–715.

What needs to be explained is the marked concentration of rewards in the top ranks. For example, the top four ranks receive 50 percent or more of the total purse in tennis tournaments. Concentration is less extreme in the executive labor market, but nonetheless earnings rise more than proportionate to rank in most firms. I show below that an elimination design requires an extra reward for the overall winner to maintain performance incentives throughout the game.

The economics of this result derives from the survival aspects of the game. A competitor's performance incentives at any stage are set by an option value. The loser's prize is guaranteed at that stage, but winning gives the option to continue on to all successive rungs in the ladder. There are fewer steps remaining to be attained as the game proceeds, and the option value plays out. It expires in the final match because advancement opportunities vanish. At that point, the difference in prize money between winning and losing must incorporate the equivalent of the survival option that maintained incentives at earlier stages. The extra weight of rewards at the top is due to the no-tomorrow aspects of the final stage of the game. It extends the horizon of players surviving to those stages, and makes the game appear of infinite length to a contestant, *as if* there are always many steps left to attain, no matter how far one has climbed in the past. This result obviously bears a family resemblance to the role of a "pension" in a finitely repeated principal and agent problem (Gary Becker and George Stigler, 1974; Lazear, 1981).

Section I describes the game, and Section II sets forth the nature of contestants' strategies. Sections III and IV analyze the problem when the inherent talents of competitors are known, while Section V analyzes the case where talents are unknown.

I. Design of the Game

For analytical tractability and simplicity, the ideas are best revealed by a paired-comparison structure, as in a tennis-ladder. The tournament begins with 2^N players and proceeds sequentially through N stages. Each stage is set of pairwise matches. Winners survive to the next round, where another pairing is drawn, and losers are eliminated from subsequent play. Half are cut from further consideration at each stage. Thus in a career game, those eligible for promotion to some rank have attained the rank immediately below it. Those who are passed over at any stage are out of the running for further promotions. The top prize W_1 is awarded to the winner of the final match, who has won N matches overall. The loser of the final match achieves second place overall and is awarded prize W_2 for having won $N - 1$ matches. Losers of the semifinals are both awarded W_3, etc.

Define s as the number of stages remaining to be played. Then all players eliminated in a match where s stages remain are awarded prize W_{s+1}. Define the interrank spread $\Delta W_s = W_s - W_{s+1}$ as the marginal reward for advancing one place in the final ranking. These increments determine incentives to advance through the stages. Prizes are increasing in survival: $\Delta W_s > 0$ for all s.

I am concerned in this work with studying how prizes affect performance and selection, and with finding some characterizations of the relative reward structure required to maintain incentives as the game proceeds. This is a piece of a larger problem of the "optimal" prize structure, the study of which requires specifying how incentives affect the social value of the game. These complex matters are not well understood. So rather than trying results to an arbitrary input-output technology, a common feature of the larger problem obviously requires that players work at least as hard, if not harder, in the later stages of the game as in the early stages. We don't want contestants to lie down near the end. For example, in a hierarchical organization, the decisions made at the top are more important than those made further down the pyramid (see my 1982 paper): shirking and lack of talent have more serious consequences at the top of the organization than at the bottom.

Rank-order schemes are encountered when individual output and input are difficult to measure on a cardinal scale, an inherent feature of managerial and many other types of talent; or when common background noise contaminates precise individual assessments of value-added. Competition is inherently head-to-head in most athletic games, and cardinality in any sense other than probability of winning has little meaning. Ordinality is inherent because the point scores used to calibrate performance contain many arbitrary elements, as in a classroom test. Many of these same considerations apply to selection of managerial talents, though competition is not strictly paired comparisons.

Given the rules, these issues may be finessed for studying the connection between prizes, incentives, and selection by specifying how players' actions affect the probability of winning. Let i index a player and let j index an opponent in some match. Consider a game in which there are m types of players. Index the ability type of the i player by I and the ability type of the opponent j player by J. Both I and J take on m possible values, $1, 2, \ldots, m$, with $m \leq 2^N$. Let x_{si} and x_{sj} denote the intensity of effort expended by players i and j in a match when s stages remain to be played, and let γ_I and γ_J represent their abilities or natural talents for the game. Then $P_s(I, J)$ is the probability that a player of type I wins in a match against a player of type J (possibly the same type) with

$$P_s(I, J) = \frac{\gamma_I h(x_{si})}{\gamma_I h(x_{si}) + \gamma_J h(x_{sj})}, \tag{1}$$

where $h(x)$ is increasing in x and $h(0) \geq 0$. A player increases the probability of winning the match by exerting greater effort, given the talent and effort of the opponent and own talent. To simplify the problem, the win technology is assumed identical at every stage (s enters only through the x's).

When both players exert the same level of effort, the win probability is $P_s(I, J) = \gamma_I/(\gamma_I + \gamma_J)$, and its inverse is a bookmaker's "morning line" or "true-to-form" actuarilly fair payoffs per dollar bet on player-type I. Notice from (1) that common, multiplicative environmental factors do not affect $P_s(I, J,)$. Let the common factor multiply $\gamma h(x)$ for both players. Then whether the commonality is match-, stage-, or tournament-specific, it factors out of the probability calculation and has no effect on either incentives or selection. Equation (1) is a logit when $h(x)$ is exponential. Alternatively, think of $\gamma h(x)$ as the arrival rate of a Poisson process. The (1) can be given a racing game interpretation, as in the recent literature on patent races (Glenn Loury, 1979).

II. Strategies

A player's decision of how much effort to expend in any match depends on weighing the benefit of greater effort (increasing the probability of surviving) against its costs. There are two complications. First, the value of advancing depends on how the player assesses future effort should eligibility be maintained. This forward-looking effect is analyzed by backward recursion. Second, current actions depend on the anticipated behavior of the current and all future possible opponents. The sequential character of the game allows this to be analyzed by adopting Nash non-cooperative strategies as the equilibrium concept. Discounting between stages is ignored and risk neutrality is assumed.

Define $V_s(I, J)$ as the value to a player of type I of playing a match against an opponent of type J when s possible stages remain to be played. Assume, for now, that all players' talents are common knowledge. Let $c(x)$ be the cost of effort in any match, assumed identical for all players, $c'(x) > 0$, $c''(x) \geq 0$, and $c(0) = 0$. The value of the match consists of two components: one is $_{s+1}$, the prize earned if the match is lost and the player is eliminated, an event which occurs with probability $1 - P_s(I, J)$. The other is the value of achieving a final rank superior to $s + 1$ if the match is won. Let $EV_{s-1}(I)$ represent the expected value of eligibility in the next stage. This is a weighted average over J of $V_{s-1}(I, J)$, where the weights are the probabilities that the I player will confront an opponent of type J in the next stage. These probabilities depend on the activities of players in other matches and the rules for drawing opponents at each stage. The probability of continuation is $P_s(I, J)$, and costs $c(x)$ are incurred for either outcome, so the fundamental equation for this problem is

$$V_s(I, J) = \max \left[P_s(I, J,)EV_{s-1}(I) \right. \tag{2}$$
$$\left. +(1 - P_s(I, J))W_{s+1} - c(x_{si}) \right].$$

The max in (2) is understood on Nash assumptions as conditioned on the given current and expected future efforts of all other players remaining alive at s and on the optimum actions taken by the player in question in subsequent matches.

Substituting (1) into (2) and differentiating with respect to x_{si} yields the first-order condition

$$\gamma_I \gamma_J h_j h_i' / (\gamma_I h_i + \gamma_J h_j)^2 \left[EV_{s-1}(I) - W_{s+1} \right] - c_i' = 0, \tag{3}$$

where $h_i = h(x_{si})$, $h_i' = dh(x_{si})/dx_{si}$, etc. The second-order condition is

$$D = c_i' \left[(h_i''/h_i') - 2\gamma_I h_i'/(\gamma_I h_i + \gamma_J h_j) \right] - c_i'' < 0. \tag{4}$$

Note that (4) allows $h'' > 0$ so long as it is bounded. There is also a global condition. Equation (3) indicates that effort in any match is controlled by $EV_{s-1}(I) - W_{s+1}$. This difference between winning and losing must be positive for the player to have an interest in maintaining eligibility into the next stage. Otherwise, it is best to default and exert no effort.

Equation (3) defines the best-response function for player i. Differentiating with respect to the current opponent's effort.

$$\partial x_i / \partial x_j = \frac{(h_j' / h_j) c_i'}{-D(\gamma_I h_i + \gamma_J h_j)} (\gamma_I h_i - \gamma_J h_j). \tag{5}$$

Player i's best reply is increasing in x_j when x_j is small enough, but is decreasing when the opponent's effort is sufficiently large. It has a turning point at $\gamma_I h(x_i) = \gamma_J h(x_j)$. The turning point occurs at $x_i = x_j$ for equally talented players ($\gamma_I = \gamma_J$). It turns at some value $x_j > x_i$ when i is playing a weaker opponent ($\gamma_I > \gamma_J$) and it turns at some $x_j < x_i$ when the opponent is the stronger player ($\gamma_I < \gamma_J$). See Figure (10.1). Analysis is confined to pure-strategy equilibria.[1]

III. Incentive-Maintaining Prizes: Equally Talented Contestants

The solution is transparent when all players are equally talented (there is only one type). Then $EV_{s-1}(I) = V_{s-1}$, because each player knows for sure that an opponent of equal skill will be confronted at every stage. From Figure 10.1, the best-reply function is the same for all players and has a turning point at $x_i = x_j$. Therefore the equilibrium is symmetric: $x_{xi} = x_{sj} = x_s$ for all i and j and $P_s = 1/2$ in equilibrium. Each match is a close call in expected value. The common level of effort when s stages remain which satisfies (3) is

$$(V_{s-1} - W_{s+1})(h'(x_s) / h(x_s)) / 4 = c'(x_s). \tag{6}$$

---

1. The best reply may jump down to zero at some point because either (4) fails beyond that point or default ($x_i = 0$) is a global optimum while (3) is local. Pure strategies characterize equilibrium when these jumps occur (if they do) at sufficiently large x_i. This requires certain bounds on the curvature of the $h(x)$ and $c(x)$ functions and some limits on the degree of heterogeneity (the γ's) among players (for example, a very weak player might just lie down against a very strong one). The rules of the game determine $c(x)$ and $h(x)$ (see O'Keefe et al.). Rules and initial screening of entrants must be suitably constrained to guarantee pure-strategy equilibria. Nalebuff and Stiglitz analyze random strategies in one-shot games. Stephen Bronars (1985) shows that a weak player might employ a riskier strategy against a stronger opponent, but (1) is not suitably parameterized to consider this.

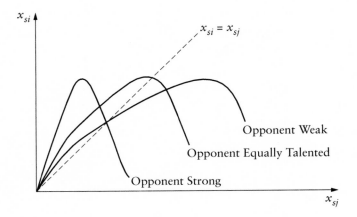

Figure 10.1

Define the elasticities

$$\eta(x) = xh'(x)/h(x),$$ (7)

$$\epsilon(x) = xc'(x)/c(x),$$

$$\mu(x) = \eta(x)/\epsilon(x).$$

Then (6) becomes

$$(V_{s-1} - W_{s+1})\eta(x_s)/4 = c(x_s).$$ (8)

Substituting (8) into (2) and using $P_s = 1/2$,

$$V_s = (1/2)(1 - \mu(x_s)/2)(V_{s-1} - W_{s+1}) + W_{s+1}$$ (9)

$$= \beta_s V_{s-1} + (1 - \beta_s)W_{s+1},$$

where

$$\beta_s = (1/2)(1 - \mu(x_s)/2).$$ (10)

The recursion (9) holds if (3) is a global maximum, and no player has incentives to default from x_s defined by (6). This requires, from (9), that $V_s - W_{s+1} = \beta_s(V_{s-1} - W_{s+1}) > 0$. Otherwise taking the sure loss is a better choice. Therefore $\beta_s > 0$, or, from (10) and (7), $\eta(x_s)/2\epsilon(x_s) < 1$, or $\eta(x) < 2$. There is no pure-strategy equilibrium in this game if any player has an incentive to default.

The sense of the no-default condition $\eta(x)/\epsilon(x) < 2$ is related to the problem of an arms race. If the elasticity of response of effort is large relative to the elasticity of its cost, then players' efforts to win results in a negative sum game in pure strategies. It is not optimal to default if the opponent does, but at the local equilibrium the costs of contesting have been escalated so much that both want to default. In fact, (9) implies that for given prizes, players are better off when there is less scope for actions to affect outcomes. V_s is decreasing in $\mu(x)$, so the rules of the game must be devised to balance two conflicting forces: games which greatly constrain the effect of actions on outcomes are inefficient and unproductive; whereas competition is destructive if these constraints are relaxed too much.[2]

Assuming $0 < \beta_s < 1$, for all s and using $V_0 = W_1$ as a boundary condition, the solution to (9) is

$$V_s = (\beta_1\beta_2 \ldots \beta_s)\Delta W_1 + (\beta_2 \ldots \beta_s)\Delta W_2 \qquad (11)$$
$$+ \cdots + \beta_s \Delta W_s + W_{s+1}.$$

The value of maintaining eligibility at any stage is the sure prize the player has guaranteed by surviving that long, plus the discounted sum of successive interrank rewards that may be achieved in future matches. Herein lies the "option" value of an elimination design. Manipulating (11) yields an expression for $V_{s-1} - W_{s+1}$, which controls performance incentives, from (8):

$$(V_{s-1} - W_{s+1}) = (\beta_1 \ldots \beta_{s-1})\Delta W_1 \qquad (12)$$
$$+ (\beta_2 \ldots \beta_{s-1})\Delta W_2 + \cdots + \Delta W_s.$$

Incentives are determined by the discounted sum of interrank spreads.

What reward structure maintains incentives to perform at a common value throughout all stages of the game? Here $x_s = x^*$ for all s and $\beta_s = \beta$ is a constant for all s, from (10). Then (12) implies

$$(V_{s-1} - W_{s+1}) - \beta(V_{s-2} - W_s) = \Delta W_s \quad \text{for } s = 2, 3, \ldots, N. \qquad (13)$$

---

2. Contestants have incentives to introduce new techniques and styles of play to create a winning edge. These are sources of technical change in career games. Athletic games use a supreme authority to maintain the integrity of the game. Innovations which escalate the collective costs of competition relative to social value are prohibited.

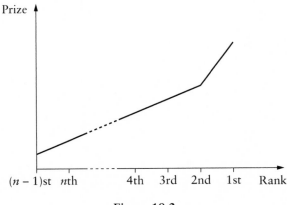

Figure 10.2

Constant performance requires that $(V_{s-1} - W_{s+1})$ is a constant. Suppose $V_{s-1} - W_{s+1} = k$, where k is determined so that $x_s = x^*$ solves (3). Then from (13),

$$k(1 - \beta) = \Delta W = \Delta W_s, \quad \text{for } s = 2, 3, \ldots, N \qquad (14)$$

and since final-round effort depends only on ΔW_1, from (12),

$$k = \Delta W_1 - \Delta W/(1 - \beta) > \Delta W. \qquad (15)$$

The incentive-maintaining prize structure requires a constant interrank spread from second place down, from (14). However, it requires a larger interrank spread at the top, from (15). Prizes rise *linearly* in increments $\Delta W = k(1 - \beta)$ from rank $N + 1$ up through rank 2, but the first-place prize takes a distinct *jump* out of sync with the general linear pattern below it. The incentive-maintaining prize distribution weighs the top prize more heavily than the rest.[3] See Figure 10.2.

The proof supports the economic interpretation of this surprising conclusion. The final-round spread has to replace the earlier option

---

3. This analysis determines only relative prizes across ranks, not their absolute level. More structure on technologies and the social value of the game must be introduced to examine the latter (for example, see Lazear's and my article). Here we require that the purse is large enough to support $V_s > 0$ for all s. This implies an upper bound on feasible x^*. Another upper bound on x^* is implied by contestants' outside opportunities, but is ignored.

value of achieving possible higher ranks at earlier stages. Substitute (14) and (15) into (12):

$$(V_{s-1} - W_{s+1}) \tag{16}$$
$$= \beta^{s-1} \Delta W_1 + \Delta W (\beta^{s-2} + \beta^{s-3} + \cdots + 1)$$
$$= \Delta W \left[\left(\beta^{s-1}/(1-\beta) \right) + \beta^{s-2} + \beta^{s-3} + \cdots + 1 \right]$$
$$= \Delta W (1 + \beta + \beta^2 + \beta^3 + \cdots) \quad \text{for all } s,$$

The extra increment at the top converts the value of the difference between winning and losing at each stage into a perpetuity of constant value at all stages. It effectively extends the horizon of the players and makes them behave *as if they are in a game which continues forever.* This horizon-extending feature of the top prize is one of the reasons why observed rewards are concentrated toward the top ranks. It is clear that concentrating even more of the purse on the top creates incentives for performance to increase as the game proceeds through its stages. For example, if the winner takes all, then every term other than the one in ΔW_1 in (12) vanished and the difference in value between winning and losing increases as the game proceeds, through the force of discounting: effort is smallest in the first stage and largest in the finals.

The result in (16) is robust to a number of modifications.

(i) *Risk Aversion.* Suppose preferences take the additive form $U(W) - \sum_s c(x_s)$, where $c(x)$ is as before and $U(W)$ is increasing, but not necessarily linear in W. Then the entire analysis goes through by replacing W_s with $U(W_s)$ wherever it appears. Incentive maintenance requires a constant difference in the utility of rewards $U(W_{s+1}) - U(W_{s+2})$ in all stages prior to the finals, but still requires a jump in the inter-rank difference in utility of winning the finals. If players are risk averse $(U''(W) < 0)$, the incentive-maintaining interrank spreads, with an even larger increment between first and second place. The prize structure is everywhere convex in rank order, with greater concentration of the purse on the top prizes than when contestants are risk neutral. The spread has to be increasing to "buy off" survivor's risk aversion and maintain their interest in advancing to higher ranks.

(ii) *Symmetric Win-Technologies.* The derivation of (14) and (15) rests only on that property that P_s is 1/2 in equilibrium. Hence Figure 10.2 is independent of the specific form of (2) and holds for *any* win technology resulting in a symmetric equilibrium. Furthermore, the result extends to more than pairwise comparisons: there might be *n*-way comparisons at each stage. In the Poisson case, the probability of advancing becomes $h(x_i)/\sum_{k=1}^{n} h(x_k)$. Then $\beta_s = (1/n)(1 - (n-1)\mu(x_s)/n)$, but the logic otherwise remains unchanged.

(iii) *Stage Effects.* The nature of competition may vary across stages. For example, in a corporate hierarchy the pass-through rate may fall at each successive rank. Similarly, μ_s may be smaller in the later stages because higher-ranking positions are more demanding than lower-ranking ones. In either case, β_s decreases as the game proceeds, and interrank spreads must be increasing to undo the incentive dilution effects of greater discounting of the future, which otherwise reduces the option value of continuation. These considerations increase the convexity of the rank/reward structure.[4]

IV. Heterogeneous Contestants with Known Talents

In heterogeneous populations, elimination designs promote *survival of the fittest* and progressive elimination of weaker contenders. The conditional mean ability of survivors tends to increase as the game proceeds and differences in survivors' talents are compressed relative to the initial field. This increasing homogeneity among surviving members across stages extends the incentive-maintenance result above to the limit of the last few stages of a long game. For by continuity of the best-reply functions in ability parameters, EV_{s-1} is approximately V_{s-1} among relatively homogeneous survivors in the final stages. The extra final-round incremental prize remains necessary to maintain incentives toward the end.

This section shows that the value of the continuation option is increasing in ability, which is why the design encourages survival of the fittest. However, analysis is complicated by progressive increasing strength-of-field effects. That stronger opponents are likely to be encountered in later stages reduces the value of continuation, while the greater likelihood of being matched against a weaker opponent in the

---

4. The analysis of direct effort spillovers across stages is complicated by the fact that there may be asymmetric as well as symmetric pure-strategy equilibria. At symmetric equilibrium it is easy to show that fatigue and "burnout" require more concentration on the top prize to penalize early-round "coasting." The force of "momentum" or learning requires less concentration at the top to maintain constant quality of play.

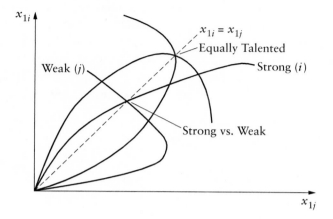

Figure 10.3

current stage increases it. Therefore, the nature of the game is affected by the rules for drawing opponents, such as a seeding. A simulation of a two-stage game illustrates these issues.[5]

To simplify, assume two player types and constant elasticity cost and $h(x)$ functions. Type 1 is stronger than type 2 ($\gamma_1 > \gamma_2$). Since we have to keep track of each player's talent, the definition of β_s must be extended to

$$\beta_s(I, J) = P_s(I, J) \left[1 - \mu P_s(J, I) \right],\qquad(17)$$

where the P's are evaluated at equilibrium. Equation (17) includes (10) when $I = J$ because $P_s(I, I) = 1/2$.

Finals. Since $EV_1 - W_2 = \Delta W_1$ for all γ_I, symmetry of (3) implies $x_{1_j} = x_{1_j}$ irrespective of players' talents: $P_1(I, J) = \gamma_I / (\gamma_I + \gamma_J)$ in equilibrium. Effort is greater in a final match involving equally talented contestants than in one which matches a stronger against a weaker player (Figure 10.3). Using the same manipulations as before, we find

$$V_1(I, J) = \beta_1(I, J) \Delta W_1 + W_1.\qquad(18)$$

---

5. Notice that a player is interested in what players in other matches are doing at any given stage because those outcomes determine who likely opponents will be in future stages. Equilibrium at each stage is a simultaneous 2^s player game: the problem does not disassemble pairwise and its complete solution must be simulated.

274 •   *Markets and Diversity*

Since $P_1(1, 2) > P_1(2, 1)$—a stronger player has a winning edge against a weak one in equilibrium, we have $\beta_1(1, 2) > \beta > \beta_1(2, 1)$.

Semifinals. Let π_1 denote the probability that the winner of the match in question will confront a strong player in the finals. This depends on the identities and efforts chosen by players in the other match, but these actions are given to the opponents in this match in the Nash solution. Therefore,

$$EV_1(I) = [\pi_1\beta_1(I, 1) + (1 - \pi_1)\beta_1(I, 2)] \Delta W_1 + W_2 \qquad (19)$$
$$= \tilde{\beta}_1(I)\Delta W_1 + W_2,$$

where

$$\tilde{\beta}_1(I) = \pi_1\beta_1(I, 1) + (1 - \pi_1)\beta_1(I, 2)$$

and

$$EV_1(I) - W_3 = \tilde{\beta}_1(I)\Delta W_1 + \Delta W_2. \qquad (20)$$

π_1 is smaller for the strong contestant implies $\tilde{\beta}_1(1) > \tilde{\beta}_1(2)$ because $\beta_1(1, 2) > \beta_1(2, 1)$.

There are two possible types of matches in the semi's. The equilibrium is symmetric if $I = J$, with $P_2(1, 1) = P_2(2, 2) = 1/2$. If $I \neq J$, the equilibrium is *not* symmetric because the stronger player has a greater value of continuation in (19) and (20). The strong player exerts greater efforts to win in equilibrium and $P_2(1, 2) > \gamma_1/(\gamma_1 + \gamma_2) = P_1(1, 2)$ (see Figure 10.4). We find

$$V_2(I, J) = \beta_2(I, J)\left[\tilde{\beta}_1(I)\Delta W_1 + \Delta W_2\right] + W_3.$$

Furthermore,

$$\beta_2(1, 2) > \beta_1(1, 2) > \beta > \beta_1(2, 1) > \beta_2(2, 1), \qquad (21)$$

which implies $V_2(1, 2) > V_2(2, 1)$ and $\tilde{\beta}_2(1) > \tilde{\beta}_2(2)$.

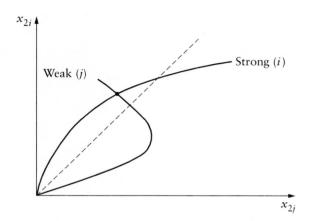

Figure 10.4

These formulas generalize for arbitrary s:

$$V_s(I, J) = \beta_s(I, J) \left[(\tilde{\beta}_1(I)\tilde{\beta}_2(I) \ldots \tilde{\beta}_{s-1}(I))\Delta W_1 \right. \tag{22}$$

$$+ (\tilde{\beta}_2(I) \ldots \tilde{\beta}_{s-1}(I))\Delta W_2 + \cdots + \Delta W_s \Big]$$

$$+ W_{s+1} E V_{s-1} - W_{s+1}$$

$$= (\tilde{\beta}_1(I)\tilde{\beta}_2(I) \ldots \tilde{\beta}_{s-1}(I))\Delta W_1 + (\tilde{\beta}_2(I) \ldots \tilde{\beta}_{s-1}(I))\Delta W_2$$

$$+ \tilde{\beta}_{s-1}(I)\Delta W_{s-1} + \Delta W_s$$

$$\tilde{\beta}_s(I) = \pi_s \beta_s(I, 1) + (1 - \pi_s)\beta_s(I, 2),$$

where π_s is the probability a strong opponent will be encountered at s. An easy induction proves $\tilde{\beta}_s(1) > \tilde{\beta}_s(2)$ for all s, so (22) implies that the value of continuation is larger for stronger players at every stage of the game. The second expression in (22) also implies that a strong player works harder in a strong-weak match than a weak player does: the weak are eliminated with probability in excess of $\gamma_1/(\gamma_1 + \gamma_2)$ at every stage except the last.

Since the value of the game is larger for stronger players, equilibrium in matches involving unequally talented players is asymmetric (except in the finals) and the definition of incentive maintenance must be extended. The most straightforward extension is a requirement that the same level of effort be maintained in all stages *within* any given type of pairing

I against *J*: it is not feasible for effort to be maintained at a constant value *across* match types due to heterogeneity. Even this question cannot be answered in its entirety without additional structure, because the inequality in (21) cannot be extended in general. However, we have the following analytical result for the last two stages:

> *If the prize distribution is linear at the top* $(\Delta W_1 = \Delta W_2)$, *effort by both players in strong-weak matches is larger in the semifinals than in the finals; and effort in matches between similar types is also larger in the semi's than in the finals.*

The first part follows from the fact that $\tilde{\beta}_1(1)$ necessarily exceeds $\tilde{\beta}_1(2)$; while the second part follows from Section III (and in fact holds true for all stages when the prize structure is linear everywhere). The best reply for each player in any type of match is larger in the semi's than in the finals when $\Delta W_1 = \Delta W_2$. Consequently the extra incremental prize at the top remains necessary to extend the horizon and help insure that the final match is the best match.

A small simulation for a two-stage game illustrates these ideas and shows some effects of seeding. To simplify the calculations, I chose $h(x) = c(x) = x$ (so $\epsilon = \eta = \mu = 1.0$). Further, $\gamma_1 = 2$ and $\gamma_2 = 1$: true-to-form odds in a $(1, 2)$ match are 2-to1 in favor of type 1. The simulation assumes that the game begins with two players of each type. The total purse is fixed at 1000 and $W_3 = 0$. The rank-prize structure is linear when $\Delta W_1 / \Delta W_2 = 1$.

The first two rows of Table 10.1 show what might happen in a random draw which pulls strong-strong and weak-weak in the initial round. This happens half the time and guarantees a strong-weak final match pairing. Column 1 demonstrates that finals effort is smaller than semifinals effort when prizes are linear. Comparing across columns, we see that the final-round increment has to be quite large for strong players to exert more effort in the finals than in the semi's. The results are qualitatively similar for the other initial-round pairing possibility. These mixed matches would be assured by seeding, but occur only half the time with random draws. Notice that effort is smaller in mixed matches than in like matches, and that effort differences across player types are smaller in mixed matches. Strong players work very hard at round 1 to knock each other off and get into the finals when they know that their next opponent will be weak.

Table 10.1 • Two-stage, two-types simulation ($\gamma_1 = 2, \gamma_2 = 1$)

	Spread: $\Delta W_1 / \Delta W_2$				
	1	2	3	5	8
A. Semifinals ($s = 2$)					
$x_2(1, 1)$	120.3	118.1	116.6	115.1	113.9
$x_2(2, 2)$	92.6	76.4	60.7	55.5	47.7
$x_2(1, 2)$	92.7	82.6	76.1	68.3	62.0
$x_2(2, 1)$	81.6	66.7	57.7	47.4	39.6
$P_2(1, 2)$	.69	.71	.73	.74	.76
B. Finals ($s = 1$)					
$x_1(1, 1) = x_1(2, 2)$	83.3	125.0	150.0	178.5	200.0
$x_1(1, 2) = x_1(2, 1)$	74.1	111.1	133.4	158.8	177.8
$\Pr(1, 1)$	.24/.48	.26/.51	.28/.53	.28/.55	.29/.57
$\Pr(2, 2)$	.04/.09	.04/.08	.03/.07	.03/.06	.03/.06
$\Pr(1, 2)$	.72/.43	.70/.41	.70/.40	.69/.39	.68/.37
C. Expected total effort					
Random	540.7	574.7	598.9	616.0	632.4
Seeds	507.4	537.2	554.4	573.3	586.9

Note: Simulation for $\gamma_1 = 2, \gamma_2 = 1, \eta = \epsilon = \mu = 1.0$. The term $x_s(I, J)$ is equilibrium effort expended by player of ability type I in match against opponent of ability type J when s stages remain; $P_2(1, 2)$ is probability strong player wins semifinal round match against weak opponent; $P_1(1, 2) = 2/3$ because final-round equilibrium is symmetric. Finals pairing probability $\Pr(I, J)$ is equilibrium probability type I against type J in finals: first number refers to *random* initial draw, second number to strong/weak *seeds* in first round. The last rows give expected effort summed over all players in all matches and stages.

The probabilities of various final match-type pairings are shown in panel B. Neither seeding nor random draw guarantees that the best players survive to the finals, but seeding *doubles* the probabilities that they do. Under random draw, the most probable (by far) final match is strong-weak. These probabilities are fairly insensitive to spread because the strong-player win-probability in a mixed first-round match is insensitive to the prize distribution with this parameter configuration. Notice that seeding makes a strong-strong final match the most probable outcome, but it comes at the cost of increasing the probability of a weak-weak final. However, this latter probability is small in either case.

Comparing across columns, we see that semifinals effort decreases and finals effort increases as the spreads grow larger. However, panel C shows that the second effect exceeds the first: expected total effort over all matches and stages increases with the spread. Most remarkably, total effort is greater when the initial draw is random than seeded. Seeding produces less variance in efforts in the first round, a lower mean in that round, and it most likely produces a better match among more talented opponents in the finals. The final interrank spread must be greatly elevated in the seeding game to produce expected total effort comparable to the no-seeding game. This suggests that seeds are observed when not simply total effort expended, but the distribution of the quality of play among players and stages, and guaranteeing the best match at the end, are important for the social productivity of the game. It justifies my reluctance to specify an additive social value function for the purposes of calculating an "optimal" prize structure.

V. Heterogeneous Contestants with Talents Unknown

Suppose we are interested in choosing the best out of T possible contestants. A round-robin design matches each player against every other and chooses the one with the largest overall win percentage. A sequential or knockout design eliminates a contender from further consideration after a certain number of losses. The sequential design promotes survival of the fittest and saves sampling costs by eliminating likely losers early in the game, but provides less precise information than the round-robin. The design choice comes down to comparing sampling costs with the value of more precision or the loss of making errors. H. A. David (1959, 1969) suggests that knockout designs have advantages over round-robins in selecting the best contestant, and Jean Gibbons, Ingram Olkin, and Milton Sobel (1977) prove it using sequential statistical decision theory. These issues are of great practical importance in medical trials. However, it is not possible to apply statistical decision theory alone to selection in human populations, because no account is taken of contestants' incentives to optimize against the experimental design.

The main ideas are best illustrated in the case of "symmetric ignorance." Consider a sequential single elimination design, in which there are m types of contestants, all of whom share the same priors on the talents of others and who are equally ignorant about their own and others' talents. The distribution of types is common knowledge, and there is no private information. Estimates of own talents and the strength of the surviving field are updated as the game proceeds. This changing information feeds back into each contestant's strategy at every stage. When contestants have no more information about themselves than their surviving opponents do, it is clear that the interesting equilibrium is symmetric, because all survivors share the same information set—the same winning record, and choose the same strategy.

Let $\alpha_s(I)$ denote the probability that a player is type I when s stages remain to be played, and let $\tilde{\alpha}_s(J)$ denote the player's assessment that the current opponent is type J. Then, from Bayes' rule, the player's assessment of himself when $s - 1$ stages remain, conditional on surviving (winning at stage s) is

$$\alpha_{s-1}(I) = \Pr(\text{win at stage } s \mid I)\alpha_2(I)/\Pr(\text{win at stage } s) \qquad (23)$$

$$= \alpha_s(I) \sum_J \tilde{\alpha}_s(J)P_s(I, J) \Big/ \sum_I \sum_J \alpha_s(I)\tilde{\alpha}_s(J)P_s(I, J)$$

where $P_s(I, J)$ is the win technology in (1); $\sum_J \tilde{\alpha}_s(J)P_s(I, J)$ is the conditional probability of winning given that one is type I. The denominator is the unconditional probability of winning at stage s. Since the initial prior is common, information is common at all stages, so $\alpha_s(I) = \tilde{\alpha}_s(I)$ in equilibrium. Furthermore, all contestants choose the same effort for given s, and $P_s(I, J) = \gamma_I/(\gamma_I + \gamma_J)$ in equilibrium: survival chances for each type run true to form at each stage. Finally, the unconditional equilibrium survival probability is always 1/2 in paired comparisons. In equilibrium (23) becomes

$$\alpha_{s-1}(I) = 2\alpha_s(I) \sum_J \alpha_s(J) \left[\gamma_I/(\gamma_I + \gamma_J)\right]. \qquad (24)$$

Equation (24) implies survival of the fittest. To illustrate, suppose there are two types, with $\gamma_1 > \gamma_2$. Let α_2 be the expected proportion of stronger (type-1) players alive at s. Then (24) is

$$\alpha_{s-1} - \alpha_s = \alpha_s(1 - \alpha_s)\omega, \qquad (25)$$

where $\omega = (\gamma_1 - \gamma_2)/(\gamma_1 + \gamma_2)\omega$ is the difference in form probabilities between types. The solution to (25) looks like a logistic. The weak are eliminated at the largest rate when $\alpha_s = 1/2$, and are eliminated at a slower rate elsewhere. The rate of elimination of the weak also depends on ω. Convergence is very fast when ω is large. For example, if $\alpha_n = 1/2$ and ω is close to unity (its maximum possible value) over 99 percent of expected survivors are strong after only three stages. More stages are required to select the fittest members of the population the smaller the initial values of α and ω.

In choosing a strategy a player must assess own and opponents' talents at each stage. The problem is illustrated for the case of two types, strong (γ_1) and weak (γ_2). We have

$$V_s(\alpha_s, \bar{\alpha}_s) = \max \left\{ \Pr(\text{win}|\alpha_s, \bar{\alpha}_s) \right. \tag{26}$$
$$\left. \times \left[V_{s-1}(\alpha_{s-1}, \bar{\alpha}_{s-1}) - W_{s+1} \right] - c(x_{si}) \right\},$$

where the win probability is conditioned on the information available at the beginning of stage s:

$$\Pr(\text{win}|\alpha_s, \bar{\alpha}_s) = \alpha_s \left[\bar{\alpha}_s P_s(1, 1) + (1 - \bar{\alpha}_s) P_s(1, 2) \right] \tag{27}$$
$$+ (1 - \alpha_s) \left[\bar{\alpha}_s P_s(2, 1) + (1 - \bar{\alpha}_s) P_s(2, 2) \right],$$

with $(\alpha_s, \bar{\alpha}_s)$ updated according to (23). Thus in choosing x, the player weighs the possibilities of own and opponent's talent pairings by the information currently available. This information depends on past data, exogenous as of stage s. The player's assessment of the future strength of an opponent, $\bar{\alpha}_{s-1}$, depends on the given efforts of players in other matches. However, the player's assessment of his own talent in the next stage depends on today's actions and outcomes, from (23), and this (the value of information) also enters the calculation for choice of x_s. The Bayesian link between stages s and $s - 1$ introduces an interstage linkage in strategies that is not present when talents are known.

The first-order condition for this problem is

$$\frac{\partial \Pr(\text{win}|.)}{\partial x_{si}} \left[V_{s-1}(\alpha_{s-1}, \bar{\alpha}_{s-1}) - W_{s+1} \right] \tag{28}$$
$$+ \Pr(\text{win}|.) \left[\partial V_{s-1}(\alpha_{s-1}, \bar{\alpha}_{s-1}) / \partial \alpha_{s-1} \right]$$
$$\times (\partial \alpha_{s-1} / \partial x_{si}) - c'(x_{si}) = 0.$$

The derivative $\partial \Pr(\text{win}|.)/\partial x_{si}$ is calculated from (27) and $\partial \alpha_{s-1}/\partial x_{si}$ is calculated from (23), both given x_{sj}. An expression for the information term $\partial V_{s-1}/\partial\alpha_{s-1}$ is found by applying the envelope property to (26):

$$\partial V_s(\alpha_s, \bar{\alpha}_s)/\partial\alpha_s \qquad (29)$$
$$= \left[V_{s-1}(\alpha_{s-1}, \bar{\alpha}_{s-1}) - W_{s+1} \right]$$
$$\times (\partial \Pr(\text{win}|\alpha_s, \bar{\alpha}_s)/\partial\alpha_s).$$

The symmetric solution is characterized by (28) evaluated at $\alpha_s = \bar{\alpha}_s$ and $x_{si} = x_{sj}$ and $x_{si} = x_{sj}$ for all s.

Writing $V_s = V_s(\alpha_s, \alpha_s)$ detailed calculations at equilibrium yield

$$\partial V_s/\partial\alpha_x = (V_{s-1} - W_{s+1})(\omega/2); \qquad (30a)$$

$$\partial \Pr(\text{win}|.)/\partial x_{si} = (h'/h)\left[(1/4) - \alpha_s(1 - \alpha_s)(\omega^2/2) \right]; \qquad (30b)$$

$$\partial\alpha_{s-1}/\partial x_{si} = -\alpha_s(1 - \alpha_s) \qquad (30c)$$

$$\times \omega\left[\left(\omega\alpha_s - \frac{\gamma_1}{\gamma_1 + \gamma_2} \right)^2 + \frac{\gamma_1\gamma_2}{(\gamma_1 + \gamma_2)^2} \right].$$

Condition (30a) shows that the value of continuation is increasing in own-assessment of talent, and that its incremental value is increasing in ω, the difference in form probabilities. The value of information is small when contestants are not very different from each other. The marginal effect of effort on winning (in (30b)) is decreasing in population heterogeneity (ω) and in the uncertainty with which players assess themselves at each stage (α). Uncertainty is a force that dampens incentives to perform and is greatest at $\alpha_s = 1/2$. This effect disappears as uncertainty is resolved. Equation (30c) shows that greater effort *reduces* the posterior assessment of strength.[6] Given the equilibrium effort of the opponent, the winning contestant is more probably of greater talent if less effort has been expended. The elimination design places extra value on strength, and private incentives to experiment to discover own strength is another force tending to make players hold back efforts at earlier stages. However, this term also vanishes as uncertainty is resolved.

---

6. Updating own-assessment of talent conditional on losing has no value because losers are eliminated. It has value in games with double or more eliminations, but equilibrium is not symmetric. Nor is it symmetric if contestants observe finer information than each player's previous win-loss record.

Substituting (30) in (28) and manipulating into elasticity form, we have

$$c(x_s) = \left[(\mu/4) - A_s\right](V_{s-1} - W_{s+1}) - B_s(V_{s-2} - W_s), \quad (31)$$

where

$$A_s = \mu\alpha_s(1 - \alpha_s)(\omega^2/2) \quad (32)$$

$$B_s = \mu(\omega^2/4)\alpha_s(1 - \alpha_s)\left[\left(\omega\alpha_s - \frac{\gamma_1}{\gamma_1 + \gamma_2}\right)^2 + \frac{\gamma_1\gamma_2}{(\gamma_1 + \gamma_2)^2}\right]$$

for $s \geq 2$

$$B_1 = 0$$

The boundary condition $B_1 = 0$ holds because information has no value in the finals. Equation (25) is used to calculate A_s and B_s. Substituting into the value function and subtracting W_{s+2} provides a recursion for the increments $V_s - W_{s+2}$ in (31):

$$V_s - W_{s+2} = (\beta - A_s)(V_{s-1} - W_{s+1}) \quad (33)$$
$$+ B_s(B_{s-2} - W_s) + \Delta W_{s+1},$$

with boundary condition $V_0 - W_2 = \Delta W_1$.

Conditions (31) and (33) plus the calculation of A and B_2 from (32) and (25) represent the complete solution of the symmetric ignorance problem. Notice that this solution converges in the limit to that of equal known talents (Section III) as α_s approaches unity, because A_s and B_s go to zero. Hence the extra increment in the final interrank spread is required for incentive maintenance in a sufficiently long game, irrespective of the initial distribution of talents.[7] By a similar token, the earlier result holds approximately when heterogeneity is small.

In fact, heterogeneity must be quite large for the value of information to have much effect on the incentive maintaining prize structure of Figure 10.2. For example, consider the case where $\gamma_1 = 2$, $\gamma_2 = 1$, and $\mu = 1$. The strong type wins two-thirds of the time and $\omega = 1/3$.

---

7. The remaining case is one of private information, where each player knows his own type, but has probabilistic assessments of opponents' types. Then Bayesian updating applies to opponents only. The analysis of this case is conceptually straightforward, but the equilibria are not symmetric and few analytical results are available. It is omitted for that reason. Still, the result on concentration of the purse on the top applies because survivors at the last few stages are relatively homogeneous.

Direct calculation reveals that B_s is of order 10^{-3}, and A_s is of order 10^{-2}. Therefore the second difference effects in (31) and (33) and negligible and Figure 10.2 is a very close approximation to the incentive maintaining prize structure. When the strong player wins three-fourths of the time, the corresponding orders of magnitude are 10^{-2} for both terms, so the approximation in Figure 10.2 remains very good: there are only a few minor wiggles.

Significant departures from Figure 10.2 occur when there are major differences between types, but this is mainly due to the incentive dilution effects of uncertainty. Even when the strong player wins 90 percent of the time, the terms in B_s remain of order 10^{-2} and the second difference (value of information) terms are negligible. But the terms in A_s show more variation with α_s. The term $(\beta - A_s)$ is smallest in those stages where uncertainty is largest. The interrank spread must be increased in those stages for x_s to be maintained, to overcome larger discounting of the future. Thus in a tournament where the proportion of strong players is relatively small in the first round, early-round incentive-maintaining prizes are approximately linear because there is little uncertainty. As the weak players are eliminated and α_s rises toward 1/2, uncertainty is *increasing* and the interrank spread has to increase to overcome this effect. If the game is long enough for α_s to exceed 1/2, uncertainty is decreasing and interrank spreads are decreasing for incentive maintenance. They increase again toward the end, due to the horizon effects. If the initial field is equally split ($\alpha_N = 1/2$), resolution-of-uncertainty acts to distribute the prize money more equally across the ranks. If the initial proportion α_N is small and the game is long, incentive-maintaining prizes redistribute from the extremes toward the middle.

Finally, the expected selection recursions in (24) show that the social value of information is independent of x_s in the symmetric equilibrium: all information in selecting strong players for survival is embedded in the elimination design itself, and incentives for contestants to produce private information come to naught. The attempt by all players to gain informational advantages in calculating their private strategies cancel each other out because of the ordered quality of competition. No one obtains an informational edge over that inherent in the design. There is a role for the prize structure to discourage these socially useless actions, and this requires less concentration of the prize money at the top, to reduce the private value of information. However, the calculations above suggest that these effects are relatively minor unless differences in talents are large.

VI. Conclusions

The chief result is identifying a unique role for top-ranking prizes to maintain performance incentives in career and other games of survival. Extra weight on top-ranking prizes is required to induce competitors to aspire to higher goals independent of past achievements. There are many rungs in the ladder to aspire to in the early stages of the game, and this plays an important role in maintaining one's enthusiasm for continuing. But after one has climbed a fair distance, there are fewer rungs left to attain. If top prizes are not large enough, those that have succeeded in achieving higher ranks rest on their laurels and slack off in their attempts to climb higher. Elevating the top prizes effectively lengthens the ladder for higher-ranking contestants, and in the limit makes it appear of unbounded length: no matter how far one has climbed, there is always the same length to go. In examining the relation between wages and marginal products, the concept of marginal productivity must be extended to take account of the value to the organization of maintaining incentives and selecting the best personnel to the various rungs, not only the contribution at each step. Payments at the top have indirect effects of increasing productivity of competitors further down the ladder.

There is another interesting class of questions in this type of competition. Adam Smith held the opinion that there is natural tendency for competitors to overestimate their survival chances ("overweaning conceit"), while Alfred Marshall held the opposite opinion. Further analysis shows how biased assessments of talent affect survival. There is a clear disadvantage to pessimism and underestimation of own talents. The pessimist doesn't try hard enough because opponents appear relatively stronger, and also because the true value of continuation is underrated. An elimination design is disadvantageous to the timid. They do not survive very long. The effects of overestimation and optimism are more complicated. For strong players and among any contestants in a field of comparable types, optimism has two effects: the optimist has a tendency to slack off due to underestimation of the relative strengths of the competition, but overestimates the own-value of continuation, which induces greater effort. Optimism has no clear-cut effects on altering survival probabilities. However, the second effect vanishes in the finals, and winning chances are reduced. Optimism has positive survival for weak players in a strong field. A weaker player who feels closer to the average field strength than is true, works harder on both counts and is not eliminated as quickly as another weak competitor with more accurate self-assessments.

When contestants' abilities are unknown, private incentives to optimize against the design for personal informational advantage lead to socially useless actions. These in the end do not produce any more information than is already embodied in the game itself and must be discouraged by concentrating less of the purse at the top. There are also private incentives for a contestant to invest in signals aimed at misleading opponents' assessments. It is in the interest of a strong player to make rivals think his strength is greater than it truly is, to induce a rival to put forth less effort. The same is true of a weak player in a weak field. However, it is in the interests of a weak player in a strong field to give out signals that he is even weaker than true, to induce a strong rival to slack off. Weighting the top prizes less heavily reduces these inefficient signaling incentives.

References

Becker, Gary S., and Stigler, George J. "Law Enforcement, Malfeasance, and the Compensation of Enforces." *Journal of Legal Studies*, January 1974, 3, 27–56.

Beckmann, Martin J. *Rank in Organizations*. Berlin: Springer-Verlag, 1978.

Bronars, Stephen. "Underdogs and Frontrunners: Strategic Behavior in Tournaments." Texas A&M University, 1985.

Carmichael, H. Lorne. "The Agent-Agents Problem: Payment by Relative Ouput." *Journal of Labor Economics*, January 1983, 1, 50–65.

David, H. A. "Tournaments and Paired Comparisons." *Biometrika*, June 1959, 46, 139–49.

—— *The Method of Paired Comparisons*. London: Charles Griffen and Co., 1969.

Gibbons, Jean D., Olkin, Ingram, and Sobel, Milton. *Selecting and Ordering Populations: A New Statistical Methodology*. New York: Wiley & Sons, 1977.

Green, Jerry R., and Stokey, Nancy L. "A Comparison of Tournaments and Contracts." *Journal of Policical Economy*. June 1983, 91, 349–65.

Holmstrom, Bengt. "Moral Hazard in Teams." *Bell Journal of Economics,* Autumn 1982, *13*, 324–40.

Lazear, Edward P. "Why Is There Mandatory Retirement?" *Journal of Political Economy,* October 1981, *89*, 841–64.

Lazear, Edward P., and Rosen, Sherwin. "Rank Order Tournaments as Optimum Labor Contracts." *Journal of Political Economy,* October 1981, *89*, 841–64.

Loury, Glenn C. "Market Structure and Innovation." *Quarterly Journal of Economics,* August 1979, *94*, 395–410.

Malcomson, James M. "Work Incentives, Hierarchy, and Internal Labor Markets." *Journal of Political Economy,* June 1984, *92*, 486–507.

Murphy, Kevin J. "Ability, Performance and Compensation: A Theoretical and Empirical Investigation of Labor Market Contracts." Unpublished doctoral dissertation, University of Chicago, 1984.

Nalebuff, Barry J., and Stiglitz, Joseph E. "Prizes and Incentives: Toward a General Theory of Compensation and Competition." *Bell Journal of Economics,* Spring 1984, *2*, 21–43.

O'Keefe, Mary, Viscusi, W. Kip, and Zeckhauser, Richard J. "Economic Contests: Comparative Reward Schemes." *Journal of Labor Economics,* January 1984, *2*, 27–56.

Rosen, Sherwin. "Authority, Control, and the Distribution of Earnings." *Bell Journal of Economics,* October 1982, *13*, 311–23.

Rosenbaum, James E. *Career Mobility in a Corporate Hierarchy.* Orlando: Academic Press, 1984.

11

Rank-Order Tournaments as Optimum Labor Contracts

EDWARD P. LAZEAR

SHERWIN ROSEN

I. Introduction

It is a familiar proposition that under competitive conditions workers are paid the value of their marginal products. In this paper we show that competitive lotteries are often efficient and sometimes superior to more familiar compensation schemes. For example, the large salaries of executives may provide incentives for all individuals in the firm who, with hard labor, may win one of the coveted top positions.

This paper addresses the relation between compensation and incentives in the presence of costly monitoring of workers' efforts and output. A wide variety of incentive payment schemes are used in practice. Simple piece rates, which have been extensively analyzed (see, e.g., Cheun 1969; Stiglitz 1975; Mirrlees 1976), gear payment to output. We consider a rank-order payment scheme which has not been analyzed but which seems to be prevalent in many labor contracts. This scheme pays prizes to the winners and losers of labor market contests. The main difference between prizes and other incentive schemes is that in a contest earnings depend on the rank order of contestants and not on "distance." That is, salaries are not contingent upon the output level of a particular game, because prizes are fixed in advance. Performance incentives are

We are indebted to Jerry Green, Merton Miller, James Mirrlees, George Stigler, Joseph Stiglitz, and Earl Thompson for helpful comments. The research was supported in part by the National Science Foundation. The research reported here is part of the NBER's research program in Labor Studies. Any opinions expressed are those of the authors and not those of the National Bureau of Economic Research.

From *Journal of Political Economy* 89, no. 5 (1981): 841–864. © 1981 by The University of Chicago.

set by attempts to win the contest. We argue that in many circumstances it is optimal to set up executive compensation along these lines and that certain puzzling features of that market are easily explained in these terms.

Central to this discussion are the conditions under which mechanisms exist for monitoring productivity (Alchian and Demsetz 1972). If inexpensive and reliable monitors of effort are available, then the best compensation scheme is a periodic wage based on input. However, when monitoring is difficult so that workers can alter their input with less than perfect detection, input-wage schemes invite shirking. The situation often can be improved if compensation is related to a more easily measured output level. In general, input-based pay is preferable because it changes the risk borne by workers in a favorable way. But when monitoring costs are so high that moral hazard is a serious problem, the gain in efficiency from using output-based pay may outweigh the risk-sharing losses. Paying workers on the basis of rank order alters costs of measurement as well as the nature of the risk borne by workers. It is for these reasons that it is sometimes a superior way to bring about an efficient incentive structure.

In the development below we start with the simplest case of risk neutrality to illustrate the basic issues. Then the more general case of risk aversion is treated in Section III. Section IV considers issues of sorting and self-selection when workers are heterogeneous.

II. Piece Rates and Tournaments with Risk Neutrality

To keep things simple and to avoid sequential and dynamic aspects of the problem, we confine attention to a single period in all that follows. Therefore, the reader should think of the incentive problem in terms of career development and lifetime productivity of workers. The worker's (lifetime) output is a random variable whose distribution is controlled by the worker himself. In particular, the worker is allowed to control the mean of the distribution by investing in costly skills prior to entering the market. However, a given productivity realization also depends on a random factor which is beyond anyone's control. Employers may observe output but cannot ascertain the extent to which it is due to investment expenditure or to good fortune or to both, though workers know their input as well as output. Worker j produces lifetime output q_j according to

$$q_j = \mu_j + \epsilon_j, \tag{1}$$

where μ_j is the level of investment, a measure of skill or average output, chosen by the worker when young and prior to a realization of the random or luck component, ϵ_j. Average skill, μ_j, is produced at cost $C(\mu)$, with $C', C'' > 0$. The random variable ϵ_j is drawn out of a known distribution with zero mean and variance σ^2.[1] Here ϵ is lifetime luck such as life-persistent person-effects or an ability factor, which is revealed very slowly over the worker's lifetime. The crucial assumption is that productivity risk is nondiversifiable by the worker himself. That is another reason for choosing a long period for the analysis. For example, if the period were very short and the random factor was independently distributed across periods, the worker could diversify per period risk by repetition and a savings account to balance off good and bad years. Evidently a persistent person or ability effect cannot be so diversified when it is undiscoverable quickly, as appears true of managerial talent, for example. It is assumed, however, that ϵ is i.i.d. across individuals, so that owners of firms can diversify risk either by pooling workers together in one firm or by holding a portfolio.

To concentrate on incentive aspects of various contractual arrangements, we adopt the simplest technology for firms. Production requires only labor and is additively separable across workers. By virtue of the independence assumptions, managers act as expected value maximizers or as if they were risk neutral. Free entry and a competitive output market set the value of the product at V per unit. Again, these assumptions are adopted to illustrate basic issues in the simplest way. The analysis also applies when there are complementarities among workers in production, which is more realistic but more difficult to exposit.

---

1. In this paper the worker has no choice over σ. This does not affect the risk-neutral solution but does have an effect if workers are risk averse, since they tend to favor overly cautious strategies. Also, virtually all the results of this paper hold true if the error structure is multiplicative rather than additive.

Piece Rates

The piece rate is very simple to analyze when workers are risk neutral. It involves paying the worker the value of his product. Let r be the piece rate. Ignoring discounting, the worker's net income is $rq - C(\mu)$. Risk-neutral workers choose μ to maximize expected net return

$$E[rq - C(\mu)] = r\mu - C(\mu).$$

The necessary condition is $r = C'(\mu)$ or the familiar requirement that investment equates marginal cost and return. On the other hand, the expected profit of a firm is

$$E(Vq - rq) = (V - r)\mu,$$

so free entry and competition for workers imply $r = V$. Consequently

$$V = C'(\mu).$$

The marginal cost of investment equals its social return, yielding the standard result that piece rates are efficient.

Rank-Order Tournaments

We shall consider two-player tournaments in which the rules of the game specify a fixed prize W_1 to the winner and a fixed prize W_2 to the loser. All essential aspects of the problem readily generalize to any number of contestants. A worker's production follows (1), and the winner of the contest is determined by the largest drawing of q. The contest is rank order because the margin of winning does not affect earnings. Contestants precommit their investments early in life, knowing the prizes and the rules of the game, but do not communicate with each other or collude. Notice that even though there are two players in a given match the market is competitive and not oligopolistic, because investment is precommitted and a given player does not know who his opponent will be at the time all decisions are made. Each person plays against the "field."

   We seek to determine the competitive prize structure (W_1, W_2). The method proceeds in two steps. First, the prizes W_1 and W_2 are fixed arbitrarily and workers' investment strategies are analyzed. Given these strategies, we then find the pair (W_1, W_2) that maximizes a worker's expected utility, subject to a zero-profit constraint by firms. It will be seen that a worker's incentives to invest increase with the spread between winning and losing prizes, $W_1 - W_2$. Each wants to improve the probability of winning because the return to winning varies with the spread. The firm would always like to increase the spread, ceteris paribus, to induce greater investment and higher productivity, because its output and revenue are increased. But as contestants invest more, their costs also rise. That is what limits the spread in equilibrium: firms offering too large a spread induce excessive investment. A competing firm can attract all of these workers by decreasing the spread because investment costs fall by more than expected product, raising expected net earnings. Increasing marginal cost of skill implies a unique equilibrium spread between the prizes that maximizes expected utility.

More precisely, consider the contestant's problem, assuming that both have the same costs of investment $C(\mu)$, so that their behavior is identical. A contestant's expected utility (wealth) is

$$(P)[W_1 - c(\mu)] + (1 - P)[W_2 - C(\mu)]$$
$$= PW_1 + (1 - P)W_2 - C(\mu), \tag{2}$$

where P is the probability of winning. The probability that j wins is

$$P = \text{prob}(q_j > q_k) = \text{prob}(\mu_j - \mu_k > \epsilon_k - \epsilon_j)$$
$$= \text{prob}(\mu_j - \mu_k > \xi) = G(\mu_j - \mu_k), \tag{3}$$

where $\xi \equiv \epsilon_k - \epsilon_j$, $\xi \sim g(\xi)$, $G(\cdot)$ is the cdf of ξ, $E(\xi) = 0$, and $E(\xi^2) = 2\sigma^2$ (because ϵ_j and ϵ_k are i.i.d.). Each player chooses μ_i to maximize (2). Assuming interior solutions, this implies

$$(W_1 - W_2)\frac{\partial P}{\partial \mu_i} - C'(\mu_i) = 0$$

and

$$(W_1 - W_2)\frac{\partial^2 P}{\partial \mu_i^2} - C''(\mu_i) < 0, \quad i = j, k. \tag{4}$$

We adopt the Nash-Cournot assumptions that each player optimizes against the optimum investment of his opponent, since he plays against the market over which he has no influence. Therefore, j takes μ_k as given in determining his investment and conversely for k. It then follows from (3) that, for player j

$$\partial P/\partial \mu_j = \partial G(\mu_j - \mu_k)/\partial \mu_j = g(\mu_j - \mu_k),$$

which upon substitution into (4) yields j's reaction function

$$(W_1 - W_2)g(\mu_j - \mu_k) - C'(\mu_j) = 0. \tag{5}$$

Player k's reaction function is symmetrical with (5).

Symmetry implies that when the Nash solution exists, $\mu_j = \mu_k$ and $P = G(0) = \frac{1}{2}$, so the outcome is purely random in equilibrium. Ex ante, each player affects his probability of winning by investing.[2]

Substituting $\mu_j = \mu_k$ at the Nash equilibrium, equation (5) reduces to

$$C'(\mu_I) = (W_1 - W_2)g(0), \quad I = j, k, \tag{6}$$

verifying the point above that players' investments depend on the spread between winning and losing prizes. Levels of the prizes only influence the decision to enter the game, which requires nonnegativity of expected wealth.

The risk-neutral firm's realized gross receipts are $(q_j + q_k) \cdot V$, and its costs are the total prize money offered, $W_1 + W_2$. Competition for labor bids up the purse to the point where expected total receipts equal costs $W_1 + W_2 = (\mu_j + \mu_k) \cdot V$. But since $\mu_j = \mu_k = \mu$ in equilibrium, the zero-profit condition reduces to

$$V\mu = (W_1 + W_2)/2. \tag{7}$$

The expected value of product equals the expected prize in equilibrium. Substitute (7) in the worker's utility function (2). Noting that $P = \frac{1}{2}$ in

---

2. However, it is not necessarily true that there is a solution, because with arbitrary density functions the objective function may not be concave in the relevant range. It is possible to show that a pure strategy solution exists provided that σ^2 is sufficiently large: contests are feasible only when chance is a significant factor. This result accords with intuition and is in the spirit of the old saying that a (sufficient) difference of opinion is necessary for a horse race. Stated otherwise, since $\partial P/\partial \mu_j = g(\mu_j - \mu_k)$ and $g(\cdot)$ is a pdf, $\partial^2 P/\partial \mu_j^2 = g'(\mu_j - \mu_k)$ may be positive, and fulfillment of second-order conditions in (4) implies sharp breaks in the reaction function. If σ^2 is small enough the breaks occur at very low levels of investment, and a Nash equilibrium in pure strategies will not exist. Existence of an equilibrium is assumed in all that follows.

equilibrium, the worker's expected utility at the optimum investment strategy is

$$V\mu - C(\mu). \tag{8}$$

The equilibrium prize structure selects W_1 and W_2 to maximize (8), or

$$[V - C'(\mu)](\partial\mu/\partial W_i) = 0, \quad i = 1, 2. \tag{9}$$

The marginal cost of investment equals its marginal social return, $V = C'(\mu)$, in the tournament as well as the piece rate. Therefore, competitive tournaments, like piece rates, are efficient and both result in exactly the same allocation of resources.

Some further manipulation of the equilibrium conditions yields an interesting interpretation in terms of the theory of agency (see Ross 1973; Becker and Stigler 1974; Harris and Raviv 1978; and Lazear 1979):

$$\begin{aligned}
W_1 &= V\mu + C'(\mu)/2g(0) = V\mu + V/2g(0) \\
W_2 &= V\mu - C'(\mu)/2g(0) = V\mu - V/2g(0).
\end{aligned} \tag{10}$$

The second equality follows from $V = C'(\mu)$. Now think of the term $C'(\mu)/2g(0) = V/2g(0)$ in (10) as an entrance fee or bond that is posted by each player. The winning and losing prizes pay off the expected marginal value product plus or minus the entrance fee. That is, the players receive their expected product combined with a fair winner-take-all gamble over the total entrance fees or bonds. The appropriate social investment incentives are given by each contestant's attempt to win the gamble. This contrasts with the main agency result, where the bond is returned to each worker after a satisfactory performance has been observed. There the incentive mechanism works though the employee's attempts to work hard enough to recoup his own bond. Here it works through the attempts to win the gamble.

Comparative statistics for this problem all follow from (9) and (10) once a distribution is specified. For example, if ϵ is normal with variance σ^2, then $g(0) = \frac{1}{2}\sigma\sqrt{\pi}$. It follows from (10) that the optimal spread varies directly with V and σ^2. While several other interesting observations can be made of this sort, we note a somewhat different but important practical implication of this general scheme. Even though the optimal prize structure determines expected marginal product through its effect on worker choice of μ and the zero-profit condition (7) implies that expected prizes equal expected productivity, nevertheless actual realized earnings definitely do not equal productivity in either an ex ante or ex post sense. Consider ex ante first. Since $\mu_j = \mu_k = \mu$, expected products are equal. Since $W_1 > W_2$ is required to induce any investment, the payment that j receives never equals the payment that k receives. It is impossible that the prize is equal to ex ante product, because ex ante products are equal. Nor do wages equal ex post products. Actual product is Vq rather than $V\mu$. But q is a random variable, the value of which is not known until after the game is played, while W_1 and W_2 are fixed in advance. Only under the rarest coincidence would $W_1 = Vq_j$ and $W_2 = Vq_k$.

Consider the salary structure for executives. It appears as though the salary of, say, the vice-president of a particular corporation is substantially below that of the president of the same corporation. Yet presidents are often chosen from the ranks of vice-presidents. On the day that a given individual is promoted from vice-president to president, his salary may triple. It is difficult to argue that his skills have tripled in that one-day period, presenting difficulties for standard theory where supply factors should keep wages in those two occupations approximately equal. It is not a puzzle, however, when interpreted in the context of a prize. The president of a corporation is viewed as the winner of a contest in which he receives the higher prize, W_1. His wage is settled on not necessarily because it reflects his current productivity as president, but rather because it induces that individual and all other individuals to perform appropriately when they are in more junior positions. This interpretation suggests that presidents of large corporations do not necessarily earn high wages because they are more productive as presidents but because this particular type of payment structure makes them more productive over their entire working lives. A contest provides the proper incentives for skill acquisition prior to coming into the position.[3]

---

3. If ϵ is a fixed effect, there is additional information from knowing the identity of winners and losers. The expected productivity of a winner is $\mu + E(\epsilon_j \mid q_j > q_k)$, while that of a loser is $\mu + E(\epsilon_j \mid q_j < q_k)$. In a one-period contest there is no possibility of taking advantage of this information. However, in a sequential contest with no firm-specific capital, the information would be valuable and would constrain subsequent wage payments in successive rounds through competition from other firms. It is not difficult to show that this does not affect the general nature of the bond-gamble solution. Alternatively, if the investment has firm-specific elements or firms adopt policies that bind workers to it (as in Lazear 1979), these restrictions do not necessarily apply.

Comparisons

Though tournaments and piece rates are substantially different institutions for creating incentives, we have demonstrated the surprising result that both achieve the Pareto optimal allocation of resources when workers are risk neutral. In fact other schemes also achieve this allocation. For example, instead of playing against an opponent, a worker might be compared with a fixed standard $\bar{q}$, with one payment awarded if output falls anywhere below $\bar{q}$ and another, higher, payment awarded if output falls anywhere above standard. Attempting to beat the standard has the same incentive effects as attempting to beat another player. Using the same methods as above, it is not difficult to show that there are spread-standard combinations that induce Pareto optimum investments. Since all these schemes involve the same investment policy, and since average payout by the firm equals average product for all of them, they all yield the same expected rewards and, therefore, the same expected utility to workers.[4]

In spite of the apparent equality of these schemes in terms of the preferences of risk-neutral workers, considerations of differential costs of information and measurement may serve to break these ties in practical situations. The essential point follows from the theory of measurement (Stevens 1968) that a cardinal scale is based on an underlying ordering of objects or an ordinal scale. In that sense, an ordinal scale is "weaker" and has fewer requirements than a cardinal scale. If it is less costly to observe rank than an individual's level of output, then tournaments dominate piece rates and standards. On the other hand, occupations for which output is easily observed save resources by using the piece rate or standard, or some combination, and avoid the necessity of making direct comparisons with others as the tournament requires. Salesmen, whose output level is easily observed, typically are paid by piece rates, whereas corporate executives, whose output is more difficult to observe, engage in contests.

In a modern, complex business organization, a person's productivity as chief executive officer is measured by his effect on the profitability

---

4. The level of the standard is indeterminate, since for any $\bar{q}$ a corresponding spread can be chosen to achieve the optimal investment. This is also true of contests among more than two players. With N contestants, the prizes of $N - 2$ of them are indeterminate. When risk neutrality is dropped, the indeterminacy vanishes in both cases.

of the whole enterprise. Yet the costs of measurement for each conceivable candidate are prohibitively expensive. Instead, it might be said that those in the running are "tested" by assessments of performance at lower positions. Realizations from such tests are sample statistics in these assessments, in much the same way that grades are assigned in a college classroom and IQ scores are determined. The point is that such tests are inherently ordinal in nature, even though the profitability of the enterprise is metered by a well-defined, cardinal ratio scale. It is in situations such as this that the conditions seem ripe for tournaments to be the dominant incentive contract institution.

Notice in this connection that the basic prize and piece-rate structures survive a broad class of revenue functions other than summable ones. Even if the production function of the firm includes complicated interactions involving complementarity or substitution among individual outputs, there exists the possibility of paying workers either on the basis of individual performance or by rank order. The revenue function itself can even involve rank-order considerations, and both possibilities still exist. For example, spectators at a horse race generally are interested in the speed of the winning horse and the closeness of the contest. Then the firm's (track) revenue function depends on the first few order statistics; yet the horses could be paid on the basis of their speed rather than on the basis of win, place, and show positions. Both methods would induce them to run fast.[5]

There has been very little treatment of the problem of tournament prize structure and incentives in the literature. Little else but the well-known paper by Friedman (1953) based on Friedman-Savage preferences for lotteries exists in economics. In the statistics literature there is an early paper by Galton (1902) that is worthy of brief discussion. Galton inquired into the ratio of first- and second-place prize money in a

---

5. The reader is reminded that throughout this section and the next workers are identical a priori and differ only ex post through the realization of ϵ. In the real world, where there is population heterogeneity, market participants are sorted into different contests. There players (and horses, for that matter) who are known to be of higher quality ex ante may play in games with higher stakes. If it can be accomplished, the sorting is by anticipated marginal products. In that sense, pay differences among contestants of known quality resemble the effect of a "piece rate." These issues are more thoroughly discussed below.

race of n contestants, assuming the prizes were divided in the following ratio:

$$W_1/W_2 = (Q_1 - Q_3)/(Q_2 - Q_3).$$

Here Q_1 is the expected value of the first- (fastest) order statistic, etc. While a moment's reflection suggests this criterion to be roughly related to marginal productivity, Galton proposed it on strictly a priori grounds. He went on to show the remarkable result that the ratio above is approximately 3 when the parent distribution of speed is normal. Hence this criterion results in a highly skewed prize structure. From what we know today about the characteristic skew of extreme value distributions, a skewed reward structure based on order statistics is less surprising for virtually any parent distribution. In the more modern statistical literature, the method of paired comparisons has tournament-like features. Samples from different populations are compared pairwise, and the object is to choose the one with the largest mean. Comparing all samples to each other is like a round-robin tournament. An alternative design is a knockout tournament with single or double elimination. The latter requires fewer samples and is therefore cheaper, but does not generate as much information as the round-robin (David 1963; Gibbons, Olkin, and Sobel 1977).

Galton's original work and the more modern developments it has given rise to are not helpful to us; they deal with samples from fixed populations, so the reward structure is irrelevant for resource allocation. The problem we have treated here is that of choosing the reward structure to provide the proper incentive and elicit the socially proper distributions.

III. Optimal Compensation with Risk Aversion

All compensation systems can be viewed as schemes which transform the distribution of productivity to a distribution of earnings. A piece rate is a linear transformation of output, so the distribution of income is the same apart from a change in location and scale. A tournament is a highly nonlinear transformation: it converts the continuous distribution of productivity into a discrete, binomial distribution of income. When workers are risk neutral, both schemes yield identical investments and expected utility because their first moments are the same. In this section, it is shown that with risk aversion one method or the other usually yields higher expected utility, because the interaction between insurance and action implies substantially different first and second moments of the income distribution in the two cases.[6]

We have been unable to completely characterize the conditions under which piece rates dominate rank-order tournaments and vice versa, but we show some examples here. Truncation offered by prizes implies more control of extreme values than piece rates but less control of the middle of the distribution. Different utility functions weight one aspect more than the other so that tournaments can actually dominate piece rates.

Optimum Linear Piece Rate

The piece-rate scheme analyzed[7] pays workers a guarantee, I, plus an incentive, rq, where r is the piece rate per unit of output. The problem for the firm is to pick an r, I combination that maximizes workers' expected utility

$$\max_{I,r}[E(U) = \max \int U(y)\theta(y)dy], \qquad (11)$$

where

$$\begin{aligned} y &\equiv I + rq - C(\mu) \\ &= I + r\mu + r\epsilon - C(\mu) \end{aligned} \qquad (12)$$

and $\theta(y)$ is the pdf of y.

The worker's problem is to choose μ to maximize expected utility given I and r. If $\epsilon \sim f(\epsilon)$, the worker's problem is

$$\max_{\mu} E(U) = \int U[I + r\mu + r\epsilon - C(\mu)]f(\epsilon)d\epsilon.$$

---

6. One might think that risks could be pooled among groups of workers through sharing agreements, but that is false because of moral hazard. A worker would never agree to share prizes since doing so would result in $\mu = 0$, and consequently $E(q_j - q_k) = 0$ and bankruptcy for the firm. As a result, firms offering tournaments or piece rates in the pure sense yield higher expected utility than the sharing arrangement.

7. The following is similar to a problem analyzed by Stiglitz (1975). A linear piece-rate structure is a simplification. A more general structure would allow for nonlinear piece rates (see Mirrlees 1976).

The first-order condition is

$$\frac{\partial E(U)}{\partial \mu} = \int [U'(y)][r - C'(\mu)]f(\epsilon)d\epsilon = 0,$$

which conveniently factors so that

$$r = C'(\mu). \tag{13}$$

Condition (13) is identical to the risk-neutral case, because ϵ is independent of investment effort, μ.

Assuming risk-neutral employers, $V\mu$ is expected revenue from a worker and $I + r\mu$ is expected wage payments. Therefore, the zero-profit market constraint is

$$V\mu = I + r\mu. \tag{14}$$

Solving (14) for I and substituting into (12), the optimum contract maximizes

$$\int U\{V\mu(r) + r\epsilon - C[\mu(r)]\}f(\epsilon)d\epsilon$$

with respect to r, where $\mu = \mu(r)$ satisfies (13). After simplification the marginal condition is

$$[V - C'(\mu)]\frac{d\mu}{dr}EU' + E\epsilon U' = 0. \tag{15}$$

Since risk aversion implies $E\epsilon U' < 0$, (15) shows that $V > C'(\mu)$ in the optimum contract for risk-averse workers. This underinvestment is the moral hazard resulting from insurance $I > 0$ and $r < V$ implied by (15).

Using familiar Taylor series approximations to the utility function and a normal density for ϵ, the optimum is approximated by

$$\mu \doteq C'^{-1}\left(\frac{V}{1 + sC''\sigma^2}\right) \tag{16}$$

and

$$\sigma_y^2 \doteq \frac{V^2\sigma^2}{(1 + sC''\sigma^2)^2} \tag{17}$$

where $s \equiv -U''/U'$ evaluated at mean income is the measure of absolute risk aversion. Investment increases (see [16]) in V and decreases in s, C'', and σ^2, because all these changes imply similar changes in the marginal piece rate r which influences investment through condition (13). The same changes in V, s, and C'' have corresponding effects on the variance of income (see [17]), but an increase in σ^2 actually reduces variance, if σ^2 is large, because it reduces r and increases I.[8]

Optimum Prize Structure

The worker's expected utility in a two-player game is

$$E(U) = P\{U[W_1 - C(\mu^*)]\} + (1 - P)\{U[W_2 - C(\mu^*)]\}, \qquad (18)$$

where $*$ denotes the outcome of the contest rather than the piece-rate scheme. The optimum prize structure is the solution to

$$\max_{W_1, W_2} \left(E(U^*) = \max_{\mu^*}\{P \cdot U[W_1 - C(\mu^*)] \right.$$
$$\left. + (1 - P) \cdot U[W_2 - C(\mu^*)]\} \right) \qquad (19)$$

subject to the zero-profit constraint

$$V\mu^* = PW_1 + (1 - P)W_2. \qquad (20)$$

The worker selects μ^* to satisfy $\partial E(U)/\partial \mu^* = 0$. Since cost functions are the same and ϵ_j and ϵ_k are i.i.d., the Nash solution implies $\mu_j = \mu_k$ and $P = \frac{1}{2}$ as before. Then the worker's investment behavior simplifies to

$$C'(\mu^*) = \frac{2[U(1) - U(2)]g(0)}{U'(1) + U'(2)}, \qquad (21)$$

where $U(\tau) \equiv U[W_\tau - C(\mu^*)]$ and $U'(\tau) \equiv U'[W_\tau - C(\mu^*)]$ for $\tau = 1, 2$. Equation (21) implies

$$\mu^* = \mu^*(W_1, W_2), \qquad (22)$$

and the optimum contract (W_1, W_2) maximizes

$$E(U^*) = \frac{1}{2}U[W_1 - C(\mu^*)] + \frac{1}{2}U[W_2 - C(\mu^*)] \qquad (23)$$

---

8. Furthermore, $r \doteq V/(1 + sC''\sigma^2)$ and $I \doteq sV^2d^2/(1 + sC''\sigma^2)^2$, so that $r = V$ and $I = 0$ in the case of risk neutrality ($s = 0$). All these approximations are first-order expansions for terms in $U'(\cdot)$ and second-order expansions for terms in $U(\cdot)$. The same is true of the approximations below for the tournament.

subject to (20), with $P = \frac{1}{2}$, and (22). Increasing marginal cost of investment and risk aversion guarantees a unique maximum to (23) when a Nash solution exists. Again, assuming a normal density for ϵ, second-order approximations yield

$$\mu^* \doteq C'^{-1}\left(\frac{V}{1 + sC''\sigma^2\pi}\right) \tag{24}$$

and

$$\sigma_{y^*}^2 \doteq \frac{\pi V^2 \sigma^2}{(1 + \pi s C''\sigma^2)^2}, \tag{25}$$

where

$$y^* \begin{cases} = W_1 - C(\mu^*) & \text{if } q_j > q_k \\ = W_2 - C(\mu^*) & \text{if } q_j < q_k \end{cases}$$

and $\epsilon_j \sim N(0, \sigma^2)$, $\epsilon_k \sim N(0, \sigma^2)$, and $\mathrm{cov}(\epsilon_j, \epsilon_k) = 0$.[9] The comparative statics of (24) and (25) are similar to the piece rate (16) and (17) and need not be repeated.

Comparisons

Equations (16) and (24) indicate the investment and expected income[10] are lower for the contest than for the piece rate at given values of s. Moreover, for values of σ^2 in excess of $1/sC''\sqrt{\pi}$, the variance of income in the tournament is smaller than for the piece rate. This would seem to suggest that contests provide a crude form of insurance when the variance of change is large enough, but the problem is significantly more complicated than that because there is no separation between tastes and opportunities in this problem: the optimum mean and variance themselves depend on utility-function parameters. Thus, for example, for the constant, absolute risk-aversion utility function $U = -e^{-sy}/s$, the insurance provided by the contest is insufficient to compensate for its smaller mean: it can be shown that the expected indirect utility of the

---

9. Furthermore, $C'(\mu^*) \doteq g(0)(W_1 - W_2)$, so the spread is still crucial for investment incentives, as in the risk-neutral case.

10. Since $y = V\mu - C(\mu)$, and since μ is below the wealth-maximizing level of μ when workers are risk averse, lower μ implies lower y because revenue falls by more than cost.

Table 11.1 • Constant relative risk aversion

σ^2	μ	μ^*	$E(U)$	$E(U^*)$
		$y_0 = 100; s(y_0) = .005$		
.1	.9995	.9984	5.012155	5.012465
.5	.9975	.9922	5.012150	5.012445
1	.9950	.9846	5.012100	5.012295
3	.9852	.9552	5.011940	5.011925
6	.9710	.9142	5.011800	5.011415
12	.9436	.8420	5.011420	5.010515
		$y_0 = 25; s(y_0) = .020$		
.1	.9980	.9938	2.524665	2.524725
.2	.9960	.9878	2.524616	2.524575
1	.9807	.9419	2.524237	2.523437
12	.8094	.5741	2.519930	2.514282

Note: $U = \alpha y^\alpha$; $y = y_0 + I + rq - C(\mu)$ for piece rate; $y = y_0 + W_1 - C(\mu)$ for contest $(i = 1, 2)$; $\alpha = .5$, $V = 1$, $C(\mu) = \mu^2/2$: σ^2.

optimal piece rate exceeds that of the optimal tournament for all values of σ^2, at least with normal distributions and quadratic investment-cost functions. However, when there is declining absolute risk aversion, we have examples where the contest dominates the piece rate.

Illustrative calculations are shown in Table 11.1 using the utility function $U = \alpha y^\alpha$, which exhibits constant relative but declining absolute risk aversion, $s(y) = (1 - \alpha)/y$. Again quadratic costs and normal errors are assumed. However, this utility function is defined for positive incomes only, so an amount of nonlabor income y_0 is assigned to the worker to avoid a major approximation error of the normal, which admits negative incomes (i.e., the possibility of losses).

Table 11.1 shows that when $y_0 = 100$ so that $s = .005$, the contest is preferred until $\sigma^2 \geq 3$. However, if $y_0 = 25$ so that $s = .020$, the contest is only preferred for $\sigma^2 < .2$. The intuition is that piece rates concentrate the mass of the income distribution near the mean, while contests place 50 percent of the weight at one value significantly below the mean and the other value significantly above. Strongly risk-averse workers seem to dislike the binomial nature of this distribution when σ^2 is high because it concentrates too much of the mass at low levels of utility. However, when σ^2 is small, the contest which truncates the tails of the income distribution associated with a linear piece rate has higher value.

Income Distributions

While it is not possible to make a general argument based on an example, Table 11.1 suggests that persons with more endowed income and smaller absolute risk aversion are more likely to prefer contests, and those with low levels of endowed wealth and larger absolute risk aversion are more likely to prefer piece rates. Consider a situation in which all persons have the same utility function, such as the one in Table 11.1, and face the same costs and luck distribution, the only difference being the fact that some workers have larger endowed incomes than others. If this difference is large enough, it can be optimal to pay piece rates to those with small values of endowed income and to pay prizes to those with large values. Individuals will self-select the payment scheme in accordance with their wealth. The distribution of earnings among those selecting the piece-rate jobs is normal with mean $V\mu$ and variance $r^2\sigma^2$. It is binomial with mean $V\mu^*$ and variance $(\Delta W)^2/4$ for those who enter tournaments. Note that μ and μ^* depend upon $s(y)$, which is smaller for workers who select contests, and it can turn out as it does in Table 11.1 that expected income is larger in the contest than in the piece rate; for example, if $\sigma^2 = 1$ then the rich prefer contests ($5.012295 > 5.012100$) and the poor prefer piece rates ($2.524237 > 2.523437$), but $\mu^* = .9846$ exceeds $\mu = .9807$. This situation is shown in Figure 11.1.

The overall distribution is the sum of a binomial and a normal with lower mean, weighted by the number of individuals in each occupation (see Fig. 11.1). It is positively skewed because $V\mu^* > V\mu$. Note also that the distribution of wage income will be less skewed than that of total income. The reason is that y_0 and mean-wage income are positively correlated because the likelihood of choosing a contest increases with y_0. These implications conform to the standard findings on the distribution of income in an economy.

This example is interesting because it is very closely related to some early results of Friedman (1953), who studied how alternative social arrangements can produce income distributions that cater to workers'

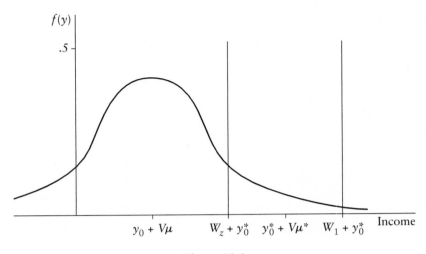

Figure 11.1

risk preferences. He showed that the Friedman-Savage utility function leads to a two-class distribution. Persons in the risk-averse region are assigned to occupations in which income follows productivity, while persons in the risk-preferring region buy lottery tickets in very risky occupations in which few win very large prizes. The overall distribution is the sum of these two and exhibits characteristic skew. The Friedman-Savage utility function implies that a person's risk preferences depend on the part of his wealth that is not at risk. Therefore, Friedman's assignment of people to jobs really follows endowed wealth (y_0), just as in our example. However, our framework offers two improvements. First, the problem of incentives is directly incorporated into the formulation of the optimum policy. Second, workers in this model are risk averse for all values of incomes, but even so gambles can be the optimal policy.

Error Structure

Relative costs of measurement are still important in choosing among incentive schemes, but the error structure plays additional roles when workers are risk averse. Suppose the output estimator for worker i in activity τ is $\hat{q}_{i\tau} = q_{i\tau} + \rho_\tau + v_{i\tau}$, where $v_{i\tau}$ is random error and ρ_τ is an error that is specific to activity τ but common to all workers within that activity. In the piece rate the common error ρ adds noise which risk-averse workers dislike, while the common noise drops out of a rank-order comparison because it affects both contestants similarly. That is, the relevant variance for the contest is $2\sigma_v^2$, while that for the piece rate is $\sigma_\rho^2 + \sigma_v^2$. It is evident that this can tip the balance in favor of tournaments if σ_ρ^2 is large enough and/or workers are sufficiently risk averse.

The common error ρ bears two interesting interpretations. One is activity-specific measurement error. For example, j and k may have the same supervisor whose biased assessments affect all workers similarly. This is similar to monitoring all workers by a mechanical counting device that might run too fast or too slow in any given trial. The other interpretation of ρ is true random variation that affects the enterprise as a whole. For example, suppose all firms produce with the same technology, but that in a given period some firms do better or worse than others. Then risk-averse workers prefer not to have their incomes vary with conditions facing the firm as a whole, and wages based on a contest eliminate this kind of variation. Without its elimination there would be excessive losses due to moral hazard.

It must be pointed out that, in the absence of measurement error, using a contest against a fixed standard $\bar{q}$ discussed above has lower variance than playing against an opponent. As shown in Section 2, the relevant variance in a contest is that of $\xi = \epsilon_k - \epsilon_j$, which has variance $2\sigma^2$ against an opponent and only σ^2 against a standard (since the standard is invariant, $\epsilon_k \equiv 0$). Consequently, we might expect risk-averse workers to prefer absolute standards.[11] Again, however, the crucial issue is the costs of measurement and the error structure. For the complex attributes required for managerial positions, it is difficult to observe output and therefore difficult to compare to an absolute

---

11. Playing against a standard is like Mirrlees's (1976) notion of an "instruction." It is clear that using standards as well as piece rates must be superior to using one alone. That scheme would allow workers to be paid $\bar{I}$ if $q < \bar{q}$ and $I_0 + rq$ for $q \geq \bar{q}$. This is important because it truncates the possibilities when $Vq < 0$. Given the technology, it is possible that very large negative values of output can offer, and since it is impossible to always tax workers the full extent of this loss, some form of truncation is desirable. A contest is an alternative way to control the tails of this distribution.

standard. Insofar as samples and tests are necessary, it bears repeating that these are inherently ordinal in nature. But this leads us back to the problem of common error, where it is often impossible to know whether a person's output is satisfactory without comparisons to other persons. Further, when there are changing production circumstances in the firm as a whole, it is difficult to know whether the person failed to meet the standard because of insufficient investment or because the firm was generally experiencing bad times, a problem of measuring "value added." Risk-averse workers increase utility by competing against an opponent and eliminating this kind of firm effect.

IV. Heterogeneous Contestants

Workers are not sprinkled randomly among firms but rather seem to be sorted by ability levels. One explanation for this has to do with complementarities in production. But even in the absence of complementarities, sorting may be an integral part of optimal labor-contract arrangements. Informational considerations imply that compensation methods may affect the allocation of worker types to firms. Therefore, this section returns to the case of risk neutrality and analyzes tournament structures when investment costs differ among persons. Two types of persons are assumed, a's and b's, with marginal costs of the a's being smaller than those of the b's: $C_a'(\mu), C_b'(\mu)$ for all μ. The distribution of disturbances $f(\epsilon)$ is assumed to be the same for both groups. Many of the following results continue to hold, with usually obvious modification of the arguments, if the a's and b's draw from different distributions. The following section addresses the question of self-selection when workers know their identities but firms do not. The next section discusses handicapping schemes when all cost-function differences can be observed by all parties.

Adverse Selection

Suppose that each person knows to which class he belongs but that this information is not available to anyone else. The principal result is that the a's and b's do not self-sort into their own "leagues." Instead, all workers prefer to work in firms with the best workers (the major leagues). Furthermore, there is no pure price-rationing mechanism that induces Pareto optimal self-selection. But mixed play is inefficient because it cannot sustain the proper investment strategies. Therefore, tournament structures naturally require credentials and other nonprice signals to differentiate people and assign them to the appropriate contest. Firms select their employees based on such information as past performances, and some are not permitted to compete.

The proof of adverse selection consists of two parts. First we show that players do not self-sort into *a* leagues and *b* leagues. Second, we show that the resulting mixed leagues are inefficient.

1. *Players do not self-sort.* Assume leagues are separated and consider the expected revenue R_i generated by playing in league $i = a, b$ with an arbitrary investment level μ. Then

$$R_i(\mu) = W_2^i + (W_1^i - W_2^i)P^i, \quad i = a, b \qquad (26)$$

where (W_1^i, W_2^i) is the prize money, and P^i is the probability of winning in league i. Recall that P^i depends on the individual's level of investment and that of his rivals. Therefore, $P^a = G(\mu - \mu_a^*)$ and $P^b = G(\mu - \mu_b^*)$, where μ_a^* is the existing players' investments in the *a* league, where $V = C_a'(\mu_a^*)$, and similarly for μ_b^*. Recalling from (6) and (9) that $W_1^i - W_2^i = V/g(0)$ and from (10) that $W_2^i = V\mu_i^* - V/2g(0)$, equation (26) becomes

$$R_i(\mu) = V\mu_i^* - \frac{V}{g(0)}[\frac{1}{2} - G(\mu - \mu_i^*)]. \qquad (27)$$

Note that $R_i(\mu) = V\mu_i^*$ when $\mu = \mu_i^*$ and that $dR_i/d\mu \equiv R_i'(\mu) = Vg(\mu - \mu_i^*)/g(0) > 0$. Since $C_a'(\mu_a^*) = V$ and $C_b'(\mu_b^*) = V$, then $\mu_a^* < \mu_b^*$ so that $R_i(\mu_a^*) > R_i(\mu_b^*)$. Furthermore, $R_b'[\mu - (\mu_a^* - \mu_b^*)] = R_a'(\mu)$. Therefore, $R_b(\mu)$ is a pure displacement of $R_a(\mu)$. Since $R_i'(\mu) = V$ for $\mu = \mu_i^*$ and $R_i'(\mu) < V$ elsewhere, and since $R_i(\mu)$ is increasing, the revenue functions never cross. So $R_b(\mu)$ lies to the southwest of $R_a(\mu)$ (see Fig. 11.2). Therefore, independent of cost curves, it is always better to play in the *a* league than the *b* league: Workers will not self-select.

2. *Mixed contests are inefficient.* Suppose the proportions of *a*'s and *b*'s in the population are α and $(1 - \alpha)$, respectively. If pairings among *a*'s and *b*'s are random, then expected utility of a player of type i is

$$\bar{W}_2 + [\alpha P_a^i + (1 - \alpha)P_b^i](W_1 - W_2) - C_i(\mu_i),$$

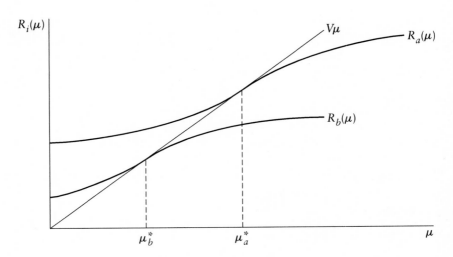

Figure 11.2

where $(\bar{W}_1, \bar{W}_2)$ is the prize money in mixed play and P^i_j is the probability that a player of type i defeats a player of type j. The first-order condition for investment of type i in this game is

$$\left[\alpha \frac{\partial P^i_a}{\partial \mu_i} + (1 - \alpha)\frac{\partial P^i_b}{\partial \mu_i}\right] \cdot (\bar{W}_1 - \bar{W}_2) = C'_i(\bar{\mu}_i).$$

A development similar to Section 2 implies equilibrium reaction functions

$$[\alpha g(0) + (1 - \alpha)g(\bar{\mu}_a - \bar{\mu}_b)](W_1 - W_2) = C'_a(\bar{\mu}_a)$$

for a's and

$$[\alpha g(\bar{\mu}_b - \bar{\mu}_a) + (1 - \alpha)g(0)](W_1 - W_2) = C'_b(\bar{\mu}_b)$$

for b's. If the solution is efficient, then $C'_b(\mu_b) = V = C'_a(\mu_a)$, which implies

$$\alpha g(0) + (1 - \alpha)g(\bar{\mu}_a - \bar{\mu}_b) = \alpha g(\bar{\mu}_b - \bar{\mu}_a) + (1 - \alpha)g(0).$$

Since g is symmetric and nonuniform, this condition can hold only if $\alpha = \frac{1}{2}$. Therefore, except in that very special case, mixed contests yield inefficient investment: one type of player overinvests and the other underinvests depending upon whether or not $\alpha \gtrless \frac{1}{2}$.

We conclude that a pure price system cannot sustain an efficient competitive equilibrium in the presence of population heterogeneity with asymmetric information. Markets can be separated, but only at a cost. Consider, for example, the case where a's want to prevent b's from contaminating their league. By making the spread, $W_1^a - W_2^a$, sufficiently large, $R_a(\mu)$ becomes steeper than $R_b(\mu)$ in Figure 11.2 and crosses it so that the envelope covers $R_b(\mu)$ at low values of μ and $R_a(\mu)$ at high values. Then, for some high levels of μ, it is more profitable to play in the a league and, for low levels of μ, the b league is preferable. Individuals may self-sort, but the cost is that a's overinvest. The result is akin to that of Akerlof (1976) and to those of Spence (1973), Riley (1975), Rothschild and Stiglitz (1976) and Wilson (1977). As they show, a separating equilibrium need not exist, but, even if it does, that equilibrium may be inferior to a nonseparating equilibrium.

The obvious practical resolution of these difficulties is the use of nonprice rationing and certification to sort people into the appropriate leagues on the basis of past performance. Similarly, firms use nonprice factors to allocate jobs among applicants. The rules for allocating those jobs may be important for at least two reasons that we can only briefly describe here.

First, sorting workers of different skill levels into appropriate positions within a hierarchy may be beneficial. In this paper, production is additive, so it does not matter who works with them. To the extent that the production technology is somewhat more complicated, sorting may well be crucial. A series of pairwise, sequential contests may efficiently perform that function. Suppose that $q_{it} = \mu_i + \delta_i + \eta_{it}$, where δ_i is an unobserved ability component for player i and η is white noise. Suppose it is efficient for the individual with the highest δ to be the chief executive. There will be a tendency to have winners play winners because

$$E(\delta_j \mid q_{j1} > q_{k1}) > E(\delta_k \mid q_{j1} > q_{k1})$$

in the first round. A sequential elimination tournament may be a cost-efficient way to select the best person.

Second, workers may not know precisely their own abilities or cost functions. A worker who is ignorant about his cost function values information before selecting a level of investment expenditure. Therefore, firms may offer "tryouts" to provide information about optimal investment strategies. In fact, one can imagine the existence of firms which specialize in running contests among young workers—the minor leagues—which provide information to be used when and if the workers opt to increase the stakes and enter a bigger league.

These issues point up an important difference between piece rates and contests. In the pure heterogeneous case, where information is asymmetric and workers are risk neutral, a piece rate always yields an efficient solution, namely, $V = C'_a(\mu_a) = C'_b(\mu_b)$. However, once slotting of workers is important because of complementarities in production, or if it is desirable for workers to gain information about their type, it is no longer obvious that a series of sequential contests does not result in a superior allocation of resources.

Handicap Systems

This section moves to the opposite extreme of the previous discussion and assumes that the identities of each type of player are known to everyone. Competitive handicaps yield efficient mixed contests.

Consider again two types a and b now known to everyone. Prize structures in a-a and b-b tournaments satisfying (11) and (12) are efficient, but those conditions are not optimal in mixed a-b play. Denote the socially optimal levels of investment by μ_a^* and μ_b^*, their difference by $\Delta\mu$, and the prizes in a mixed league by $\tilde{W}_1$ and $\tilde{W}_2$. Let h be the handicap awarded to the inferior player b. Then the Nash solution in the a-b tournament satisfies

$$g(\mu_a - \mu_b - h)\Delta\tilde{W} = C'_a(\mu_a) \tag{28}$$

and

$$g(\mu_a - \mu_b - h)\Delta\tilde{W} = C'_b(\mu_b).$$

(The second condition in [28] follows from symmetry of $g[\xi]$.) Since the efficient investment criterion is $V = C'_a(\mu_a^*) = C'_b(\mu_b^*)$, independent of pairings, the optimum spread in a mixed match must be

$$\Delta\tilde{W} = V/g(\Delta\mu - h). \tag{29}$$

From (28), condition (29) insures the proper investments by both contestants. The spread is larger in mixed than in pure contests unless a gives b the full handicap $h = \mu_a^* - \mu_b^*$. Otherwise, the appropriate spread is a decreasing function of h. Prizes $\tilde{W}_1$ and $\tilde{W}_2$ must also satisfy the zero-profit constraint $\tilde{W}_1 + \tilde{W}_2 = V \cdot (\mu_a^* + \mu_b^*)$ independent of h since the spread is always adjusted to induce investments μ_a^* and μ_b^*.

The gain to an a from playing a b with handicap h, rather than another a with no handicap, is the difference in expected prizes:

$$
\begin{aligned}
\gamma_a(h) &= \bar{P}\tilde{W}_1 + (1 - \bar{P})\tilde{W}_2 - C_a(\mu_a^*) - [(W_1^a + W_2^a)/2 - C_a(\mu_a^*)] \\
&= \bar{P}\tilde{W}_1 + (1 - \bar{P})\tilde{W}_2 - (W_1^a + W_2^a)/2,
\end{aligned}
\tag{30}
$$

where $\gamma_a(h)$ is the gain to a and $\bar{P} = G(\Delta\mu - h)$ is the probability that a wins the mixed match. The corresponding expression for b is

$$
\gamma_b(h) = (1 - \bar{P})\tilde{W}_1 + \bar{P}\tilde{W}_2 - (W_1^b + W_2^b)/2.
\tag{31}
$$

The zero-profit constraints in a-a, a-b, and b-b require that $\gamma_a(h) + \gamma_b(h) = 0$ for all admissible h. The gain of playing mixed matches to a is completely offset by the loss to b and vice versa.

If $C_a(\mu)$ is not greatly different from $C_b(\mu)$, then $\Delta\mu = \mu_a^* - \mu_b^*$ is small and $\bar{P} \doteq \frac{1}{2} + [g(\Delta\mu - h)(\Delta\mu - h)$. This approximation and the zero-profit constraint reduce (30) to

$$
\gamma_a(h) \doteq V \cdot \left(\frac{\Delta\mu}{2} - h \right).
\tag{32}
$$

The expression for $\gamma_b(h)$ is the same, except its sign is reversed, so the gain to a decreases in h, and the gain to b increases in h. Therefore $h^* = \Delta\mu/2$ is the competitive handicap, since it implies $\gamma_a(h^*) = \gamma_b(h^*) = 0$. If the actual handicap is less than h^*, then γ_a is positive and a's prefer to play in mixed contests rather than with their own type, while b's prefer to play with b's only. The opposite is true if $h > h^*$.

A two-player game is said to be fair when the players are handicapped to equalize the medians. The competitive handicap does not result in a fair game, since $h^* = \Delta\mu/2 < \Delta\mu$. The a's are given a competitive edge in equilibrium, because they contribute more to total output in mixed matches than the b's do. This same result holds if ϵ_a has a different variance than ϵ_b, but it may be sensitive to the assumption of statistical independence and output additivity.

Alternatively, h can be constrained to be zero. In this case, different wage schedules would clear the market. Since $\gamma_a(0) = -\gamma_b(0) \equiv \beta$, paying $\tilde{W}_1 - \beta$ and $\tilde{W}_2 - \beta$ to a's, while paying $\tilde{W}_1 + \beta$, $\tilde{W}_2 + \beta$ to b's, leaves the spread and, therefore, the investments unaltered. It is easy to verify that a's and b's are still indifferent between mixed and pure contests, because expected returns are equal between segregated and integrated contests for each type of player. With no handicaps, the market-clearing prizes available to a's in the mixed contest are lower than those faced by b's. Still, expected wages are higher for a's than b's in the mixed contest, because their probability of winning is larger. The b's are given a superior schedule in the mixed contest as an equalizing difference for having to compete against superior opponents. This yields the surprising conclusion that reverse discrimination, where the less able are given a head start or rewarded more lucratively if they happen to accomplish the unlikely and win the contest, can be consistent with efficient incentive mechanisms and might be observed in a competitive labor market.

V. Summary and Conclusions

This paper analyzes an alternative to compensation based on the level of individual output. Under certain conditions, a scheme which rewards rank yields an allocation of resources identical to that generated by the efficient piece rate. Compensating workers on the basis of their relative position in the firm can produce the same incentive structure for risk-neutral workers as does the optimal piece rate. It might be less costly, however, to observe relative position than to measure the level of each worker's output directly. This results in paying salaries which resemble prizes: wages which differ from realized marginal products.

When risk aversion is introduced, the prize salary scheme no longer duplicates the allocation of resources induced by the optimal piece rate. Depending on the utility function and on the amount of luck involved, one scheme is preferred to the other. An advantage of a contest is that it eliminates income variation which is caused by factors common to workers of a given firm.

Finally, we allow workers to be heterogeneous. This complication adds an important result: competitive contests do not automatically sort workers in ways that yield an efficient allocation of resources when information is asymmetric. In particular, low-quality workers attempt to contaminate firms composed of high-quality workers, even if there are no complementarities in production. Contamination results in a general breakdown of the efficient solution if low-quality workers are not prevented from entering. However, when player types are known to all, there exists a competitive handicapping scheme which allows all types to work efficiently within the same firm.

References

Akerlof, George. "The Economics of Caste and of the Rat Race and Other Woeful Tales." *Q.J.E.* 90 (November 1976): 599–617.

Alchian, Armen A., and Demsetz, Harold. "Production, Information Costs, and Economic Organization." *A.E.R.* 62 (December 1972): 777–95.

Becker, Gary S., and Stigler, George J. "Law Enforcement, Malfeasance, and Compensation of Enforcers." *J. Legal Studies* 3, no. 1 (1974): 1–18.

Cheung, Steven N. S. *The Theory of Share Tenancy: With Special Application to Asian Agriculture and the First Phase of Taiwan Land Reform.* Chicago: Univ. Chicago Press, 1969.

David, Herbert A. *The Method of Paired Comparisons.* London: Charles Griffin, 1963.

Friedman, Milton. "Choice, Chance, and the Personal Distribution of Income." *J.P.E.* 61, no. 4 (August 1953): 277–90.

Galton, Francis. "The Most Suitable Proportion between the Values of First and Second Prizes." *Biometrika* 1 (1901–2): 385–90.

Gibbons, Jean D.; Olkin, Ingram; and Sobel, Milton. *Selecting and Ordering Populations: A New Statistical Methodology.* New York: Wiley, 1977.

Harris, Milton, and Raviv Artur. "Some Results on Incentive Contracts with Applications to Education and Employment, Health Insurance, and Law Enforcement." *A.E.R.* 68 (March 1978): 20–30.

Lazear, Edward P. "Why is There Mandatory Retirement?" *J.P.E.* 87, no. 6 (December 1979): 1261–84.

Mirrlees, James A. "The Optimal Structure of Incentives and Authority within an Organization." *Bell. J. Econ.* 7 (Spring 1976): 105–31.

Riley, John G. "Competitive Signalling." *J. Econ. Theory* 10 (April 1975): 174–86.

Ross, Stephen A. "The Economic Theory of Agency: The Principal's Problem." *A.E.R. Papers and Proc.* 63 (May 1973): 134–39.

Rothschild, Michael, and Stiglitz, Joseph E. "Equilibrium in Competitive Insurance Markets: An Essay on the Economics of Imperfect Information." *Q.J.E.* 90 (November 1976): 630–49.

Spence, A. Michael. "Job Market Signaling." *Q.J.E.* 87 (August 1973): 355–74.

Stevens, S. S. "Measurement, Statistics, and the Schemapiric View." *Science* 161 (August 30, 1968): 849–56.

Stiglitz, Joseph E. "Incentives, Risk, and Information: Notes toward a Theory of Hierarchy." *Bell J. Econ. and Management Sci.* 6 (Autumn 1975): 552–79.

Wilson, Charles A. "A Model of Insurance Markets with Incomplete Information." *J. Econ. Theory* 16 (December 1977): 167–207.

12

Contracts and the Market for Executives

1. Introduction

The vital function of business executives in efficiently directing the vast amounts of resources under their control makes the executive labor market an especially interesting one to study. Berle and Means raised the fundamental contractual issue by pointing out possible conflicts of interest arising from separation of ownership and control. It has taken many years for the economics profession to put these matters in proper perspective.

The first important response was to identify a market for corporate control (Manne, 1965), whereby the threat of involuntary termination would provide incentives for managers to align their actions with shareholders' interests. The remarkable level of activity in the American corporate-control market in recent years has dispelled any lingering doubts about the importance of this mechanism. Still, there remain differences of informed opinion on its efficacy for solving the problem.

Second-generation debates on the managerial theory of the firm (Marris, 1963; Baumol, 1967) focused attention on the firm's objective function. If managers operated the firm in shareholders' interests then they would maximize profits, and if they catered to their own interests then such things as sales and the amount of assets controlled would enter into the firm's objectives. An empirical question was immediately suggested: did executive earnings respond more to profitability or to

I am indebted to the National Science Foundation for financial support. Many people have contributed helpful comments, criticism, and discussion, including discussants Bengt Holmstrom and Larry Lau; colleagues Gary Becker, Gene Fama, and Edward Lazear; and contributors to the literature, especially Kevin J. Murphy, Robert Gibbons, and Edward Glaeser. I take responsibility for interpretations and errors.

From *Contract Economics,* ed. Lars Werin and Hans Wijkander (Oxford: Blackwell, 1992), 181–211.

sales? The investigations provoked by this question were among the first empirical studies of agency.

It would be interesting to report that these studies provided an empirical basis for the extensive theory of agency that has been developed recently, but that is not the way it happened. Rather, much of that development paralleled theoretical research on information economics. Whatever its source, the executive labor market is one of the most important practical applications of the new theory. Theory in turn has provided a useful framework for thinking about the data and for showing precisely how various mechanisms may be devised to align the interests of control and ownership. I attempt to join the theoretical and empirical strands of this literature in this chapter. It is organized around the three main economic problems that the executive labor market must solve: the distribution and assignment of control among executives; providing performance incentives; and identifying talent and reassigning control in the course of career development.

Section 2 briefly takes up the problem of the allocation of control, given incentives. The idea is that personal power and influence in an organization depend on the interactions between talent and the productivity of control. If there is complementarity between the two it is efficient to assign greater control to more talented persons. In a market equilibrium, the most talented executives occupy top positions in the largest firms, where the marginal productivity of their actions is greatly magnified over the many people below them to whom they are linked. This explains why earnings of top executives in large firms are so large, and why executive pay is positively correlated with firm size. The empirical elasticity of top executive pay with respect to firm size is approximately 0.25 for all industries and time periods for which it has been estimated.

Sections 3 and 4 take up the agency and incentive question, given the allocation of control. Theory predicts that the structure of pay strikes a compromise between incentives and insurance. Much evidence supports that prediction. The direct incentive component is of particular interest. The elasticity of compensation with respect to accounting rates of return is in excess of 1.0; and the elasticity with respect to the stock market rate of return is approximately 0.10. However, there exists no theoretical benchmark to serve as a guide for the size of number that should be expected, and disputes remain on whether compensation mechanisms provide enough incentives to elicit efficient management behavior.

Section 5 joins the assignment and incentive questions. How are competent and talented managers identified and how is control reallocated over the course of careers across successive, overlapping generations? For this task the labor market must keep a running score on available talent and adjust the assignment of control accordingly. Competition is thereby induced among contenders to influence the scoring process and gain greater rank and control over their careers. Such competition, of which promotion to higher-paying and more responsible positions is an important part, is the means by which control is transferred across the generations. Career incentives serve as better substitutes for current performance incentives at earlier stages of a career than in later stages, when a rapidly diminishing horizon reduces any incentive effects of future status on current behavior. Available data support the idea that compensation is increasingly structured to reward and weigh current performance more heavily over the course of a career, as theory suggests.

The final section draws out some suggestions for further work.

2. The Marginal Productivity Theory

Great power to direct resources and the large earnings that go with it are what make the executive labor market so interesting. Power and income are related in a market economy, where remuneration is proportional to one's marginal contribution to production. Early work began to connect marginal productivity to business decisions within hierarchical control structures—see Reder's (1968) excellent survey for references. Activities of top management are magnified geometrically because they affect recursively the productivity of all who work below them in the organization. This "scale of operations" effect, multiplying little bits over each of many units, accrues to the more talented managers as economic rent in a competitive equilibrium, much like a "superstar" effect (Rosen, 1981).

Top management inputs have something in common with local public goods, consisting as they do of commands and decisions affecting the productivity of the organization as a whole. What type of goods should be built and on what scale? What niche should the firm play in the market and how should its products be priced? Although a detailed theory of the division of labor in management organization is unavailable, a simple hierarchical model illustrates the essence of the idea—see Rosen (1982) and Miller (1982) for more details.

2.1 The Model

Consider a hierarchy with a fixed span of control, s, throughout every branch. Then the organization is a strictly triangular tree with s branches at every node. Production occurs at the bottom layer. Higher levels are exclusively devoted to "management" activities, which refine and augment production worker output. Decisions made at a higher level get dissipated somewhat in percolating down the tree, but link in a multiplicative way to more production workers and have larger marginal product the higher up they start.

Let z be a worker's talent (measured as output in self-employment). Assume that a level-j manager produces $(kz_j + mz_{j-1})$ units of service jointly with each of the s immediately subordinate workers below him, where k and m are positive constants independent of j and $m + k < 1$. Then a one-management-level firm produces output of $s(kz_1 + mz_0)$. A two-level firm produces $s^2(k(kz_2 + mz_1) + mz_0)$ units, and by recursion an n-layer organization with s_n production workers produces output of

$$Y_n = s^n \left(k^n z_n + k^{n-1} m z_{n-1} + \cdots + m z_0 \right)$$
$$\equiv A^n z_n + \sum_{j=1}^{n-1} s^{n-j} A^j m z_j + s^n m z_0, \tag{1}$$

where $j = 0$ is the bottom production level layer, $j = n$ is CEO (chief executive officer) and $A = sk > 1.0$ is the net span of control. From the second expression, the CEO contributes $A^n z$ to output, a j-level manager contributes $A^j mz$ and a production worker contributes mz. That there is one CEO, s^{n-j} level-j managers, and s^n production workers, gives total production in the firm.

The marginal product of talent is larger at higher levels of a hierarchy, through a chain letter-like effect. The CEO effectively is "cloned" $(sk)^n z$ times through subordinates in the chain of command. Lower-level managers are cloned only $(sk)^j mz$ times (for $j < n$), because their input has a shorter distance to travel down the tree and is further discounted (by $m < 1$), arising from the need to spend time processing supervisors' orders.

Let $W_j(z)$ be the wage of a level-j manager of talent z. Additivity of equation (1) implies that output is linear in talent within levels. Therefore incremental product accrues as rent to talent within levels according to:

$$W_j(z) = w_j + A^j mz, \quad j = 0, 1, \dots, n-1 \tag{2}$$

where $\{w_j\}$ are constants, determined by equating market supply and demand in the assignment of workers by talent to levels.

Total rent accruing to the person at the top of an n-level organization is the difference between output and costs of lower level workers. Defining profits as revenue minus costs, using (2) and simplifying:

$$I_n(z) = A^n z_n - \sum_{j-0}^{n-1} s^{n-j} w_j. \tag{3}$$

This too is linear in z_n. The first term can be interpreted as the unit toll the CEO collects for each of the A^n times he is cloned through all subordinates. The second term is the payment the CEO must make to all level-j subordinates for that privilege while letting them collect their own ability rents through *their* subordinates.

The earnings–talent gradient is linear within levels in (2) and (3), but is highly nonlinear between levels because the market equilibrium assigns talents to positions along the upper envelope of (2) and (3). The envelope is strictly convex, following from the fact that the marginal product of talent is increasing in level in (1). Consequently, a competitive market allocates talented people to higher-level positions in larger firms. Complementarity between talent and productivity inherent in hierarchical structures ($\partial Y_n / \partial z_j$ increasing in j in (1)) is what makes this so. Scarce talents of the most capable managers are economized by assigning them to positions at or near the top of the largest firms, where their ability is magnified to greater effect by spreading it over longer chains of command and larger scales of operations. These magnification effects accrue to these executives as rent. This is what sustains high average earnings of top-level executives in large firms and also implies that firm size and executive pay should be positively related. Since the firms we are concerned with here have average assets of $5 billion and large numbers of employees and other stakeholders, multiplicative scale-of-operations effects loom large: a little extra talent at the top can have enormous effects on total output. The social gains to devising efficient incentive mechanisms and to identifying the most talented managers are likely to be correspondingly large.

2.2 The Evidence

Top executive salaries increase with the size of the firm. Most of the evidence relates to the top five executives of American corporations as reported, by law, in annual proxy statements to shareholders. Lower-ranking executives have not been studied very much because no public data are available, although a few studies have used proprietary data on such persons.

Most of the evidence on firm size and executive pay comes from empirical attempts to parcel out executive pay to firm size or growth "causes" on the one hand, and to the profitability of the firm on the other. The preceding analysis shows that such attributions of causes are conceptually ambiguous and not mutually exclusive because large firms are more likely to be headed by more able executives and this has little bearing on whether firms can be treated as sales maximizers or as profit maximizers. Unusual talents and abilities must earn scarcity rents even in the absence of agency and incentive problems.

Many of these studies have encountered multicollinearity problems. Firms with large assets and sales revenues also have large accounting profits in absolute terms. The common factor, bigness, is at work. Even in comparing a giant firm with a merely large one, the sheer effects of scale dominate comparisons in cross-firm salary regressions and often make the regressors collinear (Ciscel and Carroll, 1980; Dunlevy, 1985). There is no "solution" to a multicollinearity problem and any way they are cut, scale effects show up powerfully in the data on top executive pay.

The numerous studies that bear on the relation between pay and the scale of resources controlled represent something of an empirical zoo. The main problem in assessing the evidence is that specifications vary widely from study to study. Multicollinearity plays some role here and so do such trivialities as different choice of units of measurement and log transforms without enough sample information for readers to construct elasticities. A definitive study will be one that estimates all existing specifications on one consistent data structure.

A start in this direction for scale effects appears in Kostiuk (1989). His estimates are based on 73 large U.S. corporations over the 1969–1981 period. The elasticity of executive annual-salary-plus-bonus with respect to sales of the firm is in the 0.2 to 0.25 range. Including firm-fixed effects does not change things. The elasticity is the same in the time-series "within"-firm comparison as in the cross-section "between"-firm comparison. A firm that is 10 percent larger than another on average pays its top executives 2.5 percent more; and when the latter firm grows by 10 percent, its top executives are on average paid 2.5 percent more in salary and bonuses. Murphy (1985) reports a similar estimate on a related sample, but using a broader definition of pay that includes deferred compensation and stock options: these components of pay are not very sensitive to size and scale variables. The regression specifications are sufficiently different between the two studies to suggest that the estimated elasticity is fairly insensitive to specification.

More convincing evidence on sensitivity comes from comparing studies that used much different data. Kostiuk's and Murphy's estimates are in the vicinity of Roberts's (1956) early estimate of 0.35 for selected manufacturing firms in the USA in the late 1940s and 1950. Using American data from 1937–1939, Kostiuk (1989) finds an asset elasticity of 0.3, close to the 0.25 elasticity estimated on U.S. data in 1967–1971. Furthermore, Cosh (1975) has estimated an asset elasticity of 0.26 for Britain during 1969–1971. This is remarkably close to that found for the United States. Barro and Barro (1990) find an asset elasticity of 0.32 for CEOs of U.S. commercial banks in the 1980s. Even those studies for which elasticity cannot be computed (McGuire et al., 1962; Winn and Shoenhair, 1988; Ciscel and Carroll, 1980—exceptions are Kokkelenberg, 1988; Lewellen and Huntsman, 1970) find strongly positive effects of sales or assets on executive pay.

The relative uniformity of the elasticity of executive pay with respect to scale across firms, industries, countries, and periods of time is notable and puzzling because the technology that sustains control and scale should vary across these disparate units of comparison. Thus the uniformity of estimates is a little too good to be true. One suspects copycat behavior among firms in compensation policy, yet the Conference Board compensation surveys that possibly provide the information for such comparisons group the data by industry. And copycat behavior cannot account for the 1930s estimate because the data were scarcely available. It surely cannot extend from the USA to the UK comparison. A convincing explanation is an open question.

3. Incentive Payments

Much of the recent interest in executive labor markets comes from new conceptual developments on incentive aspects of labor supply.

3.1 Pay and Hours of Work

High-ranking executives in large corporations earn large amounts of money, averaging $500,000 per year in salary and bonus alone. Adding deferred pay, options, and pensions sometimes changes it by more than one order of magnitude. Systematic data on the hours worked by high-ranking business executives are not available, but much informal evidence indicates that both hours worked and the intensity of work are among the largest of any specific occupational group in the economy. There is no shortage of labor supply in the usual sense and in fact salaries are independent of hours worked. Apparently, self-regulation, peer pressure, and monitoring by superiors are adequate to maintain great work intensity and long hours.

3.2 Agency: Nature of the Problem

The interesting question is whether or not executive efforts are directed toward the proper goals. Do business managers and executives direct their work to serve the interests of shareholders and other stakeholders or do they work in more self-serving ways?

At heart this *agency problem* represents some limitation on possibilities for decentralizing the functions of management in market economies. Specialization of knowledge and information, and the capital requirements of large enterprises virtually dictate a managerial function that is itself specialized and separated from ownership but tied to the fortunes of one enterprise. The resources controlled by such firms are so large that they must be assembled from far and wide. Individual owners cannot shepherd their resources in that way because of lack of skill, specific production and market knowledge, and motivation. Instead, they must place a certain amount of trust in a management team to take proper actions on their behalf. Herein lies the agency problem.

The formal problem is to design contracts to induce executives to act in their shareholders' interests. Various mechanisms have been identified that might accomplish this task. Economists have confined their attention to an idealized problem where the technology, scope for actions, and outcomes are common knowledge among principals and agents and only the action taken is private information of the agent. Principals know a great deal about the business, including what actions should be taken conditional on circumstances. They simply do not know what circumstances arose in any given realization: only the agent knows that. This is a far more constrained view than the idea of Berle and Means, or even that of the law on principal and agent relations, where the agent typically is hired to render services of exclusive technical or other specialized knowledge that cannot be known to principals because it is not their business.

3.3 Penalties for Misbehavior

Incentive schemes can either penalize unwanted behavior (negative feedback) or reward desirable behavior (positive reinforcement). Ambiguity arises because rewards for good behavior imply, by lack of reward, penalties for poor behavior, and is resolved by adopting some norm of "expected behavior." The earliest approaches to agency theory suggested penalties as efficient incentives (Mirrlees, 1976). Diminishing marginal utility of money makes the monetary reward required to induce good behavior larger than the monetary penalty needed to discourage bad behavior.

3.3.1 *Bonding Solutions to Agency Problems*

A performance bond is the prototype. Malfeasance is discouraged by a potential penalty because the agent puts personal wealth in jeopardy, "up front," as the bond. If the norm of good behavior is maintained, the agent is paid opportunity costs plus interest on the bond. If malfeasance is detected, the bond is seized and the worker is fired. The potential unraveling problem at contract termination is solved by extending the worker's horizon and not returning the bond until after "retirement" as a pension (see Becker and Stigler, 1974, for a very clear account). There exists a locus or trade-off of bond, detection-probability combinations that motivate the agent to adopt good behavior. Since resources used for monitoring have opportunity costs, it is economical to make the bond as large as possible and the probability of detection as small as possible (Becker, 1968) (ignoring type II errors).

Economists have used considerable imagination in applying this model. Lazear (1979) interpreted the bond-pension scheme very broadly. In his model, workers are paid less than their value to the firm when young but more than their value when old. The negative difference between pay and value is a gradual posting of bond, with the worker effectively "investing" in the firm and becoming a "partner" for all practical purposes. This model implies a reduction in turnover. Studies of job turnover have established that, after an experimentation period at the start of the life cycle, permanent attachments are made and turnover drops precipitously. Once a stable job has been found, it persists for remarkably long periods. Unfortunately, business executives have not been singled out for study, and there are serious gaps in the executive data for this purpose. However, a few conclusions may be warranted.

Executives at or near the CEO rank in large corporations hold their positions for fairly long intervals and have been employed by the firm for a very long time. For example, in the samples used by Kostiuk (1989) and Murphy (1985), the average top-level executive was 55–57 years old, had been in the position for seven or eight years, and had worked for the company for more than 25 years. In the larger *Forbes* sample of almost 1,300 large corporations over 1974–1986, Jensen and Murphy (1990) report that CEOs who left office during that period had, on average, served for ten years. In the case studies discussed by Vancil (1987), 80 percent of "retired" CEOs remained on their firm's board of directors, and more than one-third served as chairman of the board. Barro and Barro (1990) show a marked increase in departure probabilities of commercial bank CEOs after 63 years of age and associated with normal retirement. This is probably true of most industries.

There is more turnover below the very top ranking positions and in smaller firms. Nevertheless, Leonard's (1990) proprietary sample suggests that the matching process is typically completed by age 34, the average age at which older executives were hired by their current employers in the sample. Casual evidence suggests substantial lower-level executive turnover upon succession changes of top-level management. A study by Lichtenberg and Siegel (1989) shows elimination of management/white-collar jobs when plants change ownership in leveraged buyouts. There is evidence that the same thing happens in un-friendly takeovers, mergers, and acquisitions.

These observations are consistent with bonding and firm-specific capital accumulation among business executives, but knowledge of magnitudes is not available to assess their deterrence effects. The deterrence value of a bond depends on its size compared with the value of resources at risk of mismanagement and appropriation. Since a person's rank and responsibility in an organization grow over the life cycle, it is likely that implicit bonds are more efficacious for younger executives who have not yet gained control of much of the firm's resources. And since the value of large corporations exceeds the wealth of top managers by many orders of magnitude, bonds provide less scope for solving the agency problem at the top.

3.3.2 Loss of Reputation as Bond

Reputational considerations serve a bonding function in agency relationships, and although they lurk in the background of agency theory, formal analysis has proved elusive. An important exception is Fama (1980), who considered a model where observers use an agent's prior record and past history of performance to infer some personal trait, such as honesty. Knowing this, the agent has incentives to act in ways that affect the market's beliefs. The agency value of reputation arises because current behavior has an enduring "memory" when the legacy of the past is used to update current beliefs. Then current actions have long-term consequences if the discount rate is not too large. Loss of reputation serves as a deterrent when the capital value of these consequences for earnings is greater than the benefit of malfeasance, sloth, and error in a current action.

Fama (1980) analyzed market equilibrium for a simple structure without discounting, which converged to first-best efficient managerial behavior. Holmstrom (1982b) showed that discounting and risk aversion limit the extent to which reputation polices incentives. For example, finite life limits the extent to which the legacy of the past persists into the future (see Telser (1980) for the need for random horizons in self-enforcing agreements, and Radner (1985) on discounting in multi-agent problems). Reputation plays an even smaller role in contract enforcement as the agent gets older because there is less to lose. At the end of the contract there is nothing to lose.

This horizon difficulty is reinforced by the fact that opportunities for misconduct increase as the successful agent's control over resources increases over the life cycle. One can be sympathetic, as I am, to the idea that there is much more to loss of reputation than merely financial opportunities—social opprobrium, disapproval from one's peers, and loss of self-esteem have substantial deterrence value to many people— yet remain skeptical about their overall role in enforcing agency relations. Like performance bonds, reputation is likely to be more efficacious earlier rather than later in the life cycle.

3.3.3 The Stock Market and Corporate Control

As everyone knows, changes in ownership and control achieved new heights in the 1980s. The takeover phenomenon has much independent interest in the field of finance (see Jensen, 1988) and is beyond the scope of this review. However, a few findings have direct bearing on the subject at hand. Hostile takeovers and tender offers have attracted all of the research attention. Insofar as they represent a difference of opinion between current and potential new management on the efficient use of the firm's resources, they serve to check some abuses of current management in the use of those resources.

Successful hostile takeovers result in wholesale changes in management of the object firm. Evidence on reemployment opportunities of displaced top executives is scanty, but displaced executives probably do not find many doors open to them. It is also known that even unsuccessful takeovers serve to reallocate resources to the control of others through divestiture. Evidently the implied penalties to existing management from both successful and unsuccessful takeovers serve as some discipline for aligning current stockholder and managerial interests.

Nevertheless, other findings suggest that this discipline is incomplete. For instance, there is often substantial severance pay to top executives of object firms in mergers. The stock market views these "golden parachutes" as productive in converting what would otherwise be hostile reactions to friendly ones in takeover overtures (Lambert and Larcker, 1985), yet the implied behavior for those seeking such security seems curious. Second, object firms in takeovers tend to be in declining industries, where industry effects might be difficult to disentangle from firm-specific management effects (Lichtenberg and Siegel, 1987; Morck et al., 1988a). Third, the takeover premium is about 40 percent (Jensen and Ruback, 1983). Thus it appears that existing managers can squander one-third of the firm's value before the threat of displacement becomes truly serious. Fourth, the market value of the average acquiring firm in a takeover shows little or no change. The market apparently puts small value in finder's fees and reorganization rents that might be expected from these activities. Perhaps competition among bidders accounts for this last finding, but it cannot account for all of it if these activities are costly. It is not obvious why, when outsiders eliminate inefficient managers, practically all of the return should go to the shareholders of the mismanaged firms. Finally, Bhagat et al. (1990) find that 1980s reorganizations "deconglomerized" many of the horizontal mergers assembled in 1960s and 1970s. Hostile takeovers and attempts resulted in spinning off business lines to specialist firms and not to other conglomerates. A convincing theory of why these conglomerates were formed in the first place is not yet available.

4. Rewards to Elicit Efficient Action

All of the penalty modes constrain, but do not eliminate, self-serving behavior. Hence there is scope for reward mechanisms to help align the interests of managers and shareholders.

4.1 Risk Sharing and Incentives

A fairly general approach was developed by Holmstrom (1979), who examined the following problem. Suppose an agent is hired by a principal to produce good x with production function $x = f(l, \epsilon)$, where l is effort and ϵ is a random variable with zero mean and known distribution. The agent is risk-averse with concave utility $u = U(c, l)$ where c is consumption. The principal is risk neutral. All production and utility functions are common knowledge and outcome x is jointly observed by principal and agent. However, the action l and the random variable ϵ are exclusive private information, either controlled or observed, of the agent. The principal has full property rights in x, which has unit price, and, for simplicity, supplies no inputs into the production process. The agent is paid a share $s(x)$ of the proceeds of x because l and ϵ are not separately observed by the principal: the goal is to characterize the equilibrium determination of $s(x)$.

The method of solution is interesting. It converts the market equilibrium problem into a two-stage maximum problem. The first step analyzes the agent's choice of l that maximizes expected utility given $s(x)$. This yields a mapping from $s(x)$ to labor supply l. The second step solves for the function $s(x)$ that maximizes either the principal's expected profit or the expected utility of the agent, given the labor supply behavior in the first step. If profit is taken as maximand, another constraint is that the worker must expect to receive the known utility level of another job. If expected utility is taken as maximand, the added constraint is that the principal receives at least the expected return in some other activity. These alternatives give two extreme points on the utility-possibility frontier. Intermediate points are similarly obtained. Competition in the labor market insures that the equilibrium contract lies on the utility-possibility frontier.

There is tension between efficient action and efficient insurance in this problem. Were everything observable, the two could be unbundled. Then the risk-neutral principal would supply full insurance to the risk-averse agent by paying a fixed salary independent of outcome. The agent would willingly supply optimal effort (expected marginal product equals marginal cost) and monitoring would eliminate shirking. If the agent is risk-neutral there are no gains from trade. The agent acquires ownership rights to x and supplies optimal effort as a residual income recipient in self-employment. In all other cases, payment based on output alone through $s(x)$ gives only one instrument to perform two real allocative functions. There aren't enough independent prices and margins to do either one sufficiently: the principal has to offer less than complete insurance to give the agent incentives to put forth effort.

It is remarkable that very little more can be said, in general, to characterize $s(x)$. Payments that are decreasing in x through part of its range cannot even be ruled out (Grossman and Hart, 1983)! This negative result provides very few restrictions on data and makes the theory difficult to apply. What is worse, the contracts actually observed in agency relationships are typically of very simple forms that are not predicted by this model.

The reason for these complications is difficult to describe. However, Holmstrom and Milgrom (1987) prove that $s(x)$ take the simple linear form of a two-part tariff when income effects are absent in preferences and the technology shocks ϵ are i.i.d. An intertemporal version shows intuitively how it works. Consider an indefinitely repeated problem when ϵ is white noise and the action l is chosen before ϵ is revealed in each round. With no income effects, the agent is content with the same amount of insurance each time irrespective of wealth, and similarly for the risk-neutral principal. Furthermore, i.i.d. production disturbances imply that each round looks exactly like every other from the production/incentive point of view. It is efficient for the agent to choose the same action in every period, because the agent's marginal rate of substitution between effort and consumption is independent of wealth and the expected marginal product of effort is constant. In the linear payoff schedule $s(x) = a + bx$, which implements the scheme, a serves as the insurance component and b as the incentive component (Stiglitz, 1975). If $s(x)$ were nonlinear, the agent would have undesirable incentives not to take the same action each time, for example, to accumulate work into a large pile and do it all at once in a range where $s'(x)$ is increasing.

4.2 The Optimal Piece Rate

Following Holmstrom and Milgrom (1989), consider the linear model for a risk-averse agent with constant absolute risk aversion who produces two inputs, x_1 and x_2, for a risk-neutral principal. Labor supplied by the agent is the only input. The agent receives a total payment y consisting of a fixed lump sum and revenues from production of x_1 and x_2 each with separate piece rates b_1 and b_2:

$$x_i = l_i + \epsilon_i, \quad i = 1, 2$$
$$y = a + b_1 x_1 + b_2 x_2 \tag{4}$$
$$u = U(y - c(l_1, l_2)) = -\exp\{-R[y - c(l_1, l_2)]\}$$

where R is the coefficient of risk aversion, l_i is the effort devoted to activity i, y is gross income, $c(l_1, l_2)$ is the agent's (convex) cost of effort and ϵ_1 and ϵ_2 are random variables with zero means and covariance matrix $\{\sigma_{ij}\}$.

Following the two-step procedure, take parameters (a, b_1, b_2) as given and calculate the agent's labor supply to each activity. Substituting from (4), the agent chooses l_1 and l_2 to maximize

$$Eu + EU(a + b_1 l_1 + b_2 l_2 + b_1 \epsilon_1 + b_2 \epsilon_2 - c(l_1, l_2)). \tag{5}$$

The first-order condition is $\partial Eu / \partial l_i = EU' \cdot [b_i - \partial c / \partial l_i] = 0$. Consequently,

$$b_i = \partial c(l_1, l_2) / \partial l_1, \quad \text{for } i = 1, 2 \tag{6}$$

from which the labor supply functions $l_i = l_i(b_1, b_2)$ are obtained by inversion. Comparative statics on (6) yields the familiar

$$\partial l_i/\partial b_j = (-1)^{i+j} c_{ij}/\Delta, \tag{7}$$

where $\Delta = c_{11}c_{22} - c_{12}^2 > 0$. It follows that $\partial l_i/\partial b_i > 0$; an increase in the payment for an output increases the effort devoted to it. Also, $\partial l_i/\partial b_j < 0$ for $i \neq j$ when $c_{ij} > 0$: an increase in the price of one good decreases the effort supplied to the other.

In the second step, the risk-neutral principal has profit $\pi = p_1 x_1 + p_2 x_2 - a - b_1 x_1 - b_2 x_2$, where p_i is the relative (market) price of x_i. Consider the case where the expected return to the principal is driven to zero. Then (a, b_1, b_2) is constrained by

$$E\pi = 0 = (p_1 - b_1)l_1 + (p_2 - b_2)l_2 - a. \tag{8}$$

The market equilibrium contract (a, b_1, b_2) is the one that maximizes the agent's expected utility Eu, subject to the labor supply functions derived in the first step and to (8).

Substituting (8) into Eu:

$$Eu = EU(p_1 l_1 + p_2 l_2 + b_1 \epsilon_1 + b_2 \epsilon_2 - c(l_1, l_2)), \tag{9}$$

where $l_i = l_i(b_1, b_2)$, satisfying (6), is understood. Differentiating (9) with respect to b_i and simplifying gives, for $i = 1, 2$,

$$\partial Eu/\partial b_i = [(p_1 - c_1)\partial l_1/\partial b_1 + (p_2 - c_2)\partial l_2/\partial b_i]EU' + EU'\epsilon_i = 0, \tag{10}$$

where $\partial l_i/\partial b_j$ satisfies (7). Finally, substituting the CARA utility function into (10):

$$(p_1 - c_1)\partial l_1/\partial b_i + (p_2 - c_2)\partial l_2/\partial b_1 - R(b_1 \sigma_{i1} + b_{12}\sigma_{i2}) = 0, \\ i = 1, 2, \tag{11}$$

gives two equations in two unknowns to solve for b_1 and b_2.

Equation (11) illustrates the balancing between incentives and insurance in the optimal contract. The marginal costs of effort, c_1 and c_2, would equal their marginal rewards, p_1 and p_2, in a first-best solution. In (11) there is a wedge between the marginal cost and marginal benefit of efforts in each good. These are weighted by the marginal response of effort to its internal price to arrive at an average deviation and balanced against risk considerations in the last term of (11). Relevant risk in the contract is an average of the variances of each output weighted by internal prices and the extent of risk aversion. Departures from first-best incentives increase with risk and the agent's sensitivity to it.

A little more progress can be made by manipulating (11) to

$$b_i = [R\sigma_{jj}(c_{jj} - pc_{ij}) - R\sigma_{ij}(pc_{ii} - c_{ij}) + 1]\Delta/D, \quad (12)$$

where $D = (R\sigma_{11}\Delta + c_{22})(R\sigma_{22}\Delta + c_{11}) - (R\sigma_{12}\Delta + c_{12})^2$. Even this is unwieldy, but two special cases suffice for present purposes.

First, let $c_{12} = \sigma_{12} = 0$. Then the two activities are independent of each other and (12) reads as

$$b_i^* = p_i/(R\sigma_{ii}c_{ii} + 1), \quad i = 1, 2. \quad (13)$$

Piece rates vary inversely with risk aversion, R, the size of the risk, σ_{ii}, and the relative responsiveness of labor supply to price, c_{ii}, and vary positively with the market value of output produced, p_i.

Second, let $c_{12} > 0$ and $\sigma_{12} = 0$. Now the activities compete with each other because doing more of one increases the marginal cost of the other. Substituting into (12), one eventually arrives at

$$b_i = b_i^* \quad \text{plus a term in} \quad [R\sigma_{ii}(c_{12} - c_{ii}) - 1],$$

where b^* is defined in (13). The second term in this expression is negative as long as $c_{ii} > c_{12}$, that is, if, from (7), the own-responsiveness of effort to price is larger than the cross-responsiveness. Then b_i is smaller than b_i^*. Piece rates are smaller when activities compete with each other in the agent's effort. There are negative externalities between the two activities when c_{12} is positive. These are effectively "taxed" by reducing the marginal incentive components in the contract, so substitution between activities gives rise to relatively insensitive internal incentives, to "low-powered" incentives in the sense of Williamson (1985).

4.3 Some Qualifications

Another, perhaps more fundamental, reason why the optimal contract might back off from sensitive performance incentives is that output and performance of managers are often hard to measure. The services rendered by business managers in large firms cannot be assessed on a fixed scale of attributes. If the list of variables is incomplete, then scoring performance on such a scale might exaggerate the production of those attributes that are only imperfectly correlated with the true value of the service. Important intangibles would not be rewarded sufficiently. Although the point is an old one, it has been applied only recently to labor market incentives. Baker (1989) shows that imperfect correlation between the assessment of performance and true output acts like a reduction in p_i in the formula for b^* above. It reduces the weight of marginal incentives in determining executive pay, and by implication increases the weight of fixed salary.

Such considerations are more appropriate for lower-level managers than for those close to the top of the ladder. Contributions of lower-level managers to the success of an organization are difficult to isolate, submerged as they are in the joint output of the team as a whole. Life-cycle considerations also play an important role there (see below). Incentives cannot be so diluted for high-ranking people, who take ultimate responsibility for the success of the organization as a whole. If they are rewarded on market valuation and profitability of the firm, there is no need to assess and price out each of the many activities that contribute to it. There is no need to reduce the "power" of incentives to them (Lazear, 1986).

An important qualification remains. Rewards that promote good incentives must be indexed to outcomes that managers can alter. Stock market values and current profits are only partly affected by managerial decisions. They are also affected by business conditions beyond any manager's control. Lazear and Rosen (1981) pointed out that relative comparisons wash out common components of variance among competitors and isolate specific performance-related components. The idea is analyzed most completely by Holmstrom (1982a), who showed that relative comparisons eliminate a source of extraneous risk for agents. Increasing the signal-to-noise ratio makes managerial incentives more effective and contracts more efficient.

4.4 The Evidence

Top executive compensation in a large firm is set by the board of directors, often with the assistance of management consultants (Tosi and Gomez-Mejia, 1989). The contracts themselves are not public information, but there is little doubt that remuneration is tied to the fortunes of the firm. There are, however, differences of opinion about how performance is measured for compensation purposes and about the magnitude of the effects.

The earliest studies in the sales–profits debate summarized above generally found a larger effect of sales than of profits (Roberts, 1956; McGuire et al., 1962). Later studies (Lewellen and Huntsman, 1970; Kokkelenberg, 1988; Winn and Shoenhair, 1988) tended to find stronger effects of accounting profits on compensation, but at least an equal number have found evidence for both (Meeks and Whittington, 1975; Ciscel and Carroll, 1980; Kostiuk, 1986, 1989; Leonard, 1990), with the picture slightly clouded by multicollinearity. Since size must be an important correlate of pay if more talented persons control greater resources, posing the agency question in terms of sales *versus* profits is not meaningful with the available data. The managerial hypothesis that size is larger than it *otherwise would be* is a counterfactual that cannot be answered at the moment. Looking at all the studies together I cannot see clear winners in the earlier debate. Both performance and scale are important. I confine attention to those studies where elasticities are presented or can be computed. All of the estimates refer either to the CEO or to the top five executives. Some use salary and bonus as independent variable, others a more comprehensive definition that includes deferred compensation and options.

Kostiuk (1986) estimates a semi-elasticity of the accounting rate of return on compensation (defined as dlog(compensation)/dr, where r is the rate of return) of about 1.25 for the United States in both the 1930s and early 1970s. This compares quite well with Cosh's (1975) estimate of 1.0 for Britain in the early 1970s. In recent years, empirical studies have tended to use the stock market rate of return as the performance measure rather than accounting rates of return. This reduces the elasticity estimate by almost a factor of 10.

Murphy (1985) estimates a semi-elasticity of compensation with respect to the rate of return to shareholders of 0.12–0.16 using a 73-firm sample of firms during 1969–1981. Murphy (1986) produces a similar estimate on a much larger *Forbes* sample of about 250 large firms over 1974–1984. Earlier, Masson (1971) estimated statistically significant effects of stock returns on CEO compensation from a 39-firm sample over 1947–1966, though the coefficients themselves are not reported. Coughlin and Schmidt (1985) estimated a semi-elasticity of 0.10–0.15 on a 40-firm sample from *Forbes* during 1978–1980. The study is notable for using the abnormal stock return (estimated form CAPM) instead of the raw return. Murphy (1985) tried both abnormal and total returns in a within-firm compensation regression. Most of the estimated effect goes to the raw return, and it does not seem to matter which one is used, so long as both are not used together. Again, there is evidence that this estimate is remarkably uniform from study to study; for example, consider that Barro and Barro (1990) report an estimate of 0.17 for bank CEOs over 1982–1987.

Coughlin and Schmidt (1985) were among the first to use a relative performance measure, yet Murphy's (1985) empirical competition between relative and absolute stock returns suggested that relative performance did not matter. Relative performance evaluation was principally addressed by Antle and Smith (1986) using Masson's 1947–1966 sample. They found only weak evidence to support the idea. It was definitely rejected for 15 out of 37 firms studied, while wrong signs on the systematic and firm-specific components were obtained for many others. Barro and Barro (1990) find no evidence of relative performance evaluation among bank CEOs, even though there were marked differences in fortunes among regional economies and their constituent banks during the period of analysis.

A recent study by Gibbons and Murphy (1990a) uses the largest (*Forbes*) sample and provides the most evidence supporting relative performance evaluation. They include the average rate of return on stock in the firm's industry and the firm's own rate of return in the compensation regression, rather than abnormal performance, CAPM measures. They find positive effects of own return on executive compensation and negative effects of industry average return. While it is the strongest evidence for relative performance effects yet found, anomalies remain because industry effects are larger at the most aggregate level than at the firm's own four-digit level. The estimated effect may be sensitive to how relative performance effects is somewhat more on the negative than positive side of the ledger.

Most studies so far have examined whether pay and performance have positive partial correlation. This is the natural first approximation, but there are only a few more ambitious studies that purport to examine causation. This program was begun by Masson (1971), who investigated how various components of pay affect firm performance. The method used is flawed and has not been pursued. Leonard (1990) regressed the rate of return on equity on various aspects of pay and incentives for executives within ten levels of the top in a proprietary sample. No clear general picture emerges because the effects differ in sign when estimated within and between firms. Abowd's (1990) study on these proprietary data is notable for asking whether changes in the sensitivity of pay to performance affect *subsequent* performance. Evidence of such effects is found for stock market performance indicators, but not for accounting measures. The inventory of studies is too small to make definitive judgements on causality right now. Hopefully, more studies along these lines will be forthcoming.

Finally, some studies have examined the sensitivity of pay components to performance. Most studies mentioned above conclude that current performance rewards come about through adjustment of the bonus and components of compensation other than salary. Salary is a substantial part of compensation, but acts more like the fixed term a in the development above. One thinks that salary adjustments should respond to longer-term components of performance and bonus to shorter-term components, but this is an understudied point. Eaton and Rosen (1983) consider the difference between long- and short-term incentives by examining the correlates of current and deferred pay components. However, Miller and Scholes (1982) argue convincingly that these forms of compensation are tied up with tax laws so it is difficult to distinguish the two. For instance, stock options were not used for compensation until the early 1950s, when upper–bracket marginal tax rates were very high. Morck et al. (1988b) find a curious nonmonotonic relationship between management stock ownership and firm performance. Using a cross-section of large U.S. firms in the 1980s, they find that performance measured by Tobin-Grunfeld's q increases with stock ownership of Board members (including the CEO) when it is less than 5 percent of total stock, decreases with ownership in 5–25 percent range, and perhaps increases again above that range. No compelling explanations have appeared as yet for this unusual finding.

4.5 Assessment

Although there is little doubt that top executives' incomes vary with the fortunes of their firms, the picture is mixed relative to theory. Confirming evidence from several independent studies and samples leaves us fairly secure that the effect of stock returns on log compensation is in the 0.10–0.15 range. The many estimates of accounting rates of return on compensation do not lend themselves to such ready comparisons, even though most studies do find positive effects. The best available comparable estimates are in the range 1.0–1.2, and quite a bit larger than for rates of return to stock ownership.

I cannot express a clear preference between these two alternatives. Many economists simply dismiss accounting profits as too easily manipulatable by top managers to be suitable contractual measures of performance. Such dismissal is simply wrong. Not only is it known that explicit provisions of executive contracts *are in fact* tied to accounting numbers, but the deeper intellectual question is whether market or accounting returns are more informative for executive incentives (Lambert and Larcker, 1987). It cannot be true that accounting information is worthless in the giant firms in question, since they simply could not exist without it. Finally, accounting numbers are the source of information not only for managerial decisions. They also inform the stock market. Top executives are in a repeated game, constantly observed by bird-dogs, market makers, and, even worse, raiders. This limits possible misrepresentation for compensation purposes. For sure, depreciation methods and special charges can be chosen advantageously on occasion. Yet these manipulations cannot occur very often and have future costs as well as current benefits.

Undoubtedly, stock values are less easy to manipulate in this sense, but how much information about performance do they contain? The stock price of a firm changes for many reasons that are independent of its performance. Some underlying causes, such as shifts in industry demand, have similar effects on accounting profits. Others, such as changes in the market discount rate, are specific to the stock market alone. There are parallel sources of independent noise for accounting measures. Putting them side by side, which measure has the greater signal power for managerial performance? Strong findings on relative performance evaluation would have shed light on this, but only one study has found evidence for it. Bonus and other payment mechanisms are seldom explicitly triggered by stock performance in executive contracts. Options and deferred stock appreciation rights are exceptions, but their value depends as much on the general state of the stock market, which managers cannot affect, as on firm-specific performance.

Jensen and Murphy (1990) argue that the empirical relationship between pay and performance, while positive, is too small to provide adequate incentives for managers to act in shareholders' interests. Using the *Forbes* 1974–1986 sample, they regress the arithmetic first difference in annual CEO compensation (including the change in personal wealth tied up in the firm) on current and lagged arithmetic changes in shareholder wealth and a few other variables. An attempt is made to eliminate the effects of market noise by using relative performance indicators, although they are unsuccessful here.

An estimate for dlog(compensation)/dr of 0.1 estimated in earlier studies seems "reasonable," so it comes as a considerable surprise that the estimated values in the arithmetic regression for d(compensation)/dr are extremely small. The differences are due to the fact that the ratio of CEO compensation to shareholder wealth is vanishingly small in these giant corporations (on the order of 6×10^{-4} at the median and 10^{-3} at the mean). In the simplest specification, the first difference regression implies that annual salary and bonus increase by a mere \$13.50–\$21.00 when shareholder wealth changes by \$1 million. Adding the effects of own stock holdings, options, and the like increases the estimates to \$32.50. Since mean compensation is more the \$0.5 million per annum and personal wealth is much larger than that, these are very small sums indeed, small enough to raise questions about the role for compensation mechanisms to align the interests of managers and owners.

Still, Jensen and Murphy's (1990) estimates are substantially smaller than those implied by other studies. Considering that both dividends and the number of shares of stock outstanding hardly change in a short time series, the rate of return on stock ownership, r, is approximately equal to the percentage change in total market shareholder value. Let ΔV represent the arithmetic first difference of total shareholder value and Δy the arithmetic first difference in salary and bonus. Jensen and Murphy estimate $\tilde{b}_1 = \Delta y / \Delta V \approx 1.35 \times 10^{-5}$. The semi-elasticity estimate discussed above is $\tilde{b}_2 = \Delta \log y / \Delta r = (\Delta y / y) / \Delta r$, for which 0.1 serves as lower bound. Now, since $\Delta r = \Delta V / V$, it follows that $\tilde{b}_1 \approx \tilde{b}_2 \cdot V / y$ and $\tilde{b}_1 \approx \tilde{b}_2 y / V$, where y and V are evaluated near the mean of the sample. Since $y/V = 10^{-3}$ at the mean, the implied estimate of $\tilde{b}_1$ when $\tilde{b}_2 \approx 0.1$ is 10^{-4}—or almost eight times larger than their estimate of 1.35×10^{-5}. This implies a total effect of at least \$100 salary and bonus change per \$1 million change in shareholder value, compared to their estimate of \$13.5–\$20.00. Working their estimate the other way round leads to an implied elasticity near 0.014, much smaller than the direct estimate of 0.1 found by others in these data.

Functional forms must account for these differences. Most empirical economists would argue for using log rather than arithmetic differences because the latter are dominated by large firms. Furthermore, the arithmetic effect is expected to decrease for large firms (as Jensen and Murphy confirm) because the risks are larger. Since the rate of return is largely independent of size, the directly estimated elasticity form ($\tilde{b}_2$) better controls statistically for size effects.

Going out on a limb, the 10^{-4} estimate of $\tilde{b}_1$ implied by the log version suggests that CEOs lose \$100,000 in direct pay per \$1 billion decline in stock value. Now a \$1 billion change is large—about 20 percent of the average firm's value in the sample. However, the \$100,000 is in the range of 20 percent of average compensation. Considering that CEO personal asset holdings are almost surely less diversified than those of the average stockholder (Lewellen, 1968; Deckop, 1988), CEOs risk a considerable portion of their personal wealth from the actions they take on behalf of shareholders. What is not so clear from theory is what a reasonable benchmark would be. Is the 0.1–0.15 elasticity estimate too small or too large? The theory has not focused enough on that number to provide and answer.

5. Career Incentives

Much of the literature has analyzed incentives in a timeless context. Interactions between the selection and incentive problems give rise to important new issues when the problem is examined over a person's career. Resources must be reassigned among managers over time, as older generations retire and are replaced by younger generations. Aspiring executives start their careers in low-level positions and work their way up through the ladder to higher-level positions over the life cycle. How a career develops depends on the quality of the person's previous work, what talents were demonstrated in lower positions, and the talent of other people who are available to be selected. Selection and incentives are intertwined by competition for promotion to higher-paying positions and by attempts to affect the selection process.

5.1 Nature of the Problem

Again, the manager's horizon is crucial to this problem. Career considerations are more important at the beginning of a career than at the end. Toward the end of a career, if not before, the cards have been dealt and one's hand is pretty much known. Higher-level reassignments are unlikely, or impossible. At that point the potential influence of future prospects vanishes and only current incentives matter. Analyzing the very top level executive labor market within a timeless context is a good approximation for this reason. However, learning, incentives, and aspects of competition for positions necessarily arise when examining the market as a whole.

A promising approach is taken by Gibbons and Murphy (1990b), who extend the linear piece-rate model to two periods. The model is specialized to only one activity but is generalized to include two sources of noise. Uncertainty about the agent's ability is added to the pure randomness and/or measurement error in the mapping from effort to output in the first period.

The problem is solved by backward recursion. The solution in the last period follows that outlined above, with the proviso that it is conditioned on whatever is known about the person's ability at the end of the previous period. Information has no value in the final period and there is no investment in it by either principal or agent. Information acquired in the first period does have value because it can be exploited later. Given anticipated optimal behavior in the second period, investments in information give extra first-period work incentives over and above the piece rate. Specifically, the agent has incentives to increase the signal-to-noise ratio in output to enable better assessment of ability. Raising the first-period piece rate is not so necessary for incentives because learning and piece rates are substitutes for each other. Such substitution actually occurs in Gibbons and Murphy (1990b) for risk-reducing reasons, and the piece-rate price b is actually smaller in the first period than in the second.

Earlier, Murphy (1986) had contrasted pure learning with pure incentive theories of the executive labor market. In the learning theory the manager is paid the value of expected productivity estimated from previous output. Bayesian inference implies that more is learned at the beginning of a career than at the end because additional samples hardly affect the posterior distribution when the number of observations is already large. On the other hand, the atemporal incentive problem looks much the same from one period to the next. Thus the learning model would imply less sensitivity of compensation to output for more experienced executives while the pure incentive model would not. When the two forces are combined, incentives to invest in learning still decline over time and less learning takes place, but now it is necessary to substitute current performance incentives for diminishing career incentives over the life cycle. This implies that sensitivity of pay to current performance should actually increase for more experienced executives, whose horizon is shorter than the less experienced.

5.2 Promotions and Career Incentives

Career considerations loom large in promotion of executives across ranks in the corporate structure. Evidence exists that much human capital investment is related to these kinds of job changes (Sicherman and Galor, 1990) in the labor market generally. Still, there are reasons to suspect that these aspects of work are much more important for executives than for other workers. Advancement in rank in the officer corps of a military organization is a useful rigid hierarchy version of the process to keep in mind (although the up-or-out feature is usually not encountered in firms). Large firms, such as oil companies with far-flung foreign operations, rotate high-level personnel through the system and through the ranks much like the military. No doubt differences in style and technology make it a poorer approximation for many firms, yet essential elements remain common to all of them.

Promotions focus an executive's career attention on those discrete points when a "window of opportunity" opens for possible advancement. Typically these windows fit some predetermined rough outline of the firm's organization structure and there is competition for them from contenders, both within and without the firm. This process can be modeled as a tournament (see Lazear and Rosen (1981) for an early analysis). Competitors with the highest scores on some performance criteria are declared winners and get promoted to a better job. Comparison methods in statistical experiments come to mind as a possible model, with the crucial difference that the objects of the experiment can and do take actions to influence the outcome. Where one gets classified in this competition makes an enormous economic difference to a person.

It is interesting that within-firm competition can sometimes be structured to approximate socially optimum incentives by adjusting the wage structure across job ranks. The idea is simple. Incentives to put forth effort to win are increasing with the difference in prizes between winning and losing. Since incentives vanish when the difference in compensation vanishes and increase without bound in the other direction, there exists a between-rank wage structure that promotes the optimal amount of effort (in the sense that the expected marginal product to the firm of such effort equals its marginal cost). Much has been made of setting the scope and limitations of this result. Levinthal (1984), McLaughlin (1988), and Mookherjee (1989) provide excellent surveys to which the reader is referred for details. Instead of providing another review, I use the idea to illustrate some effects of career considerations on the organizational wage structure.

Think of a career as stochastically climbing a ladder. Ultimately the person comes to rest at some rung, perhaps at the top but usually before. This scheme loosely follows a sequential design of experiments, where "losers" are successively culled from the sample and not allowed to continue. It economizes sample size and gains information efficiently. Incentive issues arise from the stopping rule. A person's horizon in this game falls to zero when being passed over for promotion enough times eliminates opportunities to continue. From that point on current monetary incentives and monitoring must motivate job performance. However, those who are still "alive" and contending in the promotion game have a longer horizon, which weighs into their decision to put out efforts to climb higher. Simple formulations of this problem have been analyzed (Rosen, 1986). The value of winning at any stage is not only the winner's prize (compensation) at that level, but also includes the value of an option to compete for larger prizes at higher levels. The value of this option reflects career considerations.

The value v_t of contending in a game in which there are t stages remaining is

$$v_t = \max \left\{ P(l, \bar{l}) v_{t-1} + [1 - P(l, \bar{l})] W_{t+1} - c(l) \right\} \qquad (14)$$

where $P(l, \bar{l})$ is the probability of winning when own effort l is expended and efforts $\bar{l}$ are expended by other competitors, W_{t+1} is the compensation paid to the loser and $c(l)$ is the (convex) cost of effort. The first-order condition for this problem is

$$(v_{t-1} - W_{t+1}) \partial P / \partial l + c'(l). \qquad (15)$$

Defining $\mu = (\partial \log P / \partial \log l)/(\partial \log c / \partial \log l)$, manipulating (15) into an elasticity form and substituting out for c in (14) yields a recursion for v_t

$$v_t = \beta_t v_{t-1} + (1 - \beta_t) W_t, \qquad (16)$$

where $\beta_t = P_t(1 - \mu_t)$ is evaluated at the Nash equilibrium effort levels and probabilities. Assuming $0 < \beta_t < 1$ and using the boundary condition that $v_0 = W_1$, where W_1 is the highest-ranking prize (the CEO's compensation), the solution to (16) is

$$
v_t = (\beta_1 \beta_2 \ldots \beta_t)\delta W_1 + (\beta_2 \ldots \beta_t)\delta W_2 \\
+ \cdots + \beta_t \delta W_t + W_{t+1},
\tag{17}
$$

where $\delta W_i = W_i - W_{i-1}$ is the difference in prizes between adjacent ranks. The option value v_t in (17) is the sure prize W_{t+1} if the contest is lost plus the discounted sum of differences in rewards between ranks in future rounds. The discount factor β_t depends on the probability of winning and the costs and technology of doing so. Subtracting W_{t+2} from both sides of (17) and comparing it with (15) shows that the incentives to win are increasing in the option value, specifically

$$
(v_{t-1} - W_{t+1}) = (\beta_1 \ldots \beta_{t-1})\delta W_1 + (\beta_2 \ldots \beta_{t-1})\delta W_2 \\
+ \cdots + \delta W_t.
\tag{18}
$$

The firm desires that effort expended by people in higher positions be at least as large as that expended at lower levels, if the multiplicative effects in Section 2 exist. This is why executives work such long hours. In a pure incentive game where the contenders are known to be of similar talent, β works out to be a constant independent of t and it can be shown that constant compensation differences between adjacent ranks below the top are necessary to induce nondecreasing effort across ranks. However, the option to continue plays out at the final round, so the difference in compensation between the CEO and the first vice-president must be increased to make up for it. There is an extra prize at the top.

The economics is that this increment acts to extend the effective horizon, "as if" the promotion ladder were of infinite length and competitors were in a game that continued forever. The idea survives many generalizations. It suggests that the wage structure in a hierarchical organization should exhibit a certain "convexity," whereby CEO compensation is out of step and elevated above the rest for motivational purposes in the organization as a whole. More generally, when managers compete to change their positions over their careers, wages at any given level have spillover effects on the incentives of contenders at lower levels.

Competition generated by these kinds of relative performance evaluation can lead to moral hazard problems. Competitors may collude (Dye, 1984) and put forth less effort than is appropriate, to the detriment of the organization as a whole. Alternatively, there may be opportunities for destructive activities of competitors to denigrate the work of others and make themselves look better by comparison (Lazear, 1989). Such antisocial behavior can be partially controlled by reducing the stakes and narrowing wage differentials between ranks, but it comes at the cost of reducing effort in the organization as a whole. It might also be controlled by recruiting personnel for these positions from outside the organization. An alternative view has been little studied: Breton and Wintrobe (1986) describe a form of competition within a patronage system. The CEO encouraged competition among his immediate subordinates, who in turn served as patrons for those lower down the hierarchy. Those further below knew the game and took actions to improve the standing of their patron in the eyes of the CEO because that could improve the subordinate's standing. The scheme has qualities of an "invisible hand," though used to totally corrupt purposes in their case study.

These moral hazards are not specific to tournament structures. Rather they apply to any incomplete scoring scheme for assessing talent. Tirole (1986) analyzes collusion between an agent and supervisor, both against the principal, Milgrom (1988) considers the effects of socially unproductive activities taken by an agent to influence the scoring system. Both considerations appear to generate incentives for more rigid and bureaucratic rules within an organization relative to using internal prices to self-regulate behavior.

5.3 Evidence

Data limitations on executive careers and incomes below the top have limited empirical work in this area. Some of the implications of these models have been borne out in experiments and a few have not (Bull et al., 1987, 1988), but there is less evidence from the market itself. Rosenbaum (1984) documented career paths through promotion in a case study of one large firm. Proxy statements of large firms often list total compensation of the highest paid 20 or 30 executives and suggest that top executives are indeed paid substantially more than those immediately below them. This is confirmed in Leonard's (1990) proprietary sample, where differences in pay increase markedly between adjacent levels in moving from bottom to top. He also reports that pay increments are negatively correlated with promotion prospects, consistent with requirements for incentive maintenance when competition is stiffer. Yet, in a single-year cross-firm comparison, O'Reilly et al. (1988) found that pay differences between CEO and vice-presidents were negatively correlated with the number of vice-presidents. A positive correlation is expected if more vice-presidents are contending for the CEO position. Perhaps some of them are not competing. The convexity implication within firms is also found by Lambert et al. (1989) in a large proprietary sample. Differences in pay between levels increase rapidly with rank in their sample, and the CEO earns on the order of $100,000 more, compared with $10,000–$30,000 median differences at lower levels.

There is evidence supporting direct substitution of current for career incentives of CEOs as time to retirement decreases. Murphy (1986) found that the relation between CEO pay and stock market rate of return was larger in earlier years of CEO tenure in both position and in the firm. Barro and Barro (1990) found declining sensitivity of pay to performance with age of CEO. However, neither study controls for CEO stock holdings, which tend to grow with age and tenure. Own stock holding in the firm gives immediate performance incentives and reduces the need for sensitivity in direct compensation. Finally, Gibbons and Murphy (1990b) examine *Forbes*'s sample CEOs who left their firms over 1974–1989. The elasticity of pay to stock market value is the usual 0.10 when these people had many years remaining, but rises to 0.18 when they had few years left.

Available evidence generally supports some of the life cycle and other implications of these models. However, more evidence is needed.

6. Conclusions

This survey demonstrates great scope for fruitful empirical and theoretical research in this area. As usual, much remains to be done.

On the empirical side, inquiry must dig deeper into the management hierarchy. In some ways our preoccupation with top executives is examining the tip of the iceberg. However, much effort at data development will be necessary for such endeavors. Empirical investigation also must be broadened beyond the United States to other countries. How will these remarkably uniform estimates compare around the world? It is commmonly alleged, for example, that Japanese business executives earn much less relative to production workers compared with their American and British counterparts. It would be very interesting to know if the compensation elasticities of 0.25 for scale and 0.10 for shareholder wealth nevertheless hold true in Japanese firms. In addition, executive ranks have recently opened up to women in many countries. The marked increase in available supplies of managerial talent should have large consequences on the executive labor market, which remain to be worked out and examined empirically.

Of the many theoretical issues on the research agenda, a few stand out. First, many alternative mechanisms for affecting managerial incentives have been identified. How should the effects of reputation, bonding, takeovers and compensation contracts be parceled out? To what extent do these alternatives act as substitutes for each other, or as complements? Second, perhaps the idea that shareholders are the only principals in the executive contracting problem is too simple. There is much to be said for the "nexus of contracts" view, because control decisions affect the wealth of many contract holders in the firm (Fama and Jensen, 1983). For example, shouldn't debt holders be included as claimants of the firm's resources and included in the empirical estimates of wealth elasticities? Furthermore, what limits the scope of control? Labor economists have increasingly recognized the importance of firm-specific human capital; and firm-specific capital is often involved in contracts with specialty suppliers and other intermediaries. All of them have a stake in how the firms in managed. Evidence on this broadened "stakeholder" view of claimants is hardly to be found, and although not compelling for the case of hostile takeovers (Shleifer and Summers, 1988; Kaplan, 1989), these issues are likely to be more generally important. They deserve more attention.

Finally, little has been done on executive succession and how incompetent executives are rooted out, short of the Draconian takeover solution. Vancil's (1987) interesting account of how CEOs are chosen in necessarily limited by the small selection of firms in its case study approach. Any executive selection process is subject to error, but little if anything is known on how mistakes are corrected. If, as I maintain, competence has extraordinary marginal product for top management positions in large firms, how incompetence is revealed and handled must be important. Formally, the job falls to the board of directors. Yet there is much opinion and some evidence (e.g., board compositions change when the CEO changes: Hermalin and Weisback, 1988) that boards are themselves controlled by the CEO. The implied limits on monitoring would appear to make the contractual approach more important.

References

Abowd, J. (1990) Does performance based management compensation affect corporate performance? *Industrial and Labor Relations Review,* 43(3), 52s–73s.

Antle, R., and Smith, A. (1986) An empirical investigation of the relative performance evaluation of corporate executives. *Journal of Accounting Research,* 24(2), 1–32.

Baker, G. P. (1989) Piece rate contracts and performance measurement error. Mimeo, Harvard Business School.

Barro, J. R., and Barro, R. J. (1990) Pay, performance, and turnover of bank CEOs. *Journal of Labor Economics,* 8(3), 448–81.

Baumol, W. J. (1967) *Business Behavior, Value, and Growth,* revised edition. New York: Harcourt Brace.

Becker, G. S. (1968) Crime and punishment: an economic approach. *Journal of Political Economy,* 76(2), 169–217.

Becker, G. S., and Stigler, G. J. (1974) Law enforcement, malfeasance, and compensation of enforcers. *Journal of Legal Studies,* 3(1), 1–18.

Bhagat, S., Shleifer, A. and Vishny, R. W. (1990) Hostile takeovers in the 1980s: the return to corporate specialization. Mimeo, University of Chicago.

Breton, A., and Wintrobe, R. (1986) The bureaucracy of murder revisited. *Journal of Political Economy,* 94(6), 905–26.

Bull, C., Schotter, A., and Weigelt, K. (1987) Tournaments and piece rates: an experimental study. *Journal of Political Economy,* 95(1), 1–33.

—— (1988) Assymetric tournaments, equal opportunity laws, and affirmative action: some experimental results. Mimeo, Wharton School, University of Pennsylvania.

Ciscel, D. H., and Carroll, T. M. (1980) The determinants of executive salaries: an econometric survey. *The Review of Economics and Statistics,* 62(1), 7–13.

Cosh, A. (1975) The remuneration of chief executives in the United Kingdom. *Economic Journal,* 85(1), 75–94.

Coughlin, A. T., and Schmidt, R. (1985) Executive compensation, management turnover, and firm performance: an empirical investigation. *Journal of Accounting and Economics,* 7(2), 43–66.

Deckop, J. R. (1988) Determinants of chief executive officer compensation. *Industrial and Labor Relations Review,* 41(2), 215–26.

Dunlevy, J. A. (1985) Econometric issues in the analysis of executive compensation. *Review of Economics and Statistics,* 67(1), 171–4.

Dye, R. (1984) The trouble with tournaments. *Economic Inquiry,* 22(1), 147–9.

Eaton, J., and Rosen, H. S. (1983) Agency, delayed compensation and the structure of remuneration. *Journal of Finance,* 38(5), 1489–505.

Fama, E. (1980) Agency problems and the theory of the firm. *Journal of Political Economy,* 88(2), 288–307.

Fama, E. F., and Jensen, M. C. (1983) Separation of ownership and control. *Journal of Law and Economics,* 26(2), 301–25.

Gibbons, R., and Murphy, K. J. (1990a) Relative performance evaluation for chief executive officers. *Industrial and Labor Relations Review,* 43(3), 30s–51s.

——— (1990b) Optimum incentive contracts in the presence of career concerns. Mimeo, University of Rochester.

Grossman, S., and Hart, O. (1983) An analysis of the principal-agent problem. *Econometrica,* 7(1), 7–45.

Hermalin, B., and Weisback, M. (1988) The determinants of board composition. *Rand Journal of Economics,* 19(4), 589–606.

Holmstrom, B. (1979) Moral hazard and observability. *Bell Journal of Economics,* 10(1), 74–91.

——— (1982a) Moral hazard in teams. *Bell Journal of Economics,* 13(2), 324–40.

——— (1982b) Managerial incentive problems–a dynamic perspective. In *Essays in Economics and Management in Honour of Lars Wahlbeck.* Helsinki: Swedish School of Economics.

Holmstrom, B., and Milgrom, P. (1987) Aggregation and linearity in the provision of intertemporal incentives. *Econometrica,* 55(2), 303–28.

——— (1989) Multi-task principal-agent problems. Mimeo, Yale School of Organization and Management.

Jensen, M. C. (1988) Takeovers: their causes and consequences. *Journal of Economic Perspectives,* 2(1), 21–48.

Jensen, M. C., and Murphy, K. J. (1990) Performance pay and top-management incentives. *Journal of Political Economy,* 98(2), 225–64.

Jensen, M. C., and Ruback, R. S. (1983) The market for corporate control: the scientific evidence. *Journal of Financial Economics,* 11(2), 5–50.

Kaplan, S. (1989) The effect of management buyouts on operating performance and value. *Journal of Financial Economics,* 24(1), 217–54.

Kokkelenberg, E. C. (1988) The behavioral objectives of firms and executive compensation. Mimeo, Department of Economics, State University of New York at Binghamton.

Kostiuk, P. F. (1986) Executive ability, corporate performance, and managerial income. Mimeo, Center for Naval Analysis, January.

———— (1989) Firm size and executive compensation. *The Journal of Human Resources,* 25(1), 90–105.

Lambert, R. A., and Larcker, D. F. (1985) Golden parachutes, executive decision-making and shareholder wealth. *Journal of Accounting and Economics,* 7(2), 179–204.

———— (1987) An analysis of the use of accounting and market measures of performance in executive contracts. *Journal of Accounting Research,* 25 (supplement), 85–123.

Lambert, R. A., Larcker, D. F., and Weigelt, K. (1989) Tournaments and the structure of organizational incentives. Mimeo, Wharton School, University of Pennsylvania.

Lazear, E. P. (1979) Why is there mandatory retirement? *Journal of Political Economy,* 87(6), 1261–84.

———— (1986) Salaries and piece rates. *Journal of Business,* 59(3), 405–31.

———— (1989) Pay, inequality, and industrial politics. *Journal of Political Economy,* 97(3), 561–80.

Lazear, E. P., and Rosen, S. (1981) Rank order tournaments as optimum labor contracts. *Journal of Political Economy,* 89(5), 841–74.

Leonard, J. S. (1990) Executive pay and firm performance. *Industrial and Labor Relations Review,* 43(3), 13s–29s.

Levinthal, D. (1984) A survey of agency models of organizations. Mimeo, Institute for Mathematical Studies in Social Science, Stanford University.

Lewellen, W. G. (1968) *Executive Compensation in Large Industrial Corporations.* New York: Columbia University Press for National Bureau of Economic Research.

Lewellen, W. G., and Huntsman, B. (1970) Managerial pay and corporate performance. *American Economic Review,* 60(4), 710–20.

Lichtenberg, F. R., and Siegel, D. (1987) Productivity and changes in Ownership of manufacturing plants. In M. N. Baily and C. Winston (eds.), *Brookings Papers in Economic Activity,* volume 3. Washington, DC: Brookings Institution, 643–73.

———— (1989) The effects of leveraged buyouts on productivity and related aspects of firm behavior. National Bureau of Economic Research Working Paper no. 3022.

McGuire, J. W., and Chiu, J. S. Y., and Elbing, A. O. (1962) Executive incomes, sales and profits. *American Economic Review,* 52(4), 753–61.

McLaughlin, K. J. (1988) Aspects of tournament models: a survey. *Research in Labor Economics,* 9, 225–56.

Manne, H. G. (1965) Mergers and the market for corporate control. *Journal of Political Economy,* 73(2), 110–20.

Marris, R. (1963) A model of the managerial enterprise. *Quarterly Journal of Economics,* 77(2), 185–209.

Masson, R. (1971) Executive motivations, earnings, and consequent equity performance. *Journal of Political Economy,* 79(6), 1278–92.

Meeks, G., and Whittington, G. (1975) Director's pay, growth, and profitability. *Journal of Industrial Economics,* 24(1), 1–14.

Milgrom, P. (1988) Employment contracts, influence activities and efficient organizational design. *Journal of Political Economy,* 96(1), 42–60.

Miller, F. H., Jr. (1982) Wages and Establishment Size. Ph.D. dissertation, University of Chicago.

Miller, M. H., and Scholes, M. S. (1982) Executive compensation, taxes and incentives. In W. F. Sharpe and C. M. Cootner (eds.), *Essays in Honor of Paul Cootner.* Englewood Cliffs, NJ: Prentice-Hall.

Mirrlees, J. A. (1976) The optimal structure of incentives and authority within an organization. *Bell Journal of Economics,* 7 (Spring), 105–31.

Mookherjee, D. (1989) Rank order competition and incentives: an organizational perspective. Mimeo, Stanford University.

Morck, R., Shleifer, A. and Vishny, R. W. (1988a) Alternative mechanisms for corporate control. Mimeo, National Bureau of Economic Research.

——— (1988b) Management ownership and market valuation. *Journal of Financial Economics,* 20, 293–315.

Murphy, K. J. (1985) Corporate performance and managerial remuneration. *Journal of Accounting and Economics,* 7(2), 11–42.

——— (1986) Incentives, learning and compensation: a theoretical and empirical investigation of managerial labor contracts. *Rand Journal of Economics,* 17(2), 59–76.

O'Reilly, C., Main, B., and Crystal, G. (1988) CEO compensation as tournament and social comparison: a tale of two theories. *Administrative Science Quarterly,* 33(3), 257–74.

Radner, R. (1985) Repeated principal-agent games with discounting. *Econometrica,* 53(5), 1173–98.

Reder, M. W. (1968) The size distribution of earnings. In J. Marchal and B. Ducros (eds.) *The Distribution of National Income.* London: MacMillan.

Roberts, D. R. (1956) A general theory of executive compensation based on statistically tested propositions. *Quarterly Journal of Economics*, 70(3), 270–94.

Rosen, S. (1981) The economics of superstars. *American Economic Review*, 71(5), 845–58.

——— (1982) Authority, control and the distribution of earnings. *Rand Journal of Economics*, 13(2), 311–23.

——— (1986) Prizes and incentives in elimination tournaments. *American Economic Review*, 76(4), 701–15.

Rosenbaum, J. (1984) *Career Mobility in a Corporate Hierarchy*. New York: Academic Press.

Shleifer, A., and Summers, L. (1988) Breach of trust in hostile takeovers. In A. J. Auerback (ed.), *Corporate Takeovers: Causes and Consequences*. Chicago: University of Chicago Press for the National Bureau of Economic Research.

Sicherman, N., and Galor, O. (1990) A theory of career mobility. *Journal of Political Economy*, 98(1), 169–92.

Stiglitz, J. E. (1975) Incentives, risk and information: notes toward a theory of hierarchy. *Bell Journal of Economics*, 6 (Autumn), 552–79.

Telser, L. G. (1980) A theory of self-enforcing agreements. *Journal of Business*, 53(1), 27–44.

Tirole, J. (1986) Hierarchies and bureaucracies: on the role of collusion in organizations. *Journal of Law, Economics, and Organization*, 2(2), 181–214.

Tosi, H., and Gomez-Mejia, L. (1989) The decoupling of CEO pay and performance: an agency theory perspective. *Administrative Science Quarterly*, 34(2), 169–89.

Vancil, R. F. (1987) *Passing the Baton: Managing the Process of CEO Succession*. Boston: Harvard Business School Press.

Williamson, O. (1985) *The Economic Institutions of Capitalism*. New York: Free Press.

Winn, D. N., and Shoenhair, J. D. (1988) Compensation-based (dis)incentives for revenue-maximizing behavior. *Review of Economics and Statistics*, 70(1), 154–8.

Author Index

Subject Index